Study Guide for Weiten's
PSYCHOLOGY
Themes and Variations

Fourth Edition

RICHARD B. STALLING
RONALD E. WASDEN

Bradley University

Brooks/Cole Publishing Company

I(T)P® *An International Thomson Publishing Company*

Pacific Grove • Albany • Belmont • Bonn • Boston • Cincinnati • Detroit • Johannesburg • London
Madrid • Melbourne • Mexico City • New York • Paris • Singapore • Tokyo • Toronto • Washington

Sponsoring Editor: Faith B. Stoddard
Editorial Assistant: Stephanie M. Andersen
Production: Dorothy Bell
Cover Design: Vernon T. Boes

Cover Art: Victor Vasarely. *Gestalt-Zoeld, 1976.* Copyright
ARS, NY. Private Collection, Paris, France.
Printing and Binding: Patterson Printing

For more information, contact:

BROOKS/COLE PUBLISHING COMPANY
511 Forest Lodge Road
Pacific Grove, CA 93950
USA

International Thomson Publishing Europe
Berkshire House 168-173
High Holborn
London WC1V 7AA
England

Thomas Nelson Australia
102 Dodds Street
South Melbourne, 3205
Victoria, Australia

Nelson Canada
1120 Birchmount Road
Scarborough, Ontario
Canada M1K 5G4

International Thomson Editores
Seneca 53
Col. Polanco
11560 México, D. F., México

International Thomson Publishing GmbH
Königswinterer Strasse 418
53227 Bonn
Germany

International Thomson Publishing Asia
221 Henderson Road
#05-10 Henderson Building
Singapore 0315

International Thomson Publishing Japan
Hirakawacho Kyowa Building, 3F
2-2-1 Hirakawacho
Chiyoda-ku, Tokyo 102
Japan

Printed in the United States of America

10   9   8   7   6   5   4   3

ISBN 0-534-35066-6

Contents

To the Student

The two of us have written about eight study guides across the last couple of decades, and we've used a number of them written by others as well. Our goal in writing this study guide was to make it the best that we have ever written or used. We're pleased with the organization, the clear way in which each component parallels each part of the text, the fact that the practice material is in close proximity to the learning objectives, and the variety of the examples. We hope you find it as helpful a resource as we have tried to make it.

The first and major section of each chapter in the study guide is the Review of Key Ideas, consisting of 20 to 30 learning objectives and several questions or exercises relating to each objective. The learning objectives tell you what you are expected to know, while the exercises quiz you, sometimes tutor you, and occasionally try to make a joke. Answers are provided at the end of each set of exercises.

The second section is the Review of Key Terms, which asks you to match 20 to 60 terms from the chapter with their definitions. The third section is the Review of key People, a matching exercise confined to the major researchers and theorists presented in each chapter. Finally, the Self-Quiz for each chapter gives you some idea of whether or not your studying has been on target.

What's the best way to work with this book? We suggest that you try this: (1) read each learning objective; (2) read the text subsection that relates to that learning objective; (3) answer the questions. After you complete the objectives, do the matching exercises and take the self-quiz. Of course, you may find a different procedure that works for you. Whatever method you use, the learning objectives will serve as an excellent review. At the end of your study of a particular chapter you can quiz yourself by reading over the learning objectives, reciting answers aloud, and checking your answers. This procedure roughly parallels the SQ3R study technique introduced in the Application section of Chapter 1 of the text.

In Chapter 16 of your text Wayne Weiten, the author, illustrates a topic in social psychology by saying that "Years ago, one of my teachers told me that I had an 'attitude problem.' " Well, years ago–about 25, to be specific–we were Wayne's teachers in college, and although we don't recall reprimanding him, if we did, we apologize. Because now the tables are turned; now we are being instructed by and taking correction from Wayne.

We wish to acknowledge the help of a few people. First, we wish to thank Wayne Weiten, our former student. It has been a pleasure to work with him; he is an excellent teacher and superb writer, which makes our task much easier. If this guide achieves what we hope it does, Wayne deserves much of the credit. Our thanks also to Faith Stoddard of Brooks/Cole, who always works patiently with the two of us, and to Gail Reynolds, who transformed our copy into its final form.

Rick Stalling and Ron Wasden

The Evolution of Psychology

REVIEW OF KEY IDEAS

FROM SPECULATION TO SCIENCE: How Psychology Developed

1. **Summarize Wundt's accomplishments and contributions to psychology.**

    1-1. If you ask most college graduates to name the founder of psychology they might well mention the name of a famous psychologist (for example, maybe Sigmund Freud), but they almost certainly would *not* say Wilhelm Wundt. Yet among psychologists Wundt is generally acknowledged to be the "_____" of our field.

    1-2. Wundt established the first experimental psychology _____ , in Leipzig, Germany, in 1879. He also established the first _____ devoted to publishing psychological research.

    1-3. What was the subject matter of Wundt's psychology? _____

    1-4. What are Wundt's major contributions to the evolution of psychology? They may be summarized as follows: He is the _____ of psychology as an independent academic field; and he insisted that psychology can and must use the _____ method.

    Answers: 1-1. founder **1-2.** laboratory, journal **1-3.** consciousness **1-4.** founder, scientific (experimental). (Personal note from RS: I visited Leipzig in the former East Germany during summer 1996 and looked for the famous founding laboratory. It wasn't there! I found Wundt Street, but no lab. Had I read World War II history more carefully I would have known that an English-U. S. bombing raid destroyed the laboratory in 1943.)

2. **Summarize Hall's accomplishments and contributions to psychology.**

    2-1. Wundt had many important students, among them the American G. Stanley Hall. In 1883, just three years after Wundt created his laboratory in Leipzig, Hall established the first American psychological _____ at Johns Hopkins. Hall also founded America's first _____ devoted to publishing material in the field of psychology.

2-2. In 1892, with 26 of his colleagues, Hall began the American Psychological Association, known by the initials _____. Hall also became the first _____ of the Association. The APA now includes more than 140,000 members.

Answers: 2-1. laboratory, journal **2-2.** APA, president.

3. Describe structuralism and its impact on the subsequent development of psychology.

3-1. Another of Wundt's students, Edward Titchener, developed the school of psychology known as _____. The major tenet of this viewpoint was that psychology should study the structure of _____, and it should do so by breaking consciousness down into its basic _____.

3-2. These basic elements were thought to be sensations. Subjects were first trained to observe some object and then, after careful introspection, to report on their conscious experience. Thus, the subject matter of structuralism was _____, and its method involved training observers in the technique of _____.

Answers: 3-1. structuralism, consciousness, elements **3-2.** introspection.

4. Describe functionalism and its impact on the subsequent development of psychology.

4-1. Rather than breaking down consciousness into basic elements, the _____ school emphasized determining the _____ or purpose of consciousness.

4-2. Functionalism was founded by William James. Influenced by the Darwin's concept of natural selection, James concluded that psychology should study the basic elements/purpose) of consciousness.

4-3. Which "school" is characterized by each of the following descriptions? Place an "S" for structuralism or "F" for functionalism in the appropriate blanks.

_____ Concerned with the purpose (or function) of consciousness.

_____ Trained observers to introspect about consciousness.

_____ Assumed that consciousness could be broken down into basic elements (in the same way that physical matter is comprised of atoms).

_____ Interested in the flow of consciousness.

_____ Focused on the adaptive (evolutionary) value of consciousness.

_____ Emphasized sensation and perception in vision, hearing, and touch.

4-4. While neither structuralism nor functionalism survived as viable theories of psychology, functionalism had a more lasting impact. What was that impact?

Answers: 4-1. functionalist, function **4-2.** purpose **4-3.** F, S, S, F, F, S **4-4.** The emphasis of functionalism on the practical (or the adaptive or purposeful) led to the development of two areas of modern psychology: behaviorism and applied psychology.

5. **Summarize Watson's view on the appropriate subject matter of psychology, nature versus nurture, and animal research.**

   5-1. A literal translation of the root words of psychology (*psyche* and *logos*) suggests that psychology is the study of the _____. For both Wundt and James, this was the case: they studied human _____. For Watson, however, the subject matter of psychology was

   _____.

   5-2. Watson believed that psychology could not be a science unless it, like the other sciences, concentrated on _____ rather than unobservable events.

   5-3. Which of the following are observable behaviors? Place an "O" in the blank if the event is observable and an "N" if it is not.

   _____ writing a letter

   _____ feeling angry

   _____ saying "Please pass the salt"

   _____ passing the salt

   _____ perceiving a round object

   _____ experiencing hunger

   _____ walking rapidly

   5-4. Watson largely discounted the importance of genetic inheritance. For Watson, behavior was governed by the _____.

   5-5. Watson also made a shift away from human introspection by using _____ as the subjects for research. Why the change in orientation? First, animal behavior is observable; human consciousness is not. Second, the environment of laboratory animals, in contrast to that of humans, is subject to much more _____.

   Answers: 5-1. soul (or mind), consciousness, behavior **5-2.** observable **5-3.** O, N (you can't see or hear your own or another person's feelings of anger; you may see the results of anger), O, O, N (you can't see or hear perception), N (you can't see or hear hunger), O **5-4.** environment **5-5.** animals, control (manipulation).

6. **Explain how Gestalt psychologists challenged the views of structuralism and behaviorism.**

   6-1. Before taking up Gestalt psychology, let's briefly review structuralism and behaviorism.

   (a) As defined by the structuralists, what was the <u>subject matter</u> of psychology?

   (b) For behaviorists, what was the subject matter of psychology?

   (c) While structuralists and behaviorists differed in their views of the subject matter of psychology, their approach to the new field was similar in one major respect. In what way were the two systems similar?

6-2.   With the example of the *phi phenomenon* the gestalt theorists demonstrated one of their basic tenets involving parts and wholes.

(a) What is the phi phenomenon and what Gestalt principle does it illustrate?

(b) What, then, was Gestalt psychology's major objection both to structuralism and to behaviorism?

Answers: 6-1. (a) conscious experience (consciousness), (b) animal or human behavior, (c) They studied "parts" rather than "wholes." Both systems believed that the task of psychology was to break down psychological phenomena into their smallest elements. (For the structuralists the smaller elements were the sensations or images that made up consciousness; for the behaviorists the elements were the stimulus-response bonds thought to make up behavior.) **6-2.** (a) The phi phenomenon is the illusion of movement created by presenting non-moving stimuli in rapid succession (as occurs in "motion" pictures). The illusion demonstrates that the whole (i.e., the illusion of movement) does not derive from the sum of its parts (the separate, non-moving stimuli), (b) Gestalt psychology asserted that by trying to study the parts of consciousness or the parts of behavior, one would miss important aspects of the whole phenomenon.

7. Summarize Freud's principal ideas and why they inspired controversy.

7-1.   Recall that for Wundt, the subject matter of psychology was human consciousness. For Freud, a major subject of study was what he termed the _____. With this concept, Freud asserted that human beings are (<u>aware/unaware</u>) of most of the factors that influence their thoughts and behavior.

7-2.   There is a word beginning with *s* that means the same thing as feces. This word, however, may be more likely to cause laughter, embarrassment, or anger than the word feces. Why do two words that mean the same thing produce such differing reactions? Freud would assert that our more emotional response to one of the words would be caused by the _____.

7-3.   Although generally not accessible to us, the unconscious is revealed in several ways, according to Freud. Freud thought, for example, that the unconscious is revealed in mistakes, such as "_____ of the tongue," or the symbolism in nighttime _____.

7-4.   Freud's ideas were (and still are) considered quite controversial. The general public tended to find Freud's ideas unacceptable because of his emphasis on _____. And scientific psychologists, with their increasing emphasis on observable behavior, rejected Freud's notion that we are controlled by _____ forces. Nonetheless, Freud's theory gradually gained prominence and survives today as an influential theoretical perspective.

Answers: 7-1. unconscious, unaware **7-2.** unconscious **7-3.** slips, dreams **7-4.** Sex (sexuality, sexual instincts), unconscious.

8. Summarize Skinner's work, views, and influence.

8-1.   Summarize Skinner's viewpoint with regard to the following topics.

(a) Mental events:

(b) The fundamental principle of behavior:

(c) Free will:

(d) The factors that control human (and lower animal) behavior:

Answers: 8-1. (a) They cannot be studied scientifically and are not useful in building a science of behavior. (b) Organisms will tend to repeat responses followed by positive outcomes (and *not* to repeat responses followed by neutral or negative outcomes). (c) Free will is an illusion (because, he says, behavior is under the lawful control of the environment). (d) external stimuli (or environmental events).

9. Summarize Rogers's and Maslow's ideas and the contributions of humanistic psychology.

9-1. Both Rogers and Maslow, like other _____ psychologists, emphasized the (similarities/ differences) between human beings and the other animals.

9-2. While Freud and Skinner stressed the way in which behavior is *controlled* (by unconscious forces or by the environment), Rogers and Maslow emphasized human beings' _____ to determine their own actions.

9-3. Rogers and Maslow also asserted that human beings have a drive to express their inner potential, a drive toward personal _____.

9-4. Perhaps the greatest contribution of the humanistic movement has been in producing (scientific findings/ new approaches) in psychotherapy.

Answers: 9-1. humanistic, differences **9-2.** freedom **9-3.** growth (expression) **9-4.** new approaches.

10. Explain how historical events since World War I have contributed to the emergence of psychology as a profession.

10-1. World War I ushered in the field of applied psychology, primarily the extensive use of _____ testing of military recruits.

10-2. World War II brought an increased need for screening recruits and treating emotional casualties. With the increased demand, the Veterans Administration began funding many new training programs in the field of _____ psychology.

10-3. In contrast to its founding in the 19th century as a research or academic endeavor, psychology in the 20th century developed a prominent _____ branch devoted to solving practical problems. These applied fields, which emerged in large part as a result of two world wars, included psychological _____ and _____ psychology.

Answers: 10-1. intelligence (psychological, mental), clinical **10-2.** clinical **10-3.** applied (or professional), testing, clinical.

11. **Describe two recent trends in research in psychology that reflect a return to psychology's intellectual roots.**

11-1. Two recent trends in research in psychology involve the reemergence of areas largely discarded or ignored by the behaviorists. What are these two areas?

11-2. Think about sucking on a lemon. When you do, the amount of saliva in your mouth will increase measurably. While it would be enough to describe your observable response as a function of my observable instruction, it is also obvious that thinking, or cognition, is involved: My instruction changed your _____ image, which was accompanied by a change in salivation.

11-3. The study of mental imagery, problem solving, and decision making involves _____ processes. The second more recent trend also concerns "internal" processes: Research on electrical stimulation of the brain, brain specialization, and biofeedback involves _____ processes.

Answers: **11-1.** cognition (consciousness or thinking) and physiological (or biological) processes **11-2.** mental **11-3.** cognitive, physiological (biological).

12. **Explain why Western psychology traditionally had scant interest in other cultures and why this situation has begun to change.**

12-1. Several factors contributed to the narrow focus of Western, and especially United States, psychology:

(a) First, studying other cultures is expensive and time consuming. It's much _____ for researchers to study people in their own country (and especially middle-class students at their own schools).

(b) Second, psychology has traditionally been more interested in the study of _____ than groups.

(c) Third, some psychologists may worry that study of diverse groups may foster _____ of those groups.

(d) Fourth, there may be a tendency among Western psychologists to view their own group as superior, the group tendency referred to as _____.

12-2. The situation has begun to change in recent years for two primary reasons:

(a) increased communication and trade worldwide, the so-called _____ economy or global interdependence; and (b) increased diversity of ethnic groups within the countries of the Western World, including the _____ mosaic characteristic of the United States.

Answers: **12-1.** (a) cheaper (easier), (b) individuals, (c) stereotypes, (d) ethnocentrism **12-2.** global; multicultural.

13. **Summarize the basic tenets of evolutionary psychology.**

13-1. The most recent major perspective to arise in psychology is _____ psychology, a field that examines behavioral processes in terms of survival value for a species.

6

13-2. According to evolutionary psychologists, all aspects of human behavior—including not only aggression and mate selection but perception, language, personality, and cognition—are strongly influenced by the _____ value that these factors have had for the human species.

13-3. While Darwin's influence is clear in other psychological theories (e.g., James, Freud, and Skinner), the new emphasis on natural selection is (less/more) comprehensive and widely researched than the earlier versions.

–13-4. The viewpoint has its critics. Some charge that the theory is not subject to scientific _____ and that evolutionary conceptions are simply post hoc accounts rather than explanations. Nonetheless, evolutionary psychology has gained a high degree of acceptance as a major new perspective in psychology.

Answers: **13-1.** evolutionary **13-2.** survival (adaptive) **13-3.** more **13-4.** test (evaluation)

PSYCHOLOGY TODAY: VIGOROUS AND DIVERSIFIED

14. Discuss the growth of psychology and the most common work settings for contemporary psychologists.

    14-1. Psychology is a thriving field that has experienced a remarkable growth since its founding in 1879. Which of the following statements about that growth are true? (Use a T or F to indicate true or false for the following statements.)

        _____ Including graduate student members APA membership now numbers more than 140,000.

        _____ 10 percent of all doctoral degrees awarded in science and the humanities are in psychology.

        _____ Psychology is the second most popular undergraduate major.

        _____ Over 1100 journals worldwide publish articles in psychology.

    14-2. Psychology was founded in a University, and earlier in this century almost all psychologists were employed as academics. Today, however, more than two-thirds of psychologists are employed in (university/non-academic) settings that include hospitals, business and industry, schools, and government agencies.

Answers: **14-1.** T, T, T, T **14-2.** applied.

15. List and describe seven major research areas in psychology.

    15-1. Read over the descriptions of the research areas in Figure 1.7. Then match the names of the areas with the correct research topics by placing the appropriate letters in the blanks. (Note that the separation between these areas is not always perfect. For example, a personality theorist might also be a psychometrician who has a physiological focus in explaining behavior. Nonetheless, the following topics have been chosen so that one answer is correct for each.)

    A. Experimental   _G_ attitude change, group behavior

    B. Physiological   _____ personality and intelligence assessment, test design, new statistical procedures

    C. Cognitive   _F_ personality assessment, personality description

    D. Developmental   _____ "core" topics (e.g., perception, conditioning, motivation)

    E. Psychometrics   _B_ influence of the brain, bodily chemicals, genetics

    F. Personality   _D_ child, adolescent, and adult development

    G. Social   _C_ memory, decision making, thinking

15-2. In case you want to remember the list of seven research areas, here's a mnemonic device: *Peter Piper Picked Some Exquisite California Dills.* List the seven research areas by matching them with the first letter of each word.

Answers: 15-1. G, E, F, A, B, D, C **15-2.** physiological, psychometrics, personality, social, experimental, cognitive, developmental.

16. List and describe the four professional specialties in psychology.

16-1. Review Figure 1.8. Then match the following specialties with the descriptions by placing the appropriate letter in the blanks.

A. Clinical _____ Treatment of less severe problems and problems involving family, marital, and career difficulties.

B. Counselin _____ Treatment of psychological disorders, behavioral and emotional problems

C. Educational and school _____ Involves work on curriculum design and achievement testing in school settings.

D. Industrial and organizational _____ Psychology applied to business settings; deals with personnel, job satisfaction, etc.

16-2. What is the difference between psychology and psychiatry? The major difference is a matter of degree (this is a pun, folks). Psychiatrists have _____ degrees. Clinical psychologists generally have _____ degrees (although some clinical psychologists have Ed.D. or Psy.D. degrees).

16-3. The major portion of psychiatrists' training occurs in _____ schools and in the residency programs in psychiatry that follow medical school. Clinical psychologists' training occurs in _____ schools.

16-4. While clinical psychologists and psychiatrists frequently use the same psychotherapeutic treatment procedures, only _____, as physicians, are licensed to prescribe drugs and engage in other medical treatment.

Answers: 16-1. B, A, C, D **16-2.** medical (M.D.), Ph.D. **16-3.** medical, graduate **16-4.** psychiatrists.

PUTTING IT IN PERSPECTIVE: SEVEN KEY THEMES

17. Summarize the text's three unifying themes relating to psychology as a field of study.

17-1. When my (R. S.'s) older daughter Samantha was about three years old, she pulled a sugar bowl off a shelf and broke it while I was not present. Later, when I surveyed the damage, I said, "I see you've broken something." She said, "How do yer know, did yer see me do it?" I was amused, because while it was obvious who had broken it, her comment reflected psychology's foundation in direct observation. **Theme 1** is that psychology is _____. Empiricism is the point of view that knowledge should be acquired through _____.

17-2. My daughter's comment caused me to think about one other aspect of empiricism: she expressed *doubt* (albeit somewhat self-serving with regard to the sugar bowl). One can describe belief systems along a continuum from *credulity*, which means ready to believe, to *skepticism*, which means disposed toward doubt. Psychology, and the empirical approach, is more disposed toward the _____ end of the continuum.

17-3. We would ordinarily think that if one theory is correct, any other used to explain the same data must be wrong. While scientists do pit theories against each other, it is also the case that apparently contradictory theories may both be correct—as with the explanation of light in terms of both wave and particle theories. Thus, **Theme 2** indicates that psychology is theoretically _____ _____.

17-4. Psychology tolerates and in fact encourages) different theoretical explanations because:

17-5. As is the case with science in general, psychology does not evolve in a vacuum. It is influenced by and influences our society. For example, the current interest in cultural diversity has prompted increased interest in cross-cultural research, which in turn affects the viewpoints in our society. As stated in **Theme 3**, psychology evolves in a _____ context.

Answers: **17-1.** empirical, observation **17-2.** skepticism **17-3.** theoretically diverse **17-4.** more than one theory may be correct; or, one theory may not adequately explain all of the observations **17-5.** sociohistorical

18. Summarize the text's four unifying themes relating to psychology's subject matter.

18-1. When looking for an explanation of a particular behavior, someone might ask: "Well, why did he do it? What was *the reason*? Was it greed or ignorance?" The question implies that if one cause is present another cannot be, and it illustrates the human tendency to reason in terms of (one cause/multiple causes).

18-2. What influences the course of a ball rolled down an inclined plane? Gravity. And also friction. And the presence of other objects, and a number of other factors. That is the point of **Theme 4**: even more than is the case for physical events, behavior is determined by _____ _____.

18-3. Among the multiple causes of human behavior is the category of causes referred to as *culture*. Cultural factors include the customs, beliefs, and values that we transmit across generations—what we eat, how we walk, what we wear, what we say, what we think, and so on. **Theme 5** indicates that our behavior is shaped by our _____ heritage.

18-4. For example, I (R. S.) have observed that many American students traveling abroad initially think that their European lecturers talk down to them; the lecturers, in turn, may regard our students as spoiled and insolent. Perhaps closer to the truth is that there is a clash of customs invisible to both cultures. While we are shaped by our _____ _____ we are often _____ (aware/unaware) of the precise rules and customs that affect us.

18-5. **Theme 6** relates to the influence of heredity and environment. What is the consensus among psychologists about the effect of heredity and environment on behavior?

18-6. The scientific method relies on observation, but observation by itself isn't sufficient. Why isn't it?

18-7. **Theme 7** indicates that our experience is subjective. What does this mean?

Answers: 18-1. one cause **18-2.** multiple causes **18-3.** cultural **18-4.** cultural heritage, aware **18-5.** Theme 6 states that behavior is affected by both heredity and environment operating jointly. While the relative influence of each is still debated, theorists no longer assert that behavior is entirely a function of one or the other **18-6.** because (Theme 7) people's experience of the world is highly subjective **18-7.** Different people experience different things; even if we observe the same event at the same time, we do not "see" the same things; we selectively focus on some events and ignore others.

APPLICATION: IMPROVING ACADEMIC PERFORMANCE

19. **Discuss three important considerations in designing a program to promote adequate studying.**

19-1. Three features of successful studying are listed below. Elaborate on them by providing some of the details asked for.

(a) A schedule: When should you plan your study schedule? Should you write it down?

(b) A place: What are the major characteristics of a good study place?

(c) A reward: When should you reward yourself? What kinds of rewards are suggested?

Answers: 19-1. (a) It's probably useful to set up a general schedule for a particular quarter or semester and then, at the beginning of each week, plan the specific assignments you intend to work on during each study session. Put your plans in writing. (b) Find a place to study with minimal distractions: little noise, few interruptions. (c) Reward yourself shortly after you finish a particular amount of studying; snacking, watching TV, or calling a friend are suggested. **Suggestion:** You are studying now. Is this a good time for you? If it is, why not *write out your weekly schedule now*. Include schedule preparation as part of your study time.

20. Describe the SQ3R method and explain what makes it effective.

20-1.   Below are descriptions of an individual applying the five steps of the SQ3R method to Chapter 1 of your text. The steps are not in the correct order. Label each of the steps and place a number in the parentheses which indicates the correct order.

( )   _____ Vanessa looks at the title of the first subsection of the chapter. After wondering briefly what it means for psychology to have "parents," she formulates this question: How was the field of psychology influenced by philosophy and physiology?

( )   _____ Vanessa turns to the back of Chapter 1 and notes that there is a chapter review. She turns back to the first page of the chapter, sees that the outline on that page matches the review at the end, and browses through some of the other parts of the chapter. She has a rough idea that the chapter is going to define the field and discuss its history.

( )   _____ Keeping in mind the question she has posed, Vanessa reads the section about the meeting of psychology's "parents" and formulates a tentative answer to her question. (She also formulates some additional questions: "Who was Descartes?" and "What method did philosophers use?")

( )   _____ Vanessa answers her first question as follows: "Philosophy (one of the parents) posed questions about the mind that made the study of human thinking and actions acceptable; physiology (the other parent) contributed the scientific method." She decides to note down her answer for later review.

( )   _____ When she has finished step 4 for all sections, Vanessa looks over the entire chapter, section by section. She repeats the questions for each section and attempts to answer each one.

20-2.   What makes the SQ3R technique so effective?

Answers: 20-1. (2) Question (1) Survey (3) Read (4) Recite (5) Review **20-2.** It breaks the reading assignment into manageable segments; it requires understanding before you move on.

21. Summarize advice provided on how to get more out of lectures.

21-1.   Using a few words for each point, summarize the four points on getting more out of lectures.

Answers: 21-1. Listen actively—focus full attention on the speaker; for complex material, read ahead; take notes in your own words and attend to clues about what is most important; consider asking questions during lectures.

22. Summarize advice provided on improving test-taking strategies.

22-1.   Is it better to change answers on multiple-choice tests or to go with one's first hunch?

22-2.   Following are situations you might encounter while taking a test. Reread the section on general test-taking tips and then indicate what you would do in each situation.

(a) You run into a particularly difficult item:

(b) The answer seems to be simple, but you think you may be missing something:

(c) The test is a timed test:

(d) You have some time left at the end of the test:

22-3. Following are samples of the situations mentioned under the discussion of tips for multiple-choice and essay exam questions. Based on the suggestions, what would you do?

(a) In a multiple-choice test, item *c* seems to be correct, but you have not yet read items *d* and *e*: What would you do next?

(b) You know that items *a* and *b* are correct, are unsure of items *c* and *d*, and item *e* is an "all of the above" option. Which alternative (a, b, c, d, or e) would you choose?

(c) You have no idea which multiple-choice alternative is correct. You note that option *a* has the word "always" in it, items *b* and *c* use the word "never," and item *d* says "frequently."

(d) You have read the stem of a multiple-choice item but you have not yet looked at the options.

(e) You think you know a concise answer to an essay question. You wonder whether to pad your answer with a long introduction or get right to the point.

(f) You know that the answer to an essay question has many parts. You wonder whether or not to simply begin writing and let the ideas flow or spend a minute in organization.

Answers: 22-1. In general, changing answers seems to be better. Available research indicates that people are more than twice as likely to go from a wrong answer to a right one as from a right answer to a wrong one. **22-2.** (a) Skip it and come back to it if time permits. (b) Maybe the answer is simple! Don't make the question more complex than it was intended to be. (c) Budget your time, checking the proportion of the test completed against the time available. (d) Review, reconsider, check over your answers. **22-3.** (a) Read all options. (b) Answer *e*. (c) Answer *d*. (Still good advice and generally the best procedure to follow. But note that some professors, aware of the strategy, may throw in an item in which "always" is part of a correct answer! It's sort of like radar detectors: someone builds a better detector and someone else tries to build radar that can't be detected.) (d) Try to anticipate the correct answer *before* reading the options. (e) It is best to get right to the point. At the same time, be sure that your answer is complete, that it contains all of the points called for in the question. (f) Spend a few minutes planning, organizing, or possibly even outlining. Many examiners will appreciate your use of headings or numbers to identify points made.

REVIEW OF KEY TERMS

Applied psychology
Behavior
Behaviorism
Clinical psychology
Cognition
Culture
Empiricism
Ethnocentrism

Evolutionary psychology
Functionalism
Gestalt psychology
Humanism
Introspection
Natural selection
Phi phenomenon
Psychiatry

Psychoanalytic theory
Psychology
SQ3R
Stimulus
Structuralism
Testwiseness
Theory
Unconscious

_____ 1. Any detectable input from the environment.

_____ 2. The branch of psychology concerned with practical problems.

_____ 3. School of thought based on notion that the task of psychology is to analyze consciousness into its basic elements.

_____ 4. Observation of one's own conscious experience.

_____ 5. School of thought asserting that psychology's major purpose was to investigate the function or purpose of consciousness.

_____ 6. The theoretical orientation asserting that scientific psychology should study only observable behavior.

_____ 7. An observable activity or response by an organism.

_____ 8. Examines behavioral processes in terms of their adaptive or survival value for a species.

_____ 9. School of psychology asserting that the whole is greater than the sum of its parts.

_____ 10. The illusion of movement created by presenting visual stimuli in rapid succession.

_____ 11. Freudian theory that explains personality and abnormal behavior in terms of unconscious processes.

_____ 12. According to psychoanalytic theory, that portion of the mind containing thoughts, memories, and wishes not in awareness but nonetheless exerting a strong effect on human behavior.

_____ 13. The psychological theory asserting that human beings are unique and fundamentally different from other animals.

_____ 14. The tendency to view one's own group as superior to other groups.

_____ 15. Widely shared customs, beliefs, values, norms, and institutions that are transmitted socially across generations.

_____ 16. The branch of psychology concerned with the diagnosis and treatment of psychological disorders.

_____ 17. Mental processes or thinking.

_____ 18. The science that studies behavior and the physiological and cognitive processes that underlie it, and it is the profession that applies this knowledge to solving various practical problems.

_____ 19. The branch of medicine concerned with the diagnosis and treatment of psychological problems and disorders.

_____ 20. The point of view that knowledge should be based on observation.

_____ 21. A system of ideas used to link together or explain a set of observations.

_____ 22. A five-step procedure designed to improve study skills.

_____ 23. Ability to use the characteristics and formats of a test to maximize one's score.

_____ 24. The Darwinian principle that characteristics that have a survival advantage for a species are more likely to be passed on to subsequent generations.

Answers: 1. stimulus **2.** applied psychology **3.** structuralism **4.** introspection **5.** functionalism **6.** behaviorism **7.** behavior **8.** evolutionary psychology **9.** Gestalt psychology **10.** phi phenomenon **11.** psychoanalytic theory **12.** unconscious **13.** humanism **14.** ethnocentrism **15.** culture **16.** clinical psychology **17.** cognition **18.** psychology **19.** psychiatry **20.** empiricism **21.** theory **22.** SQ3R **23.** testwiseness **24.** natural selection.

REVIEW OF KEY PEOPLE

Sigmund Freud   Carl Rogers   John B. Watson
G. Stanley Hall   B. F. Skinner   Wilhelm Wundt
William James

_____ 1. Founded experimental psychology and the first experimental psychology laboratory.

_____ 2. Established the first American research laboratory, launched America's first psychological journal, was first president of the APA.

_____ 3. Chief architect of functionalism; described a "stream of consciousness."

_____ 4. Founded behaviorism.

_____ 5. Devised the theory and technique known as psychoanalysis.

_____ 6. Identified operant conditioning.

_____ 7. A major proponent of "humanistic" psychology.

Answers: 1. Wundt **2.** Hall **3.** James **4.** Watson **5.** Freud **6.** Skinner **7.** Rogers.

SELF-QUIZ

1. Structuralism is the historical school of psychology that asserted that the purpose of psychology was to:
   a. study behavior
   b. discover the smaller elements that comprise consciousness
   c. explore the unconscious
   d. examine the purposes of conscious processes

2. Of the two parents of psychology, physiology and philosophy, which provided the method? What is the method?
   a. philosophy; logic, reasoning
   b. philosophy; intuition, introspection
   c. physiology; observation, science
   d. physiology; anatomy, surgery

3. Who is Wilhelm Wundt?
   a. He founded the first experimental laboratory.
   b. He founded the American Psychological Association.
   c. He discovered the classically conditioned salivary reflex.
   d. He founded behaviorism.

4. For John B. Watson, the appropriate subject matter of psychology was:
   a. animal behavior
   b. the unconscious
   c. consciousness
   d. human physiology

5. Which of the following represents a major breakthrough in the development of applied psychology?
   a. the use of the method of introspection
   b. Binet's development of the intelligence test
   c. establishment of the first animal laboratory
   d. Wundt's founding of experimental psychology

6. Within the field of psychology, Freud's ideas encountered resistance primarily because he emphasized:
   a. human consciousness
   b. human behavior
   c. introspection
   d. the unconscious

7. Which of the following would be considered the major principle of operant conditioning?
   a. Human behavior derives in part from free will; animal behavior is determined by the environment.
   b. Humans and other animals tend to repeat responses followed by positive outcomes.
   c. The majority of human behavior is based on thoughts, feelings, and wishes of which we are unaware.
   d. Human beings are fundamentally different from other animals.

8. Which of the following theorists would tend to emphasize explanations in terms of freedom and potential for personal growth?
   a. Carl Rogers
   b. Sigmund Freud
   c. B. F. Skinner
   d. All of the above

9. Recent research trends in psychology involve two areas largely ignored by early behaviorists. These two areas are:
   a. observable and measurable responses
   b. cognition (thinking) and physiological processes
   c. classical and operant conditioning
   d. the effect of environmental events and the behavior of lower animals

10. Which core psychological research area is primarily devoted to the study of such topics as memory, problem solving, and thinking?
    a. physiological
    b. social
    c. cognitive
    d. personality

11. Which of the following schools of psychology objected both to attempts to break consciousness into constituent elements and to attempts to analyze behavior into stimulus-response bonds?
    a. structuralism
    b. functionalism
    c. behaviorism
    d. Gestalt

12. The assertion that "psychology is empirical" means that psychology is based on:
a. introspection
b. logic
c. observation
d. mathematics

13. In looking for the causes of a particular behavior, psychologists assume:
a. one cause or factor
b. multifactorial causation
c. free will
d. infinite causation

14. Contemporary psychologists generally assume that human behavior is determined by:
a. heredity
b. environment
c. heredity and environment acting jointly
d. heredity, environment, and free will

15. What does SQ3R stand for?
a. search, question, research, recommend, reconstitute
b. silence, quietude, reading, writing, arithmetic
c. summarize, quickly, read, research, reread
d. survey, question, read, recite, review

Answers: 1. b **2.** c **3.** a **4.** a **5.** b **6.** d **7.** b **8.** a **9.** b **10.** c **11.** d **12.** c **13.** b **14.** c **15.** d.

Chapter Two

The Research Enterprise in Psychology

REVIEW OF KEY IDEAS

LOOKING FOR LAWS: THE SCIENTIFIC APPROACH TO BEHAVIOR

1. **Explain science's main assumption and describe the goals of the scientific enterprise in psychology.**

   1-1. A major assumption of science is that events occur in an orderly or _____ manner.

   1-2. The three interrelated goals of psychology and the other sciences are: (a) measurement and description, (b) understanding and prediction, and (c) application and control. Match each of the following descriptions with the goal it represents by placing the appropriate letters in the blanks. (There is considerable overlap among these goals; pick the closest match.)

   _____ Muscle relaxation techniques are found to be useful in reducing anxiety and improving concentration and memory.

   _____ A psychologist develops a test or procedure that measures anxiety.

   _____ Researchers find that when individuals are exposed to an object they happen to fear (e.g., a cliff, rats, roaches, snakes, spiders, etc.), their concentration and memory deteriorate.

   Answers: 1-1. lawful (predictable, consistent, regular) **1-2.** absolute (final, concrete), lawful (orderly, etc.) **1-3.** c, a, b.

2. **Explain the relations between theory, hypotheses, and research.**

   2-1. What's a theory? Your text defines a theory as a system of ideas that is used to explain a set of observations. So, a theory is a *system*, which means that it integrates (or organizes or classifies) a series of observations; and it helps _____ those observations. And, it does one thing more: it suggests ideas, or predictions, or _____, to be tested future research.

   2-2. Researchers can't test a theory all at once, but they can test one or two hypotheses derived from the theory. This, then, is the relationship between theory, hypothesis, and research: theories suggest _____ (questions or predictions), which are then tested in _____. If the hypotheses are supported, then confidence in the concepts of the _____ is strengthened.

3. Describe psychology's relations to other sciences.

3-1.　What psychology has in common with the other sciences is the assumption that events in the world around us are best explored through empirical _____. Thus, the major aspect of similarity among the sciences is the scientific method; the major difference concerns the (<u>subject matter/method</u>).

3-2.　While psychology and the other sciences to a large extent study different phenomena, there is overlap. For example, both psychologists and _____ may study brain function and genetic inheritance. As your text points out, Herbert Simon and Roger Sperry, both professors of _____, have won Nobel prizes in, respectively, economics and physiology.

4. Outline the steps in a scientific investigation.

4-1.　Following are the five steps generally used in performing a scientific investigation. Fill in the missing key words.

(a) Formulate a testable _____.

(b) Select the research _____ and design the study.

(c) _____ the data.

(d) _____ the data and draw conclusions.

(e) _____ the findings.

4-2.　Following are descriptions of various phases in the project by Holmes and his co-workers (Wyler et al., 1968). Indicate which step of this study is being described by placing a letter from the previous question (a, b, c, d, or e) in the appropriate blank.

_____ The authors prepared a report of their findings that was accepted for publication in a technical journal.

_____ The patients' responses were expressed as numbers and analyzed with statistics. The data indicated that high scores on the life change questionnaire were associated with high scores on physical illness.

_____ Holmes and his co-workers thought that life change might be associated with increased illness. Before they began they made precise operational definitions of both life change and illness.

_____ The researchers decided to use a survey procedure involving administering questionnaires to a large number of people.

_____ The researchers gathered questionnaire data from 232 patients.

5. Discuss the advantages of the scientific approach.

5-1.　We all tend to agree with the idea that "haste makes waste." We are also likely to agree with a commonsense saying that has the opposite implication: "a stitch in time saves nine." What are the two major advantages of the scientific approach over the commonsense approach?

Answers: 5-1. First, scientific descriptions generally have a clarity and precision lacking in commonsense proverbs. While we have a general idea about the meaning of haste, for example, we don't know precisely when or in what way or how much haste we should avoid. Second, science has an intolerance for error or for contradictory conclusions, and commonsense sayings are likely to be contradictory. (Note that the proverbs in our example have contradictory messages: one says to slow down, the other says to hurry up.)

LOOKING FOR CAUSES: EXPERIMENTAL RESEARCH

6. **Describe the experimental method of research, explaining independent and dependent variables, experimental and control groups, and extraneous variables.**

6-1. Schachter proposed that affiliation is caused (in part) by level of anxiety. What was his independent variable? _____ Dependent variable? _____

6-2. The variable that is manipulated or varied by the experimenter is termed the _____ variable. The variable that is affected by, or is dependent on, the manipulation is termed the _____ variable.

6-3. What is the name of the variable that *results from* the manipulation? _____ What is the name of the variable that *produces* the effect? _____

6-4. The group of subjects that receives the experimental treatment is known as the _____ group; the group that does not is known as the _____ group.

6-5. Control and experimental groups are quite similar in most respects. They differ in that the experimental group receives the experimental _____ and the control group does not. Thus, any differences found in the measure of the _____ variable are assumed to be due to differences in manipulation of the _____ variable.

6-6. An extraneous variable is any variable other than the _____ variable that seems likely to cause a difference between groups as measured by the _____ variable.

6-7. To review the parts of an experiment: Suppose a researcher is interested in the effect of a drug on the running speed of rats. The _____ group is injected with the drug and the _____ group is not. Whether or not the rats received the drug would be the _____ variable, and running speed would be the _____ variable.

6-8. Suppose also that the average age of the experimental rats is two years while the average age of the control rats is 3 months. What is the extraneous variable in this experiment? _____ Why does this variable present a problem?

6-9. Researchers generally control for extraneous variables through random _____ of subjects to groups. Write a definition of this procedure:

7. **Describe the Featured Study on hypnosis and eyewitness memory.**

   7-1.   (a) What did subjects observe as part of the procedure?

   (b) What were the two independent variables?

   7-2.   Which group was more accurate, in terms of either correctly identifying the thief or indicating that he was not in the lineup? _____ Which group had somewhat more confidence in its judgments? _____ Which group recalled more details on the ten-item test? _____

   7-3.   What is the major implication to be drawn from this study?

8. **Explain the major advantages and disadvantages of the experimental method.**

   8-1.   What is the major advantage of the experimental method?

   8-2.   What are the two major disadvantages of the experimental method?

   8-3.   Suppose a researcher is interested in the effect of drinking large amounts of alcohol on health (e.g., 15 glasses of wine per day over an extended period of time). What would be a major *disadvantage* of using the experimental method to examine this particular question?

Answers: 8-1. The major advantage is that it permits researchers to make cause-effect conclusions. **8-2.** The major disadvantages are that (a) precise experimental control may make the situation so artificial that it does not apply to the real world, and (b) ethical or practical considerations may prevent one from manipulating independent variables of interest. **8-3.** It would be unethical and perhaps impossible to require an experimental group to drink that much per day.

LOOKING FOR LINKS: DESCRIPTIVE RESEARCH

9. **Discuss three descriptive/correlational methods: naturalistic observation, case studies, and surveys.**

   9-1. Naturalistic observation involves study of human beings or animals in their natural environments conducted (<u>with/without</u>) direct intervention from the observer.

   9-2. A case study is an in-depth and generally highly subjective or impressionistic report on (<u>a group of people/a single individual</u>) that may be based on interviews, psychological testing, and so on.

   9-3. The third descriptive procedure is the survey technique. *Surveys* use _____ to find out about specific aspects of human attitudes or opinions.

   9-4. List the three descriptive/correlational methods in the space below.

   Answers: 9-1. without **9-2.** a single individual **9-3.** questionnaires (or interviews) **9-4.** naturalistic observation, case studies, surveys.

10. **Explain the major advantages and disadvantages of descriptive/correlational research.**

    10-1. The major difference between the experimental method and descriptive research is that with descriptive/correlational research the experimenter cannot _____ variables. For this reason, the descriptive methods do not permit one to demonstrate _____ relationships between variables.

    10-2. For example, suppose you have data indicating that people who happen to drink a lot of coffee tend to have cardiovascular problems. Is this experimental or descriptive/correlational research? _____ Would it be correct to infer (from these data) that coffee drinking causes cardio-vascular problems? _____

    10-3. An advantage of the descriptive/correlational methods is that they allow researchers to study phenomena that they could not study with experimental methods. Thus, the descriptive/correlational methods (<u>narrow/broaden</u>) the scope of phenomena studied. A major disadvantage of these techniques is that one generally cannot make _____ conclusions from the resulting data.

    Answers: 10-1. manipulate (control), cause-effect (causal) **10-2.** descriptive/correlational, because the variables are not manipulated by the experimenter; no **10-3.** broaden, cause-effect (causal).

LOOKING FOR CONCLUSIONS: STATISTICS AND RESEARCH

11. **Describe three measures of central tendency and one measure of variability.**

    11-1. To review the meaning of the three measures of central tendency, determine the mean, median, and mode of the following scores: 3, 5, 5, 5, 6, 6, 7, 9, 80.

Mean: _____

Median: _____

Mode: _____

11-2. One can describe a group of data with a single number by using one of the measures of central tendency. In the blanks below indicate which measure of central tendency is being described.

_____ The score that occurs most frequently.

_____ The sum of all scores divided by the total number of scores.

_____ Half the scores fall above this measure and half below.

_____ Very sensitive to extreme scores.

_____ Usually the most useful because it may be used in further statistical manipulations.

_____ The middle score.

11-3. What is the median of data set A, below? _____ of set B? _____ Which of these sets is more variable, A or B? _____

A. 30, 40, 50, 60, 70 B. 10, 30, 50, 70, 90

11-4. What is the name of the statistic used as a measure of variability? _____

_____.

Answers: 11-1. 14, 6, 5 **11-2.** mode, mean, median, mean, mean, median **11-3.** 50, 50, B **11-4.** standard deviation.

12. Distinguish between positive and negative correlations.

12-1. Some examples help illustrate the difference between positive and negative correlations. Which of the following relationships are positive (direct) and which are negative (inverse)? (Indicate with a + or – sign.)

____ The better that students' grades are in high school, the better their grades tend to be in college.

____ The more alcohol one has drunk, the slower his or her reaction time.

____ The higher the anxiety, the poorer the test performance.

____ The greater the fear, the greater the need for affiliation.

12-2. Which of the following indicates the *strongest correlational relationship*?

a. 1.12

b. –.92

c. .58

d. .87

Answers: 12-1. +, –, –, + **12-2.** b (not *a*, because correlations cannot exceed +1.00 or –1.00).

13. Discuss correlation in relation to prediction and causation.

13-1. Suppose you have some data indicating that the more money people make (i.e., the higher their annual incomes), the less depressed feelings they report on a mood survey. Thus, if you know the incomes of people in that group you should be able to _____, with some degree of accuracy, their self-reported depressed mood.

13-2. The accuracy of your prediction will depend on the size of the correlation coefficient. Which of the following correlation coefficients would allow you to predict with the greatest accuracy?

    a. +.41

    b. +.54

    c. −.65

13-3. What kind of conclusion is justified on the basis of the previous relationship, a conclusion involving prediction or one involving a statement about causation? _____

13-4. Consider the same relationship as in the previous question: You discover that the more money people make, the greater their happiness. Which of the following conclusions is justified? Explain why.

    a. Money makes people happy.

    b. Happiness causes people to earn more money.

    c. Both happiness and money result from some unknown third factor.

    d. None of the above.

13-5. Again consider the relationship between money and happiness. Assume that money does not cause happiness and happiness does not cause money. What possible *third factor* can you think of that could cause both? (I'm asking you to make a wild speculation here just to get the idea of how third variables may operate.)

13-6. We aren't justified in making causal conclusions from a correlation, but we can predict. Let's examine what prediction means in the case of our hypothetical example. If the relationship really exists, what prediction would you make about people who are rich? What prediction would you make concerning people who are unhappy?

Answers: 13-1. predict **13-2.** c. **13-3.** prediction (Generally one can't make causal conclusions from a correlation.) **13-4.** d. Any of the statements is a possible *causal* explanation of the relationship, but we don't know which one(s) may be correct because the data are correlational. Therefore, *no causal conclusions* are justified. **13-5.** For example, poor health might cause one to be both unhappy *and* poverty stricken (while good health would cause one to be both happy and wealthy). Intelligence or aggressiveness or stubbornness or a number of other physiological or behavioral factors could be causally related *both* to income and to happiness without those two factors being causes of one another. **13-6.** You would predict that a group that was rich would also be happy and that a group that was unhappy would be poor. No causation is implied in these statements.

14. Explain the logic of hypothesis testing and the meaning of statistical significance.

14-1. In the hypothetical experiment described in your text there are two groups, largely equivalent except that the _____ group receives the computerized tutoring sessions and the _____ group does not. What is the hypothesis of this experiment?

14-2. Researchers statistically evaluate the hypothesis by comparing means and determining the likelihood or probability that a difference between means of the size obtained (or larger) would occur by _____. If the probability that such a difference would occur by chance is very low, say less than 5 times in 100, the researchers would conclude that the difference (<u>is/is not</u>) due to chance. They would declare the difference statistically _____ at the _____ level of significance.

14-3. Statistically significant does not mean important or significant in the usual sense of that word. What does statistically significant mean?

14-4. How do we reach a conclusion when the results of different studies often produce contradictory results? One method for doing so is the relatively new technique known as _____. What is meta-analysis?

Answers: **14-1.** experimental, control, The hypothesis is that special tutoring would increase reading scores. **14-2.** chance, is not, significant, .05 **14-3.** It means that a difference that large would be rare on a chance basis, so it is assumed *not* to be due to chance; or, more simply, it is assumed that the difference between means is due to treatment. **14-4.** Meta-analysis, a statistical technique for combining results from many different studies.

LOOKING FOR FLAWS: EVALUATING RESEARCH

15. Explain what makes a sample representative and discuss the problem of sampling bias.

15-1. Dr. Brutalbaum distributes a questionnaire in an attempt to find out how the students in a particular course react to his teaching. The day that he chooses for the evaluation is the day before a scheduled vacation, and about half the students are absent. He is aware that he does not have to test the entire class, that he may use a representative sample. The question is: is the sample that attended class that day a representative sample? _____ Why or why not?

Answers: **15-1.** No. A representative sample is one that is similar in composition to the population from which it is drawn. In this case, it seems likely that students who attend are different from those who do not (e.g., perhaps more enthusiastic, harder working, more fearful, etc.). Since the sample is not representative, the flaw illustrated is *sampling bias*.

16. Explain when placebo effects are likely to be a problem.

16-1. A student in Brutalbaum's class orders some audio tapes that promise to produce sleep learning. (Brutalbaum is dubious, because from his observations students sleep a lot in class but still don't seem to learn very much. Nonetheless . . .)

The student runs the experiment in Brutalbaum's class. She describes the anticipated sleep-learning benefits to the class and then gives the sleep tapes to a random half of the students and nothing to the other half. After the next test she analyzes the results. The mean test score of the experimental group is statistically significantly higher than that of the control group. What is the flaw in this experiment? .

(a) sampling bias

(b) possible placebo effects

(c) distortions in self-report

(d) None of the above.

16-2. What are placebo effects?

16-3. How would you change the study described above to reduce or eliminate the possibility of placebo effects?

Answers: **16-1.** b **16-2.** Placebo effects: the tendency for people's behavior to change because of their expectation that the treatment will have an effect **16-3.** Include a placebo treatment. For example, the experimenter might have given the control group a placebo tape that was the same as the sleep tape in every respect except for the supposedly critical information.

17. Describe the typical kinds of distortions that occur in self-report data.

17-1. Brutalbaum is now concerned about class attendance and decides to find out what proportion of students miss class regularly. He distributes a questionnaire asking students to indicate how many classes they have missed. Which of the four common flaws is he likely to encounter? _____

17-2. For a number of reasons, people may not answer questions correctly, including the fact that they may not understand the question or don't _____ the information accurately. Respondents also frequently want to create a favorable impression, the response tendency known as the social _____ bias. Somewhat surprisingly, people may also be predisposed to respond in particular ways regardless of the question (e.g., tendencies to agree or disagree regardless of content). This type of response tendency is known as a response _____.

Answers: **17-1.** distortions in self-report **17-2.** remember, desirability, set.

18. Describe Rosenthal's research on experimenter bias.

18-1. When we ask a question, we frequently expect a particular answer. The same thing is true with scientists, and sometimes their hypotheses or expectations influence the answers that they obtain. When a researcher's expectations about the outcome of a study influence the results, then the flaw in procedure known as _____ has occurred.

18-2. Experimenter bias or influence may occur in subtle ways, and Rosenthal has repeatedly demonstrated that when the experimenter merely knows which treatment condition a subject is in, the fact of that knowledge or expectation alone may influence the subject's behavior. For this reason it is extremely important in research to maintain the _____ procedure, in which neither subjects nor experimenters know which treatment condition the subject is in.

Answers: **18-1.** experimenter bias **18-2.** double-blind

LOOKING AT ETHICS: DO THE ENDS JUSTIFY THE MEANS?

19. Discuss the pros and cons of deception in research with human subjects.

19-1. In the space below present one or two of the arguments in favor of using deception and one or two arguments against.

Answers: **19-1.** On the con side, deception is, after all, lying; it may undermine people's trust in others; it may cause distress. On the pro side, many research issues could not be investigated without deception; the "white lies" involved are generally harmless; research indicates that deception studies are not actually harmful to subjects; the advances in knowledge obtained may improve human well-being.

20. Discuss the controversy about the use of animals as research subjects.

20-1. What is the major reason that some people object to using animal subjects in research? In view of this objection, what moral considerations are raised by those who favor using animals in research?

Answers: **20-1.** Many people believe that it is morally wrong to use animals in research, especially in painful or harmful treatments that would be unacceptable for human subjects. In defense of the practice, others cite the significant advances in treatment of a variety of mental and physical disorders that have resulted from animal research. The question to some degree involves the issue of whether or not saving human lives or finding remedies for human illnesses justifies the sacrifice of or pain inflicted on research animals.

PUTTING IT IN PERSPECTIVE

21. Explain how this chapter highlighted two of the text's unifying themes.

21-1. One of the text's unifying themes is that psychology is _____ , which means that its conclusions are based on systematic _____ and that it tends to be (skeptical/credulous).

21-2. In what way did the discussion of methodology suggest that psychology tends to be skeptical of its results?

21-3. Another theme refers to psychology's awareness of the subjectivity of personal experience. In this chapter were described four problems or flaws frequently encountered in research. Describe the two methodological problems discussed that refer to the theme involving subjectivity.

Answers: 21-1. empirical, observation (experience), skeptical **21-2.** The field pays attention only to results considered highly unlikely to have occurred by chance; it constantly searches for methodological flaws; it subjects results to critical scrutiny by other scientists. **21-3.** Scientists try to guard against subjective reactions, both those of the participants as well as their own, by building in controls for placebo effects and experimenter bias.

APPLICATION: FINDING AND READING JOURNAL ARTICLES

22. Describe the nature of technical journals.

22-1. A technical journal publishes scholarly material in a field, generally the results of original empirical _____ . Some journals also publish articles that summarize findings from a large number of studies, articles known as _____ articles.

22-2. Journals represent the core intellectual activity of a field and are generally highly selective, in many cases rejecting more than 90% of manuscripts submitted by researchers. Since the articles are written primarily for (the layman/other professionals), they are frequently difficult for people with little background in a field to read.

23. Explain how to use *Psychological Abstracts* and discuss the advantages of computerized literature searches.

23-1. *Psychological Abstracts* contains abstracts or concise _____ of articles published in psychological journals. To find information about a particular article, consult either the author index or the _____ index found at the back of each monthly issue of the *Abstracts*. Cumulative _____ are published annually.

23-2. If you know the author's name you can easily find the article. Next to the author's name, each article he or she has published within the period is identified by a particular number, its _____ number.

23-3. Once you know the index number you can find the abstract. As you can see in Figure 2.19 in your text, the abstract provides not only a summary but the exact reference for the article, including publication date, page numbers, and name of the _____ in which the article was published.

23-4. The subject index works the same way as the author index, but it's a little more like looking through the yellow pages of a phone book (e.g., do you look under cars, automobiles, or rental?). As with the author index, you can locate the abstract once you find the index _____ of a particular article. A quick glance at the abstract will then tell you whether the article is likely to be of interest.

23-5. The availability of personal computers has made the search easier. The information contained in *Psychological Abstracts* from 1976 on is stored in the _____ databases PsycINFO and PsychLIT. The advantage of computerized over manual searches is that the former are much faster, precise, and thorough. For example, using a computerized search you are much (<u>less/more</u>) likely to miss relevant articles, and by pairing two topics you can find precisely those articles that are relevant to your particular question.

Answers: 23-1. summaries, subject, indexes **23-2.** index **23-3.** journal **23-4.** number **23-5.** computerized, less.

24. Describe the standard organization of journal articles reporting on psychological research.

24-1. In the blanks below list the six parts of the standard journal article in the order in which they occur. (As a hint, the initial letters of each section are listed on the left.)

A _____

I _____

M _____

R _____

D _____

R _____

24-2. In the blanks below match the names of the sections of the standard journal article with the descriptions.

_____ States the hypothesis and reviews the literature relevant to the hypothesis.

_____ A list of all the sources referred to in the paper.

_____ A summary.

_____ Presents the data; may include statistical analyses, graphs, and tables.

_____ Describes what the researchers did in the study; includes subjects, procedures, and data collection techniques.

_____ Interprets or evaluates the data and presents conclusions.

Answers: 24-1. abstract, introduction, method, results, discussion, references **24-2.** introduction, references, abstract, results, method, discussion.

REVIEW OF KEY TERMS

Case study
Confounding of variables
Control group
Correlation
Correlation coefficient
Data collection techniques
Dependent variable
Descriptive statistics
Double-blind procedure
Experiment
Experimental group
Experimenter bias
Extraneous variables
Hypothesis

Independent variable
Independent variable
Inferential statistics
Journal
Mean
Median
Meta-analysis
Mode
Naturalistic observation
Operational definition
Participants
Placebo effects
Population
Random assignment

Replication
Research methods
Response set
Sample
Sampling bias
Social desirability bias
Standard deviation
Statistical significance
Statistics
Survey
Theory
Variability
Variables

_____ 1. Any of the factors in an experiment that are controlled or observed by an experimenter or that in some other way affect the outcome.

_____ 2. A tentative statement about the expected relationship between two or more variables.

_____ 3. Precisely defines each variable in a study in terms of the operations needed to produce or measure that variable.

_____ 4. Persons or animals whose behavior is being studied.

_____ 5. Differing ways of conducting research, which include experiments, case studies, surveys, and naturalistic observation.

_____ 6. A research method in which independent variables are manipulated and which permits causal interpretations.

_____ 7. A condition or event that an experimenter varies in order to observe its impact.

_____ 8. The variable that results from the manipulation in an experiment.

_____ 9. The group in an experiment that receives a treatment as part of the independent variable manipulation.

_____ 10. The group in an experiment that does not receive the treatment.

_____ 11. Any variables other than the independent variables that seem likely to influence the dependent measure in an experiment.

_____ 12. Distribution of subjects in an experiment in which each subject has an equal chance of being assigned to any group or condition.

_____ 13. A link or association between variables such that one can be predicted from the other.

_____ 14. The statistic that indicates the degree of relationship between variables.

_____ 15. A research method in which the researcher observes behavior in the natural environment without directly intervening.

_____ 16. An in-depth, generally subjective, investigation of an individual subject.

_____ 17. A questionnaire or interview used to gather information about specific aspects of subjects' behavior.

_____ 18. Procedures for making empirical observations, including questionnaires, interviews, psychological tests, and physiological recordings.

_____ 19. Mathematical techniques that help in organizing, summarizing, and interpreting numerical data.

_____ 20. Statistics helpful in organizing and summarizing (but not interpreting) data.

_____ 21. Statistical procedures used to interpret data in an experiment and draw conclusions.

_____ 22. A statistical procedure that combines the results of many studies.

_____ 23. A descriptive statistic and measure of central tendency that always falls in the exact half-way point of a distribution of data.

_____ 24. The arithmetic average.

_____ 25. The score that occurs most frequently.

_____ 26. The spread or dispersion of data, including the extent to which scores vary from the mean.

_____ 27. A measure of variability in data.

_____ 28. A judgment inferred from statistics that the probability of the observed findings occurring by chance is very low.

_____ 29. A repetition of a study to determine whether the previously obtained results can be duplicated.

_____ 30. A group of subjects taken from a larger population.

_____ 31. A larger group from which a sample is drawn and to which the researcher wishes to generalize.

_____ 32. Exists when a sample is not representative of the population from which it was drawn.

_____ 33. Also known as subjects, the persons or animals whose behavior is systematically observed in a study.

_____ 34. Occurs when a researcher's expectations influence the results of the study.

_____ 35. Effects that occur when subjects experience a change due to their expectations (or to a "fake" treatment).

_____ 36. The tendency to respond in a particular way (e.g., agreeing) that is unrelated to the content of questions asked.

_____ 37. Occurs when an extraneous variable makes it difficult to sort out the effects of the independent variable.

_____ 38. The tendency to answer questions about oneself in a socially approved manner.

_____ 39. A research strategy in which neither the subjects nor experimenters know which condition or treatment the subjects are in.

_____ 40. A periodical that publishes technical and scholarly material within a discipline.

_____ 41. A system of interrelated ideas used to explain a set of observations.

Answers: 1. variables **2.** hypothesis **3.** operational definition **4.** subjects **5.** research methods **6.** experiment **7.** independent variable **8.** dependent variable **9.** experimental group **10.** control group **11.** extraneous variables **12.** random assignment **13.** correlation **14.** correlation coefficient **15.** naturalistic observation **16.** case study **17.** survey **18.** data collection techniques **19.** statistics **20.** descriptive statistics **21.** inferential statistics **22.** meta-analysis **23.** median **24.** mean **25.** mode **26.** variability **27.** standard deviation **28.** statistical significance **29.** replication **30.** sample **31.** population **32.** sampling bias **33.** participants **34.** experimenter bias **35.** placebo effects **36.** response set **37.** confounding of variables **38.** social desirability bias **39.** double-blind procedure **40.** journal **41.** theory.

REVIEW OF KEY PEOPLE

Thomas Holmes   Robert Rosenthal
Neal Miller   Stanley Schachter

_____   **1.** Examined the relationship between stress and physical illness.

_____   **2.** Studied the effect of anxiety on affiliation.

_____   **3.** Studied experimenter bias, a researcher's unintended influence on the
                                      behavior of subjects.

_____   **4.** Asserted that the benefits of animal research (e.g., the resulting treatments for
                                      mental and physical disorders) far outweigh the harm done.

Answers: 1. Holmes **2.** Schachter **3.** Rosenthal **4.** Miller.

SELF-QUIZ

1. Which of the following is a major assumption of science?
a. Events occur in a relatively orderly or predictable manner.
b. Cause and effect is indicated by correlational relationships.
c. In contrast to the behavior of lower animals, human behavior is in part a function of free will.
d. Events are largely randomly determined.

2. An experimenter tests the hypothesis that physical exercise helps people's mood (makes them happier). Subjects
in the experimental group participate on Monday and Tuesday and those in the control group on Wednesday and
Thursday. What is the _independent_ variable?
a. the hypothesis
b. day of the week
c. the exercise
d. the mood (degree of happiness)

3. Regarding the experiment described in the previous question: What is the _dependent_ variable?
a. the hypothesis
b. day of the week
c. the exercise
d. the mood (degree of happiness)

4. Regarding the experiment described above: What is an _extraneous_ (confounding) variable?
a. the hypothesis
b. day of the week
c. the exercise
d. the mood (degree of happiness)

5. The major advantage of the experimental method over the correlational approach is that the experimental method:
a. permits one to make causal conclusions
b. allows for prediction
c. is generally less artificial than correlational procedures
d. permits the study of people in groups

6. In looking through some medical records you find that there is a strong relationship between depression and chronic pain: the stronger the physical pain that people report, the higher their scores on an inventory that measures depression. Which of the following conclusions are justified?
   a. Depression tends to produce chronic pain.
   b. Chronic pain tends to produce depression.
   c. Both chronic pain and depression result from some unknown third factor.
   d. None of the above.

7. What is the mode of the following data? 2, 3, 3, 3, 5, 5, 7, 12
   a. 3
   b. 4
   c. 5
   d. 6

8. What is the median of the following data? 1, 3, 4, 4, 5, 6, 9,
   a. 3
   b. 4
   c. 4.57
   d. 6

9. Researchers find an inverse relationship between alcohol consumption and speed of response. Which of the following fictitious statistics could possibly represent that correlation?
   a. −4.57
   b. −.87
   c. .91
   d. .05

10. The term *statistical significance* refers to:
    a. how important the data are for future research on the topic
    b. the conclusion that there are no reasonable alternative explanations
    c. the inference that the observed effects are unlikely to be due to chance
    d. the representativeness of the sample

11. An instructor wishes to find out whether a new teaching method is superior to his usual procedures, so he conducts an experiment. Everyone in his classes is quite excited about the prospect of learning under the new procedure, but of course he cannot administer the new teaching method to everyone. A random half of the students receive the new method and the remaining half receive the old. What is the most obvious flaw in this experiment?
    a. Subjects should have been systematically assigned to groups.
    b. The sample is not representative of the population.
    c. Placebo effects or experimenter bias are likely to affect results.
    d. Distortions in self-report will affect results.

12. What procedure helps correct for experimenter bias?
    a. extraneous or confounding variables
    b. sleep learning or hypnosis
    c. a higher standard for statistical significance
    d. use of the double-blind procedure

13. With regard to the topic of deception in research with human subjects, which of the following is true?
    a. Researchers are careful to avoid deceiving subjects.
    b. Some topics could not be investigated unless deception was used.
    c. It has been empirically demonstrated that deception causes severe distress.
    d. All psychological research must involve some deception.

14. Which of the following is among the six standard parts of a psychological journal article?
    a. conclusions
    b. bibliography
    c. data summary
    d. results

15. The Author Index in the *Psychological Abstracts* provides:
    a. names of current APA members
    b. registration and biographical information about frequent authors
    c. index numbers that locate article summaries
    d. names of authors who specialize in abstractions

Answers: 1. a **2.** c **3.** d **4.** b **5.** a **6.** d **7.** a **8.** b **9.** b **10.** c **11.** c **12.** d **13.** b **14.** d **15.** c.

Chapter Three

The Biological Basis of Behavior

REVIEW OF KEY IDEAS

COMMUNICATION IN THE NERVOUS SYSTEM

1. **Describe the main functions of the two types of nervous tissue.**

   1-1. One of the major types of nervous tissue provides very important services to the other type: such removing waste, supplying nutrients, insulating, and providing structural support. Individual members of this kind of nervous tissue are called _____.

   1-2. The other type of nervous tissue receives, integrates, and transmits information. Individual members of this type of tissue are called _____.

   1-3. While most neurons just receive and transmit information from one neuron to another, two kinds of neurons are specialized for additional tasks. Name the two types and describe their specialization below.

   Answers: 1-1. glia cells **1-2.** neurons **1-3.** Sensory neurons receive information from the outside environment, while motor neurons activate the muscles.

2. **Describe the various parts of the neuron and their functions.**

   2-1. The neuron has three basic parts, the <u>dendrites</u>, the <u>cell body</u> or <u>soma</u>, and the <u>axon</u>. The major mission of the average neuron is to receive information from one neuron and pass it on to the next neuron. The receiving part is the job of the branch-like parts called _____. They then pass the message along to the nucleus of the cell, called the <u>cell body</u>, or _____. From there the message is sent down the _____ to be passed along to other neurons.

   2-2. Many axons are wrapped in a fatty jacket called the _____, which permits for faster transmission of information and prevents messages from getting on to the wrong track. Like the covering on an electrical cord, myelin acts as an _____ material.

2-3. When the neural message reaches the end of the axon it excites projections called <u>terminal</u> _____, which then release a chemical substance into the junction that separates them from other neurons. This junction between neurons is called the _____.

2-4. Identify the major parts of a neuron in the figure below. Note that the arrow indicates the direction of the flow of information.

(a) _____ (b) _____ (c) _____ (d)_____

Answers: **2-1.** dendrites, soma, axon **2-2.** myelin sheath, insulating **2-3.** buttons, synapse **2-4.** (a) dendrites, (b) cell body or soma, (c) axon, (d) terminal buttons.

3. Describe the neural impulse.

3-1. When it is at rest, the neuron is like a tiny battery in that it contains a weak (<u>negative/positive</u>) charge. When the neuron is stimulated, the cell membrane becomes more permeable. This allows positively charged _____ ions to flow into the cell, thus lessening the cell's negative charge.

3-2. The change in the charge of the cell caused by the inflow of positively charged sodium ions, called an _____, travels down the _____ of the neuron. After the firing of an action potential, there is a brief period in which no further action potentials can be generated. This brief period is called the <u>absolute</u> _____period.

3-3. The text likens the neuron to a gun in that it either fires or it does not fire. This property of the neuron is called the _____ law. Neurons transmit information about the strength of a stimulus by variations in the number of action potentials generated. For example, in comparison to a weak stimulus, a strong stimulus will generate a (<u>higher/lower</u>) rate of action potentials.

Answers: **3-1.** negative, sodium **3-2.** action potential, axon, refractory **3-3.** all or none, higher.

4. Describe how neurons communicate at chemical synapses.

4-1. A neuron passes its message on to another neuron by releasing a chemical messenger into the gap or _____ that separates it from other neurons. The sending neuron, called the _____, releases a chemical messenger into the synaptic cleft, which then excites the _____neuron.

4-2. The chemical messenger that provides this transmitting service is called a _____. The chemical binds with specifically tuned receptor sites on the postsynaptic neurons. In other words, the receptor sites accept some neurotransmitters and reject _____. Thus a specific receptor site and a specific neurotransmitter act in the manner of a lock and _____.

Answers: **4-1.** synaptic cleft, presynaptic, postsynaptic **4-2.** neurotransmitter, others, key.

5. Describe the two types of postsynaptic potentials and how cellls integrate these signals

5-1. When the neurotransmitter combines with a molecule at the receptor site it causes a voltage change at the receptor site called a _____ potential (PSP). One type of PSP is excitatory and (<u>increases</u>/ <u>decreases</u>) the probability of producing an action potential in the receiving neuron. The other type is inhibitory and _____ the probability of producing an action potential.

5-2. Whether or not a neuron fires depends on the number of excitatory PSPs it is receiving and the number of _____ PSPs it is receiving. PSPs (<u>do/do not</u>) follow the all or none law.

5-3. Put the five steps of communication at the synapse in their correct order (by using the numbers 1 through 5):

_5_ (a) The reuptake of transmitters by the presynaptic neuron.

_4_ (b) The enzyme inactivation or drifting away of transmitters in the synapse

_1_ (c) The synthesis and storage or transmitters.

_3_ (d) The binding of transmitters at receptor sites on the postsynaptic membrane.

_2_ (e) The release of transmitters into the symaptic cleft.

5-4. If enough excitatory PSPs occur in a neuron, the electrical currents can add up cauing the neuron to generate an action potential. Excitatory PSPs can add up in two ways. When several PSPs follow and another in rapid succession at a receptor site, _____ summation can occur. When several PSPs occur simultaneously at different receptor sites, _____ summation can occur.

Answers: **5-1.** postsynaptic, increases, decreases **5-2.** inhibitory, do not **5-3.** (a) 5, (b) 4, (c) 1, (d) 3, (e) 2.
5-4. temporal, spatial.

6. Discuss some of the functions of acetylcholine and the monoamine neurotransmitters.

6-1. Our moods, thoughts and actions all depend on the action of neurotransmitters. For example, the movement of all muscles depends on _____ (ACh). An inadequate supply of acetylcholine has also been implicated in the memory losses seen in _____ disease.

6-2. Three neurotransmitters, dopamine, norepinephrine, and serotonin, are collectively known as _____. Both Parkinsonism and schizophrenia have been linked with alterations in _____ activity, while the mood changes found in depression have been linked to receptor sites for _____ and serotonin. Serotonin also plays a key role in the regulation of _____ and wakefulness.

Answers: **6-1.** acetylcholine, Alzheimer's **6-2.** monoamines, dopamine, norepinephrine, sleep.

7. **Discuss how GABA and endorphins are related to behavior.**

7-1.   Still another group of neurotransmitters, including GABA and glycine, are unlike other neurotransmitters in that they only have (excitatory/inhibitory) effects at receptor sites. Most other neurotransmitters can have either inhibitory or excitatory effects. Lowered levels of GABA in the brain may allow for heightened neural activity which translates into feelings of _____. Tranquilizers appear to work by facilitating the binding of _____ to its receptors.

7-2.   Endorphins are neuropeptides produced by the body that have effects similar to those produced by the drug _____and its derivatives. That is, they are able to reduce pain and also induce _____. Endorphins work in two different ways. Some bind to specific receptor sites and thus serve as _____. Most endorphins, however, work by modulating the activity of specific neurotransmitters. In this role they are said to serve as _____.

Answers: 7-1. inhibitory, anxiety, GABA **7-2.** opium, pleasure, neurotransmitters, neuromodulators.

ORGANIZATION OF THE NERVOUS SYSTEM

8. **Provide an overview of the peripheral nervous system, including its subdivisions.**

With approximately 85 to 180 billion individual neurons to control, it is important that the central nervous system have some kind of organizational structure. This organizational structure is depicted in Figure 3.8 of the text, and it will prove helpful if you have this figure in front of you while answering the following questions.

8-1.   Answer the following questions regarding the organization of the peripheral nervous system.

(a) What constitutes the peripheral nervous system?

(b) What two subdivisions make up the peripheral nervous system?

(c) What is the role of the afferent and efferent nerve fibers?

(d) What two subdivisions make up the autonomic nervous system?

(e) Describe the opposing roles of the sympathetic and parasympathetic nervous systems.

Answers: 8-1. (a) All of the nerves that lie outside of the brain and spinal cord. (b) The somatic nervous system and the autonomic nervous system. (c) Afferent fibers carry information inward from the periphery, while efferent fibers carry information outward to the periphery. (d) The sympathetic nervous system and the parasympathetic nervous system. (e) The sympathetic system prepares the body for fight or flight and the parasympathetic system conserves the body's resources.

9. **Distinguish between the central nervous system and the peripheral nervous system.**

    9-1.   What are the two parts of the central nervous system?

    9-2.   What is the name given to all of the nerves that lie outside of the central nervous system?

    Answers: 9-1. The brain and the spinal cord **9-2.** The peripheral nervous system.

LOOKING INSIDE THE BRAIN: RESEARCH METHODS

10. **Describe how the EEG, lesioning, and ESB are used to investigate brain function.**

    10-1.   The electroencephalograph, or _____, is a device that can measure the brain's _____ activity. Electrodes are placed on the scalp and the brain's electrical activity is then monitored by the EEG machine and transformed into line tracings called _____waves.

    10-2.   Answer the following questions regarding the use of lesioning and ESB to investigate brain function.

        (a) What technique involves the actual destruction of brain tissue in order to examine the resulting effect on behavior?

        (b) What technique would most likely be employed by a neurosurgeon to map the brain of a patient?

        (c) Which techniques employ the use of electrodes and electrical currents?

        (d) In what fundamental way does lesioning differ from ESB?

    Answers: 10-1. EEG, electrical, brain **10-2.** (a) lesioning (b) ESB (c) lesioning and ESB (d) Lesioning is used to actually destroy tissue, whereas ESB is used to merely elicit behavior.

11. **Describe the new brain-imaging methods that are used to study brain structure and function.**

    11-1.   There are three new kinds of brain-imaging procedures that have come into recent use. One of these procedures consists of a computer enhanced X-ray machine that compiles multiple X-rays of the brain into a single vivid picture. The resulting images are called _____ scans. An even newer device that produces clearer three dimensional images of the brain goes by the name of magnetic resonance imaging scanner, and the images it produces are known as _____ scans.

11-2. Unlike CT and MRI scans, which can only show the structure of the brain, the positron emission tomography scanner can portray the brain's actual _____ across time. The images produced by this procedure are called _____ scans.

Answers: **11-1.** CT, MRI **11-2.** activity, PET.

THE BRAIN AND BEHAVIOR

12. Summarize the key functions of the medulla, pons, and cerebellum.

12-1. Three separate structures make up the hindbrain: the cerebellum, the pons, and the medulla. Identify these structures from the descriptions given below.

(a) This structure is essential for executing and coordinating physical movement.

(b) This structure attachs to the top of the spinal cord and controls many essential functions such as breathing and circulation.

(c) This structure forms a bridge of fibers between the brainstem and cerebellum and plays an important role in both sleep and arousal.

Answers: **12-1.** (a) cerebellum (b) medulla (c) pons.

13. Summarize the key functions of the midbrain.

13-1. Helping to locate objects in space and execute voluntary movements are two of the major roles of the _____. It also shares a structure with the hindbrain that is essential for the regulation of sleep and wakefulness as well as modulation of muscular reflexes, breathing, and pain perception. This structure is called the _____ formation.

Answers: **13-1.** midbrain, reticular.

14. Summarize the key functions of the thalamus and hypothalamus.

14-1. The structure which serves as a way station for all sensory information headed for the brain is called the _____. The thalamus also appears to play an active role in _____ sensory information.

14-2. In addition to its role in controlling the autonomic nervous system and linking the brain to the endocrine system, the hypothatamus also plays a major role in regulating basic biological drives such as fighting, _____, feeding, and _____.

Answers: **14-1.** thalamus, integrating **14-2.** fleeing, mating.

15. **Describe the nature and location of the limbic system and summarize some of its key functions.**

15-1.   An interconnected network of structures involved in the control of emotion, motivation, and memory are collectively known as the _____ system. Damage to one of these structures, the hippocampus, is found in Alzheimer's disease patients; thus it must play a key role in the formation of _____. However, the limbic system is best known for its role as the seat of _____. Electrical stimulation of particular areas of the limbic system in rats, monkeys, and human beings appears to produce intense pleasure, but the pleasure seems to be least intense in _____. The key neurotransmitter in these pleasure centers appears to be _____.

Answers: **15-1.** limbic, memories, emotion, humans, dopamine.

16. **Name the four lobes in the cerebral cortex and identify some of their key functions.**

_16-1.   The cerebrum is the brain structure that is responsible for our most complex _____ activities. Its folded outer surface is called the _____ cortex. The cerebrum is divided into two halves, known as the _____ and _____ cerebral hemispheres. The two hemispheres communicate with each other by means of a wide band of fibers called the _____ _____.

⌐16-2.   Each cerebral hemisphere is divided into four parts called lobes. Match these four lobes (occipital, parietal, temporal, and frontal) with their key function:

_____ (a) Contains the primary motor cortex that controls the movement of muscles.

_____ (b) Contains the primary visual cortex which initiates the processing of visual information.

_____ (c) Contains the primary auditory cortex which initiates the processing of auditory information.

_____ (d) Contains the primary sensory cortex that registers the sense of touch.

Answers: **16-1.** mental, cerebral, right, left, corpus callosum **16-2.** (a) frontal (b) occipital (c) temporal (d) parietal.

RIGHT BRAIN/LEFT BRAIN: CEREBRAL LATERALITY

17. **Summarize evidence that led scientists to view the left hemisphere as the dominant hemisphere and describe how split-brain research changed this view.**

⌐17-1.   Until recent years, it was believed that the left hemisphere dominanted a submissive right hemisphere. Evidence for this belief came from several sources which all seemed to indicate that the left hemisphere played the dominant role with respect to the use of _____. For example, damage to an area in the frontal lobe known as _____ area was associated with speech deficits. Also, damage to another area located in the temporal lobe was found to be associated with difficulty in speech comprehension. This area is called _____ area. Both of these areas are located in the _____ cerebral hemisphere.

17-2.   Answer the following questions regarding split-brain research.

(a) What was the result of severing the corpus callosum in these patients?

(b) Which hemisphere was found to be primarily responsible for verbal and language tasks in general?

(c) Which hemisphere was found to be primarily responsible for visual and spatial tasks?

17-3. What can be concluded with respect to hemispheric domination from split-brain studies?

Answers: 17-1. language, Broca's, Wernicke's, left **17-2.** (a) The two cerebral hemispheres could no longer communicate with each other. (b) The left cerebral hemisphere. (c) The right cerebral hemisphere **17-3.** Neither hemisphere dominates, rather each has its own specialized tasks.

18. Describe how neuroscientists conduct research on cerebral specialization in normal subjects and what this research has revealed.

18-1. Researchers have looked at left-right imbalances in the speed of visual or auditory processing in the two hemispheres and have observed perceptual _____ in normal subjects.

18-2. Answer the following questions regarding the conclusions that can be drawn from the research on hemispheric asymmetry.

(a) Are you more likely to identify quickly and accurately verbal stimuli when presented to the right visual field or right ear (left hemisphere), or when presented to the left visual field or left ear (right hemisphere).

(b) Are you more likely to identify quickly and accurately visual/spatial information, such as recognizing a face, when the stimuli are presented to the right visual field (left hemisphere) or when presented to the left visual field (right hemishphere).

(c) What conclusions can be drawm from the research on normal subjects regarding hemispheric specialization with respect to cognitive tasks?

Answers: 18-1. asymmetries **18-2.** (a) When presented to the right visual field or right ear (left hemisphere). (b) When presented to the left visual field (right hemisphere). (c) The two hemispheres handle different cognitive tasks.

19. **Summarize evidence on the origins and correlates of handedness. Describe the Featured Study on reduced longevity in left-handers.**

19-1.   The fact that a vast majority of people in all cultures are right-handed argues against a/an (<u>environmental/genetic</u>) theory of handedness.

19-2.   The fact that left-handedness occurs in only about 35 percent of children whose parents are both left-handed argues against a purely _____ basis for handedness. Thus the explanation of handedness remains _____.

Answers: 19-1. environmental **19-2.** genetic, unknown.

20. **Answer the following questions regarding the Featured Study.**

(a) Who provided the information on the questionnaires as to the handedness of recently deceased persons?

(b) How many reduced years in longevity were found among females who were either left-handed or mixed-handed?

(c) How many reduced years in longevity were found among males who were either left-handed or mixed-handed?

(d) What two factors might account for the reduced survival of left- or mixed-handed persons?

Answers: 20-1. (a) The next of kin as listed on death certificates (b) 5 years (c) 10 years (d) They may be involved in more accidents, and left-handedness may be a marker associated with neurological damage due to birth trauma.

THE ENDOCRINE SYSTEM: ANOTHER WAY TO COMMUNICATE

21. **Describe some of the ways in which hormones regulate behavior.**

21-1.   Answer the following questions regarding the workings of the endocrine system.

(a) What is the role played by the hormones in the endocrine system?

(b) While many glands comprise the endocrine system, which one functions as a master gland to control the others?

(c) What structure is the real power behind the throne here?

21-2. Fill in the boxes in the diagram below showing the role of the pituitary gland in the "fight or flight" response to stress.

Hypothalamus	→		→	ACTH hormone	→	

21-3. What is the role of sexual hormones:

(a) Prior to birth?

— (b) At puberty?

Answers: 21-1. (a) They serve as chemical messengers (b) The pituitary gland. (c) The hypothalamus
21-2. pituitary, adrenal cortex **21-3.** (a) They direct the formation of the external sexual organs. (b) They are responsible for the emergence of the secondary sexual characteristics.

HEREDITY AND BEHAVIOR: IS IT ALL IN THE GENES?

22. Describe the structures and processes involved in genetic transmission.

22-1. When a human sperm and egg unite at conception they form a one-celled organism called a
_____. This cell contains 46 chromosomes, half of which are contributed by each _____,
thus making 23 pairs. Each member of a pair operates in conjunction with its _____ member. The
zygote then evolves to form all of the cells in the body, each of which, except for the sex cells, have
_____ pairs of chromosomes.

22-2. Each chromosome is actually a threadlike strand of a _____ molecule, and along this threadlike
structure are found the individual units of information, called _____, that determine our biological
makeup. Like chromosomes, genes operate in _____. For example, eye color is determined by
a pair of genes. If both parents contribute a gene for the same color, the child will inherit this eye color,
and the two genes are said to be _____. If the parents contribute two different genes for eye color,
the genes are said to be _____, and the child will inherit the eye color carried by the dominant
gene. When heterozygous genes are paired, the dominant gene masks the _____ gene.

Answers: 22-1. zygote, parent, opposite **22-2.** DNA, genes, pairs, homozygous, heterozygous, recessive.

23. **Explain the difference between genotype and phenotype and the meaning of polygenic inheritance.**

23-1. Answer the following questions about the difference between genotype and phenotype.

(a) What are the two genes that make up your eye color said to be?

(b) What is your resulting eye color said to be?

(c) Can your genotype or phenotype change over time?

23-2. What is meant when it is said that most human traits are polygenic?

Answers: 23-1. (a) Your genotype (b) Your phenotype (c) Only your phenotype can change **23-2.** They are determined by two or more pairs of genes.

24. **Explain the special methods used to investigate the influence of heredity on behavior.**

24-1. If a trait is due to heredity, then more closely related members of a family should show (lesser/greater) resemblance on this trait than less closely related family members. Studies using this method are called _____ studies. Data gathered from family studies (can/cannot) furnish conclusive proof as to the heritability of a specific trait. Even when it is demonstrated that a particular trait is highly related to the degree of family relationship, the cause for this relationship could be either heredity or _____.

24-2. A second method in this line of investigation is to compare specific traits across identical twins and fraternal twins. This method, called _____ studies, assumes that inherited traits are much more likely to be found among _____ twins than among fraternal twins. These studies do in fact show that for many characteristics, such as intelligence and extraversion, the resemblance is closest for _____ twins. However, since identical twins are far from identical on these characteristics, _____ factors must also play a role here.

24-3. A third method in this line of investigation is to study children who have been separated from their biological parents at a very early age and raised by adoptive parents. The idea behind these _____ studies is that if the adoptive children more closely resemble their biological parents with respect to a specific trait, then it can be assumed that _____ plays a major role. On the other hand, if the adoptive children more closely resemble their adoptive parents with respect to a specific trait it would indicate that _____ plays a major role. Studies using this method to study the inheritabilty of intelligence have found that adoptive children more closely resemble their _____ parents on this particular trait, but not by much. This would indicate that a trait such as intelligence is influenced by both heredity and _____.

25. Explain how heredity may influence behavior and how its influence may be moderated by environment.

25-1. The answer to the question, "Is it all in the genes"?, now appears to be quite clear. The answer is No. However, neither is it all in the environment. What does this mean with respect to most behavioral traits?

25-2. How can the interaction between heredity and environment be used to explain the development of schizophrenic disorders?

PUTTING IT IN PERSPECTIVE

26. Explain how this chapter highlighted three of the texts unifying themes.

26-1. Indicate which of the three unifying themes (heredity and environment jointly influence behavior, behavior is determined by multiple causes, and psychology is empirical, is particularly illustrated in each of the following situations.

(a) The development of schizophrenic disorders.

(b) The use of many techniques and instruments that led to the discovery of cerebral specialization.

(c) The development of personal characteristics such as intelligence and extraversion.

APPLICATION: THINKING CRITICALLY ABOUT THE CONCEPT OF "TWO MINDS IN ONE"

27. **Outline five popular ideas linking cerebral specialization to cognitive processes.**

   27-1.   Your text lists five popular ideas that have found support among some neuroscientists and psychologists. These ideas are:

   (a) The two hemispheres are _____ to process different cognitive tasks.

   (b) Each hemisphere has its own independent stream of _____.

   (c) The two hemispheres have _____ modes of thinking.

   (d) People vary in their _____ on one hemisphere as opposed to the other.

   (e) Schools should place more emphasis on teaching the _____ side of the brain.

   Answers: 27-1. (a) specialized (b) consciousness (c) different (d) reliance (dependence) (e) right.

28. **Critically evaluate each of the five ideas on cerebral specialization and cognitive porcesses in light of currently available data.**

   28-1.   We will now proceed through each of these five assumptions to show how each has to be qualified in light of currently available evidence.

   (a) The idea that the left and right brains are specialized to handle different kinds of information (is/is not) supported by research. However, there is evidence that this specialization hardly occurs in some persons, while in other persons the specialization is reversed, particularly among _____handed persons. Moreover, most tasks require the ongoing cooperation of _____ hemispheres.

   (b) The evidence that each hemisphere has its own mind, or stream of consciousness, is actually very weak, except for persons who have undergone _____-_____surgery. The resulting "two minds" in these patients appears to be a byproduct of the surgery.

   (c) The assertion that each hemisphere has its own mode of thinking is (plausible/confirmed). A big problem here, however, is that mode of thinking, or cognitive style, has proven difficult to both _____and _____.

   (d) The assertion that some people are left-brained while other are right-brained (is/is not) conclusive at this time. Abilities and personality characteristics (do/do not) appear to be influenced by brainedness.

   (e) The notion that most schooling overlooks the education of the right brain (does/does not) really make sense. Since both hemispheres are almost always sharing in accomplishing an ongoing task, it would be _____ to teach only one hemisphere at at time.

   Answers: 28-1. (a) is, left, both (b) split-brain (c) plausible, define, measure (d) is not, do not (e) does not, impossible.

REVIEW OF KEY TERMS

Absolute refractory period
Action potential
Adoption studies
Afferent nerve fibers
Agonist
Antagonist
Autonomic nervous system (ANS)
Axon
Behavioral genetics
Blood-brain barrier
Central nervous system (CNS)
Cerebral cortex
Cerebral hemispheres
Cerebral laterality
Cerebrospinal fluid (CSF)
Chromosomes
Corpus callosum
Dendrites
Dominant gene
Efferent nerve fibers
Electrical stimulation of the brain (ESB)
Electroencephalograph (EEG)
Endocrine System
Endorphins

Excitatory PSP
Family studies
Forebrain Fraternal (dizygotic) twins
Genes
Genetic mapping
Genotype
Glia
Handedness
Heterozygous condition
Hindbrain
Homozygous condition
Hormones
Hypothalamus
Identical (monozygotic) twins
Inhibitory PSP
Interneurons
Lesioning
Limbic system
Midbrain
Motor neurons
Myelin sheath
Nerves
Neuromodulators
Neurons

Neurotransmitters
Parasympathetic division
Perceptual asymmetries
Peripheral nervous system
Phenotype
Pituitary gland
Polygenic traits
Postsynaptic potential (PSP)
Recessive gene
Resting potential
Sensory neurons
Soma
Somatic nervous system
Spatial summation
Split ƒ brain surgery
Stereotaxic instrument
Symnpathetic division
Synapse
Synaptic cleft
Temporal summation
Terminal buttons
Thalamus
Twin studies
Zygote

_____ 1. Neurons that receive information from outside the nervous system.

_____ 2. Neurons that transmit information to the muscles that actually move the body.

_____ 3. Cells found throughout the nervous system that provide structural support and insulation for neurons.

_____ 4. Individual cells in the nervous system that receive, integrate, and transmit information.

_____ 5. Neuron part that contains the cell nucleus and much of the chemical machinery common to most cells.

_____ 6. Branchlike parts of a neuron that are specialized to receive information.

_____ 7. A long, thin fiber that transmits signals away from the soma to other neurons, or to muscles or glands.

_____ 8. An insulating jacket, derived from glia cells, that encases some axons.

_____ 9. Small knobs at the end of the axon that secrete chemicals called neurotransmitters.

_____ 10. A junction where information is transmitted between neurons.

_____ 11. The stable, negative charge of an inactive neuron.

_____ 12. A brief change in a neuron's electrical charge.

_____ 13. The minimum length of time after an action potential during which another action potential cannot begin.

_____ 14. A microscopic gap between the terminal buttons of the sending neuron and the cell membrane of another neuron.

_____ 15. Chemicals that transmit information from one neuron to another.

_____ 16. A voltage change at the receptor site of a neuron.

_____ 17. An electric potential that increases the likelihood that a postsynaptic neuron will fire action potentials.

_____ 18. An electric potential that decreases the likelihood that a postsynaptic neuron will fire action potentials.

_____ 19. A technique for assessing hereditary influence by examining blood relatives to see how much they resemble each other on a specific trait.

_____ 20. A chemical that mimics the action of a neurotransmitter.

_____ 21. A chemical that opposes the action of a neurotransmitter.

_____ 22. An entire family of internally produced chemicals that resemble opiates in structure and effects.

_____ 23. Chemicals that increase or decrease (modulate) the activity of specific neurotransmitters.

_____ 24. System that includes all those nerves that lie outside the brain and spinal cord.

_____ 25. Bundles of neuron fibers (axons) that travel together in the peripheral nervous system.

_____ 26. System made up of the nerves that connect to voluntary skeletal muscles and sensory receptors.

_____ 27. Axons that carry information inward to the central nervous system from the periphery of the body.

_____ 28. Axons that carry information outward from the central nervous system to the periphery of the body.

_____ 29. System made up of the nerves that connect to the heart, blood vessels, smooth muscles and glands.

_____ 30. The branch of the autonomic nervous system that mobilizes the body's resources for emergencies.

_____ 31. The branch of the autonomic nervous system that generally conserves bodily resources.

_____ 32. System that consists of the brain and spinal cord.

_____ 33. A solution that fills the hollow cavities (ventricles) of the brain and circulates around the brain and spinal cord.

_____ 34. A semipermeable membranelike mechanism that stops some chemicals from passing between the bloodstream and brain cells.

_____ 35. A device that monitors the electrical activity of the brain over time by means of recording electrodes attached to the surface of the scalp.

_____ 36. Assessing hereditary influence by comparing the resemblance of identical twins and fraternal twins on a trait.

_____ 37. Method that involves destroying a piece of the brain by means of a strong electric current delivered through an electrode.

_____ 38. A device used to implant electrodes at precise locations in the brain.

_____ 39. Method that involves sending a weak electric current into a brain structure to stimulate (activate) it.

_____ 40. Part of the brain that includes the cerebellum and two structures found in the lower part of the brainstem–the medulla and the pons.

_____ 41. The segment of the brainstem that lies between the hindbrain and the forebrain.

_____ 42. Part of the brain encompassing the thalamus, hypothalamus, limbic system, and cerebrum.

_____ 43. A structure in the forebrain through which all sensory information (except smell) must pass to get to the cerebral cortex.

_____ 44. A structure found near the base of the forebrain that is involved in the regulation of basic biological needs.

_____ 45. A densely connected network of structures located beneath the cerebral cortex, involved in the control of emotion, motivation and memory.

_____ 46. The convulated outer layer of the cerebrum.

_____ 47. The right and left halves of the cerebrum.

_____ 48. The structure that connects the two cerebral hemispheres.

_____ 49. Assessing hereditary influence by examining the resemblance between adopted children and both their adoptive and biological parents.

_____ 50. Surgery in which the the corpus callosum is severed to reduce the severity of epileptic seizures.

_____ 51. System of glands that secrete chemicals into the bloodstream that help control bodily functioning.

_____ 52. The chemical substances released by the endocrine glands.

_____ 53. The "master gland" of the endocrine system.

_____ 54. Threadlike strands of DNA molecules that carry genetic information.

_____ 55. A one-celled organism formed by the union of a sperm and an egg.

_____ 56. DNA segments that serve as the key functional units in hereditary transmission.

_____ 57. A gene that is expressed when the paired genes are different (heterozygous).

_____ 58. A gene that is masked when paired genes are heterozygous.

_____ 59. A person's genetic makeup.

_____ 60. The ways in which a person's genotype is manifested in observable characteristics.

_____ 61. Characteristics that are influenced by more than one pair of genes.

_____ 62. Neurons that communicate only with other neurons.

_____ 63. The degree to which the left or right hemisphere controls various cognitive and behavioral functions.

_____ 64. Left-right imbalances between the cerebral hemispheres in the speed of visual or auditory processing.

_____ 65. A preference for using one's right or left hand in most activities.

_____ 66. An interdisciplinary field that studies the influence of genetic factors on behavioral traits.

_____ 67. The two genes in a specific pair are the same.

_____ 68. The two genes in a specific pair are different.

_____ 69. Twins that emerge from one zygote that splits.

_____ 70. Twins that result when two eggs are fertilized simultaneously by different sperm cells, forming two separate zygotes.

_____ 71. The process of determining the location and chemical sequence of specific genes on specific chromosomes.

_____ **72.** Can occur when several or more PSPs follow one another in rapid succession as a receptor site.

_____ **73.** Can take place when several or more PSPs occur simultaneously at different receptor sites.

Answers: 1. sensory neurons **2.** motor neurons **3.** glia **4.** neurons **5.** soma **6.** dendrites **7.** axon **8.** myelin sheath **9.** terminal buttons **10.** synapse **11.** resting potential 12. action potential **13.** absolute refractory period **14.** synaptic cleft **15.** neurotransmitters **16.** postsynaptic potential (PSP) **17.** excitatory PSP **18.** inhibitory PSP **19.** family studies **20.** agonist **21.** antagonist **22.** endorphins **23.** neuromodulators **24.** peripheral nervous system **25.** nerves **26.** somatic nervous system **27.** afferent nerve fibers **28.** efferent fibers **29.** autonomic nervous system (ANS) **30.** sympathetic division **31.** parasympathetic division **32.** central nervous system (CNS) **33.** cerebrospinal fluid (CSF) **34.** blood-brain barrier **35.** electroencephalograph (EEG) **36.** twin studies **37.** lesioning **38.** stereotaxic instrument **39.** electrical stimulation of the brain (ESB) **40.** hindbrain **41.** midbrain **42.** forebrain **43.** thalamus **44.** hypothalamus **45.** limbic system **46.** cerebral cortex **47.** cerebral hemispheres **48.** corpus callosum **49.** adoption studies **50.** split-brain surgery **51.** endocrine system **52.** hormones **53.** pituitary gland **54.** chromosomes **55.** zygote **56.** genes **57.** dominant gene **58.** recessive gene **59.** genotype **60.** phenotype **61.** polygenic traits **62.** interneurons **63.** cerebral laterality **64.** perceptual asymmetries **65.** handedness **66.** behavioral genetics **67.** homozygotic condition **68.** heterozygotic condition **69.** identical (monozygotic) twins **70.** fraternal (dizygotic) twins **71.** genetic mapping **72.** temporal summation **73.** spatial summation.

REVIEW OF KEY PEOPLE

Alan Hodgkin & Andrew Huxley   Candice Pert & Solomon Snyder   Roger Sperry & Michael Garzzaniga
James Olds & Peter Milner   Robert Plomin

_____ **1.** Unlocked the mystery of the neural impulse.

_____ **2.** Known for their work with the split-brain.

_____ **3.** Showed that morphine works by binding to specific receptors.

_____ **4.** Discovered "pleasure-centers" in the limbic system.

_____ **5.** One of the leading behavior genetics researchers in the last decade.

Answers : 1. Hodgkin & Huxley **2.** Sperry & Garzzaniga **3.** Pert & Snyder **4.** Olds & Milner **5.** Plomin.

SELF-QUIZ

1. Most neurons are involved in transmitting information:
a. from one neuron to another
b. from the outside world to the brain
c. from the brain to the muscles
d. none of the above

2. Neurons that are specialized to communicate directly with the muscles of the body are called:
   a. sensory neurons
   b. motor neurons
   c. actuator neurons
   d. muscle neurons

3. Which part of the neuron has the responsibility for receiving information from other neurons?
   a. the cell body
   b. the soma
   c. the axon
   d. the dendrites

4. The myelin sheath serves to:
   a. permit faster transmission of the neural impulse
   b. keep neural impulses on the right track
   c. both of the above
   d. none of the above

5. The change in the polarity of a neuron that results from the inflow of positively charged ions and the outflow of negatively charged ions is called the:
   a. presynaptic potential
   b. postsynaptic potential
   c. synaptic potential
   d. none of the above

6. The task of passing a message from one neuron to another is actually carried out by:
   a. the myelin sheath
   b. the glia cells
   c. the action potential
   d. neurotransmitters

7. Which of the following neurotransmitters can only have an inhibitory effect at receptor sites?
   a. GABA
   b. dopamine
   c. norepinephrine
   d. serotonin

8. Which of the following techniques is often used by neurosurgeons to map the brain when performing brain surgery?
   a. EEG recordings
   b. ESB
   c. lesioning
   d. all of the above

— 9. The seat of emotion is to be found in the:
   a. reticular formation
   b. hindbrain
   c. limbic system
   d. forebrain

10. Persons having difficulty with language and speech following an accident that resulted in injury to the brain are most likely to have sustained damage in the:
   a. right cerebral hemisphere
   b. left cerebral hemisphere
   c. right cerebral hemisphere if they are a male and left cerebral hemisphere if they are a female
   d. I have no idea what you are talking about

11. Which of the following best explain the origins of handedness?
    a. cultural preferences
    b. family preferences
    c. genetic factors
    d. none of the above

12. In carrying out the "fight or flight" response, the role of supervisor is assigned to the:
    a. adrenal gland
    b. pituitary gland
    c. hypothalamus
    d. parasympathetic nervous system

13. A person's current weight and height could be said to exemplify his or her:
    a. genotype
    b. phenotype
    c. both of the above
    d. none of the above

14. Which of the following kinds of studies can truly demonstrate that specific traits are indeed inherited?
    a. family studies
    b. twin studies
    c. adoption studies
    d. none of the above

15. Current evidence indicates that schizophrenia results from:
    a. genetic factors
    b. environmental factors
    c. multiple causes that involve both genetic and environmental factors
    d. completely unknown factors

16. Psychology as a science can be said to be:
    a. empirical
    b. rational
    c. analytic
    d. both b and c

17. Which of the following statements is/are correct?
    a. the right side of the brain is the creative side
    b. the right and left brains are specialized to handle different kinds of information
    c. language tasks are always handled by the left brain
    d. all of the above

Answers: 1. a 2. b 3. d 4. c 5. d 6. d 7. a 8. b 9. c 10. b 11. d 12. c 13. b 14. d 15. c 16. a 17. b.

Chapter Four

Sensation and Perception

REVIEW OF KEY IDEAS

1. **Explain how thresholds are determined and how stimulus intensity is related to absolute thresholds.**

   1-1. You are sitting on a secluded beach at sundown with a good friend. You make a bet as to who can detect the first evening star. Since you have just recently covered this chapter in your text, you explain to your friend that doing so involves the detection of a stimulus _____. In this case, the first star that provides the minimal amount of stimulation which can be detected is said to have crossed the _____ threshold. All of our senses have absolute thresholds, but research clearly shows that the minimal amount of stimulation necessary to be detected by any one of our senses (is/is not) always the same. Therefore, the absolute threshold is defined as the stimulus intensity that can be detected _____ percent of the time.

   Answers: 1-1. threshold, absolute, is not, 50.

2. **Explain Weber's law and Fechner's law.**

   2-1. Weber's law states that the size of a just noticeable difference (JND) is a constant proportion of the intensity (size) of the initial stimulus. This means that as a stimulus increases in intensity, the JND increases proportionally as well. Therefore, it would be more difficult to detect a slight increase in the length of a (1-inch/20-inch) line, a slight decrease in a (quiet/loud) tone, or a slight increase in the weight of a (30-ounce/90-ounce) object.

   2-2. Fechner's law states that larger and larger increases in stimulus intensity are required to produce perceptible increments, or _____, in the magnitude of sensation. What this means is that as the intensity of a stimulus increases, the size of the JND we are able to detect (decreases/increases).

   Answers: 2-1. 20-inch, loud **2-2.** JNDs, increases.

3. **Explain the basic thrust of signal-detection theory.**

   3-1. The major idea behind signal detection theory is that our ability to detect signals depends not only on the initial intensity of a stimulus, but also on other sensory and decision processes as well. What two factors are particularly important here?

   3-2. Thus, according to signal detection theory, the concepts of absolute thresholds and JNDs need to be replaced by the notion that the probability of detecting any given stimulus will depend on all of the above factors; this is called the concept of _____.

   Answers: 3-1. background noise and subjective factors within the perceiver **3-2.** detectability.

4. **Describe some evidence on perception without awareness and discuss the practical implications of subliminal perception.**

   4-1. Answer the following questions about the study conducted by Jon Krosnick and his colleages.

      (a) What two different kinds of subliminal information accompanied the slides of the target person?

      (b) Which group rated the target group in a more favorable manner?

   4-2. What general conclusions can be drawn from the research om sibliminal perception with respect to its potential persuasive effects?

   Answers: 4-1. (a) emotion arousing stimuli that would elicit either positive or negative emotions (b) the group exposed to positive emotional stimuli **4-2.** The effects are very weak.

5. **Discuss the meaning and significance of sensory adaptation.**

   5-1. Which of the following examples best illustrates what is meant by sensory adaptation?

      (a) You are unable to clearly hear the conversation at the next table even though it sounds intriguing and you are straining to listen.

      (b) The strawberries you eat at grandma's farm at the age of 20 seem not to taste as good as when you ate them at the age of 6.

      (c) The wonderful smell you encounter upon first entering the bakery seems to have declined considerably by the time you make your purchase and leave.

5-2. If you answered c to the above question you are right on track and understand that sensory adaptation involves a gradual _____ in sensitivity to prolonged stimulation. This automatic process means that we are not as likely to be as sensitive to the constants in our sensory environments as we are to the _____.

Answers: **5-1.** c **5-2.** decrease, changes.

OUR SENSE OF SIGHT: THE VISUAL SYSTEM

6. List the three properties of light and the aspects of visual perception that they influence.

6-1. Before we can see anything, _____ must be present. There are three characteristics of lightwaves that directly effect how we perceive visual objects; match each of these characteristics with its psychological effect.

_____ (a) wavelength   1. color

_____ (b) amplitude   2. saturation (or richness)

_____ (c) purity   3. brightness

Answers: **6-1.** lightwaves or light, (a) 1 (b) 3 (c) 2.

7. Describe the role of the lens and pupil in the functioning of the eye.

7-1. Getting light rays entering the eye to properly focus on the retina is the job of the _____. It accomplishes this task by either thickening or flattening its curvature, a process called _____. Controlling the amount of light entering the eye is the job of the _____. It accomplishes this task by opening or closing the opening in the center of the eye called the _____.

Answers: **7-1.** lens, accomodation, iris, pupil.

8. Describe the role of the retina in light sensitivity and in visual information processing.

8-1. The structure that transduces the information contained in light rays into neural impulses that are then sent to the brain is called the _____. All of the axons carrying these neural impulses exit the eye at a single opening in the retina called the optic _____. Since the optic disk is actually a hole in the retina, this part of the retina cannot sense incoming visual information and for this reason it is called the _____.

8-2. The specialized receptor cells that are primarily responsible for visual acuity and color vision are called the _____. The cones are mainly located in the center of the retina in a tiny spot called the _____. The specialized receptor cells that lie outside of the fovea and towards the periphery of the retina are called the _____. The rods are primarily responsible for peripheral vision and for _____ vision.

8-3. Both dark and light adaptation are primarily accomplished through _____ reactions in the rods and cones. This chemical reaction occurs more quickly in the _____, so they are quicker to show both dark adaptation and light adaptation.

8-4. Light rays striking the rods and cones initiate neural impulses that are then transmitted to _____ cells and then to _____cells. From here the visual information is transmitted to the brain via the axons running from the retina to the brain, collectively known as the _____ nerve.

8-5. The processing of visual information begins within the receiving area of a retinal cell called the _____ field. Stimulation of the receptive field of a cell causes signals to be sent inward towards the brain and sideways, or _____, to nearby cells, thus allowing them to interact with one another. The most common of these interactive effects, the inhibition of one cell by another, is called lateral _____. Lateral antagonism allows the visual system to compute the (absolute/relative) amount of light; it occurs in the retina and along the pathway to and including the visual cortex.

Answers: 8-1. retina, disk, blind spot **8-2.** cones, fovea, rods, night **8-3.** chemical, cones **8-4.** bipolar, ganglion, optic **8-5.** receptive, laterally, antagonism, relative.

9. Describe the routing of signals from the eye to the brain and the brain's role in visual information processing.

9-1. Visual information from the right side of the visual field (see Figure 4-14 in the text) exits from the retinas of both eyes via the optic nerves and meet at the _____ chiasma, where it is combined and sent to the _____ side of the brain. Visual information from the left side of the visual field follow a similar pattern, meeting at the optic chiasma, and then on to the _____ side of the brain.

9-2. After leaving the optic chiasma on their way to the visual cortex, the optic nerve fibers diverge along two pathways. Fill in the missing parts of these pathways in the figures below.

Major pathway

(a) Optic chiasma _____ _____ Visual cortex

Secondary pathway

(b) Optic chiasma _____ _____ Visual cortex

9-3. What purpose is served by having these two separate pathways dumping their information into different areas of the visual cortex?

9-4. Because the cells in the visual cortex respond very selectively to specific features of complex stimuli, they have been described as _____detectors. There are three major types of cells in the visual cortex: simple cells, complex cells, amd hypercomplex cells. Identify them from their descriptions given on the following page.

(a) These cells are particular about the width and orientation of a line but respond to any position in their receptive field.

(b) These cells are very particular about the width, orientation, and position of a line.

(c) These cells are like complex cells, but they are particular about the length of the lines that will cause them to fire.

9-5. Each of these groups of cells respond to particular features of incoming stimuli. This means that the cells in the visual cortex (do/do not) provide a photographic-like picture of the outside world. Rather they provide a coding system that can then be transformed into such a picture.

Answers: 9-1. optic, left, right **9-2.** (a) thalamus, lateral geniculate nucleus (b) superior colliculus, thalamus **9-3.** It allows for parallel processing (simultaneously extracting different information from the same input) **9-4.** (a) complex cells (b) simple cells (c) hypercomplex cells **9-5.** do not.

10. Discuss the trichromatic and opponent process theories of color vision, and the modern reconciliation of these theories.

10-1. The trichromatic theory of color vision, as its name suggests, proposes three different kinds of receptors (channels) for the three primary colors red, _____, and _____. The opponent process theory of color vision also proposes three channels for color vision, but these channels are red versus _____, yellow versus _____, and black versus

_____.

10-2. These two theories of color vision can be used to explain different phenomenon. Use T (trichromatic) or O (opponent process) to indicate which theory best explains the following phenomena.

_____ (a) The color of an afterimage is the complement of the original color.

_____ (b) The different kinds of color blindness suggest three different kinds of receptors.

_____ (c) Any three appropriately spaced colors can produce all other colors.

_____ (d) People describing colors often require at least four different names.

10-3. The evidence is now clear that both theories are (incorrect/correct). Each is needed to explain all of the phenomena associated with color vision. Three different kinds of cones have been found in the retina which are sensitive to one of the three primary colors; this supports the _____ theory. It has also been found that visual cells in the retina, the LGN, and the visual cortex respond in opposite (antagonistic) ways to complementary colors, thus supporting the _____

_____ theory.

Answers: 10-1. green, blue, green, blue, white **10-2.** (a) O (b) T (c) T (d) O **10-3.** correct, trichromatic, opponent process.

11. Distinguish between top-down processing and bottom-up processing.

    11-1.   Answer the following questions regarding top-down and bottom-up processing.

        (a) Which process appears to assume feature analysis, the process of detecting specific elements in visual input and assembling them into a more complex whole?

        (b) Which process appears to account for our ability to rapidly recognize and read long strings of words?

        (c) Which process appears to account for our ability to see contours when no physical edges or lines are present (subjective contours)?

    11-2.   Anne Treisman has proposed that visual information is processed in two stages. During the preattentive stage the physical features of stimuli are analyzed using _____ processing. During the focused attention stage, the features are organized into recognizeable objects using _____ processing.

    Answers: 11-1. (a) bottom-up processing (b) top-down processing (c) top-down processing **11-2.** bottom-up, top-down.

12. Explain the basic premise of Gestalt psychology and describe Gestalt principles of visual perception.

    12-1.   The Gestalt view of form perception assumes that form perception is not constructed out of individual elements; rather the form, or whole, is said to be _____ than the sum of its individual elements. The illusion of movement, called the _____ phenomenon, is used to support the Gestalt view of form perception because the illusion of movement (is/is not) completely contained in the individual chunks of stimuli that give rise to it. In other words, the illusion, or whole, appears to be _____ than the sum of its parts.

12-2. Five Gestalt principles of visual perception are illustrated below. Match each illustration with its correct name.

Proximity

Similarity

Continuity

Closure

Simplicity

(a) _proximity_

(b) _simplicity_

(c) _similarity_

(d) _closure_

(e) _continuity_

12-3. What Gestalt principle is illustrated by:

(a) The words printed on this page appear to stand out from the white paper they are printed on?

(b) Things moving in the same direction together get grouped together?

Answers: 12-1. greater (more), phi, is not, greater (more) **12-2.** (a) proximity (b) closure (c) similarity (d) simplicity (e) continuity **12-3.** (a) figure and ground (b) common fate.

13. Explain how form perception can be a matter of formulating perceptual hypotheses.

13-1. The objects that surround us in the world outside of our bodies are called _____ stimuli; the images the objects project on our retinas are called _____ stimuli. When perceived from different angles or distances, the same distal stimulus projects (similar/different) proximal images on the retina. This forces us to make perceptual _____ about the distal stimulus.

Answers: 13-1. distal, proximal, different, hypotheses or guesses.

14. Describe the monocular and binocular cues employed in depth perception and cultural variations in depth perception.

14-1. There are two general kinds of cues that allow us to perceive depth and they are easy to remember because one kind involve the use of both eyes and are called ___ cues; the other kind require the use of only one of the eyes and are called _____ cues. Depth perception (<u>does/does not</u>) require the use of both binocular and monocular cues.

14-2. Here are examples of two different kinds of binocular cues, retinal disparity and convergence. Identify each from these examples:

(a) As a person walks towards you your eyes turn inward.

(b) The images are slightly different on each retina and the differences change with distance.

14-3. There are two general kinds of monocular cues. One kind involves the active use of the eye, such as the accomodation used for focusing the eye. The other general kind is used to indicate depth in flat pictures and thus is called a _____ cue.

14-4. Identify the following pictoral cues below:

(a) Parallel lines grow closer as they recede into the distance.

(b) More distant objects are higher in the field than nearer objects.

(c) When objects appear to be of the same size, closer ones appear larger than more distant ones.

(d) Near objects block or overlap more distant ones.

(e) Texture appears to grow finer as viewing distance increases.

(f) Patterns of light and dark suggest shadows that can create an impression of three-dimensional space.

14-5. What differences have been found in a few cultures without previous experience in viewing two-dimensional figures and photographs?

Answers: 14-1. binocular, monocular, does not **14-2.** (a) convergence (b) retinal disparity **14-3.** pictorial **14-4.** (a) linear perspective (b) height in plane (c) relative size (d) interposition (e) texture gradients (f) light and shadow **14-5.** They have difficulty in perceiving depth (using only two-dimensional cues).

15. Summarize the Featured Study and follow-up research on the perception of geographical slant.

15-1. After reading the Featured Study you should be able to qnswer the following questions.

(a) Which method of judgement of geographical slant, verbal, visual, or haptic, was the most accurate?

(b) In what way might overestimates of geographical slant by the visual and verbal methods be of value?

(c) In what way might the better accuracy of haptic estimates be of value?

Answers: 15-1. (a) haptic (b) They prevent people from undertaking climbs they are not equipped to handle. (c) It prevents stumbling (when climbing or descending a geographical slant).

16. Describe perceptual constancies and illusions in vision, and discuss cultural variations in susceptibility to certain illusions.

16-1. The tendency to experience stable perceptions in spite of constantly changing sensory input is called perceptual _____. The text lists several of these visual perceptual constancies; identify the ones being illustrated below.

(a) Even though the retinal image shrinks as a friend walks away, she continues to appear her usual height.

(b) The retinal image warps as you track a basketball through the air, but the ball always appears perfectly round.

(c) Indoors or on the ski slope a light blue sweater always looks light blue.

16-2. Being fooled by the discrepancy between the appearance of a visual stimulus and its physical reality is what is meant by an optical _____. Both perceptual constancies and optical illusions illustrate the point we are continually formulating _____ about what we perceive and also that these perceptions can be quite (<u>subjective/objective</u>).

16-3. What do the variations in cultural susceptibility to certain illusions tell us about our perceptual inferences?

Answers: 16-1. constancy, (a) size constancy (b) shape constancy (c) color constancy **16-2.** illusion, hypotheses, subjective **16-3.** They can be shaped by our experience.

OUR SENSE OF HEARING: THE AUDITORY SYSTEM

17. List the three properties of sound and the aspects of auditory perception that they influence.

17-1. Name the perceived qualities that are associated with the following properties of sound waves.

Physical property	Description	Perceived Quality
(a) purity	kind of mixture	_____
(b) amplitude	wave height	_____
(c) wavelength	wave frequency	_____

Answers: 17-1. (a) timbre (b) loudness (c) pitch.

18. Summarize the information on human hearing capacities and describe how sensory processing occurs in the ear.

18-1. Below are questions concerning human hearing capacities. Match the questions with their correct answers.

Answers	Questions
1. 90 to 120 decibels (dB).	____ (a) What is the frequency range of human hearing?
2. 1,000 to 5,000 Hz.	____ (b) How loud do sounds have to be to cause damage to human hearing?
3. 20 to 20,000 Hz.	____ (c) To what frequency range is human hearing the most sensitive?

18-2. Below is a scrambled sequence of events that occurs when a sound wave strikes the ear. Put these events in their correct order using the numbers 1 through 4.

_____ Fluid waves travel down the choclea causing the hair cells on the basilar membrane to vibrate.

_____ The pinna directs air to the eardrum.

_____ The hair cells convert fluid motion into neural impulses and send them to the brain.

_____ The motion of the vibrating eardrum is converted to fluid motion by the ossicles.

Answers: 18-1. (a) 3 (b) 1 (c) 2 **18-2.** 3, 1, 4, 2.

19. **Describe the routing of auditory signals from the ear to the brain.**

19-1. After leaving the ear, the auditory nerves ascend through the lower _____ and then through the thalamus before ending in the _____ cortex.

19-2. Answer the following questions regarding this pathway.

(a) Which cerebral hemisphere receives the information from the left ear more directly and immediately?

(b) What three kinds of information are largely extracted during the ascension through the lower brain centers?

(c) What kind of information does the auditory cortex appear to process?

Answers: 19-1. brainstem, auditory **19-2.** (a) the right cerebral hemisphere (b) location in space, pitch, and loudness (c) complex patterns of sound such as speech.

20. **Compare and contrast the place and frequency theories of pitch perception and discuss the resolution of the debate.**

20-1. One theory of pitch perception assumes that the hair cells respond differentially to pitch depending on their location along the basilar membrane. This is the main idea of the _____ theory of pitch perception. A second theory assumes a one to one correspondence between the actual frequency of the sound wave and the frequency at which the entire basilar membrane vibrates. This is the main idea of the _____ theory of pitch perception.

20-2. Below are several facts uncovered by research. Tell which theory of pitch is supported by each of these facts.

(a) The hair cells vibrate in unison and not independently.

(b) Even when they fire in volleys, auditory nerves can only handle up to 5000 Hz.

(c) A wave pattern caused by the vibrating basilar membrane peaks at a particular place along the membrane.

20-3.   The above facts mean that the perception of pitch depends on both _____ and
_____ coding.

Answers: 20-1. place, frequency **20-2.** (a) frequency theory (b) place theory (c) place theory **20-3.** place and
frequency.

21. Discuss the cues employed in auditory localization.

21-1.   The sound shadow cast by the head is in a large part responsible for enhancing two important cues used
for auditory localization. What are these two cues?

21-2.   What do the eyes have to do with locating sound in space.?

Answers: 21-1. There are differences in the intensity and time of arrival of sound waves reaching each ear **21-2.** They
are used to locate sources of sound.

OUR CHEMICAL SENSES: TASTE AND SMELL

22. Describe the stimulus and receptors for taste and discuss a factor that influences perceived flavor.

22-1.   The stimuli for taste perception are _____ absorbed in the saliva that stimulate taste cells
located in the tongue's _____. It is generally thought that there are
four fundamental tastes; these are _____,_____,_____,_____.

22-2.   What additional effect is added to the flavor of wine by first swirling it in the glass?

Answers: 22-1. chemicals, taste buds, sweet, sour, salty, bitter **22-2.** It helps to release the wine's odor and odor is a
major determinant of flavor.

23. Describe the stimulus and receptors for smell.

23-1.   The stimuli for the sense of smell are _____ molecules floating in the air. The receptors for
smell are hairlike structures located in the nasal passages called _____
_____. If there are any primary odors, they must be (large/small) in number. Human
sensitivity to smell (does/does not) compare favorably with that of many other animals, although some
animals surpass us in this respect.

Answers: 23-1. chemical, olfactory cilia, large, does.

24. Describe processes involved in the perception of pressure and temperature.

24-1. The statements below pertain to either the sense of pressure (P) or the sense of temperature (T). Indicate the correct answers below using the letters P or T.

_____ (a) The somatosensory area of the cortex is the primary receiving area for this sense.

_____ (b) Has receptors specific for either warmth or cold.

_____ (c) The free nerve endings in the skin are in patches that act like receptive fields in vision.

_____ (d) The free nerve endings in the skin fire spontaneously when no stimulus change is being experienced

Answers: 24-1. (a) p (b) t (c) p (d) t.

25. Describe the two pathways along which pain signals travel and discuss evidence that the perception of pain is subjective.

25-1. Pain signals travel to the brain by two slightly different pathways. One pathway sends signals directly and immediately to the cortex and is called the _____ pathway. The other first sends signals through the limbic system and then on to the cortex and is called the _____ pathway. Lingering, less localized pain is mediated by the _____ pathway.

25-2. Many studies have demonstrated that the perception of pain can be affected by factors such as mood, ethninticity, and culture. Thus, the perception of pain is _____.

Answers: 25-1. fast, slow, slow **25-2.** subjective.

26. Explain the gate—control theory of pain perception and recent findings on the descending pathway that regualtes pain

26-1. Answer the following questions regarding the perception of pain.

(a) What phenomenon did the gate-control theory of pain perception attempt to explain?

(b) What effect do endorphins have with respect to pain?

(c) What seeems to be the role of the descending neural pathway that appears to originate in the periaqueductual gray (PAG) area in the midbrain?

Answers: 26-1. (a) Why the perception of pain is so subjective. (b) An analgesic, or pain-relieving, effect. (c) It sends signals down the spinal cord that block incoming pain signals.

OUR OTHER SENSES

27. Describe the perceptual experiences mediated by the kinesthetic and vestibular senses.

27-1. The system that monitors the positions of various parts of the body is called the _____ system. This systems sends information to the brain about body position and movement obtained from receptors located in the joints and _____.

27-2. The system that monitors the body's location in space is called the _____ system. The receptors for the vestibular system are primarily hair cells contained within the _____ canals in the inner ear.

27-3. What point does the text make about the kinesthetic and vestibular systems, and indeed all sensory systems, in carrying out their tasks?

Answers: 27-1. kinesthetic, muscles **27-2.** vestibular, semicircular **27-3.** They integrate information from other senses (in carrying out their tasks).

PUTTING IT IN PERSPECTIVE

28. Explain how this chapter highlighted three of the text's unifying themes.

28-1. The fact that competing theories of both color vision and pitch were eventually reconciled attests to the value of theoretical diversity. Why is this?

28-2. Why must our experience of the world always be highly subjective?

28-3. What do cultural variations in depth perception, taste preferences, and pain tolerance tell us about the physiological basis of perception?

Answers: 28-1. Competing theories drive and guide the research that resolved the conflicts **28-2.** The perceptual processes themselves are inherently subjective **28-3.** That it is subject to cultural influences.

29. Discuss how painters create an illusion of three-dimensional reality.

29-1. What two pictorial depth cues are of particular importance in creating the illusion of depth in Figure 4.60?

Answers: 29-1. linear perspective and relative size.

30. **Discuss how the impressionists, Cubists, and Surrealists used various principles of visual perception.**

30-1.   After reading the Application section in your text, try and answer the following questions by only looking at the paintings.

_____ (a)   Which painting depends particularly on the Gestalt principles of continuity and common fate for its effect?

_____ (b)   Which painting makes use of a reversible figure to enchance a feeling of fantasy?

_____ (c)   Which two paintings make use of color mixing to illustrate how different spots of colors can be blended into a picture that is more than the sum of its parts?

_____ (d)   Which painting uses proximity, similarity, and closure to allow you see its abstract subject (feature analaysis applied to canvas)?

Answers: 30-1. (a) Figure 4.64 (b) Figure 4.65 (c) Figures 4.61 and 4.62 (d) Figure 4.63.

31. **Discuss how Escher, Vasarely, and Magritte used various principles of visual perception.**

31-1.   After reading the Application section in your text, try and answer the following questions by only looking at the paintings?

_____ (a)   Which painting uses variations in context to make identical triangles appear very different?

_____ (b)   Which two paintings incorporate impossible figures to achieve their effect?

_____ (c)   Which painting manipulates the figure and ground relationship to achieve its special effect?

_____ (d)   Which painting makes particular use of texture gradient and light and dark shadow to convey the impression of depth?

Answers: 31-1. (a) Figure 4.70 (b) Figures 4.67 and 4.68 (c) Figure 4.66 (d) Figure 4.69.

REVIEW OF KEY TERMS

Absolute threshold
Additive color mixing
After image
Auditory localization
Basilar membrane
Binocular depth cues
Bottom-up processing
Cochlea
Color blindness
Complimentary colors
Cones
Convergence
Dark adaptation
Depth perception
Distal stimuli
Farsightedness
Feature analysis

Feature detectors
Fechner's law
Fovea
Frequency theory
Gate-control theory
Gustatory system
Impossible figures
Just noticeable difference (JND)
Kinesthetic system
Lateral antagonism
Lens
Light adaptation
Monocular depth cues
Motion parallax
Nearsightedness
Olfactory system
Opponent process theory of color vision

Optical illusion
Optic chiasm
Perception
Perceptual constancy
Perceptual hypothesis
Perceptual set
Phi phenomenon
Pictorial depth cues
Place theory
Proximal stimuli
Psychophysics
Pupil
Receptive field of a visual cell
Retina
Retinal disparity
Reversible figure
Rods

Sensation
Sensory adaptation
Signal-detection theory
Subjective contours

Subliminal perception
Subtractive color mixing
Threshold
Top-down processing

Trichromatic theory of color vision
Vestibular system
Volley principle
Weber's law

_____ 1. The stimulation of sense organs.

_____ 2. The selection, organization, and interpretation of sensory input.

_____ 3. The study of how physical stimuli are translated into psychological (sensory) experience.

_____ 4. A dividing point between energy levels that do and do not have a detectable effect.

_____ 5. The minimum amount of stimulation that can be detected by an organism for a specific type of sensory input.

_____ 6. The smallest amount of difference in the amount of stimulation that can be detected in a sense.

_____ 7. States that the size of a just noticeable difference is a constant proportion of the size of the initial stimulus.

_____ 8. Proposes that sensory sensitivity depends on a variety of factors besides the physical intensity of the stimulus.

_____ 9. Involves a gradual decline in sensitivity to prolonged stimulation.

_____ 10. States that larger and larger increases in stimulus intensity are required to produce perceptible increments in the magnitude of sensation.

_____ 11. The transparent eye structure that focuses the light rays falling on the retina.

_____ 12. The opening in the center of the iris that helps regulate the amount of light passing into the rear chamber of the eye.

_____ 13. The neural tissue lining the inside back surface of the eye that absorbs light, processes images, and sends visual information to the brain.

_____ 14. Specialized receptors that play a key role in daylight vision and color vision.

_____ 15. Specialized receptors that play a key role in night vision and peripheral vision.

_____ 16. A tiny spot in the center of the retina that contains only cones, where visual acuity is greatest.

_____ 17. The process in which the eyes become more sensitive to light in low illumination.

_____ 18. The process in which the eyes become less sensitive to light in high illumination.

_____ 19. A variety of deficiencies in the ability to distinguish among colors.

_____ 20. The retinal area that, when stimulated, affects the firing of a particular cell.

_____ 21. Occurs when neural activity in a cell opposes activity in surrounding cells.

_____ 22. Neurons that respond selectively to very specific features of more complex stimuli.

_____ 23. Works by removing some wavelengths of light, leaving less light than was originally there.

_____ 24. Works by superimposing lights, leaving more light in the mixture than in any one light by itself.

_____ 25. Proposes that the human eye has three types of receptors with differing sensitivities to different wavelengths.

_____ 26. Pairs of colors that can be added together to produce gray tones.

_____ 27. A visual image that persists after a stimulus is removed.

_____ 28. Proposes that color is perceived in three channels, where an either-or response is made to pairs of antagonistic colors.

_____ 29. A drawing compatible with two different interpretations that can shift back and forth.

_____ 30. A readiness to perceive a stimulus in a particular way.

_____ −31. A process in which we detect specific elements in visual input and assemble these elements into a more complex form.

_____ 32. A progression from individual elements to the whole.

_____ 33. A progression from the whole to the elements.

_____ −34. An apparently inexplicable discrepancy between the appearance of a visual stimulus and its physical reality.

_____ 35. The illusion of movement created by presenting visual stimuli in rapid succession.

_____ 36. Stimuli that lie in the distance (in the world outside us).

_____ 37. The stimulus energies that impinge directly on our sensory receptors.

_____ −38. An inference about what distal stimuli could be responsible for the proximal stimuli sensed.

_____ 39. Involves our interpretation of visual cues that tell us how near or far away objects are.

_____ 40. Clues about distance that are obtained by comparing the differing views of two eyes.

_____ 41. Clues about distance that are obtained from the image in either eye alone.

_____ 42. A tendency to experience a stable perception in the face of constantly changing sensory input.

_____ 43. Locating the source of a sound in space.

_____ 44. A fluid-filled, coiled tunnel that makes up the largest part of the inner ear.

_____ 45. A membrane running the length of the cochlea that holds the actual auditory receptors, called hair cells.

_____ 46. Holds that our perception of pitch corresponds to the vibration of different portions, or places, along the basilar membrane.

_____ 47. Holds that our perception of pitch corresponds to the rate, or frequency, at which the entire basilar membrane vibrates.

_____ 48. Holds that groups of auditory nerve fibers fire neural impulses in rapid succession, creating volleys of impulses.

_____ 49. Our sense of taste.

_____ 50. Our sense of smell.

_____ 51. Objects that can be represented in two-dimensional figures but cannot exist in three-dimensional space.

_____ 52. Holds that incoming pain sensations pass through a "gate" in the spinal cord that can be opened or closed.

_____ 53. The sense that monitors the positions of the various parts of the body.

_____ 54. The system that provides the sense of balance.

_____ 55. The point at which the optic nerves from the inside half of each eye cross over and then project to the opposite half of the brain.

_____ 56. Clues about distance that can be given in a flat picture.

_____ 57. The registration of sensory input without conscious awareness.

_____ 58. Involves the perception of contours where there really are none.

_____ 59. A case in which close objects are seen clearly but distant objects appear blurry.

_____ 60. A case in which distant objects are seen clearly but close objects are blurry.

_____ 61. A depth cue which refers to the fact that objects within 25 feet project images to slightly different locations on your right and left retinas, so the right and left eyes see slightly different images.

_____ 62. A binocular cue which involves sensing the eyes convergin toward each other as they focus on closer objects.

_____ 63. A monocular depth cue which involves images of objects at different distances moving accross the retina at different rates.

Answers: 1. sensation **2.** perception **3.** psychophysics **4.** threshold **5.** absolute threshold **6.** just noticeable difference (JND) **7.** Weber's law **8.** signal detection theory **9.** sensory adaptation **10.** Fechner's law **11.** lens **12.** pupil **13.** retina **14.** cones **15.** rods **16.** fovea **17.** dark adaptation **18.** light adaptation **19.** color blindness **20.** receptive field of a visual cell **21.** lateral antagonism **22.** feature detectors **23.** subtractive color mixing **24.** additive color mixing **25.** trichromatic theory of color vision **26.** complementary colors **27.** afterimage **28.** opponent process theory of color vision **29.** reversible figure **30.** perceptual set **31.** feature analysis **32.** bottom-up processing **33.** top-down processing **34.** optical illusions **35.** phi phenomenon **36.** distal stimuli **37.** proximal stimuli **38.** perceptual hypothesis **39.** depth perception **40.** binocular cues **41.** monocular cues **42.** perceptual constancy **43.** auditory localization **44.** cochlea **45.** basilar membrane **46.** place theory **47.** frequency theory **48.** volley principle **49.** gustatory system **50.** olfactory system **51.** impossible figures **52.** gate-control theory **53.** kinesthetic sense **54.** vestibular system **55.** optic chiasm **56.** pictorial depth cues **57.** subliminal perception **58.** subjective contours **59.** nearsightedness **60.** farsightedness **61.** retinal disparity **62.** convergence **63.** motion parallax.

REVIEW OF KEY PEOPLE

Linda Bartoshuk
Gustav Fechner
Herman von Helmholtz

David Hubel and Torston Weisel
Ronald Melzack and Patrick Wall
Anne Treisman

Ernst Weber
Max Wertheimer

_____ 1. Pioneered the early work in the detection of thresholds.

_____ 2. His law states that the size of a just noticeable difference is a constant proportion of the size of the initial stimulus.

_____ 3. These two men won the Nobel prize for their discovery of feature detector cells in the retina.

_____ 4. One of the originators of the trichromatic theory of color vision.

_____ 5. Made use of the phi phenomenon to illustrate some of the basic principles of gestalt psychology.

_____ 6. Has proposed that the perception of objects involves two stages characterized by different types of processing.

_____ **7.** A leading authority on taste research.

_____ **8.** Proposed a gate-control theory of pain.

Answers: 1. Fechner **2.** Weber **3.** Hubel and Weisel **4.** Helmholtz **5.** Wertheimer **6.** Treisman **7.** Bartoshuk **8.** Melzack and Wall.

SELF-QUIZ

1. Stimuli cannot be perceived when they are presented below the absolute threshold. This statement is:
   a. true
   b. false

2. Research shows that subliminal perception:
   a. cannot be reliably demonstrated
   b. produces only moderate persuasive effects
   c. can exert powerful persuasive effects
   d. does not show adaptation effects
   e. both c and d

3. Which of the following places a major emphasis on subjective factors in the perception of thresholds?
   a. Weber's law
   b. Fechner's law
   c. Steven's power factor
   d. signal detection theory

4. The receiving area of a retinal cell is called the:
   a. cone
   b. fovial field
   c. rod
   d. receptive field

5. The fact that we are generally much more aware of the changes in our sensory environments rather than the constants is the general idea behind:
   a. signal detection theory
   b. sensory adaptation
   c. the method of constant stimuli
   d. sensory equalization

6. The major difference between a green light and a blue light is the:
   a. wave frequency
   b. wave purity
   c. wavelength
   d. wave saturation

7. If the eye is compared to a camera, the role of the retina would most closely resemble the role of the:
   a. lens
   b. film
   c. shutter
   d. flash cube

8. Which theory of color vision best explains why the color of an afterimage is the complement of the original color?
   a. the trichromatic theory
   b. the opponent process theory
   c. both theories explain this phenomenon equally well
   d. neither theory adequately explains this phenomenon

9. When watching a wild car chase scene in a movie we can be thankful for:
   a. chunking
   b. lateral processing
   c. bottom-up processing
   d. the phi phenomenon

10. Which of the following is not one of the pictorial depth cues?
    a. convergence
    b. linear perspective
    c. relative height
    d. texture gradients

11. Which of the following is an example of what is meant by perceptual constancy?
    a. moths are always attracted to light
    b. a round pie tin always appears to us as round
    c. proximal and distal stimuli are always identical
    d. none of the above

12. Gate-control theory is an attempt to explain:
    a. why the perception of pain is so subjective
    b. how subliminal perception works
    c. how receptive fields influence one another
    d. how the optic chiasm directs visual information

13. Research has shown that the perception of pitch depends on:
    a. the area stimulated on the basilar membrane
    b. the frequency at which the basilar membrane vibrates
    c. both of the above
    d. none of the above

14. Which of the following is not considered to be one of the four fundamental tastes?
    a. sour
    b. sweet
    c. burnt
    d. bitter

15. Our sense of balance depends upon:
    a. the semicircular canals
    b. the kinesthetic senses
    c. visual cues
    d. all of the above

16. Which of the following terms perhaps best describes human perception?
    a. accurate
    b. objective
    c. subjective
    d. unknowable

Answers: 1. b **2.** b **3.** d **4.** d **5.** b **6.** c **7.** b **8.** b **9.** d **10.** a **11.** b **12.** a **13.** c **14.** c **15.** d **16.** c.

Chapter Five

Variations in Consciousness

REVIEW OF KEY IDEAS

ON THE NATURE OF CONSCIOUSNESS

1. **Discuss the nature of consciousness.**

   1-1. The personal awareness of internal and external events is how psychologists define _____. Consciousness is like a moving stream in that it is constantly_____.

   1-2. Not only is consciousness constantly changing, but it also exists at different levels. Freud believed that at its deepest level we would find the _____. Moreover, there is a _____ of levels of awareness from the conscious to the unconscious. There (is/is not) some awareness during sleep and while under anesthesia.

   Answers: 1-1. consciousness, changing **1-2.** unconscious, continuum, is.

2. **Discuss the relationship between consciousness and EEG activity.**

   2-1. EEG recordings reveal that there (is/is not) some relationship between brain waves and levels of consciousness. There are four principal bands of brain wave activity, based on the frequency of the wave patterns, these are alpha, beta, delta, and theta. Identify these wave patterns from their descriptions given below.

   _____ (a) alert (13-24 cps)   _____ (c) deep sleep (4-7 cps)

   _____ (b) drowsy (8-12 cps)   _____ (d) deepest sleep (1-4 cps)

   Answers: 2-1. is (a) beta (b) alpha (c) theta (d) delta.

3. **Summarize what is known about our biological clocks and their relationship to sleep.**

   3-1.   What are the approximate time periods for the following cyclical patterns in human beings?

      _____ (a) Female menstrual cycle

      _____ (b) Circadian rhythm

      _____ (c) Mood swings and sexual activity

      _____ (d) Fluctuations in alertness and hunger

   3-2.   The daily, or 24-hour, circadian rhythm is responsible for the regulation of sleep and wakefulness. This is accomplished through the regulation of several bodily processes, including body temperature. Describe below what happens to body temperature when we:

(a) begin to fall asleep.

(b) continue into deeper sleep.

(c) begin to awaken.

   3-3.   There is evidence that exposure to _____ is responsible for regulating the 24-hour circadian clock. Sunlight affects the suprachiasmatic nucleus in the hypothalamus which in turn signals the _____ gland. The pineal gland then secretes the hormone melatonin which is a major player in adjusting biological clocks. There is also evidence that most persons tend to drift from a 24-hour cycle to a _____ hour cycle.

   3-4.   Getting out of time with the circadian rhythms can greatly affect the quality of _____. This is commonly found among persons suffering from jet lag. Research on jet lag has shown that there are two kinds of alterations in circadian rhythms. One kind called phase-delay shift occurs when the day is _____. Another kind, called phase-advance shift, occurs when the day is _____. Since there already seems to be a natural tendency to shift to a 25-hour circadian cycle, most people find it is easier to make a phase _____ shift. This explains why air travel is likely to be less disturbing when flying in a _____ direction.

Answers: 3-1. (a) 28 days (b) 24 hours (c) 1 year (d) 90 minutes **3-2.** (a) temperature decreases (b) temperature continues to decrease (c) temperature begins to increase **3-3.** sunlight, pineal, 25 **3-4.** sleep, lengthened, shortened, delay, westerly.

4. **Describe the Featured Study on how to make shift rotation less disruptive and evidence on the value of melatonin for resetting biological clocks.**

   4-1.   The Featured Study looked at two different factors that may help to make shift rotation more compatible with circadian rhythms. One factor was to change from phase-advance shift rotations to phase-_____ shift rotations. The investigators also looked at what differences may occur between weekly shift rotations and rotations that ocurred every _____ weeks. All of the workers in the experimental group were switched to phase delay shift rotations and were compared to similar workers not subjected to shift rotations. In addition, some of the workers in the experimental group experienced shift rotations every 3 weeks, while others were rotated on a _____ basis. Measures of worker satisfaction, health, and productivity served as the _____ variables.

   4-2.   What did the results of this study show regarding worker satisfaction for the workers changed to phase-delay shift rotations?

   4-3.   What group showed the greatest improvement in worker satisfaction?

   4-4.   Research has shown that low doses of melatonin can (check those that apply):

   a. alleviate the effects of jet lag and shift rotation.

   b. serve as an effective sedative for some people.

   c. slow the aging process.

   d. enhance sex.

   e. fight AIDS and cancer.

   Answers: 4-1. delay, 3, weekly, dependent **4-2.** Worker satisfaction improved **4-3.** Workers rotated at 3-week intervals **4-4.** Only a and b are correct.

THE SLEEP AND WAKING CYCLE

5. **Describe how sleep research is conducted.**

   5-1.   Sleep research is conducted by electronically monitoring various bodily activities such as brain waves, muscular activity, eye movements, and so on, while persons actually _____ in a specially prepared laboratory setting. Through the use of a television camera or a window, researchers also the subjects during sleep.

   Answers: 5-1. sleep, observe (watch).

6. **Describe how the sleep cycle evolves through the night**

   6-1.   Answer the following questions regarding the sleep cycle.

           (a) How many stages are there in one sleep cycle?

           (b) Which two stages make up slow-wave sleep?

           (c) Which brain waves are prominant during slow-wave sleep.

   Answers: 6-1. (a) four (b) 3 and 4 (c) delta.

7. **Compare and contrast REM and NREM sleep.**

   7-1.   What particularly differentiates NREM sleep from rapid eye movement sleep, or _____ sleep,
           is that during REM sleep the brain wave pattern resembles that of a person who is wide _____.
           However, REM sleep is actually a deep stage of sleep in which the muscle tone is extremely relaxed and
           the sleeper is virtually _____. It is also during REM sleep that _____ is most
           likely to occur.

   7-2.   The sleep cycle is representative of one of the _____ minute biological rhythms and is repeated
           approximately four times during an average night of sleep. NREM sleep dominates the early part of the
           sleep period, but _____ sleep and dreaming dominate the later stages of sleep. As one
           progresses though the night the depth of NREM sleep tends to progressively (<u>increase/decrease</u>).

   Answers: 7-1. REM, awake, paralyzed, dreaming **7-2.** 90, REM, decrease.

8. **Summarize age trends in patterns of sleep.**

   8-1.   Not only do newborns sleep more frequently and for more total hours during a day than do adults, but
           they also spend a greater proportion of time in _____ sleep. As they grow older, the
           children move toward longer but (<u>more/less</u>) frequent sleep periods and the total proportion of REM
           sleep declines from about 50 percent to the adult level of about _____ percent. During
           adulthood there is a gradual shift towards the (<u>lighter/deeper</u>) stages of sleep.

   Answers: 8-1. REM, less, 20, lighter.

9. **Summarize how culture influences sleep patterns.**

   9-1.   Answer the following questions regarding sleeping patterns across cultures.

           (a) Which pattern, children sleeping with their parents (co-sleeping) or children sleeping alone, is the
               most widely practiced?

(b) Where are the "siesta cultures" generally located?

(c) What is the effect of industrialization on the practice of siestas?

Answers: 9-1. (a) co-sleeping (b) tropical regions (c) The practice declines.

10. Discuss the neural basis of sleep.

—**10-1.** Sleep and wakefulness is apparently under the control of several neural structures, but one that appears to be particularly essential for both sleep and wakefulness is the reticular _____. When a part of this system, called the ascending _____ system (ARAS) is severed in cats, the cats remain in continuous _____. When the ARAS is stimulatd in normal cats, they act _____.

—**10-2.** There are also at least five neurotransmitters that appear to influence the sleep-wakefulness cycle, but the neurotransmitters _____ and _____ appear to be particularly important. Even so, it should be remembered that sleep depends on the interaction between _____ brain structures and _____ neurotransmitters.

Answers: 10-1. formation, reticular activating, sleep, alert or awake **10-2.** acetycholine, serotonin, several (or many), several (or many).

11. Summarize evidence on the effects of complete and partial sleep deprivation.

11-1. Answer the following questions regarding the effects of different kinds of sleep deprivation.

(a) What is the major effect of both complete and partial sleep deprivation?

(b) In what way might increased sleepiness be a major problem with respect to the workplace?

Answers: 11-1. (a) weariness or sleepiness (b) It can lead to increased accidents.

12. Discuss the effects of selective deprivation of REM sleep and slow-wave sleep.

12-1. Studies in which subjects were selectively deprived of REM sleep, leaving NREM sleep undisturbed, found (substantial/little) negative effects from REM deprivation. One curious effect that has been noted from selective REM deprivation is that subjects tend to increase their amount of (NREM/REM) sleep when given the first opportunity to do so. This same rebound effect has also been found with stage 4 or _____-_____ sleep.

Answers: 12-1. little, REM, slow-wave.

13. **Explain restorative and circadian theories of sleep.**

  13-1. Some theories as to why we sleep believe the purpose is to recharge the body. These are known as _____ theories. Other theories propose that sleep has survival value since it conserves energy and protects from danger. These theories are known as _____ theories.

  13-2. After reading the text you should be able to answer the following questions regarding Borbely's theory of sleep.

  (a) Borbely's theory assumes that:

    (1) Restorative theories are correct.

    (2) Circadian theories are correct.

    (3) Both theories are correct.

  (b) According to Borbely's theory, the need for sleep will be highest when (see Fig. 5.11c):

    (1) Process C (circadian rhythm) is high.

    (2) Process S (hours awake) is high.

    (3) Both process C and Process S are high.

  (c) Research evidence shows that:

    (1) Time spent in slow wave sleep depends on

    _____ .

    (2) Time spent in REM sleep depends on

    _____ .

  (d) If the theory and the research evidence are correct then a person suffering from jet lag will most likely experience a need for (REM/slow-wave) sleep.

  13-3. What additional factor did Webb suggest to account for the ability to adapt to flexible work and sleeping schedules?

Answers: **13-1.** restorative, circadian **13-2.** (a) 3, (b) 3, (c) 1. hours spent awake 2. the circadian rhythm. (d) REM **13-3.** behavioral controls (actions taken to inhibit or facilitate sleep).

14. **Discuss the prevalence, causes, and treatments of insomnia.**

  14-1. While practically everybody will suffer from occasional bouts of insomnia, it is estimated that chronic problems with insomnia occur in about _____ percent of all adults and another _____ percent complain of occasional insomnia. There are three basic types of insomnia, which are easily remembered because one type occurs at the beginning of sleep, one type during sleep, and the third type at the end of sleep. Thus, one type involves difficulty in _____asleep; one type involves difficulty in _____ asleep; and one type involves persistent _____ awakening.

  14-2. There are a number of different causes of insomnia, but perhaps the most common one results from events and problems that generate excessive _____. Another frequent cause results from pain or difficulty in breathing due to _____. Certain drugs are also implicated in insomnia.

14-3.   Since there are many different causes of insomnia, it seems reasonable that there (is/is not) a single form of treatment. However, researchers agree that the most commonly used form of treatment, using sedatives, or _____ pills, is not the treatment of choice. Evidence shows that while sleeping pills do promote sleep, they also interfere with both the slow-wave and _____ part of the sleep cycle.

Answers: 14-1. 15, 15, falling, remaining, early **14-2.** stress, health problems **14-3.** is not, sleeping, REM.

15. Describe the symptoms of narcolepsy, sleep apnea, night terrors, nightmares, and somnambulism.

15-1.   Described below are five different case histories of persons suffering from five different sleep disorders. Make the appropriate diagnosis for each one.

(a) Throckmorton is a young child who frequently wakes up during the night with a loud piercing cry, but can not describe what happened to him; he usually returns quickly to sleep. A night spent at the sleep clinic discloses that the episodes generally occur during NREM sleep. Throckmorton is most likely suffering from _____ _____.

(b) Galzelda reports that occasionally, even when typing a term paper or driving a car, she will quickly drop into a deep sleep. The sleep is often accompanied by dreams, which indicates REM sleep. Gazelda is most likely suffering from _____.

(c) Ajax is a young child who frequently wakes up terrified and relates vivid dreams to his parents who rush to comfort him. The family physician tells the parents there is probably nothing to worry about, unless these episodes persist, and that the child will most likely outgrow this problem. The diagnosis here is probably _____.

(d) Mr. Whistletoe will occasionally get up late at night and walk around the house. Unfortunately, Mr. Whistletoe is completely unaware of this behavior and usually returns to bed without awakening. Upon awakening the next morning he is surprised by a new bruise on his leg and he wonders how the chair in the living room got tipped over. Mr. Whistletoe would be diagnosed as suffering from _____, or sleep walking.

(e) Hendrieta complains that during a night's sleep she frequently wakes up grasping for breath. A visit to the sleep clinic discloses that indeed she does stop breathing for brief periods all through the night. Hendrieta undoubtably suffers from _____ _____.

Answers: 15-1. (a) night terrors (b) narcolepsy (c) nightmares (d) somnambulism (e) sleep apnea.

THE WORLD OF DREAMS

16. Discuss the nature of dreams.

16-1.   The conventional view of dreams is that they are mental experiences during REM sleep and often have a bizarre storylike quality and vivid imagery. What do many theorists now think of this view?

Answers: 16-1. They question many aspects of this view.

17. **Summarize findings on dream content.**

17-1. Calvin Hall, who analyzed the contents of more than 10,000 dreams, concluded that the content of most dreams is (<u>exotic/mundane</u>). Moreover, he found that dreams seldom involve events that are not centered around _____. Hall also found that dreams tend to be like soap operas in that they revolve around such common themes as misfortune, _____, and _____.

17-2. Answer the following questions regarding the differences in dream content betweem men and women. Which sex is more likely to dream about:

_____ (a) acting aggressively?

_____ (b) sex with strangers?

_____ (c) children?

17-3. What did Freud mean when he stated that our dreams reflect day residue?

17-4. What other factor has an inconsistent effect on our dreams?

Answers: 17-1. mundane, ourselves, sex, aggression **17-2.** (a) men (b) men (c) women **17-3.** Dream content is influenced by what happens to us in our daily lives. **17-4.** external stimuli (driping water, ringing phones, etc.).

18. **Describe some cultural variations in beliefs about the nature and importance of dreams.**

18-1. Say which of the following statements about dreams is more characteristic of Western cultures (W) or non-Western cultures (NW).

_____ (a) Little significance paid as to the meaning of dreams.

_____ (b) Remembering dreams is important.

_____ (c) Believe that dreams may provide information about the future.

_____ (d) Are likely to report frquent dreams involving food.

Answers: 18-1. (a) W (b) NW (c) NW (d) Persons from any culture who are chronically hungry.

19. **Describe the three theories of dreaming covered in the chapter.**

19-1. The text mentions three theories as to why we need to dream. Tell what cognitive purpose, if any, each of these theories proposes as to the purpose of dreaming.

(a) This was Sigmund Freud's theory about the need to dream.

(b) This theory proposed by Rosalind Cartwright is cognizant of the fact that dreams are not restricted by logic or reality.

— (c) The activation-synthesis theory of Hobson and McCarley proposes that dreams occur as side effects of neural activation of the cortex by lower brain centers.

Answers: 19-1. (a) Dreams serve the purpose of wish fulfillment. (b) Dreams allow for creative problem-solving. (c) Dreams serve no cognitive purpose.

HYPNOSIS: ALTERED CONSCIOUSNESS OR ROLE PLAYING?

20. **Discuss hypnotic susceptibility, list some prominant effects of hypnosis, and explain the role-playing and altered-state theories of hypnosis.**

— 20-1.   While there are many different hypnotic induction techniques, they all lead to a heightened state of _____. Research shows that individuals (do/do not) vary in their susceptibility to hypnotic induction. In fact, approximately ____ percent of the population does not respond at all and approximately _____ percent are highly susceptible to hypnotic induction. People who are highly susceptible tend to have (vivid/poor) imaginations and a (rich/poor) fantasy life.

— 20-2.   The text lists several of the more prominent effects that can be produced by hypnosis. Identify these effects from their descriptions given below.

   (a) Reducing awareness of pain. _____

   (b) Engaging in acts one would not ordinarily do. _____

   (c) Perceiving things that do not exist or failing to perceive things that do exist. _____

   (d) Claiming that sour foods taste sweet. _____ _____

   (e) Carrying out suggestions following the hypnotic induction session. _____ _____

   (f) Claiming to forget what occured during the induction session. _____

Answers: 20-1. suggestibility, do, 10, 10, vivid **20-2.** (a) anesthetic (b) disinhibition (c) hallucinations (d) sensory distortions (e) posthypnotic suggestions (f) amnesia.

21. **Explain the role-playing and altered-states theories of hypnosis.**

   21-1.   A theory of hypnosis proposed by Barber and Orne is that hypnosis is really a form of acting or role playing in which the subjects are simply playing as if they are hypnotized. What two lines of evidence support this theory?

21-2. A theory of hypnosis proposed by Hilgard is that hypnosis does in fact result in an altered state of conscious. This theory holds that hypnosis results in a dissociation or _____ of consciousness into two parts. One half of the divided consciousness communicates with the hypnotist while the other half remains _____, even from the hypnotized subject. In this case, pain perceived by the "hidden" part of the consciousness (is/is not) reported to the "aware" part of consciousness. The divided state of consciousness proposed by Hilgard (is/is not) a common experience in everyday life. One such example of this commonly experienced state is appropriately called highway _____."

Answers: 21-1. Nonhypnotized subjects can duplicate the feats of hypnotized subjects and it has been shown that hypnotized subjects are merely carrying out their expectations of how hypnotized subjects should act. **21-2.** spliting or dividing, hidden, is not, is, hypnosis.

MEDITATION: PURE CONSCIOUSNESS OR RELAXATION?

22. Summarize the evidence on the short-term and long-term effect of meditation.

22-1. Certain short-term physiological changes may occur during meditation. One of the most prominent of these changes is that EEG brain waves change from the rapid beta waves to the slower _____ and theta waves. This change to slower waves is accompanied by (an increase/a decrease) in metabolic activity, such as heart rate, oxygen consumption, etc. All of these physiological changes are characteristic of a normal state of _____. This state of relaxation (is/is not) unique to meditation.

22-2. The claims made for the long-term effects of meditation may have some merit in that studies have shown that subjects have shown improved mood and lessened anxiety and fatigue, as well as better physical health and increased longevity. These changes can (also/not) be induced by other commonly used methods for inducing relaxation. Moreover, the claim that meditation can produce a unique state of pure consciousness (has/has not) been conclusively proven.

Answers: 22-1. alpha, a decrease, relaxation, is not **22-2.** also, has not.

ALTERING CONSCIOUSNESS WITH DRUGS

23. List and describe the major types of abused drugs and their effects.

23-1. The text list six different categories of psychoactive drugs; identify these drugs from the descriptions given below.

(a) This drug is the most widely used, and abused, of all psychoactive drugs and produces a relaxed euphoria that temporarily boosts self-esteem. Wince and beer are both examples of the drug _____.

(b) While this class of drugs derived from opium is effective at relieving pain, it can also produce a state of euphoria, which is the principal reason that opiates, or _____, are attractive to recreational users.

(c) The drugs in this class, such as LSD, mescaline and psilocybin, are known for their ability to distort sensory and perceptual experiences, which is why they are given the collective name of

_____.

—(d) The drugs in this class include marijuana, hashish and THC. Although they vary in potency each of them can produce a mild and an easy going state of euphoria along with enhanced sensory awareness and a distorted sense of time. This class of drugs gets its name from the hemp plant _____ from which they are all derived.

—(e) This class of drugs is known for its sleep-inducing (sedation) and behavioral depression effects, resulting in tension reduction and a relaxed state of intoxication. While there are several different drugs in this class, the barbiturates are the most widely abused. Commonly known as "downers", they are more properly called _____.

—(f) This class of drugs produces arousal in the central nervous system and ranges from mildly arousing drugs like caffeine and nicotine, to strongly arousing drugs like cocaine and the amphetamines. Known for their ability to produce an energetic euphoria, the drugs in this class go by the name of _____.

Answers: 23-1. (a) alcohol (b) narcotics (c) hallucinogens (d) cannabis (e) sedatives (f) stimulants.

24. Explain why drug effects vary and how psychoactive drugs exert their effects on the brain.

24-1.   Taking a specific drug (will/will not) always have the same effect on the same person. This is because drug effects have _____ causation; individual, environmental, and drug factors can combine in many ways to produce the final effect. For example, one's expectations can strongly affect reactions to a drug. This is known as the _____ effect. Moreover, as one continues to take a specific drug, it requires a greater amount of the drug to achieve the same effect. This phenomenon is called drug _____.

24-2.   Psychoactive drugs affect the CNS by selectively inflluencing _____ systems in a variety of ways. The action takes place at the juncture between neurons called the _____. Some psychoactive drugs mimic the effects of naturally occuring neurotransmitters, while others act by increasing or decreasing the availability of selective _____. Both sedatives and alcohol exert their key effects at GABA synapses. When these two drugs are taken together their combined depressive effect on the CNS may be greater than the sum of their individual effects. Drugs having this effect are said to be _____.

Answers: 24-1. will not, multifactorial, placebo, tolerance 24-2. neurotransmitter, synapse, neurotransmitters, synergistic.

25. Summarize which drugs carry the greatest risk of tolerance, physical dependence, and psychological dependence.

25-1.   When a person must continue taking a drug to avoid withdrawal illness, addiction, or _____ dependence is said to occur. When a person must continue taking a drug to satisfy intense emotional craving for the drug, then _____ dependence is said to occur.

25-2.   As can be seen in Table 5.5 in the text, the three riskiest drugs in terms of tolerance and physical and psychological dependence are:

25-3. What appears to be the critical force behind both physical and psychological addiction?

Answers: 25-1. physical, psychological **25-2.** narcotics/opiates, sedatives, stimulants **25-3.** The pursuit of pleasant effects.

26. Summarize evidence on the major physical health risks associated with drug abuse.

26-1. What two physical effects were found in the study in which rats were allowed unlimited access to heroin or cocaine and which drug was the most deadly?

26-2. There are three major ways in which drugs may affect physical health. The most dramatic way is when a person takes too much of a drug, or drugs, and dies of an _____. Another way is when drug usuage directly damages bodily tissue; this is referred to as a _____ effect. The third way is when drug usage results in accidents, improper eating and sleeping habits, infections, etc. These effects are collectively called _____effects.

26-3. Say whether the following statements concerning marijuana are true or false.

_____ (a) Marijuana can cause chromosome breakage and birth defects in human beings.

_____ (b) Pregnant women should not smoke marijuana.

_____ (c) Marijuana produces only a slight and insignificant decrease in the immune response.

_____ (d) Marijuana can have lasting effects on a male-smoker's sexual functioning.

Answers: 26-1. loss of body weight and death, cocaine **26-2.** overdose, direct, indirect **26-3.** (a) false (b) true (c) true (d) false.

27. Discuss how drug abuse is related to psychological health.

27-1. While there is good evidence of a linkage between excessive drug abuse and poor mental health, the data are only correlational. What interpretive problem does this pose?

27-2. Shedler and Block showed in their study of eighteen-year-olds that frequent users of illicit drugs were more likely to have had a prior history of maladjustment in their childhood than less frequent users. One conclusion is that prior maladjustment leads to excessive drug use. What is another possible conclusion?

Answers: 27-1. Its difficult to say which causes which. **27-2.** Ineffective child rearing leads to both maladjustment and excessive drug use.

PUTTING IT IN PERSPECTIVE

28. Explain how the chapter highlighted four of the text's unifying themes.

28-1.   Identify which of the underlying themes (psychology evolves in a sociohistorical context, experience is subjective, cultures mold some aspects of behavior, and psychology is theoretically diverse) is illustrated by the following statements.

(a) Psychologists have followed many different approaches and developed many different theories in their attempt to understand consciousness.

(b) The study of consciousness by psychologists followed rather than preceded renewed public interest in this topic.

(c) There are striking individual differences in the way people respond to hypnosis, meditation and drugs.

(d) The significance given to dreams and sleep patterns can be influenced by this factor.

Answers: 28-1. (a) Psychology is theoretically diverse. (b) Psychology evolves in a sociohistorical context. (c) Experience is subjective. (d) Culture molds some aspects of behavior.

APPLICATION: ADDRESSING PRACTICAL QUESTIONS ABOUT SLEEP AND DREAMS

29. Summarize evidence on common questions about sleep discussed in the Application.

29-1.   Answer the following questions about sleep and napping.

(a) How much sleep do we require?

(b) While napping can be refreshing for most people, in what way can it prove inefficient?

(c) Why are drugs such as sedatives and alcohol likely to interfere with refreshing sleep?

(d)   What does evidence show about the effectiveness of attempting to learn complex material, such as a foreign language, during deep sleep?

29-2.   In addition to developing sensible daytime habits, there are numerous methods for facilitating actually going to sleep. A common feature in all of them is that they generate a feeling of _____. Some methods generate a feeling of boredom, which is akin to relaxation. The important point here is that one (<u>does/does not</u>) concentrate on the heavy events in life when attempting to go to sleep.

Answers: 29-1. (a) It varies across individuals. (b) Insufficient time is spent in deeper sleep. (c) They interfere with REM and slow-wave sleep. (d) It is very ineffective. **29-2.** relaxation or calmness, does not.

30.   Summarize evidence on the common questions about dreams discussed in the Application.

30-1.   While there are some persons who claim they never dream, what is really happening is that they cannot _____ their dreams. Dreams are best recalled when waking occurs during or immediately following (REM/ NREM) sleep. Determination and practice (<u>can/cannot</u>) improve one's ability to recall dreams. A dream whose action takes place over a 20-minute period will actually last for approximately _____ minutes.

30-2.   Freud believed that dreams do require interpretation because their true meaning, which he called the _____ content, is symbolically encoded in the obvious plot of the dream, which he called the _____ content. Freud's theory that dreams carry hidden symbolic meaning would mean that dream interpretation (<u>is/is not</u>) a very complicated affair. More recent researchers now believe that dreams are (<u>more/less</u>) complicated than Freud believed. Calvin Hall makes the point that dreams require some interpretation simply because they are mostly (<u>visual/verbal</u>).

30-3.   In what way does lucid dreaming differ from regular dreaming?

30-4.   Indicate whether the following statements are "true" or "false."

____   (a)   Evidence shows that some control over one's dreams is possible, but it is not easy and results are not always consistent.

____   (b)   There have been several reported cases of persons reporting their own deaths as the result of fatal dreams.

____   (c)   It has been shown that subjects can communicate with researches using prearranged eye signals during lucid dreaming.

Answers: 30-1. remember (or recall), can, 20 **30-2.** latent, manifest, is, less, visual **30-3.** In lucid dreaming one is aware that one is dreaming. **30-4.** (a) true (b) false (c) true.

REVIEW OF KEY TERMS

Alcohol
Ascending reticular activating system (ARAS)
Biological rhythms
Cannabis
Circadian rhythms
Dissociation
Dream
Stimulants
Tolerance

Electroencephalograph (EEG)
Electromyograph (EMG)
Electro-oculograph (EOG)
Hallucinogens
Hypnosis
Insomnia
Latent content
Lucid dreams
Manifest content
Meditation
Narcolepsy

Narcotics or opiates
Nightmares
Night terrors
Non-REM sleep
Physical dependence
Psychoactive drugs
Psychological dependence
REM sleep
Sedatives
Sleep apnea
Slow-wave sleep (SWS)
Somnambulism

_____EEG_____ **1.** A device that monitors the electrical activity of the brain.

_____EMG_____ **2.** A device that records muscle activity and tension.

_____EOG_____ **3.** A device that records eye movements.

___biological rhythms___ **4.** Periodic fluctuations in physiological functioning.

_____Circadian_____ **5.** The 24-hour biological cycles found in humans and many other species.

_____REM_____ **6.** Sleep involving rapid eye movements.

_____SWS_____ **7.** Sleep stages 1 through 4, which are marked by an absence of rapid eye movements.

_____ARAS_____ **8.** Consists of the afferent fibers running through the reticular formation that influence physiological arousal.

__narcotics/opiates__ **9.** Drugs that are derived from opium that are capable of relieving pain. These drugs are also called narcotics.

_____Insomnia_____ **10.** Involves chronic problems in getting adequate sleep.

_____narolepsy_____ **11.** A disease marked by sudden and irresistible onsets of sleep during normal waking hours.

____sleep apnea____ **12.** Reflexive grasping for air that awakens a person and disrupts sleep.

_____terrors_____ **13.** Abrupt awakenings from NREM sleep accompanied by intense autonomic arousal and feelings of panic.

____nightmares____ **14.** Anxiety arousing dreams that lead to awakening, usually from REM sleep.

_____ **15.** Occurs when a sleeping person arises and wanders about in deep NREM sleep.

_____dream_____ **16.** A mental experience during sleep that includes vivid visual images.

_____hypnosis_____ **17.** A systematic procedure that typically produces a heightened state of suggestibility.

____dissociation____ **18.** Involves a splitting off of mental processes into two separate, simultaneous streams of awareness.

_____meditation_____ **19.** A family of medical exercises in which a conscious attempt is made to focus attention in a nonanalytical way.

psychoactive   **20.** Chemical substances that modify mental, emotional or behavioral functioning.

    21. Sleep stages 3 and 4 in which low-frequency delta waves become prominent in EEG recordings.

sedatives   **22.** Drugs that have sleep-inducing and behavioral depression effects.

stimulants   **23.** Drugs that tend to increase central nervous system activation and behavioral activity.

hallucinogens   **24.** A diverse group of drugs that have powerful effects on mental and emotional functioning, marked most prominently by distortions in sensory and perceptual experience.

    25. The hemp plant from which marijuana, hashish, and THC are derived.

alcohol   **26.** A variety of beverages containing ethyl alcohol.

tolerance   **27.** A progressive decrease in a person's responsiveness to a drug.

physical   **28.** A condition that exists when a person must continue to take a drug to avoid withdrawal illness.

psychology   **29.** A condition that exists when a person must continue to take a drug to satisfy mental and emotional craving for the drug.

latent   **30.** Freud's term that refers to the plot of a dream at the surface level.

manifest   **31.** Freud's term that refers to the hidden or disguised meaning of events in a dream.

lucid   **32.** Dreams in which persons are aware that they are dreaming.

Answers: 1. electroencephalograph (EEG) **2.** electromyograph (EMG) **3.** electro-oculograph (EOG) **4.** biological rhythms **5.** circadian rhythms **6.** REM sleep **7.** non-REM sleep **8.** ascending reticular activating system (ARAS) **9.** narcotics or opiates **10.** insomnia **11.** narcolepsy **12.** sleep apnea **13.** night terrors **14.** nightmares **15.** somnambulism **16.** dream **17.** hypnosis **18.** dissociation **19.** meditation **20.** psychoactive drugs **21.** slow-wave sleep (SWS) **22.** sedatives **23.** stimulants **24.** hallucinogens **25.** cannabis **26.** alcohol **27.** tolerance **28.** physical dependence **29.** psychological dependence **30.** manifest content **31.** latent content **32.** lucid dreams.

REVIEW OF KEY PEOPLE

Theodore Barber	Sigmund Freud	J. Alan Hobson
Alexander Borbely	Calvin Hall	William James
Rosalind Cartwright	Ernest Hilgard	Wilse Webb
Willian Dement		

James   **1.** Originated the term, "the stream of consciousness".

Freud   **2.** Argued for the existence of the unconscious and the hidden meaning of dreams.

    3. As one of the pioneers in early sleep research, he coined the term REM sleep.

    4. His theory is an integration of restorative and circadian theories as to why we sleep.

    5. After analyzing thousands of dreams, he concluded that their contents are generally quite mundane.

_____ **6.** Proposes a problem-solving view as a reason for dreaming.

_____ **7.** One of the authors of the role playing theory of hypnosis.

_____ **8.** A proponent of the altered state (divided consciousness) theory of hypnosis.

_____ **9.** His activation-synthesis model proposes that dreams are only side effects of neural activation.

_____ **10.** Suggests a three process model of sleep regulation that factors behavior control into the picture.

Answers: 1. James **2.** Freud **3.** Dement **4.** Borbely **5.** Hall **6.** Cartwright **7.** Barber **8.** Hilgard **9.** Hobson **10.** Webb

SELF-QUIZ

1. Which brain wave is probably operating while you are taking this quiz?
   a. alpha
   b. beta
   c. theta
   d. delta

2. The circadian rhythm operates around a:
   a. 1-year cycle
   b. 28-day cycle
   c. 24-hour cycle
   d. 90-minute cycle

3. Most dreams occur during:
   a. REM sleep
   b. NREM sleep
   c. the early hours of sleep
   d. both b and c

4. Severing the ascending reticular activating system in cats caused them to:
   a. become very aggressive
   b. become very fearful
   c. remain in continuous wakefulness
   d. remain in continuous sleep

5. Which of the following is likely to be found among persons deprived of sleep for a long period of time?
   a. slower reaction times
   b. slurred speech
   c. both of the above
   d. none of the above

6. If you fly fron New York City to San Francisco you will experience:
   a. a phase-advance shift
   b. a phase-delay shift

c. disturbed REM sleep

d. long lines at the airports.

7. According to Borbely's theory of sleep, the need for sleep is due to:
   a. the need to recharge the body
   b. circadian rhythms
   c. both a and b
   d. none of the above

8. The content of most dreams is usually:
   a. mundane
   b. exotic
   c. exciting
   d. both b and c

9. Which of the following sleep disorders is most life threatening?
   a. nightmares
   b. narcolepsy
   c. sleep apnea
   d. somnambulism

10. Persons can be made to act as if they are hypnotized even without the use of hypnotic induction. This statement
    is:
    a. true
    b. false

11. Which of the following physiological changes is unique to meditation?
    a. increased alpha rhythms
    b. decreased heart rate
    c. decreased oxygen consumption
    d. none of the above

12. Psychoactive drugs exert their effect on the brain by:
    a. decreasing blood supply to the brain
    b. altering neurotransmitter activity
    c. breaking down essential brain amino acids
    d. penetrating the nucleus of the neurons

13. The most widely abused drug in the United States is:
    a. alcohol
    b. cocaine
    c. heroin
    d. hallucinigens

14. Which of the following is likely to produce highly subjective events?
    a. hypnosis
    b. meditation
    c. psychoactive drugs
    d. all of the above

15. In order to maintain good psychological adjustment one should:
    a. sleep at least 8 hours per day
    b. take a short nap each afternoon

c. both of the above

d. none of the above are necessarilly essential

16. Which of the following statements is correct?
    a. Most people do not dream in color.
    b. Practice will not improve the ability to recall dreams.
    c. Dreams generally last only 1 or 2 minutes at most.
    d. From birth until deathy everyone dreams.

Answers: **1.** b **2.** c **3.** a **4.** d **5.** d **6.** b **7.** c **8.** a **9.** b **10.** a **11.** d **12.** b **13.** a **14.** d **15.** d **16.** d.

Chapter Six

Learning Through Conditioning

REVIEW OF KEY IDEAS

1. **Describe Pavlov's demonstration of classical conditioning and the key elements in this form of learning.**

   1-1. Classical conditioning is a type of learning that occurs when two stimuli are paired or associated closely in time. In Pavlov's initial demonstration, the two stimuli were a bell and _____.

   1-2. The response to one of the two stimuli occurs naturally and does not have to be learned or acquired through conditioning. This "unlearned" stimulus, in this case the food, is technically known as the _____ stimulus.

   1-3. The other stimulus is said to be neutral in the sense that it does not initially produce a response. When a response to this neutral stimulus is *acquired* or *learned*, the technical name for it is the _____ stimulus. In Pavlov's initial study the conditioned stimulus was the sound of a _____.

   1-4. The unconditioned stimulus in Pavlov's original study was the _____ and the conditioned stimulus was the _____. Salivation to the meat powder is known as the _____ response; salivation to the bell is termed the _____ response.

   1-5. Label the parts of the classical conditioning sequence. Place the commonly used abbreviations for these terms in the parentheses.

   (a) meat _____ (   )

   (b) salivation to meat: _____ (   )

   (c) bell: _____ (   )

   (d) salivation to bell: _____ (   )

   Answers: 1-1. meat powder (food) **1-2.** unconditioned **1-3.** conditioned, bell **1-4.** meat powder, bell, unconditioned, conditioned **1-5.** (a) unconditioned stimulus (UCS) (b) unconditioned response (UCR) (c) conditioned stimulus (CS) (d) conditioned response (CR).

2. **Discuss how classical conditioning may shape phobias, other emotional responses, and physiological processes.**

2-1.   The kids in the neighborhood where I (R. S.) grew up used to dig tunnels in a neighbor's backyard. One day a boy got stuck in the tunnel and couldn't get out. Eventually he got out, but after that he didn't want to play in tunnels again. To this day that person still has an intense fear not only of tunnels but of closed-in spaces in general. Label the parts of the classical conditioning process involved in the acquisition of the phobia of closed-in spaces. (Hint: Even though "getting stuck" certainly involves a behavior or response, it also has stimulus components.)

(a) Getting stuck:

(b) Fear produced by getting stuck:

(c) Tunnels and closed-in spaces:

(d) Fear of tunnels and closed-in spaces:

2-2.   The individual described above had developed an intense fear or phobia, acquired in part through the process of _____ conditioning. Other emotions can be conditioned as well. For example, the smell of smoke and Beemans gum described in your text, the playing of "our song," and the sight of one's home after a long absence could all produce a pleasant emotional response (or perhaps a slightly weepy, sentimental feeling). Such smells, sounds, or sights would be considered _____ stimuli.

2-3.   Similarly, certain physiological responses can be conditioned. Label the parts of the conditioning process in the study on immunosuppression in rats described in the text. (Use the abbreviations CS, CR, UCS, and UCR.)

_____ The immunosuppressive drug.

_____ Unusual taste.

_____ Decreased antibody production produced by the drug.

_____ Decreased antibody production produced by the taste.

Answers: 2-1. (a) unconditioned stimulus (UCS) (b) unconditioned response (UCR) (c) conditioned stimulus (CS) (d) conditioned response (CR) **2-2.** classical, conditioned **2-3.** UCS, CS, UCR, CR.

3. **Describe the classical conditioning phenomena of acquisition, extinction, and spontaneous recovery.**

3-1.   *Acquisition* of a conditioned response occurs when the CS and UCS are contiguous, or paired. Not all pairings result in conditioning, however. What characteristics of a CS are more likely to produce acquisition of a CR?

3-2. Timing is also important for acquisition. In the diagram below the UCS is shown at the top in bold and three possible arrangements of the CS are shown below it. Label the CS-UCS presentations as *trace, simultaneous,* or *short-delayed.*

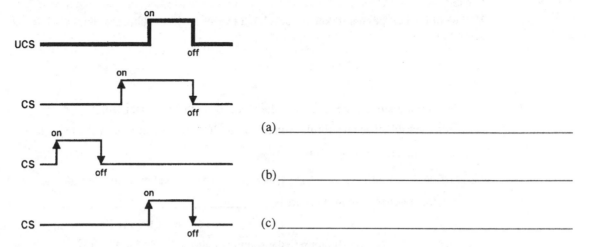

(a) _____

(b) _____

(c) _____

3-3. Which of the above arrangements is most effective for establishing a conditioned response?

3-4. Acquisition refers to the formation of a conditioned response. What is the term that refers to the weakening or disappearance of a CR?

3-5. Describe the procedure that results in extinction of a CR.

3-6. CRs may be acquired, and they may extinguish. After they extinguish they may also reappear, even without further conditioning.

(a) What is the name of this "reappearance"?

(b) When, or under what circumstance, is this recovery likely to occur?

Answers: 3-1. A novel or particularly intense CS is more likely to produce conditioning. **3-2.** (a) short-delayed (b) trace (c) simultaneous **3-3.** short-delayed **3-4.** extinction **3-5.** The CS is presented for a series of trials alone, without the UCS. **3-6.** (a) spontaneous recovery (b) after extinction, following a period of nonexposure to the CS

4. Describe the processes of stimulus generalization and discrimination and summarize the classic study of Little Albert.

4-1. With regard to the case of Little Albert:

(a) What was the CS?

(b) The UCS?

4-2. Albert was also afraid of white dogs and white rabbits. What is the name of the process that resulted in his acquisition of these fear responses?

4-3. Why would Albert be more likely to develop a fear of a white rabbit, say, than a white car or a dark horse?

4-4. The more similar stimuli are to the CS, the more likely the organism will _____ from the CS to the other stimuli. The less similar stimuli are to the CS, the more likely the organism is to _____ them from the CS.

4-5. Casey (R. S.'s cat) salivates when she hears the sound of food being dumped into her bowl. The process by which this learned response occurs is _____. The food is a(an) _____ _____. The sound of the food is a(an) _____ _____. Salivation to the sound is a(an) _____ _____.

4-6. Pets are also likely to salivate when they hear other, similar sounds, such as bags rustling in the kitchen or dishes being pulled from the cupboard. Salivation to these other sounds represents stimulus _____.

4-7. With continued training, in which food is paired only with the sound of food entering the bowl and not with the other sounds, the animal will learn to salivate only to the rattling bowl. The process of learning to respond only to one particular stimulus and not to a range of similar stimuli is termed _____.

Answers: **4-1.** (a) a white rat (b) a loud noise **4-2.** stimulus generalization (or just generalization) **4-3.** Because of similarity. The more similar the other stimuli to the CS, the more likely generalization is to occur. **4-4.** generalize, discriminate **4-5.** classical conditioning, unconditioned stimulus, conditioned stimulus, conditioned response **4-6.** generalization **4-7.** discrimination.

5. Explain what happens in higher-order conditioning.

5-1. Suppose that a bell and meat powder are paired, as in the original Pavlovian study, until a conditioned salivary response occurs to the bell. Suppose that in a new series of trials the bell is then with a clicking sound. Assuming that the stimuli are potent enough, that the timing is right, and so on:

(a) Will a CR now occur to the clicking sound?

(b) What is the name of this conditioning procedure?

(c) Which stimulus acts as the UCS under this new arrangement?

Answers: **5-1.** (a) yes (b) higher-order conditioning (c) The bell. In the original pairing of bell and food, the bell was the CS; in the new pairing of clicking sound and bell, the bell acts as a UCS.

6. **Discuss the nature of operant responding in comparison to the types of responding typically governed by classical conditioning.**

   6-1. A major aspect of Pavlovian or classical conditioning is that responses are controlled largely by stimuli that precede the responses. For example, food (precedes/follows) the response of salivation to the food, and the sound of the bell (precedes/follows) salivation to the bell.

   6-2. In contrast, in operant conditioning, learning or conditioning results from stimuli that

   _____ the response, the stimuli that are the "payoff" or _____ of that particular behavior.

   6-3. Learning theorists originally supposed that the two types of conditioning controlled different types of responses, that classical conditioning controlled reflexive or (voluntary/involuntary) responses (such as salivation or leg flexion) while operant conditioning controlled voluntary responses. While this distinction holds up (all of the time/much of the time), it is now clear that the only absolute distinction is in terms of procedure.

   Answers: 6-1. precedes, precedes **6-2.** follow (come after), consequence **6-3.** involuntary, much of the time.

7. **Describe Thorndike's work and explain his law of effect.**

   7-1. E. L. Thorndike's pioneering work on what he referred to as _____ learning provided the foundation for Skinner's _____ conditioning.

   7-2. According to Thorndike's law of _____, if a response leads to a satisfying effect in the presence of a stimulus, the association between the stimulus and response is strengthened. Thorndike's law of effect is similar to Skinner's concept of reinforcement: both emphasize the _____ of behavior.

   Answers: 7-1. instrumental, operant **7-2.** effect, consequences.

8. **Describe Skinner's principle of reinforcement and the prototype experimental procedures used in studies of operant conditioning.**

   8-1. A reinforcer is a stimulus or event that (1) is presented *after* a response and that (2) increases the tendency for the response to be repeated. Apply that definition to this example: Grundoon, a captive monkey, occasionally swings on a bar in his cage. Suppose that at some point Grundoon's trainers decide to give him a spoonful of applesauce whenever he swings. Is the applesauce a reinforcer? In terms of the definition above, how do you know that applesauce is a reinforcer?

   8-2. The trainers switch to vinegar. Grundoon, an unusual primate, swings quite frequently when this behavior is followed by vinegar. Is vinegar a reinforcer here? How do you know?

8-3. The trainers try another approach. They present Grundoon with fresh fruit *just before* they think he is likely to jump. It so happens that Grundoon's rate of jumping does increase. Is the fruit a reinforcer here? Why or why not?

8-4. The prototypic apparatus used in operant conditioning studies is the operant chamber, better known as the _____. On one wall of the chamber is mounted a manipulandum, a device that makes for an easily discernible response. For rats, the manipulandum is usually a small _____; for pigeons, the device is a _____ that the bird learns to peck.

8-5. A press of the lever or peck at the disk may produce a reinforcer, generally a small bit of food dispensed into the food cup mounted to one side or below the manipulandum. Each of these responses is recorded on a _____ _____, a device that creates a graphic record of the number of responses per unit time.

8-6. The cumulative recorder records the *rate* of the behavior, that is, the number of _____ made per unit _____.

8-7. Below is a highly stylized version of a cumulative record. About how many responses were made during the first 40 seconds? _____ Which section of the graph (a, b, c, d, or e) has the steepest slope? _____ Which section of the graph illustrates the fastest rate of responding? _____ About how many responses were made between the 40th and 70th seconds? _____

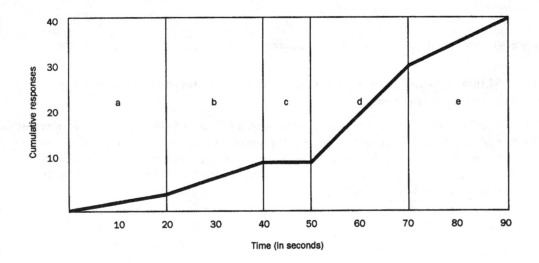

Answers: 8-1. Yes. If the animal's rate of swinging increases when followed by applesauce, then applesauce is a reinforcer. **8-2.** Yes. Because the vinegar is presented *after the response*, and because the *response rate increases*. (Note that this is an imaginary example to illustrate the point that reinforcement is defined in terms of *consequences*, not by our subjective judgment. I don't know of any monkeys that will respond for vinegar.) **8-3.** No. Reinforcing stimuli, by definition, *follow* the response. (Again, this is a contrived example just to illustrate the definition.) **8-4.** Skinner box, lever (or bar), disk **8-5.** cumulative recorder **8-6.** responses, time **8-7.** 10, d, d, 20.

9. **Describe the operant conditioning phenomena of acquisition, shaping, and extinction.**

9-1. Acquisition refers to the formation of new responses. In classical conditioning, acquisition occurs through a simple pairing of the CS and UCS. In operant conditioning, acquisition involves the procedure known as _____.

9-2. What is shaping? When is it used?

9-3. Extinction in classical conditioning involves removing the UCS while still presenting the CS.

(a) What is the extinction procedure in operant conditioning?

(b) What is the effect of extinction on behavior (response rate)?

(c) What does the term *resistance to extinction* mean?

Answers 9-1. shaping **9-2.** Shaping involves reinforcing closer and closer approximations to the desired behavior. It is used in the formation of a new response. **9-3.** (a) Extinction refers to the decrease and eventual cessation of responding that occurs when the reinforcers are no longer presented. (b) Response rate decreases; the behavior may eventually stop occurring altogether. (c) Animals may continue to respond, for a period of time, even when reinforcers are no longer presented. The extent to which they will respond during extinction is referred to as resistan*ce to extinction*.

10. **Explain how stimuli govern operant behavior and how generalization and discrimination occur in operant conditioning.**

10-1. Suppose that a rat has been shaped so that when it presses a lever it receives a food pellet. With further training, the rat may respond only when a light (or sound, etc.) in the chamber is on and not when it is off. The food pellet (which follows the response) is a _____. The light (which precedes the response) is a _____ stimulus.

10-2. Reinforcers occur _____ (after/before) the response occurs. Discriminative stimuli occur _____ the response occurs.

10-3. To create a discriminative stimulus, one reinforces a response only in the presence of a particular stimulus and not in its absence. In time that stimulus will gain control of the response: Animals will tend to emit the response only if the discriminative stimulus is (present/absent) and not if it is _____.

10-4. For example, rats can be trained to press a lever when a light comes on and not to press when the light is off. Lever presses that occur when the light is on are followed by a food pellet; those that occur in the dark are not. Label each component of this operant-conditioning process by placing the appropriate letters in the blanks below.

_____ light   a. discriminative stimulus

_____ lever press   b. response

_____ food   c. reinforcer

10-5. "Heel Fido!" says Ralph. Fido runs to Ralph's side. Fido gets a pat on the head. Label the parts of the operant conditioning sequence by placing the appropriate letters in the blanks. (To avoid confusion, the behavior or response of interest in this example is already labeled.)

_____ Heel Fido!"   a. discriminative stimulus

_____ Fido gets a pat on the head.   b. response

__b___ Fido runs to Ralph's side.   c. reinforcer

10-6. Phyllis will lend money to Ralph, but only after Ralph promises to pay her back. Ralph is also careful to thank Phyllis for her help. The behavior we are looking at here is Phyllis's lending behavior.

_____ Thank you very much, Phyllis."   a. discriminative stimulus

__b___ Phyllis lends.   b. response

_____ "I promise I'll pay you back."   c. reinforcer

10-7. Generalization occurs in operant as well as classical conditioning. For example, when I put dishes in the sink, our cat will *run to her bowl* looking for food. In technical terms, our cat _____

between the sound of food dropping in her bowl and the similar sound of dishes going into the sink.

Despite the fact that food does not follow the sound of clattering dishes, our cat has not yet learned to

_____ between the sounds in our kitchen.

Answers: 10-1. reinforcer, discriminative **10-2.** after, before **10-3.** present, absent **10-4.** a, b, c **10-5.** a, c, (b) **10-6.** c, (b), a **10-7.** generalizes, discriminate.

11. Discuss the role of delayed reinforcement and conditioned reinforcement in operant conditioning.

11-1. People who smoke like to smoke. Giving up the habit, however, also has its rewards. Given the information about delay of reinforcement, why is the behavior of giving up smoking so difficult to acquire?

11-2. Define the following:

(a) Primary reinforcer:

(b) Secondary or conditioned reinforcer:

Answers: 11-1. Because we, probably like the rest of the animal kingdom, are more affected by reinforcers that follow our behavior *immediately* than those that follow after a delay. Reinforcement for smoking is immediate; reinforcement for giving up smoking may occur only after a long delay. **11-2.** (a) A primary reinforcer satisfies biological needs, such as needs for food, water, warmth and sex. (b) A secondary, or conditioned, reinforcer is one that is learned or acquired through association with a primary reinforcer. In humans, secondary reinforcers include applause, praise, attention, and money.

12. Identify various types of schedules of reinforcement and discuss their typical effects on responding.

12-1. Schedules of reinforcement are either continuous or intermittent. If reinforcers follow each response, the schedule is referred to as a _____ reinforcement schedule. If reinforcers only follow some responses and not others (e.g., FR, VR), or occur as a function of the passage of time (e.g., FI, VI), the schedule is referred to as a/an _____ schedule.

12-2. Identify the following schedules of reinforcement by placing the appropriate abbreviations in the blanks: continuous reinforcement (CRF), fixed ratio (FR), variable ratio (VR), fixed interval (FI), variable interval (VI).

_____ A pigeon is reinforced whenever it has pecked a disk exactly 200 times.

_____ A pigeon is reinforced for pecking a disk, on the average, 200 times.

_____ A rat is always reinforced for the first response that follows a two-minute interval.

_____ A slot machine delivers a payoff, on the average, after every 10th pull of the lever.

_____ Every time the pigeon pecks a disk, it receives a pellet of food.

_____ A rat is reinforced, on the average, for the first response following a two-minute interval.

_____ A pig is reinforced for the first response after 30 seconds, then for the first response after 42 seconds, then for the first response after 5 seconds, and so on.

_____ Every two weeks Ralph picks up his payroll check at the office.

_____ A rat is reinforced after the 73rd response, then after the 22nd response, then after the 51st response, and so on.

12-3. Resistance to extinction refers to the extent to which responses occur during a period of extinction. What is the general effect of the intermittent schedules of reinforcement on resistance to extinction?

12-4. In terms of the effect on patterns of responding, what is the general difference between the *ratio* schedules (FR and VR) and the *interval* schedules (FI and VI)?

12-5. In terms of the effect on patterns of responding, what is the general difference between *fixed* schedules and *variable* schedules?

Answers: 12-1. continuous, intermittent (or partial) **12-2.** FR, VR, FI, VR, CRF, VI, VI, FI, VR **12-3.** The intermittent schedules increase resistance to extinction. **12-4.** The ratio schedules tend to produce more rapid responding than the interval schedules. **12-5.** The variable schedules tend to produce more regular patterns of responding, without pauses or scalloping, than do their fixed counterparts. They also result in more resistance to extinction.

13. Explain the distinction between positive and negative reinforcement.

13-1. Some Skinner boxes may be set up so that a mild electric shock can be delivered to the feet of the animal through the floor of the box. Suppose that whenever the animal presses the bar, the shock is turned *off* for a period of time. Will the lever-pressing behavior be *strengthened* or *weakened*?

13-2. By definition, what effect does reinforcement have on behavior? What is the effect of positive reinforcement on behavior? Negative reinforcement?

13-3. With positive reinforcement, a stimulus is *presented* after the response. What is the procedure with negative reinforcement?

Answers: 13-1. strengthened   **13-2.** Reinforcement strengthens (increases the frequency of) behavior. Both positive and negative reinforcement strengthen behavior.   **13-3.** The stimulus (an aversive stimulus) is *removed* after the response.

14. Describe and distinguish between escape learning and avoidance learning.

14-1. In escape learning the animal first experiences the aversive stimulus and then makes a response that escapes it. In avoidance learning the animal responds to a cue that permits it to respond before the aversive stimulus is delivered, thereby avoiding it altogether. Label the following examples E for escape and A for avoidance.

_____ The weather has changed, and Fahrquhart is getting extremely cold. He goes inside.

_____ Little Sandy rapidly removes her hand from the hot stove.

_____ A cue light comes on in the dog's shuttle box. It jumps the hurdle to the other side.

_____ Randolph has been told that he will be mugged if he goes outside, so he stays inside.

_____ Sue has learned a new bit of verbal behavior. If she simply says, "No, I don't want that" shortly after a salesman starts his pitch, the salesman will stop bothering her.

_____ Alice sees Ruppert in the distance. If Ruppert see her he will ask for her course notes, which she doesn't want to lend him. She heads in the other direction.

14-2. What is the major difference between escape learning and avoidance learning?

Answers: 14-1. E, E, A, A, E, A **14-2.** The major difference is that with escape learning there is no cue stimulus, so that the animal must first experience the aversive stimulus and then *escape* it. In the case of avoidance learning, a cue preceding the aversive stimulus permits the animal to *avoid* the aversive event altogether.

15. **Explain Mowrer's two-process theory and the role of negative reinforcement in avoidance behavior.**

15-1. In successful avoidance learning, the organism never experiences the aversive stimulus. So why doesn't the response gradually extinguish? Why does the animal continue to avoid? Mowrer proposed the answer more than 40 years ago: The dog in the shuttle box isn't just avoiding the shock, it is avoiding (or escaping) something else as well. What else is it avoiding?

15-2. In Mowrer's explanation the cue stimulus becomes an aversive stimulus that elicits fear. Through what learning process does the cue stimulus acquire the capacity to produce a fear response?

15-3. Why is Mowrer's theory called a two-process theory?

15-4. Some years ago Ajax was bitten by a dog on a couple of occasions. Even though he hasn't been bitten by a dog in years, the sight of a dog will send chills through his body, and he runs away. Use Mowrer's theory to explain why this phobic response hasn't extinguished.

Answers: 15-1. the cue light, or conditioned fear of the cue light   **15-2.** classical conditioning **15-3.** Because it integrates two processes, classical and operant conditioning. **15-4.** The sight of the dog produces a classically conditioned fear response. Ajax can avoid this aversive stimulus and the fear it produces (an internal stimulus) by running away.

16. **Describe punishment and its effects.**

16-1. Punishment involves weakening a response by presenting an aversive stimulus after the response has occurred. Review the concepts of reinforcement and punishment by labeling each of the following with one of these terms: positive reinforcement, negative reinforcement, or punishment.

(a) A stimulus is presented after the response; response rate increases:

(b) A stimulus is presented after the response; response rate decreases:

(c) A stimulus is removed after the response; response rate increases:

16-2. Response rate *increases*. Which of the following procedure or procedures may have been used?

a. positive reinforcement

b. negative reinforcement

c. punishment

d. either *a* or *b* above

16-3. Response rate *decreases*. Which of the following procedure or procedures may have been used?

a. positive reinforcement

b. negative reinforcement

c. punishment

d. either *b* or *c* above

16-4. When a rat presses a bar in an operant chamber, the electric shock stops. Bar pressing increases. What procedure has been used?

a. positive reinforcement

b. negative reinforcement

c. punishment

d. extinction

16-5. When the dog ran after the car, his master immediately threw a bucket of water on him. This sequence of events was repeated only twice, and the dog stopped running after the car. What has occurred?

a. positive reinforcement

b. negative reinforcement

c. punishment

d. extinction

16-6. When Randolph stepped out in his new outfit, everyone stared. If Randolph tends *not* to wear this outfit in the future, what has occurred?

a. positive reinforcement

b. negative reinforcement

c. punishment

d. extinction

16-7. Skinner has argued that punishment does not have a particularly potent effect on behavior. Recent research has found which of the following?

a. Punishment has as strong an influence on behavior as reinforcement.

b. The effects of punishment are weaker than those of reinforcement.

c. Punishment only temporarily suppresses behavior.

d. Punishment is even more effective than reinforcement.

16-8. In the space below list three negative side effects of punishment.

Answers: 16-1. (a) positive reinforcement (b) punishment (c) negative reinforcement **16-2.** d, because if response rate increases, *either* positive *or* negative reinforcement may be involved **16-3.** c. Not d, because negative reinforcement *increases* response rate. **16-4.** b **16-5.** c **16-6.** c **16-7.** a **16-8.** Punishment may (1) suppress responses in general rather than just the response punished, (2) produce unwanted emotional responses, including fear and anger, and (3) increase aggressive behavior.

17. List six guidelines for making punishment more effective.

17-1. Following are six hints that refer to the guidelines for making punishment more effective. Beneath each hint describe the appropriate guideline.

(a) When?

(b) How strong?

(c) How consistently?

(d) What explanations?

(e) Alternative responses?

(f) Spanking, or withdrawal of privileges?

Answers: 17-1. (a) If possible, punishment should be delivered immediately after the behavior. (b) Since undesirable side effects increase with the intensity of punishment, it should be *only as strong as needed* to be effective. (c) To be effective punishment should be given *consistently*, after each instance of the behavior. (d) If the *reasons for the punishment* are given to children, the punishment tends to be more effective. (e) Punishment tends to be more effective if *alternative behaviors are reinforced* at the same time. (f) In most situations *physical punishment should be avoided* because it tends to increase aggressive behavior in children. In addition, in many cases physical punishment may be less effective than withdrawal of privileges.

NEW DIRECTIONS IN THE STUDY OF CONDITIONING

18. Discuss the phenomena of instinctive drift, conditioned taste aversion, and preparedness.

18-1. What is instinctive drift?

18-2. Why was the occurrence of instinctive drift surprising to operant psychologists? Discuss this question in terms of the supposed *generality* of the laws of learning.

18-3. What is conditioned taste aversion?

18-4. Why is the occurrence of conditioned taste aversion surprising? Discuss this question in terms of classical conditioning relating to (1) CS-UCS delays and (2) the sense of taste compared with other senses.

18-5. Preparedness is Seligman's idea that there are *species-specific* tendencies to be conditioned in some ways and not in others. Both of the findings discussed above, the phenomena of _____ and _____, involve the concept of _____.

18-6. People are much more likely to die in a car than in an airplane, but phobias related to flying are much more common than phobias about driving. Why is that the case? Try to account for this oddity using Seligman's notion of preparedness.

Answers: **18-1.** The tendency for instinctive or innate behavior to interfere with the process of conditioning. **18-2.** Before the 1960s, operant psychologists assumed that any response that an animal could emit could be conditioned. This turned out not to be true. It was surprising to find that conditioning was not as general a process as they had supposed—that because of inherent characteristics of an animal some responses are difficult or impossible to condition. **18-3.** It is the fact that if the distinctive taste of a particular food is followed some hours later by sickness (and nausea, vomiting, etc.), then that taste will become aversive and will also elicit the response of nausea. **18-4.** It is surprising because (1) classical conditioning generally does not occur if there are long CS-UCS delays, and (2) taste is only one of several senses stimulated in this situation. Garcia concluded that animals have an innate tendency to associate taste (rather than sight, sound, etc.) with sickness even though the sickness may occur much later. **18-5.** instinctive drift, conditioned taste aversion, preparedness **18-6.** Seligman's notion of preparedness includes the idea that we are genetically predisposed to develop phobic responses more readily to some stimuli than to others—to spiders, rodents, and heights more readily than baseballs, lamps, and backyards. Probably because of the heights that are part of flying, flying seems to be more conditionable than driving.

19. Explain the evolutionary perspective on learning.

19-1. Psychologists used to believe that there were highly general "laws" of learning. More recently, studies like those just referred to and the emerging field of evolutionary psychology indicate that there probably (are/are not) principles of learning that apply to all species.

19-2. Instead, the new viewpoint emerging among psychologists is that ways of learning have evolved along different paths in different species, so that classical and operant conditioning, for example, are to some extent (universal/specific-specific). Finding food, avoiding predators, and reproducing allow a species to survive, but the ways of learning that accomplish these outcomes depend on the _____ value of these processes.

Answers: 19-1. are not **19-2.** species-specific **19-3.** adaptive (survival, evolutionary).

20. **Describe research on blocking and signal relations in classical conditioning and explain their theoretical importance.**

20-1. With regard to blocking: In phase one of the study described, a tone is paired with shock in a classical conditioning arrangement.

   (a) What was paired with shock in phase two?

   (b) What happens when the tone and light are presented together (without the shock)?

   (c) What happens when the light is presented alone?

   (d) In terms of traditional thinking about classical conditioning and the conditioned reflex, why is the blocking phenomenon surprising and of theoretical importance?

20-2. In the example of a signal relations study described, the number of conditioning trials in which CS and UCS were paired was the same for two groups. The difference between the two treatment groups was that for one group the (CS/UCS) was presented *alone* for a series of trials.

20-3. Theorists originally assumed that classical conditioning is an automatic, reflexive phenomenon that does not depend at all on higher mental processes. If this actually were the case, then what, supposedly, would have been the effect of presenting the UCS alone?

   a. Extinction would occur.

   b. The UCS-alone trials would weaken conditioning.

   c. The UCS-alone trials would have no effect on conditioning.

20-4. In fact, what did occur in the signal relations studies?

   a. Extinction.

   b. The UCS-alone trials weakened conditioning.

   c. The UCS-alone trials had no effect on conditioning.

20-5. Why are the blocking and signal relations studies surprising and of theoretical importance?

Answers: 20-1. (a) A tone and light were presented together prior to the UCS. (b) A conditioned response was elicited. (c) There was no CR to the light alone. (d) The finding that the light did not become a CS, even though it was paired with shock, is surprising if one takes the traditional view that classical conditioning is an au*tomatic, mechanical* process. After all, a light alone paired with shock will produce classical conditioning, so why should the addition of the tone CS block conditioning? The blocking phenomenon suggests that some sort of *cognitive* processes are at work, that the animal is able to understand that the light provides no new information. **20-2.** UCS! (If the CS were presented alone, it would be extinction.) **20-3.** c **20-4.** b **20-5.** These studies indicate that conditioning is not, as assumed earlier, an automatic process but instead depends to a considerable degree on higher mental processes.

21. **Explain how response-outcome relations (including noncontingent reinforcement) may influence operant behavior.**

21-1. "Response-outcome relations" refers to the connection between a response and its consequences. For example, for a rat in a Skinner box the relationship between the lever press (the response) and the food pellet (the outcome) is this: the rat gets the food *only if* it presses the lever. In other words, the reinforcer is (contingent/not contingent) on the response.

21-2. But suppose the rat is reinforced so that the food pellet is delivered on a timed basis, without regard to what the animal is doing. Whether the rat is jumping, sniffing, scratching, turning, or whatever, when the time comes it will receive a pellet of food. In this case the reinforcer is delivered (contingently/ noncontingently).

21-3. As is the case with contingent reinforcement, when a reinforcer is delivered noncontingently the organism will tend to repeat what it was doing just before it was reinforced. Athletes, for example, may develop superstitious rituals (hat tugging, sock pulling, pants adjusting, etc.) that have been reinforced accidentally (by making a basket, hitting a home run, etc.). This accidental reinforcement is technically termed _____ reinforcement.

21-4. While noncontingent reinforcement does strengthen behavior, noncontingent reinforcement is (more/less) effective than reinforcement that is logically connected to the response. Even studies with animals have found that responses are more affected by reinforcers that appear to be _____ by the response than by those which do not.

21-5. Reinforcement, then, is not such an automatic process. Some *response-outcome relations* are more plausible than others, and the more plausible ones are (just as/more) likely to be strengthened than the less plausible ones.

21-6. Thus, research on blocking, signal relations, and response-outcome relations has forced the development of new theories which emphasize a much more _____ explanation of conditioning, an explanation in which organisms actively attempt to detect the *relationship* between their behaviors and environmental events.

Answers: 21-1. contingent   21-2. noncontingently   **21-3.** noncontingent   **21-4.** less, caused (produced)   **21-5.** more
21-6. cognitive (information processing, mental).

OBSERVATIONAL LEARNING

22. **Discuss the nature and importance of observational learning.**

22-1. Observational learning occurs when an organism learns by observing others, who are called _____. This type of learning occurs in (humans/animals/both).

22-2. Why is the concept of observational learning so important? For one thing the idea was surprising to theorists who assumed that all learning could be accounted for by operant and classical conditioning. For another, it extends classical and operant conditioning to include not only *direct* experience but _____ or vicarious experience. We learn not only when we behave but when we _____ the behavior of others.

22-3. Bandura's theory has helped explain some puzzling aspects of conditioning in human behavior. For example, what happens when parents punish aggressive behavior in their children? While punishment by definition (increases/decreases) the behavior it follows, a parent using punishment also serves as a _____ for aggressiveness. In this way events intended to decrease aggression may, in the longer run, _____ aggression through the process of _____ learning.

Answers: **22-1.** models, both **22-2.** indirect, observe **22-3.** decreases, model, increase, observational.

23. List the basic processes in observational learning and discuss Bandura's view on whether reinforcement affects learning or performance.

23-1. In the space below list and define the four processes that Bandura has identified as crucial components of observational learning. The first letter of each concept is listed at the left.

A_____:

R_____:

R_____:

M_____:

23-2. Is reinforcement essential for learning? Many learning theorists used to think so, but in Bandura's view reinforcement is essential only for (learning/performance). Bandura asserts that we may learn without being reinforced simply by _____ the behavior of a model but are unlikely to perform the response unless we are _____ for doing so.

Answers: **23-1.** Attention: Paying attention to a model's behavior and consequences. Retention: Retaining in memory a mental representation of what onc has observed. Reproduction: Having the ability to reproduce what one sees, to convert the image to behavior. Motivation: Having the inclination, based on one's assessment of the likely payoff, to reproduce the observed behavior. **23-2.** performance, observing, reinforced.

24. Describe the Featured Study on observational learning and aggression.

24-1. The major purpose of the study was to test the hypothesis that children who saw models _____ for aggression would imitate the aggressive behavior to a greater extent than those who saw the models _____ for their aggression.

24-2. There were four televised scenes presented in the study, as follows.

(a) In one condition four-year-old subjects saw Rocky beat up Johnny, following which Rocky was seen happily playing with toys while consuming cookies and pop. This was the Aggressive-Model-_____ condition.

(b) In a second condition subjects saw Rocky engaged in the same aggressive behavior, but this time Johnny returned the aggression, following which Rocky was seen cowering in a corner. This was the Aggressive-Model_____ condition.

(c) In a third condition Rocky and Johnny are engaged in vigorous play, but there is no aggression. This was the Nonaggressive-Model-_____ condition.

(d) In the fourth condition the children did not watch TV. This was the No-Model-_____ condition.

24-3. After participating in one of the four conditions, the children were left in a room filled with toys for 20 minutes. Among the toys were two five-foot tall Bobo dolls. What were the results of this study?

Answers: 24-1. rewarded, punished **24-2.** (a) Rewarded (b) Punished (c) Control (d) Control **24-3.** Children in the Aggressive-Model-Rewarded condition displayed significantly more aggression than did children in the other conditions. Observers are more likely to imitate behavior followed by positive consequences than behavior followed by negative consequences.

PUTTING IT IN PERSPECTIVE

25. Explain how this chapter highlighted two of the text's unifying themes.

25-1. Skinner emphasized the importance of *environmental* events (reinforcers, punishers, discriminative stimuli, schedules of reinforcement) as the determinants of behavior. One of our unifying themes, however, is that heredity and environment interact. In support of this theme list the names of three phenomena that show that *biology* has a powerful effect on *conditioning*.

25-2. The second theme well illustrated in this chapter is that psychology evolves in a sociohistorical context. To illustrate this theme, list three areas in which operant psychology has influenced our everyday lives.

Answers: 25-1. instinctive drift, conditioned taste aversion, preparedness **25-2.** Operant psychology has probably influenced (1) parents' tendency to prefer reinforcement over punishment, (2) increased emphasis on the use of positive reinforcement in management in business , and (3) programmed learning and individualized instruction (including, by the way, the procedure of using learning objectives in your text and study guide).

APPLICATION: ACHIEVING SELF-CONTROL THROUGH BEHAVIOR MODIFICATION

26. Describe how to specify your target behavior and gather baseline data for a self-modification program.

26-1. What behavior do you want to change? The question sounds simple, but the task of defining a _____ behavior is frequently quite tricky.

26-2. The behavior that you select must be defined very specifically so that you will know if and when it changes. For example, for the problem of anger control, which of the following would be the most directly observable definition of "angry outbursts"?

  a. inner turmoil

  b. temper tantrums

  c. loud voice and clenched fists

26-3. Once you specify the target behavior you must gather _____ data on your behavior prior to the intervention. At this time you should also keep track of events that precede the target behavior, the _____ events, and also the positive and negative reinforcers that follow it, the _____ events.

Answers: **26-1.** target   **26-2.** <u>c</u>, although even those behaviors would probably be described even further in a behavior modification program. Alternative <u>a</u> is not really observable. Alternative <u>b</u> could be behaviorally defined, but as it stands it is hard to know precisely which behaviors temper tantrums refers to   **26-3.** baseline, antecedent, consequent.

27. Discuss your options for increasing or decreasing a response in designing a self-modification program.

27-1. To increase a target behavior you would use _____. The reinforcer (ca<u>n/can not</u>) be something that you already are receiving. For example, you probably already watch T.V., go to movies, or buy things for yourself, so you could make one of these events _____ on an increased frequency of the target behavior.

27-2. You would specify exactly what behavioral goals must be met before you receive the reinforcer; that is, you would arrange the _____. If your goal is to increase studying, you might specify that T.V. watching for one hour is _____ on having studied for two hours.

27-3. Or, you might specify that for each hour you studied you would earn points that could be "spent" for watching T.V., or going to movies, or talking with friends, and so on. This type of arrangement is referred to as a _____ economy.

27-4. In some cases you might want to approach the target response gradually, to reinforce successive approximations to the target behavior using the procedure known as _____.

27-5. To decrease a target behavior you could make some sort of _____ contingent on the behavior. The problem with this approach is that it is difficult to follow through by punishing oneself, so there are two guidelines to keep in mind: (1) Use punishment only in conjunction with _____ reinforcement; and (2) use a relatively _____ punishment that you, or perhaps a third party, will be able to administer.

27-6. For some situations you may be able to identify events that reliably precede the behaviors you are trying to stop. For example, for some people smoking is at least under partial control of certain types of social events. So, one strategy for decreasing a behavior is to identify the (<u>antecedent/consequent</u>) events that may control the behavior.

Answers: **27-1.** reinforcement, can, contingent   **27-2.** contingency, contingent   **27-3.** token   **27-4.** shaping
27-5. punishment, positive, mild   **27-6.** antecedent.

28. **Discuss how to execute, evaluate, and end a self-modification program.**

28-1.   Successful execution of the program depends on several factors. To avoid "cheating" try creating a formal written behavioral _____. Or, make an arrangement so that (only you/someone else) delivers the reinforcers and punishments.

28-2.   If your program isn't working, some small revision may turn it around. Try increasing the strength of the reinforcer or else try _____ the delay between the behavior and delivery of the reinforcer.

28-3.   It is generally a good idea to specify in advance the conditions under which you would end the program. You may wish to phase it out by having (a gradual/an immediate) reduction in the frequency or potency of reinforcers, although for some successful programs the new behaviors become self-maintaining on their own.

   Answers: **28-1.** contract (agreement), someone else   **28-2.** decreasing   **28-3.** a gradual.

REVIEW OF KEY TERMS

Acquisition
Antecedents
Avoidance learning
Behavioral contract
Behavior modification
Blocking
Classical conditioning
Conditioned reinforcers
Conditioned response (CR)
Conditioned stimulus (CS)
Continuous reinforcement
Cumulative recorder
Discriminative stimuli
Elicit
Emit
Preparedness
Escape learning
Extinction
Fixed-interval (FI) schedule

Fixed-ratio (FR) schedule
Higher-order conditioning
Instinctive drift
Instrumental learning
Intermittent reinforcement
Law of effect
Learning
Negative reinforcement
Noncontingent reinforcement
Observational learning
Operant chamber
Operant conditioning
Partial reinforcement
Pavlovian conditioning
Phobias
Positive reinforcement
Primary reinforcers
Programmed learning
Punishment

Reinforcement
Reinforcement contingencies
Resistance to extinction
Respondent conditioning
Schedule of reinforcement
Secondary reinforcers
Shaping
Skinner box
Spontaneous recovery
Stimulus contiguity
Stimulus discrimination
Stimulus generalization
Token economy
Trial
Unconditioned response (UCR)
Unconditioned stimulus (UCS)
Variable-interval (VI) schedule
Variable-ratio (VR) schedule

_____learning_____   1.   A relatively durable change in behavior or knowledge that is due to experience.

_____phobias_____   2.   Irrational fears of specific objects or situations.

classical conditioning   3.   The most common name of a type of learning in which a neutral stimulus acquires the ability to evoke a response that was originally evoked by another stimulus.

Pavlovian conditioning   4.   Another name for classical conditioning derived from the name of the person who originally discovered the conditioning phenomenon.

respondent   5.   A third name for classical conditioning that emphasizes the importance of the response.

uncondition UCS   6.   A stimulus that evokes an unconditioned response.

_____UCR_____	7. The response to an unconditioned stimulus.
_____CS_____	8. A previously neutral stimulus that has acquired the capacity to evoke a conditioned response.
_____CR_____	9. A learned reaction to a conditioned stimulus that occurs because of previous conditioning.
_____elicit_____	10. To draw out or bring forth, as in classical conditioning.
_____	11. Any presentation of a stimulus or pair of stimuli in classical conditioning.
_____acquisition_____	12. The formation of a new response tendency.
_____	13. Occurs when there is a temporal (time) association between two events.
_____extinction_____	14. The gradual weakening and disappearance of a conditioned response tendency.
spontaneous recovery	15. The reappearance of an extinguished response after a period of nonexposure to the conditioned stimulus.
stimulus generalization	16. Occurs when an organism responds to new stimuli that are similar to the stimulus used in conditioning.
" discrimination	17. Occurs when an organism learns not to respond to stimuli that are similar to the stimulus used in conditioning.
_____	18. Occurs when a conditioned stimulus functions as if it were an unconditioned stimulus.
operant conditioning	19. This term, introduced by Skinner, refers to learning in which voluntary responses come to be controlled by their consequences.
instrumental	20. Another name for operant conditioning, this term was introduced earlier by Edward L. Thorndike.
law of effect	21. Law stating that if a response in the presence of a stimulus leads to satisfying effects, the association between the stimulus and the response is strengthened.
reinforcement	22. Occurs when an event following a response strengthens the tendency to make that response.
skinner box	23. A standard operant chamber in which an animal's responses are controlled and recorded.
_____	24. Production of voluntary responses in responding in operant conditioning.
_____	25. The circumstances or rules that determine whether responses lead to presentation of reinforcers; or, the relationship between a response and positive consequences.
cumulative recorder	26. Device that creates a graphic record of operant responding as a function of time.
shaping	27. The reinforcement of closer and closer approximations of the desired response.
_____	28. An approach to self-instruction in which information and questions are arranged in a sequence of small steps to permit active responding by the learner.
resistance to extinction	29. Occurs when an organism continues to make a response after delivery of the reinforcer for it has been terminated.
_____	30. Cues that influence operant behavior by indicating the probable consequences (reinforcement or nonreinforcement) of a response.
primary reinforcers	31. Stimulus events that are inherently reinforcing because they satisfy biological needs.

secondary reinforcers	**32.**	Stimulus events that acquire reinforcing qualities by being associated with primary reinforcers.
schedule of reinforcement	**33.**	A specific pattern of presentation of reinforcers over time.
continuous	**34.**	Occurs when every instance of a designated response is reinforced.
fixed interval intermittent	**35.**	The name for all schedules of reinforcement in which a designated response is reinforced only some of the time.
fixed ratio	**36.**	The schedule in which the reinforcer is given after a fixed number of nonreinforced responses.
variable ratio	**37.**	The schedule in which the reinforcer is given after a variable number of nonreinforced responses.
variable interval	**38.**	The schedule in which the reinforcer is given for the first response that occurs after a fixed time interval has elapsed.
fixed interval	**39.**	The schedule in which the reinforcer is given for the first response that occurs after a variable time interval has elapsed.
+ve reinforcement	**40.**	Occurs when a response is strengthened because it is followed by the arrival of a rewarding (presumably pleasant) stimulus.
−ve reinforcement	**41.**	Occurs when a response is strengthened because it is followed by the removal of an aversive (unpleasant) stimulus.
escape	**42.**	Occurs when an organism engages in a response that brings aversive stimulation to an end.
avoidance	**43.**	Occurs when an organism engages in a response that prevents aversive stimulation from occurring.
punishment	**44.**	Occurs when an event that follows a response weakens or suppresses the tendency to make that response.
instinctive drift	**45.**	Occurs when an animal's innate response tendencies interfere with conditioning processes.
blocking	**46.**	Occurs when a stimulus paired with a UCS fails to become a CS because it is redundant with an established CS.
observational learning	**47.**	Occurs when a response is strengthened even though the delivery of the reinforcer is not a result of the response.
observational	**48.**	Occurs when an organism's responding is influenced by the observation of others, who are called models.
behaviour mod	**49.**	A systematic approach to changing behavior through the application of the principles of conditioning.
antecedents	**50.**	Events that typically precede your target behavior and may play a major role in governing your target response; also, another term for discriminative stimuli.
token economy	**51.**	A system for distributing symbolic reinforcers that are exchanged later for a variety of genuine reinforcers.
behavioural contract	**52.**	A written agreement outlining a promise to adhere to the contingencies of a behavior-modification program.
partial	**53.**	When a designated response is reinforced only some of the time; another name for intermittent reinforcement.
	54.	Another name for secondary reinforcers.
Preparedness	**55.**	A species-specific predisposition to be conditioned in certain ways and not in others.
operant chamber	**56.**	A small enclosure in which an animal's responses are recorded and followed by specified consequences; a Skinner box.

REVIEW OF KEY PEOPLE

Albert Bandura
John Garcia
Ivan Pavlov

Robert Rescorla
Martin Seligman
B. F. Skinner

E. L. Thorndike
John B. Watson

_____ 1.   The first to describe the process of classical conditioning.

_____ 2.   Founded behaviorism; examined the generalization of conditioned fear in a boy known as "Little Albert."

_____ 3.   Developed a principle known as the law of effect; coined the term _instrumental learning_.

_____ 4.   Elaborated the learning process known as operant conditioning; investigated schedules of reinforcement; developed programmed learning.

_____ 5.   Asserted that environmental stimuli serve as signals and that some stimuli in classical conditioning are better signals than others.

_____ 6.   Described and extensively investigated the process of observational learning.

_____ 7.   Discovered that taste aversion was conditioned only through taste and nausea pairings and not through other stimulus pairings, such as taste and shock.

_____ 8.   Proposed the theory of preparedness, the notion that there are species-specific predispositions to condition to certain stimuli and not to others.

SELF-QUIZ

1. In Pavlov's original demonstration of classical conditioning, salivation to the bell was the:
    a. conditioned stimulus
    b. conditioned response
    c. unconditioned stimulus
    d. unconditioned response

2. Sally developed a fear of balconies after almost falling from a balcony on a couple of occasions. What was the conditioned response?
    a. the balcony
    b. fear of the balcony
    c. almost falling
    d. fear resulting from almost falling

3. When the UCS is removed and the CS is presented alone for a period of time, what will occur?
   a. classical conditioning
   b. generalization
   c. acquisition
   d. extinction

4. Sally developed a fear of balconies from almost falling. Although she has had no dangerous experiences on bridges, cliffs, and the view from tall buildings, she now fears these stimuli as well. Which of the following is likely to have produced a fear of these other stimuli?
   a. instinctive drift
   b. spontaneous recovery
   c. generalization
   d. discrimination

5. A researcher reinforces closer and closer approximations to a target behavior. What is the name of the procedure she is using?
   a. shaping
   b. classical conditioning
   c. discrimination training
   d. extinction

6. John says, "Please pass the salt." Ralph passes the salt. "Thank you," says John. John's request precedes a behavior (salt passing) that is reinforced ("Thank you"). Thus, the request "Please pass the salt" is a _____ for passing the salt:
   a. discriminative stimulus
   b. response
   c. positive reinforcer
   d. conditioned stimulus (CS)

7. A rat is reinforced for the first lever-pressing response that occurs, *on the average*, after 60 seconds. Which schedule is the rat on?
   a. FR
   b. VR
   c. FI
   d. VI

8. When the rat presses a lever, the mild electric shock on the cage floor is turned off. What procedure is being used?
   a. punishment
   b. escape
   c. discrimination training
   d. avoidance

9. A cue light comes on in the dog's shuttle box. It jumps the hurdle to the other side. What procedure is being used?
   a. punishment
   b. escape
   c. discrimination training
   d. avoidance

10. In Mowrer's explanation of avoidance, the cue stimulus acquires the capacity to elicit fear through the process of:
    a. operant conditioning
    b. classical conditioning
    c. generalization
    d. discrimination

11. The contingencies are as follows: if the response occurs, a stimulus is *presented*; if the response does not occur, the stimulus is not presented. Under this procedure the strength of the response *decreases*. What procedure is being used?
    a. positive reinforcement
    b. negative reinforcement
    c. punishment
    d. avoidance training

12. In terms of the traditional view of conditioning, research on conditioned taste aversion was surprising because:
    a. there was a very long delay between CS and UCS
    b. the dislike of a particular taste was operantly conditioned
    c. conditioning occurred to all stimuli present when the food was consumed
    d. the sense of taste seems to be relatively weak

13. Animal trainers (the Brelands) trained pigs to put coins in a piggy bank for a food reward. The animals learned the response but, instead of depositing the coins immediately in the bank, the pigs began to toss them in the air, drop them, push them on the ground, and so on. What had occurred that interfered with conditioning?
    a. conditioned taste aversion
    b. blocking
    c. instinctive drift
    d. S & L scandal

14. A stimulus paired with a UCS fails to establish a CR because it is redundant with an already established CS. What is involved?
    a. spontaneous recovery
    b. stimulus generalization
    c. instinctive drift
    d. blocking

15. Earlier learning viewpoints considered classical and operant conditioning to be automatic processes involving environmental events that did not depend at all on biological or cognitive factors. Research in which of the following areas cast doubt on this point of view?
    a. blocking and signal relations
    b. instinctive drift and conditioned taste aversion
    c. response-outcome relations
    d. all of the above

Answers: 1. b 2. b 3. d 4. c 5. a 6. a 7. d 8. b 9. d 10. b 11. c 12. a 13. c 14. d 15. d.

Chapter Seven

Human Memory

REVIEW OF KEY IDEAS

ENCODING: GETTING INFORMATION INTO MEMORY

1. List and describe the three basic human memory processes.

    1-1.   The three basic human memory processes are:

        (a) Putting the information in, a process called _____.

        (b) Holding onto the information, a process called _____.

        (c) Getting the information back out, a process called _____.

Answers: 1-1. (a) encoding (b) storage (c) retrieval.

2. Discuss the role of attention in memory and contrast the early- and late-selection theories of attention.

    2-1.   If you are being introduced to a new person and you want to remember her name, it is first necessary to give selective _____ to this information. This requires_____ out irrelevent sensory input. The debate between early and late selection theories of attention is an argument over when this filtering takes place, before or after _____ is given to the arriving material.

    2-2.   While there is ample evidence to support both early- and late-selection theories of attention, what conclusion have some theorists been led to?

Answers: 2-1. attention, filtering, meaning **2-2.** The location of the attention filter may be flexible rather than fixed.

3. **Describe the three levels of information processing proposed by Craik and Lockhart.**

— 3-1.   Craik and Lockhart propose three levels for encoding incoming information, with ever increasing retention as the depth of processing increases. In their order of depth these three levels are:

(a) _____   —(b) _____   (c) _____

— 3-2.   Below are three-word sequences. Tell which level of processing each sequence illustrates and why.

(a) cat   IN   tree   _____

(b) car   BAR   czar   _____

(c) CAN CAP   CAR   _____

—3-3.   If this theory is correct then we would expect most persons to best remember the sequence in _____. This is because the words in this sequence have greater_____ than do the other two sequences. It has been found that processing time (is/is not) a reliable index of depth of processing, and thus what constitutes "levels" remains vague.

Answers: 3-1. (a) structural (b) phonemic (c) semantic **3-2.** (a) Semantic because we immediately give meaning to the words. (b) Phonemic because the words sound alike. (c) Structural because the words look alike. **3-3.** cat in tree, meaning, is not.

4. **Discribe three techniques for enriching _e encoding process and research on each.**

—4-1.   Elaboration helps us to better remember the words RUN FAST CAT than the words WORK SLOW TREE. Why is this?

—4-2.   According to Paivio's dual-coding theory, why is it easier to remember the word APPLE rather than the word PREVAIL?

4-3.   What is the general idea behind self-referent encoding?

Answers: 4-1. Because the words RUN FAST CAT allow us to make richer and more elaborate associations among them than do the other three words (for example you can imagine a cat running fast). **4-2.** Because it is easier to form a visual image of the word APPLE thus allowing for storage of both the word and image. **4-3.** We are more likely to remember information when it is relevant to ourselves.

STORAGE: MAINTAINING INFORMATION IN MEMORY

5. Describe the role of the sensory store in memory.

5-1. Sensory memory allows for retention of a very (<u>large</u>/small) amount of information for a very (<u>brief</u>/long) period of time. The retention time for vision is less than_____, although for other senses, such as hearing and touch, it may last more than a second. In other words, sensory memory allows us to retain almost all incoming information long enough to allow for further processing. However, most of the processing of incoming information probably (does/<u>does not</u>) take place in the sensory store.

Answers: 5-1. large, brief, one second, does not.

6. Describe the characteristics of short-term memory.

6-1. Indicate whether the following statements regarding short-term memory are true or false.

_____ (a) Has a virtually unlimited storage capacity.

_____ (b) Has a storage capacity of seven, plus or minus two, items.

_____ (c) Requires continuous rehearsal to maintain information in store for more than 20 or 30 seconds.

_____ (d) Stores information more or less permanently.

_____ (e) Chunking can help to increase the capacity of this system.

Answers: 6-1. (a) false (b) true (c) true (d) false (e) true.

7. Discuss Baddely's model of working memory.

7-1. Say which component of Baddely's working memory, rehearsal loop, visuospatial sketchpad, or executive control system, is operating in the following situations.

(a) You are mentally weighing the pros and cons of attending a particular university

(b) You continue to recite a phone number as you walk towards the phone.

(c) You are describing the location of a resturant to a friend.

Answers: 7-1. (a) executive control system (b) rehearsal loop (c) visuospatial sketchpad.

8. Evaluate the hypothesis that all memories are stored permanently in long-term memory (LTM).

8-1. There are two views regarding the durability of information in LTM. One is that no information is ever lost and the other is that _____. Those who favor the "no-loss" view explain forgetting as a failure of _____. The information is still there, we just cannot get it out.

8-2. How do the some-loss proponents counter the following three lines of evidence cited by the no-loss proponents?

(a) Flashbulb memories of previous events?

(b) The remarkable recall of hypnotized subjects?

(c) Penfield's electrically triggered memories?

Answers: 8-1. some information is lost, retrieval **8-2.** (a) They often tend to be inaccurate and less detailed with the passage of time. (b) Their recall of information is often found to be incorrect. (c) The memories were often incorrect and resembled dreams or hallucinations more than real events.

9. Explain how verbal rehearsal relates to LTM storage and discuss the likely causes of the serial position effect.

9-1. Perhaps the major way in which information is transferred from STM to LTM is through the use

of_____. The longer information is retained in STM through verbal rehearsal, the

(less/more) likely it is to be transferred to LTM.

9-2. Roughly sketch the serial position effect onto the figure below. Then label the area on the sketch with a P that shows the primacy effect and with an R that shows the recency effect.

9-3. What appears to account for the primacy effect?

9-4. What appears to account for the recency effect?

Answers: 9-1. verbal rehearsal, more **9-2.** The curve you drew should be in the shape of a U. The primacy effect should be at the beginning (upper left side) and the recency effect at the end (upper right side). **9-3.** Words at the beginning get rehearsed more often. **9-4.** Words at the end still remain in STM.

10. **Describe clustering, conceptual hierarchies, semantic networks, and their role in long-term memory (LTM).**

   10-1. Group the following words into two groups or categories:

   rose　　dog　　grass　　cat　　tree　　rat

   You probably grouped the words into plants and animals, which is the general idea behind
   _____. Thus clustering leads to forming categories (concepts) and in turn the the categories
   are organized into _____ hierarchies. For example, the categories of plants and animals can
   be placed under the higher category (hierarchy) of _____ things.

   10-2. In addition to conceptual categories, it appears that LTM also stores information in terms of semantic
   networks. If you understand the idea behind semantic networks and its related idea of spreading activation, you should be able to answer the questions below.

   Person A attends an urban university and frequently studies while riding a bus to and from school.

   Person B attends a university located in a rural area and frequently studies outside in one of the many
   park-like areas surrounding the school.

   (a) When asked to think of words associated with the word STUDY, which of the students is most likely
   to think of the word GRASS?_____

   (b) Which person is most likely to think of the word TRAFFIC?_____

   (c) Which person is most likely to think of the word PEACEFUL?_____

   Answers: 10-1. clustering, conceptual, living **10-2.** (a) person B (b) person A (c) person B.

11. **Describe schemas and scripts and their role in long-term memory.**

   11-1. It also appears that LTM also stores information in an organized clusters of knowledge about particular
   objects or events called _____. For example, in the study cited by the text, the subjects who
   falsely recalled seeing books did so because of their schema of what a professor's _____
   looks like.

   11-2. A particular kind of schema that organizes what people know about common activities, such as grocery
   shoping or washing clothes, is called a _____.

   Answers: 11-1. schemas, office **11-2.** script.

12. Describe how retrieval cues and context cues influence retrieval.

12-1.   In the following examples indicate whether retrieval cues or context cues are being used to retrieve information from long-term memory.

(a)   In trying to recall the name of a high school classmate, you get the feeling that his first name began with an "L" and begin saying names like Larry, Leroy, Lionel, etc.

(b)   Or you may attempt to recall the high school classmate by imagining the history class in which he sat in the row next to you.

Answers: 12-1. (a) retrieval cues (b) context cues.

13. Distinguish between mood-dependent memory effects and mood-congruence effects.

13-1.   The following situations depict either a mood-dependent effect or a mood-congruence effect. Identify them.

(a)   While sitting at a resturant enjoying a great meal you suddenly recall another pleasant experience from last summer.

(b)   As an experimental subject you are asked to recall a list of words you learned while in an induced sad state. You find your recall improves when the sad state is reinduced.

Answers: 13-1. (a) mood-congruence effect (b) mood-dependent effect.

14. Discuss Bartlett's work and research on the misinformation effect.

14-1.   Bartlett's work with the "The War of the Ghosts," found that the subjects reconstructed the original tale to fit with their already established _____.

14-2.   Since we use schemas to move information in and out of long-term memory, it is not too surprising that retrieved information may be altered by the schema. This is the general idea behind the _____ nature of memory.

14-3.   For example, Elizabeth Loftus found that subjects were much more likely to falsely recall seeking broken glass on a videotaped scene when they were originally asked, "How fast were the cars going when they (hit/smashed) into each other". In this case the word "smashed" resulted in a different _____ than did the word "hit". The distortion of memory by the word "smashed" is an example of the post-event _____ effect.

14-4. While research evidence clearly shows that post-event misinformation does cause alterations in memory, it not so clear about the underlying mechanisms. What two theories covered so far have been proposed to account for this phenomenon?

Answers: 14-1. schemas **14-2.** reconstructive **14-3.** smashed, schema, misinformation **14-4.** The misinformation replaces and destroys the original memory. The misinformation interferes with retrieving the original information.

15. Discuss the implications of evidence on source monitoring and reality monitoring.

15-1. A third explanation for distorted memory retrieval involves source monitoring. Both source monitoring and its subtype, reality monitoring, require us to make attributions about the _____ of memories. Errors in memory from both kinds of monitoring are (<u>rare/common</u>).

15-2. Say whether the situations below are examples of source monitoring (S) or reality monitoring (R).

_____ (a) You become convinced that you broke your arm when you were five years old, but your mother tells you that it never happened.

_____ (b) You attribute a funny story to your good friend Tom when in fact it was Fred, whom you don't really care for, who told you the story.

_____ (c) You believe that you received an "A" in college algebra, but your transcript shows a "C".

Answers: 15-1. origins, common **15-2.** (a) R (b) S (c) R.

FORGETTING: WHEN MEMORY LAPSES

16. Describe Ebbinghaus's forgetting curve and three measures of retention.

16-1. Ebbinghau's forgetting curve, using nonsense syllables and himself as the subject, showed that forgeting was most rapid in the (<u>first/second</u>) 9 hours after learning the material. Latter research has shown that the dramatic decline is (<u>the same/much less</u>) when more meaningful material is involved.

16-2. Which of the three different methods of measuring forgetting is illustrated in each of the following situations?

(a) You are asked to identify a suspect in a police lineup.

(b) You time yourself while learning 20 new French words. After a week you find you have forgotten some of the words, and you again time yourself while learning the list a second time.

(c) You are asked to draw a floor plan of your bedroom from memory.

Answers: 16-1. first, much less **16-2.** (a) recognition (b) relearning (c) recall.

17. Explain how forgetting may be due to ineffective encoding.

- 17-1.   Why are most people unable to recognize the correct penny shown at the beginning of this chapter in the text?

- 17-2.   What is another name for information loss due to ineffective coding of this kind?

17-3.   Why is semantic coding better than phonemic coding for enhancing future recall of written material?

Answers: 17-1. They never encoded the correct figure in their memories. **17-2.** pseudoforgetting **17-3.** Semantic coding will lead to deeper processing and more elaborate associations.

18. Compare and contrast decay and interference as potential causes of forgetting.

- 18-1.   Two other theories of forgetting propose additional factors that may be involved in retrieval failure. One theory holds that retrieval failure may be due to the impermanence of the memory storage itself. This is the notion behind the _____ theory of forgetting. Decay theory is best able to explain retrieval failure in _____ memory and to a lesser extent in (<u>short-term/long-term</u>) memory.

- 18-2.   The other theory attributes retrieval failure to other information already in the memory or to information arriving at a later time. This is the notion behind the _____ theory of forgetting. According to interference theory, the failure may be caused by interference from information already in the memory, a phenomenon called _____ <u>interference</u>, or the failure may be caused by interference occuring after the original memory was stored, a phenomenon called _____ <u>interference</u>. Interference is most likely to occur when the materials being stored are very (<u>similar/different</u>).

Answers: 18-1. decay, sensory store, short-term **18-2.** interference, proactive, retroactive, similar.

19. Explain how forgetting may be due to factors in the retrieval process.

- 19-1.   Breakdowns in the retrieval process can occur when the encoding specificity principle is violated. This means there has been a mismatch between the _____ <u>cue</u> and the _____ code. A common instance of this violation is seen when one attempts to retrieve a semantically coded word with (<u>semantic/phonetic</u>) retrieval cues.

19-2. Retrieval failure may also occur when there is a poor fit between initial encoding processing and the processing required by the measure of retention. In other words, the two kinds of processing are not transfer-_____.

19-3. Sigmund Freud felt that some breakdowns in the retrieval process could be attributed to purposeful suppression of information by unconscious forces, a phenomenon called _____ forgetting. Freud called motivated forgetting _____.

Answers: 19-1. retrieval, memory, phonemic **19-2.** appropriate **19-3.** motivated, repression.

20. Summarize the repressed memories controversy.

20-1. The major controversy regarding the recovery of previously repressed memories is whether or not they are authentic. One possibility is that the recovered memories are indeed authentic. What is another possible explanation, particularly for persons who have been undergoing psychotherapy?

Answers: 20-1. The memories may have been (unintentionally) implanted by the therapists.

21. Describe the Featured Study on the creation of false memories.

21-1. Answer the following questions regarding the Featured Study.

(a) What kinds of persons made up the two groups in this study.

(b) What three factors increased the probability of the psuedomemory effect?

Answers: 21-1. (a) Persons who scored high or low in hypnotic susceptibility. (b) Being highly susceptible to hypnosis, being hypnotized, and experiencing rapport with the hypnotist.

IN SEARCH OF THE MEMORY TRACE: THE PHYSIOLOGY OF MEMORY

22. Summarize evidence on the biochemistry and neural circuitry underlying memory.

22-1. Which of the following biochemical changes have been implicated in the physiology of memory?

(a) An increase or decrease in the release of neurotransmitters.

(b) Induced changes in RNA.

(c) Inadequate synthesis of acetylcholine.

(d) Interference with protein synthesis.

22-2. Answer the following questions regarding the neural circuity of memory.

(a) What neural changes were found in rats that learned to run a series of mazes?

(b) What caused a rabbit to lose its memory of a conditioned eye blink?

(c) What do localized neural circuits have to do with memory?

Answers: **22-1.** a, c, d **22-2.** (a) Increased growth of neuronal dendritic trees. (b) Destruction of an area in the cerebellum. (c) Specific memories may have specific localized neural circuits.

23. Distinguish between two types of amnesia and indentify the anatomical structures implicated in memory.

23-1. Amnesia cases due to head injury provide clues about the anatomical basis of memory. There are two basic types of head-injury amnesia. When the memory loss is for events prior to the injury, it is called _____ amnesia. When the memory loss is for events following the injury, it is called _____ amnesia.

23-2. Damage to what three areas in or near the limbic system have been found to result in amnesia?

23-3. The limbic system also appears to play a role in the hypothesized consolidation process, which assumes that the consolidation of memories begins in the _____ system. These memories are then stored in the same areas that were originally involved in processing the sensory input in the _____.

Answers: **23-1.** anterograde, retrograde **23-2.** amygdala, hippocampus, thalamus **23-3.** limbic, cortex.

ARE THERE MULTIPLE MEMORY SYSTEMS?

24. Distinguish between implicit versus explicit memory and their relationship to declarative and procedural memory.

24-1. Label the two following situations as to whether they are examples of implicit or explicit memory.

_____ (a) After studying for your history test, you were able to easily recall the information during the exam.

_____ (b) While studying for your history exam, you unexpectedly recall an incident from the previous summer.

24-2. Another division of memory systems has been hypothesized for declarative memory and procedural memory. Identify these two divisions from their descriptions given below.

_____ (a) This system allows you to drive a car or play a piano with minimal attention to the execution of movements that are required.

_____ (b) This system allows you to explain how to drive a car or play a piano to a friend.

24-3. It has been suggested that there is an apparent relationship between implicit memory and _____ memory and between explicit memory and _____ memory.

Answers: 24-1. (a) explicit (b) implicit **24-2.** (a) procedural (b) declarative **24-3.** (a) procedural (b) declarative.

25. Explain the distinctions between episodic memory versus semantic memory and prospective versus retrospective memory.

25-1. It has also been hypothesized that declarative memory can be further subdivided into semantic and episodic memory. Identify these two kinds of memory from the following descriptions:

_____ (a) This kind of memory acts like an encyclopedia, storing all of the factual information you possess.

_____ (b) This kind of memory acts like an autobiography, storing all of your personal experiences.

25-2. Still another possibility is that we have separate memory systems for prospective and retrospective memory. The distinction here is between our ability to remember events from the past or previously learned information, _____ memory, and our ability to remember or perform actions in the future, _____ memory.

Answers: 25-1. (a) semantic (b) episodic **25-2.** retrospective, prospective.

PUTTING IT IN PERSPECTIVE

26. Explain how this chapter highlighted two of the text's unifying themes.

26-1. The two unifying themes highlighted in this chapter were that experience is subjective and that behavior has multifactoral causation. The text mentions three major areas in which subjectivity may influence memory. Identify them below.

(a) We often see what we want, or are conditioned, to see and thus our _____ is selective.

(b) Every time we tell about a particular experience, details are added or subtracted because of the _____ nature of memory.

(c) Particularly painful personal events may lead to _____ forgetting.

26-2. Since the memory of a specific event can be influenced by many factors, operating in each of the three memory stores, it is obvious that memory, like most behavior, has _____

_____.

Answers: 26-1. (a) attention (b) reconstructive (c) motivated **26-2.** multifactorial causation.

APPLICATION: IMPROVING EVERYDAY MEMORY

27. **Discuss the importance of rehearsal, distributed practice, and interference in efforts to improve everyday memory.**

   27-1. The text lists three general strategies for improving everyday memory. Identify which strategy is being employed in the following examples.

   (a) Most persons can remember their phone number because of extensive_____.

   (b) Willie Nurd the bookworm always takes breaks between study periods when changing subject matter. Willie must realize the importance of _____.

   (c) Ajax never studies any other material besides mathematics on the day of his math exams in order to minimize _____.

   Answers: 27-1. (a) rehearsal (b) distributed practice (c) interference.

28. **Discuss the value of deep processing, transfer-appropriate processing, and good organization in efforts to improve everyday memory.**

   28-1. Answering question such as these is much better than simply underlining the same material in the text because it forces you to engage in _____.

   28-2. The self-quiz at the end of this chapter will help you prepare for a similar multiple-choice test because you are taking advantage of _____-_____ processing.

   28-3. Outlining material from textbooks can enhance retention because it leads to better _____ of the material.

   Answers: 28-1. deep processing **28-2.** transfer-appropriate **28-3.** organization.

29. **Describe some verbal and visual mnemonic devices that can be used to improve everyday memory.**

   29-1. Specific strategies for enhancing memory are called _____ devices. Examples of strategies which do not employ visual images are listed below. See if you can identify which strategy is being employed in each illustration.

   (a) Using the phrase, "My Very Excellent Mother Just Sells Nuts Under Protest", to remember the names and positions of the planets illustrates the use of an _____.

   (b) International Business Machines is easily identified by its _____ IBM.

   (c) The phrase, "One two three four, I left my keys in the drawer" illustrates the use of _____.

   (d) Since you are going to the store your roommate asks you to bring her a bar of Ivory soap, a box of Kleenex and a Snickers bar. You then make up a story which begins, "On my way to the Ivory Coast to check on the latest shipment of Kleenex, I ....." Here you're making use of a _____ method as a mnemonic device.

29-2. Three techniques involving visual imagery can also serve as helpful mnemonic devices: the link method, the method of loci, and the keyword method. Identify them in the examples below.

(a) You want to remember the name of your bus driver, Ray Blocker, who has especially large forearms. You form an image of a man using his large arms to block light rays from his face._____.

(b) You want to remember to buy bananas, eggs, milk, and bread. You visualize walking in your front door and triping on a bunch of bananas. Stumbling forward into the hallway you notice broken eggs on the table etc._____.

(c) You imagine yourself using a banana to break eggs, which you then pour into a bowl of milk and bread._____.

Answers: 29-1. mnemonic (a) acrostic (b) acronym (c) rhyming (d) narrative **29-2.** (a) keyword method (b) method of loci (c) link method.

REVIEW OF KEY TERMS

Anterograde amnesia
Attention
Chunk
Clustering
Conceptual hierarchy
Consolidation
Decay theory
Declarative memory system
Dual-coding theory
Elaboration
Encoding
Encoding specificity principle
Episodic memory system
Explicit memory
Flashbulb memories
Forgetting curve
Implicit memory
Interference theory
Keyword method
Levels of processing theory

Link method
Long-term memory (LTM)
Long-term potentiation (LTP)
Method of loci
Mnemonic devices
Mood-congruence effect
Nondeclarative memory
Nonsense syllables
Overlearning
Primacy effect
Proactive interference
Procedural memory system
Prospective memory
Reality monitoring
Recall
Recency effect
Recognition
Rehearsal
Relearning
Repression

Retention
Retrieval
Retroactive interference
Retrograde amnesia
Retrospective memory
Schema
Script
Sel-referent encoding
Semantic memory system
Semantic networks
Sensory memory
Serial-position effect
Short-term memory
Source-monitoring
Source-monitoring error
State-dependent memory
Storage
Tip-of-the-tongue phenomenon
Transfer-appropriate processing.

_____Storage_____ 1. Putting coded information into memory.

_____ 2. Maintaining coded information in memory.

_____retrieval_____ 3. Recovering information from memory stores.

_____attention_____ 4. The process of focusing awareness on a narrowed range of stimuli or events.

prospective memory 5. Involves remembering to perform actions in the future.

retrospective 6. Involves remembering events from the past or previously learned information.

_____ 7. The initial processing of information is similar to the type of processing required by the subsequent measure of retention.

_____ 8. Occurs when memory is better for information that is consistent with one's ongoing mood.

elaboration 9. Memory which involves the intentional recollection of previous experiences.

levels of 10. A theory that proposes that deeper levels of processing result in longer lasting memory codes.

11. Involves linking a stimulus to other information at the time of encoding.

dual code 12. A theory that memory is enhanced by forming both semantic and visual codes since either can lead to recall.

sensory storage 13. Preserves information in the original sensory form for a very brief time.

short term 14. A limited capacity memory store that can maintain unrehearsed information for 20 to 30 seconds.

rehearsal 15. The process of repetitively verbalizing or thinking about new information.

cluster 16. A group of familiar stimuli stored as a single unit.

LTM 17. An unlimited capacity memory store that can hold information over lengthy periods of time.

flashbulb 18. Unusually vivid and detailed recollections of momentous events.

primacy 19. Occurs when subjects show better recall of items at the beginning and end of a list than for items in the middle.

recency primacy 20. Occurs when items at the beginning of a list are recalled better than other items.

recency 21. Occurs when items at the end of a list are recalled better than other items.

declarative 22. Memory for factual information.

procedural 23. Memory for actions, skills, and operations.

episodic 24. Memory made up of chronological, or temporally dated, recollections of personal experiences.

explicit 25. Memory that contains general knowledge that is not tied to the time when the information was learned.

26. The tendency to remember similar or related items in a group.

link 27. These consist of concepts joined together by links that show how the concepts are related.

28. A long lasting increase in neural excitability at synapses along a specific neural pathway.

29. An organized cluster of knowledge about a particular object or sequence of events.

script 30. A particular kind of schema that organizes what people know about common activities.

tip of the tongue 31. A temporary inability to remember something you know accompanied by the feeling that it's just out of reach.

state-dependent 32. Improved recall that is attributed to being in the same emotional state during encoding and subsequent retrieval.

nonsense syllables 33. Consonant-vowel-consonant letter combinations that do not correspond to words (NOF, KER, etc.).

forgetting curve 34. A curve graphing retention and forgetting over time.

retention 35. The proportion of material remembered.

recall 36. The ability to remember information without any cues.

recognition 37. Requires the selection of previously learned information from an array of options (e.g., multiple-choice tests).

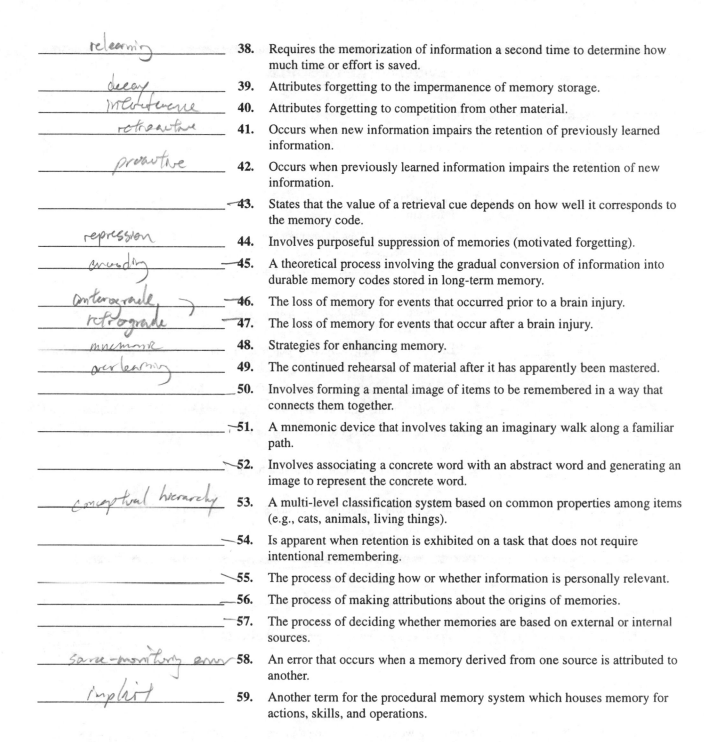

_____relearning_____ **38.** Requires the memorization of information a second time to determine how much time or effort is saved.

_____decay_____ **39.** Attributes forgetting to the impermanence of memory storage.

_____interference_____ **40.** Attributes forgetting to competition from other material.

_____retroactive_____ **41.** Occurs when new information impairs the retention of previously learned information.

_____proactive_____ **42.** Occurs when previously learned information impairs the retention of new information.

_____ **43.** States that the value of a retrieval cue depends on how well it corresponds to the memory code.

_____repression_____ **44.** Involves purposeful suppression of memories (motivated forgetting).

_____encoding_____ **45.** A theoretical process involving the gradual conversion of information into durable memory codes stored in long-term memory.

_____anterograde_____ **46.** The loss of memory for events that occurred prior to a brain injury.

_____retrograde_____ **47.** The loss of memory for events that occur after a brain injury.

_____mnemonic_____ **48.** Strategies for enhancing memory.

_____overlearning_____ **49.** The continued rehearsal of material after it has apparently been mastered.

_____ **50.** Involves forming a mental image of items to be remembered in a way that connects them together.

_____ **51.** A mnemonic device that involves taking an imaginary walk along a familiar path.

_____ **52.** Involves associating a concrete word with an abstract word and generating an image to represent the concrete word.

_____conceptual hierarchy_____ **53.** A multi-level classification system based on common properties among items (e.g., cats, animals, living things).

_____ **54.** Is apparent when retention is exhibited on a task that does not require intentional remembering.

_____ **55.** The process of deciding how or whether information is personally relevant.

_____ **56.** The process of making attributions about the origins of memories.

_____ **57.** The process of deciding whether memories are based on external or internal sources.

_____source-monitoring error_____ **58.** An error that occurs when a memory derived from one source is attributed to another.

_____implicit_____ **59.** Another term for the procedural memory system which houses memory for actions, skills, and operations.

Answers: 1. encoding **2.** storage **3.** retrieval **4.** attention **5.** prospective memory **6.** retrospective memory **7.** transfer-appropriate processing **8.** mood-congruence effect **9.** explicit memory **10.** levels of processing theory **11.** elaboration **12.** dual-coding theory **13.** sensory memory **14.** short-term memory (STM) **15.** rehearsal **16.** chunk **17.** long-term memory (LTM) **18.** flashbulb memories **19.** serial position effect **20.** primacy effect **21.** recency effect **22.** declarative memory system **23.** procedural memory system **24.** episodic memory system **25.** semantic memory system **26.** clustering **27.** semantic networks **28.** long-term potentiation **29.** schema **30.** script **31.** tip-of-the-tongue phenomenon **32.** state-dependent memory **33.** nonsense syllables **34.** forgetting curve **35.** retention **36.** recall **37.** recognition **38.** relearning **39.** decay theory **40.** interference theory **41.** retroactive interference **42.** proactive interference **43.** encoding specificity principle **44.** repression **45.** consolidation **46.** retrograde amnesia **47.** anterograde amnesia **48.** mnemonic devices **49.** overlearning **50.** link method **51.** method of loci **52.** keyword method **53.** conceptual hierarchy **54.** implicit memory **55.** self-referral encoding **56.** source monitoring **57.** reality monitoring **58.** source-monitoring error **59.** nondeclarative memory.

REVIEW OF KEY PEOPLE

Richard Atkinson & Richard Shiffrin   Herman Ebbinghaus   George Miller
Gordon Bower   Marcia Johnson   Brenda Milner
Fergus Craik and Robert Lockhart   Elizabeth Loftus   Endel Tulving.

_____   **1.**   Proposed three progressively deeper levels for processing incoming information.

_____   **2.**   Influential in the development of the model of three different kinds of memory stores (sensory, STM and LTM).

_____   **3.**   She, and her colleagues, proposed the notions of source and reality monitoring.

_____   **4.**   Proposed the idea that categorical information is organized into conceptual hierarchies.

_____   **5.**   Demonstrated that the reconstructive nature of memory can distort eyewitness testimony.

_____   **6.**   Used nonsense syllables to become famous for his forgetting curve.

_____   **7.**   One of his many contributions was the encoding specificity principle.

_____   **8.**   Proposed the concept of chunking for storing information in short-term memory.

_____   **9.**   Followed the case of HM, who had his hippocampus removed.

Answers: 1. Craik & Lockhart **2.** Atkinson & Shiffrin **3.** Johnson **4.** Bower **5.** Loftus **6.** Ebbinghaus **7.** Tulving **8.** Miller **9.** Milner.

SELF-QUIZ

1. Which of the following is not one of the three basic human memory processes?
   a. storage
   b. retrieval
   c. decoding
   d. encoding

2. Which one of the three levels of processing would probably be employed when attempting to memorize the following three-letter sequences WAB WAC WAD?
   a. structural
   b. semantic
   c. phonemic
   d. chunking

3. Retrieval from long-term memory is usually best when the information has been stored at which level of processing?
   a. structural
   b. semantic
   c. phonemic
   d. chunking

4. According to Paivio's dual-coding theory:
    a. words are easier to encode than images
    b. abstract words are easier to encode than concrete words
    c. visual imagery may hinder the retrieval of words
    d. none of the above

5. Which of the memory stores can store the least amount of information?
    a. sensory store
    b. short-term memory
    c. long-term memory

6. Which of the following statements is the most accurate evaluation as to the authenticity of the recall of repressed memories?
    a. Research confirms that they are authentic.
    b. Research confirms that they are not authentic.
    c. Researchers cannot confirm or deny their authenticity.

7. Information is primarily transferred from short-term memory to long-term memory through the process of:
    a. elaboration
    b. verbal rehearsal
    c. clustering
    d. sensory coding

8. In learning a list of 20 new Spanish words you are likely to experience:
    a. a primacy effect
    b. a recency effect
    c. a serial position effect
    d. all of the above

9. Which of these appear to be intimately related?
    a. implicit and procedural memory
    b. implicit and semantic memory
    c. explicit and procedural memory
    d. implicit and declarative memory

10. When you attempt to recall the name of a high school classmate by imagining yourself back in the English class with her, you are making use of:
    a. retrieval cues
    b. context cues
    c. schemas
    d. recognition cues

11. Taking this particular self-test measures your:
    a. constructive errors
    b. reconstructive errors
    c. recall
    d. recognition

12. Ineffective encoding of information may result in:
    a. the primacy effect
    b. the recency effect
    c. pseudoforgetting
    d. chunking

13. Decay theory is best able to explain the loss of memory in:
    a. sensory store
    b. long-term memory
    c. short-term memory
    d. both sensory store and short-term memory

—14. When you violate the encoding specificity principle, you are likely to experience an inability to:
    a. encode information
    b. store information
    c. retrieve information
    d. none of the above

15. Evidence continues to grow that RNA may provide the chemical code for memory. This statement is:
    a. true
    b. false

16. It is very easy to recall the name of your high school because it has been subjected to extensive:
    a. deep processing
    b. clustering
    c. chunking
    d. overlearning

Answers: **1.** c **2.** a **3.** b **4.** d **5.** b **6.** c **7.** c **8.** d **9.** a **10.** b **11.** d **12.** c **13.** d **14.** c **15.** b **16.** d.

Chapter Eight

Language and Thought

REVIEW OF KEY IDEAS

THE COGNITIVE REVOLUTION IN PSYCHOLOGY

1. **Describe the "cognitive revolution" in psychology.**

    1-1. Answer the following questions regarding the cognitive revolution in psychology.

    (a) In what decade did this revolution get underway?

    (b) Why were earlier cognitive approaches abandoned?

    (c) What theoretical school openly opposed the cognitive approach?

    (d) What accounts for the success of the cognitive revolution?

    Answers: 1-1. (a) The 1950s (b) They were too subjective (as opposed to being empirical or objective) (c) Behaviorism (d) The employment of empirical (or objective) methods to study cognitive processes.

LANGUAGE: TURNING THOUGHTS INTO WORDS

2. **Summarize evidence on language acquisition in chimpanzees, including Kanzi.**

    2-1. Indicate whether each of the following is true or false.

    _____ (a) Researchers have been able to teach chimpanzees to use symbols to communicate.

    _____ (b) Chimpanzees find it difficult to catch onto the rules of language.

    _____ (c) Language acquisition in chimpanzees appears to be very similar to language acquisition in children.

__ **2-2.** The Featured Study was a developmental account of how a chimp, Kanzi, learned to communicate with his caretakers.

(a) What were Kanzi's ages during the period of the study?

(b) How did Kanzi communicate with his caretakers?

(c) How did the caretakers communicate with each other and with Kanzi when in his presence?

(d) What previous experience with language did Kanzi have?

Answers: 2-1. (a) true (b) true (c) false **2-2.** (a) 2 1/2 to 5 years (b) by touching geometric symbols representing words (c) in this same manner (d) passively watching his mother communicate with the caretakers.

3. Outline the key properties of language and use these to reevaluate the ape-language controversy.

3-1. Language is characterized by four properties; it is symbolic, semantic, generative, and structured. Identify each of these properties in the following statements.

(a) Applying rules to arrange words into phrases and sentences illustrates the_____ property of language.

(b) Using words, or geomentric forms, to represent objects, actions or events illustrates the _____ property of language.

(c) Making different words out of the same letters, such as NOW and WON, illustrates the _____ property of language.

(d) Giving the same meaning to different words, such as chat, katz, and cat, illustrates the _____ aspect of language.

3-2. Identify the following parts (units) of language.

(a) With around 40 of these basic sounds you can say all of the words in the English language.

_____

(b) Phonemes are combined into these smallest units of meaning in a language, which may include root words as well as prefixes and suffixes. _____

(c) These rules specify how words can be combined into phrases and sentences. _____

3-3. Which of the four key properties of language did Kanzi appear to use, at least in a rudimentary form?

Answers: 3-1 (a) structured (b) symbolic (c) generative (d) semantic **3-2.** (a) phonemes (b) morphemes (c) syntax
3-3. all four.

4. Discuss the possible evolutionary bases of language.

4-1. To what does Steven Pinker attribute the remarkable language ability of human beings?

4-2. What evolutionary advantage might language provide according to Pinker and Bloom?

Answers: 4-1. It is a species-specific (genetic) trait that is the product of natural selection. **4-2.** It might lead to a
decrease in mortality rates.

5. Outline the development of human language during the first year.

5-1. Answer the following question regarding the development of language during the first year of life.

(a) What are a child's three major vocalizations during the first 6 months of life?

(b) What is the range in months for the babbling stage of language development?

(c) What gradually occurs as the babbling stage progresses?

Answers: 5-1. (a) Crying, laughing, and cooing (b) 6 to 18 months (c) The babbling increasingly resembles spoken
language.

6. Describe children's early use of single words and word combinations.

6-1. What does the text mean when it states that the receptive vocabulary of toddlers is much larger than their
productive vocabulary?

6-2. Identify the following phenomenon observed in children's early use of language.

  (a) What phenomenon is illustrated when a child calls all four-legged creatures "doggie"?_____

  (b) What phenomenon is illustrated when a child correctly communicates her desire to know where the family dog is simply by asking, "doggie"?_____

  (c) What phenomenon is illustrated when a child complains to her mother, "doggie eat cookie"?_____

  (d) What phenomenon is illustrated when a child says, "doggie runned away"?

  (e) What phenomenon is illustrated when a child puns, "I love your I's"?_____

  (f) Solve the following anagram that best describes how children acquire language skills. FWSYLIFT_____

Answers: **6-1.** They can understand more spoken words than they can reproduce themselves. **6-2.** (a) overextensions (b) holophrases (c) telegraphic speech (d) overregularization (e) metalinguistic awareness (f) swiftly.

7. Compare and contrast the behaviorist, nativist, and interactionist perspectives on the acquisition of language.

7-1. Identify the following perspectives on the acquisition of language.

  (a) This perspective places great emphasis on the role of reinforcement and imitation._____

  (b) This perspective assumes that children make use of a language acquisition device (LAD) to acquire transformational rules which enable them to easily translate between surface structure and deep structure._____

  (c) This interactionist perspective argues that language development is tied to progress in thinking and general cognitive development._____

  (d) This interactionist perspective argues that language development is directed to some extent by the social benefits children derive from interaction with mature language users._____

7-2. Which perspective places greatest emphasis on:

  (a) nurture _____

  (b) nature _____

  (c) nature interacting with nurture _____

Answers: **7-1.** (a) behaviorist (b) nativist (c) cognitive theories (d) social communication theories **7-2.** (a) behaviorist (b) nativist (c) interactionist.

8. Discuss culture and language and the status of the linguistic relativity hypothesis.

8-1. What is the major idea behind Benjamin Whorf's linguistic relativity hypothesis?

8-2. What did Eleanor Rosch's experiment show when she compared the color recognition ability of English-speaking people and Dani people, who have only two words for color?

8-3. While language does not appear to invariably determine thought, it does appear to exert some influence over the way we approach an idea. In other words, one's language may make it either_____or more_____to think along certain lines.

Answers: 8-1. Language determines thought. **8-2.** She found no difference in the ability to deal with colors. **8-3.** easier, difficult.

PROBLEM SOLVING: IN SEARCH OF SOLUTIONS

9. List and describe the three types of problems proposed by Greeno.

9-1. Greeno has proposed three types of problems (arrangement, inducing structure and transformation). Identify each of these categories from their descriptions given below.

(a) This type of problem requires the problem solver to discover the relations among the parts of the problem.

(b) This type of problem requires the problem solver to place the parts in a way that satisfies some specific criterion.

(c) This type of problem requires the problem solver to carry out a sequence of changes or rearrangements in order to reach a specific goal.

9-2. Which types of Greeno's problems are represented in the following situations?

(a) What two three-letter English words can be made from the letters TBU?

(b) Fill in the missing word in, grass is to green as snow is to _____".

(c) You need to take your child to a pediatrician, your dog to the veterinarian, and your mother to the hairdresser all within a limited time period. You think to yourself, "I'll take the kid and the dog and pick up Mom. Mom can stay with the kid at the doctor's office while I take the dog to the vet. Then I'll.....

9-3. Which type of problems are often solved in a sudden burst of insight?

Answers: 9-1. (a) arrangement (b) inducing structure (c) transformation **9-2.** (a) inducing structure (b) arrangement (c) transformation **9-3.** arrangement.

10. Explain the difference between well-defined problems and ill-defined problems.

10-1. When your task is to find how many times 13 can be divided in 936 then you are dealing with a

_____-_____ problem. When your task is to manage the election campain for your friend

who is running for college president then you are dealing with an _____-_____ problem.

Answers: 10-1. well-defined, ill-defined.

11. Explain how irrelevant information and functional fixedness can hinder problem solving.

11-1. Which of the barriers to effective problem solving, irrelevant information or functional fixedness, are you
overcoming when you:

(a) make a financial decision without first consulting your horoscope?

(b) use a page of newspaper as a wedge to keep a door open?

Answers: 11-1. (a) irrelevant information (b) functional fixedness.

12. Explain how mental set and unnecessary constraints can hinder problem solving.

12-1. Which of the barriers to effective problem solving, mental set or unnecessary constrains, are you overcoming when you:

(a) color outside the lines to create a more interesting picture?

(b) teach an old dog a new trick?

Answers: 12-1. (a) unnecessary constraints (b) mental set.

13. Describe a variety of general problem-solving strategies.

13-1. The text describes a variety of different problem-solving techniques, or_____. Which of these

heuristics (means/ends analysis, forming subgoals, working backward, searching for analogies, or

changing the representation of the problem) would be most applicable in solving the following problems?

(a) While opening your car door you drop the keys. The keys hit your foot and bounce underneath the
car, too far to reach. It has stopped raining so you close your umbrella and ponder how to get your
keys.

(b) You have accepted the responsibility for chairing the homecoming celebration at your school.

(c) Alone at night in the office you observe that the ribbon is missing from a printer you want to use. After obtaining a new ribbon you can't figure out how to install it correctly. Glancing around you see a similar printer with the ribbon installed.

(d) As an entering freshman in college, you have already chosen a field of study and a specific graduate school you wish to attend. Now all you have to do is accomplish this goal.

(e) You have agreed to become the campaign chairwoman of a friend who wants to run for student body president. Obviously your goal is to make your friend look like a good choice to students, but which heuristic do politicians often employ here?

Answers: 13-1. heuristics (a) search for analogies (the umbrella can be used as a rake) (b) form subgoals (c) work backwards (see how the ribbon comes out) (d) means/ends analysis (e) change the representation of the problem (make the opponents look like a bad choice).

14. Summarize evidence on the roots of expertise.

14-1. Pchologists have found several differences in the approaches taken by experts and novices when faced with similar problems. For example, master chess players are far better able to group chess pieces into familiar groups or patterns, a process called _____.

14-2. It has also been found that in comparison to novices, experts are less likely to jump right into a complex problem. Rather they will first make effective use of _____ an approach to a solution. Experts are also more likely to think about their own thoughts when planning a solution, a process called

_____.

14-3. In comparison to novices, experts are also much more likely to recognize analogies in problems and to categorize problems according to their analogous (situations/solutions). In other words, they look beyond the surface aspects and focus on the _____ structures of problems

14-4. Finally, experts are much more likely to engage in deliberate and extensive training and

_____.

Answers: 14-1. chunking **14-2.** planning, metacognition **14-3.** solutions, deeper **14-4.** practice.

15. Discuss the distinction between field independence and dependence.

15-1. Answer the following true-false questions regarding the distinctions between field dependent and field independent persons.

(a) Field dependent persons are more likely to use internal cues to orient themselves in space.

(b) Field independent persons are more likely to recognize the component parts of a problem rather than just seeing it as a whole.

Answers: 15-1. (a) false (b) true.

16. **Discuss cultural variations in cognitive style as they relate to problem solving.**

   16-1.   Answer the following true-false questions regarding cultural variations in cognitive style.

   (a) Persons living in cultures that depend on hunting and gathering for their subsistence are generally more field dependent than persons living in more stable agricultural societies.

   (b) Persons raised in cultures with lenient child-rearing practices and an emphasis on personal autonomy tend to be more field independent.

   Answers: 16-1. (a) false (b) true.

DECISION MAKING: CHOICES AND CHANCES

17. **Compare the additive and elimination by aspects approaches to selecting an alternative.**

   17-1.   Indicate which of these two approaches to decision making would be best when:

   (a) The task is complex and there are numerous alternatives to choose from.

   (b) You want to allow attractive attributes to compensate for unattractive attributes.

   Answers: 17-1. (a) elimination by aspects (b) additive.

18. **Discuss conflict in decision making and the idea that one can think too much about a decision.**

   18-1.   What do persons often do when faced with a conflict in which they can't decide between alternative choices?

   18-2.   Recent studies have shown that thinking too much about a problem (will/may not) lead to a better solution. One reason suggested for this is that gathering more and more information that is less and less important _____ the picture.

   Answers: 18-1. They delay their decision. **18-2.** may not, clutters or confuses.

19. **Explain the factors that individuals typically consider in risky decision-making.**

   19-1.   What differentiates risky decision making from other kinds of decision making?

   19-2.   What is the most you can know when making a risky decision?

   19-3.   What two things must be known in order to calculate the expected value of making a risky decision when gambling with money?

   19-4.   How does the concept of subjective utility explain why some persons still engage in risky decision making when the expected value predicts a loss?

   Answers: 19-1. The outcome is uncertain. **19-2.** The probability of a particular outcome. **19-3.** The average amount of money you could expect to win or lose with each play and the probability of a win or loss. **19-4.** The personal worth of the outcome may outweigh the probability of losing.

20. **Describe the availability and representativeness heuristics.**

   20-1.   Estimating the probability of an event on the basis of how often one recalls it has been experienced in the past is what Tversky and Kahneman call a (an) _____ heuristic.

   20-2.   When most people are asked if there are more words that begin with N or words that have N as the third letter, they apply the availibity heurestic and guess incorrectly. Explain why they do this.

   20-3.   Estimating the probability of an event on the basis of how similar it is to a particular model or stereotype of that event is what Tversky and Kahneman call a _____ heuristic.

   20-4.   "Steve is very shy. He has a high need for structure and likes detail. Is Steve more likely to be a salesperson or a librarian?" When persons are given this problem, they usually guess that he is a librarian even though there are many more salespersons than there are librarians. Explain why they do this.

   Answers: 20-1. availability **20-2.** Because they can immediately recall many more words that begin with N than words having N as the third letter. **20-3.** representativeness **20-4.** Because they employ the representativess heuristic and Steve fits the stereotype of a librarian.

21. **Discuss the effects of framing and anticipatory regret on decision making.**

   21-1.   Asking persons if they would prefer their glass of wine to be half-full or half-empty illustrates the general idea behind the_____ of questions.

   21-2.   Are persons more likely to take risky options when the problem is framed so as to obtain gains, or when when it is framed so as to cut losses?

21-3. Answer the following questions regarding the effects of anticipatory guilt on decision making.

(a) How does a high vulnerability to regret affect a person's decision making?

(b) What appears to be a dominant characteristic of persons who are vulnerable to anticipatory guilt?

Answers: 21-1. framing **21-2.** When it is framed so as to cut losses **21-3.** (a) They tend to make safer decisions. (b) low self-esteem.

PUTTING IT IN PERSPECTIVE

22. Explain how this chapter highlighted four of the text's themes.

22-1. Indicate which one of the four unifying themes (the influence of heredity and the environment, similarities and differences across cultures, the empirical nature of psychology, and the subjectivity of experience) are best represented by the following statements.

(a) Psychologists developed objective measures for higher mental processes thus bringing about the cognitive revolution.

(b) The manner in which questions are framed can influence cognitive appraisal of the questions.

(c) Neither pure nativist theories nor pure nurture theories appear to adequately explain the development of language.

(d) The ecological demands of one's environment appear to somewhat affect one's cognitive style.

Answers: 22-1. (a) the empirical nature of psychology (b) the subjectivity of experience (c) the influence of heredity and the environment (d) similarities and differences across cultures.

UNDERSTANDING PITFALLS IN DECISION MAKING

23. Explain what is meant by the gambler's fallacy and ignoring base rates.

23-1. Identify which example of the flawed use of the resentativeness heuristic, the gambler's fallacy or ignoring base rates, is being described below.

(a) Using the representativeness heuristic and guessing that "Steve" is a librarian and not a salesperson.

(b) The belief that the odds of a chance event increases if the event hasn't occurred recently.

Answers: 23-1. (a) ignoring base rates (b) the gambler's fallacy.

24. **Explain the conjunction fallacy and the law of small numbers.**

24-1. Identify which example of flawed reasoning, the conjunction fallacy or ignoring the law of small numbers, is being described below.

(a) The belief that a small sampling of cases can be as valid as a large sampling of cases.

(b) Estimating that the odds of two uncertain events happening together are greater than the odds of either event happening alone.

Answers: 24-1. (a) ignoring the law of small numbers (b) the conjunction fallacy.

25. **Describe the propensity to overestimate the imporbable, seek confirming evidence, and overrate confidence.**

25-1. What flaw in reasoning often results from intense media coverage of dramatic, vivid, but infrequent events.

25-2. What omission leads to the confirmation bias when making decisions?

25-3. How is this same phenomenon related to belief perserverance?

25-4. Answer the following true/false questions regarding the overconfidence effect.

(a) We are much less subject to this effect when making decisions about ourselves as opposed to more worldly matters.

(b) Scientists are not generally prone to this effect when making decisions about information in their own fields.

(c) In the study of college students cited by the text it was observed that the gap between personal confidence and actual accuracy of decisions increased as the confidence level increased.

Answers: 25-1. The propensity to overestimate the improbable. 25-2. Failure to seek out disconfirming evidence. 25-3. Disconfirming evidence is subjected to skeptical evaluation. 25-4. (a) false (b) false (c) true.

REVIEW OF KEY TERMS

Algorithm
Availability heuristic
Belief perseverance
Cognition
Compensatory decision models
Confirmation bias
Conjunction fallacy
Decision making
Deep structure
Expertise
Fast mapping
Field dependence-independence
Framing
Functional fixedness

Gambler's fallacy
Heuristic
Holophrases
Ill-defined problems
Insight
Language
Language acquisition device (LAD)
Linguistic relativity
Mean length of utterance (MLU)
Means/ends analysis
Mental set
Metacognition
Metalinguistic awareness
Morphemes

Noncompensatory decision models
Overextension
Overregularization
Phonemes
Problem solving
Problem space
Psycholinguistics
Representativeness heuristic
Risky decision making
Surface structure
Syntax
Telegraphic speech
Trial and error
Well-defined problems

_____ 1. The study of the psychological mechanisms underlying the acquisition and use of language.

_____ 2. A collection of symbols, and rules for combining those symbols, that can be used to create an infinite variety of messages.

_____ 3. The smallest units of sound in a spoken language.

_____ 4. The smallest units of meaning in a language.

_____ 5. The rules that specify how words can be combined into phrases and sentences.

_____ 6. Using a word incorrectly to describe a wider set of objects or actions than it is meant to.

_____ 7. Single-word utterances that represent the meaning of several words.

_____ 8. Consists mainly of content words with articles, prepositions, and other less critical words omitted.

_____ 9. The ability to reflect on the use of language.

_____ 10. Basing the estimated probability of an event on the ease with which relevant instances come to mind.

_____ 11. Basing the estimated probability of an event on how similar it is to the typical prototype of that event.

_____ 12. The mental processes involved in acquiring knowledge.

_____ 13. The tendency to perceive an item only in terms of its most common use.

_____ 14. The sudden discovery of a correct solution to a problem following incorrect attempts.

_____ 15. Identifying differences that exist between the current state and the goal state and making changes that will reduce these differences.

_____ 16. A strategy for solving problems.

_____ 17. The process by which children map a word on an underlying concept after only one exposure to the word.

_____ 18. The average of youngsters' spoken statements (measured in morphemes).

_____ 19. Generalizing grammatical rules to irregular cases where they do not apply.

_____ 20. Decision making models which allow for attractive attributes to compensate for unattractive attributes.

_____ 21. Decision making models that do not allow for some attributes to compensate for others.

_____ 22. Making decisions under conditions of uncertainty.

_____ 23. A hypothetical innate mechanism or process that facilitates the learning of language.

_____ 24. Persisting in using problem-solving strategies that have worked in the past.

_____ 25. The theory that one's language determines one's thoughts.

_____ 26. The active efforts to discover what must be done to achieve a goal that is not readily attainable.

_____ 27. Trying possible solutions sequentially and discarding those that are in error until one works.

_____ 28. Evaluating alternatives and making choices among them.

_____ 29. How issues are posed or how choices are structured.

_____ 30. The underlying meaning of a sentence or statement.

_____ 31. The word arrangement used in expressing a sentence or statement.

_____ 32. A methodical, step-by-step procedure for trying all possible alternatives in searching for a solution to a problem.

_____ 33. The tendency to hang onto beliefs in the face of contradictory evidence.

_____ 34. The tendency to seek information that supports one's decisions and beliefs while ignoring disconfirming evidence.

_____ 35. Occurs when people estimate that the odds of two uncertain evets happening are greater than the odds of either event happening alone.

_____ 36. Refers to individuals' tendency to rely primarily on external versus internal frames of reference when orienting themselves in space.

_____ 37. The belief that the odds of a chance event increase if the event hasn't occurred recently.

_____ 38. Problems in which one or more elements among the initial state, the goal state, and the constraints are incompletely or unclearly specified.

_____ 39. Problems in which the initial state, the goal state, and the constraints are clearly specified.

_____ 40. Refers to the set of possible pathways to a solution considered by the problem solver.

_____ 41. Involves thinking about one's thinking.

_____ 42. Refers to consistently superior performance on a specified set of tasks or problems.

Answers: 1. psycholinguistics **2.** language **3.** phonemes **4.** morphemes **5.** syntax **6.** overextensions **7.** holophrases **8.** telegraphic speech **9.** metalinguistic awareness **10.** availability heuristic **11.** representativeness heuristic **12.** cognition **13.** functional fixedness **14.** insight **15.** means/end analysis **16.** heuristic **17.** fast mapping **18.** mean length of utterances (MLU) **19.** overregularization **20.** compensatory decision models **21.** noncompensatory decision models **22.** risky decision-making **23.** language acquisition device (LAD) **24.** mental set **25.** linguistic relativity **26.** problem solving **27.** trial and error **28.** decision making **29.** framing **30.** deep structure **31.** surface structure **32.** algorithm **33.** belief perseverance **34.** confirmation bias **35.** conjunction fallacy **36.** field dependence-independence **37.** gambler's fallacy **38.** ill-defined problems **39.** well-defined problems **40.** problem space **41.** metacognition **42.** expertise.

REVIEW OF KEY PEOPLE

Noam Chomsky   Sue Savage-Rumbaugh   B. F. Skinner
Daniel Kahneman & Amos Tversky   Herbert Simon

_____ 1. Won the Nobel Prize for his research on decision making and artificial intelligence.

_____ 2. Proposed that children learn language through the established principles of learning.

_____ 3. Proposed that children learn language through a biologically built-in language acquisition device.

_____ 4. Performed research that showed people base probability estimates on heurestics that do not always yield reasonable estimates of success.

_____ 5. Along with her colleagues she taught the chimp, Kanzi, to communicate in a way that made use of all the basic properties of language.

Answers: 1. Simon **2.** Skinner **3.** Chomsky **4.** Kahneman & Tversky **5.** Savage-Rumbaugh.

SELF-QUIZ

1. Which of the following explanations best explains the success of the cognitive
   a. the refining of introspection as a research method
   b. the development of empirical methods
   c. the use of psychotherapy to explore the unconscious
   d. the success in teaching chimps to use language

2. Which perspective on the acquisition of language places the greatest emphasis on nuture?
   a. nativist theories
   b. social communication theories
   c. behaviorist theories
   d. cognitive theories

3. The word SLOWLY would be an example of a:
   a. metalinguistic
   b. phoneme
   c. syntactical unit
   d. morpheme

4. Children and chimpanzees appear to learn language in the same manner. This statement is:
   a. true
   b. false

5. When a child says that TUB and BUT are constructed of the same three letters, she is showing an awareness of:
   a. morphemes
   b. phonemes
   c. metalinguistics
   d. syntax

6. The fact that children appear to learn rules, rather than specific word combinations, when acquiring language skills argues most strongly against which theory of language development?
   a. cognitive
   b. behaviorist
   c. nativist

7. Which of the following is not one of the basic properties of language?
   a. generative
   b. symbolic
   c. structured
   d. alphabetical

8. Which of the following heuristics would you probably employ if assigned the task of carrying out a school election?
   a. work backwards
   b. representativeness
   c. search for analogies
   d. form subgoals

9. Which one of Greeno's problems is exemplified by the anagram?
   a. arrangement
   b. inducing structure
   c. transformation
   d. chunking

10. Experts differ from novices in their problem solving in that they are more likely to make use of:
   a. planning
   b. chunking
   c. focusing on the deeper structures
   d. all of the above

11. People generally prefer a choice that provides an 80 percent chance of success over one that provides a 20 percent chance of failure. This illustrates the effect of:
   a. the availability heuristic
   b. the representativeness heuristic
   c. framing
   d. confirmation bias

12. When faced with having to choose among numerous alternatives, most persons will opt for:
   a. an elimination by aspects approach
   b. an additive approach
   c. a means/end analysis
   d. a subjective-utility model

13. Field independent persons are most likely to come from cultures that:
   a. encourage strict child-rearing practices
   b. have a stable agricultural base
   c. encourage lenient child-rearing practices
   d. both a and b

14. Most persons mistakenly believe that more people die from tornadoes than from asthma. This is because they mistakenly apply:
    a. a means/end analysis
    b. a compensatory decision model
    c. an availability heuristic
    d. a representativeness heuristic

15. Failure to actively seek out contrary evidence may lead to:
    a. overestimating the improbable
    b. the conjunction fallacy
    c. the gambler's fallacy
    d. confirmation bias

16. Which of the following perhaps best illustrates the interaction effect of both heredity and environment on behavior?
    a. the development of language skills in a child
    b. the development of field independence in nomadic cultures
    c. the development of problems-solving skills in experts
    d. the development of the overconfidence effect in all of us

Answers: 1. b **2.** c **3.** d **4.** b **5.** c **6.** b **7.** d **8.** d **9.** a **10.** d **11.** c **12.** a **13.** c **14.** c **15.** d **16.** a

Chapter Nine

Intelligence and Psychological Testing

REVIEW OF KEY IDEAS

KEY CONCEPTS IN PSYCHOLOGICAL TESTING

1. **List and describe the principle categories of psychological tests.**

   1-1. Most psychological tests can be placed into one of two very broad categories. These two categories are: _____ tests and _____ tests.

   1-2. There are three categories of mental abilities tests. Below are examples of each of these categories. Identify them.

      (a) The ACT and SAT tests you may have taken before entering college are examples of _____ tests.

      (b) The exams you frequently take in your introductory psychology class are examples of _____ tests.

      (c) Tests used to demonstrate general intellectual giftedness are examples of _____ tests.

   1-3. Personality tests allow an individual to compare himself or herself to other persons with respect to particular personality _____. Personality tests generally (<u>do/do not</u>) have right and wrong answers.

   Answers: 1-1. mental ability, personality **1-2.** (a) aptitude (b) achievement (c) intelligence **1-3.** characteristics or traits, do not.

2. **Discuss the concepts of standardization and test norms.**

   2-1. Developing test norms and uniform procedures for use in the administration and scoring of a test is the general idea behind test _____.

   2-2. In order to interpret a particular score on a test it is necessary to know how other persons score on this test. This is the purpose of test <u>_____</u>. An easy method for providing comparisons of test scores is to convert the raw scores into _____ scores.

3. **Explain the meaning of test reliability and how it is estimated.**

   3-1. The ability of a test to produce consistent results across subsequent measurements of the same persons is known as its _____. Psychological tests (<u>are/are not</u>) perfectly reliable.

   3-2. Readministering the same test to the same group of persons in a week or two following the original testing allows one to estimate the _____ of a test. If a test is highly reliable, then a person's scores on the two different administrations will be very similar. The amount of similarity can be assessed by means of the _____ <u>coefficient</u>.

   Answers: **3-1.** reliability, are not **3-2.** reliability, correlation

4. **Explain the three types of validity and how they are assessed.**

   4-1. The ability of a test to actually measure what it claims to measure is known as its _____. The term validity is also used to refer to the accuracy or usefullness of the _____ based on a test.

   4-2. There are three general kinds of validity. Identify each of these kinds from the descriptions given below.

      (a) This kind of validity will tend to be high when, for example, scores on the ACT and SAT actually predict success in college. _____

      (b) This kind of validity will be of particular importance to you when taking your exams for this class. It will be high if the exam sticks closely to the explicitly assigned material. _____

      (c) This kind of validity is more vague than the other two kinds and refers to the ability of a test to measure abstract qualities, such as intelligence. _____.

   4-3. As with the estimation of reliability, the estimation of validity makes use of the _____.

   Answers: **4-1.** validity, inferences or decisions **4-2.** (a) criterion-related validity, (b) content validity, (c) construct validity **4-3.** correlation coefficient.

THE EVOLUTION OF INTELLIGENCE TESTING

5. **Summarize the contributions of Galton and Binet to the evolution of intelligence testing.**

   5-1. Identify each of the above men from the descriptions of their contributions given below.

      (a) This man developed the first useful intelligence test. His tests were used to predict success in school, and scores were expressed in terms of mental age. _____

      (b) This man began the quest to measure intelligence. He assumed that intelligence was mainly inherited and could be measured by assessing sensory acuity. He also invented correlation and percentile test scores. _____

   Answers: **5-1.** (a) Binet (b) Galton.

6. **Summarize the contributions of Terman and Wechsler to the evolution of intelligence testing.**

   6-1. Identify each of the above men from the descriptions of their contributions given below.

      (a) This man revised Binet's tests to produce the Stanford-Binet Intelligence Scale, the standard for all future intelligence tests. He also introduced the intelligence quotient (IQ).

         _____

      (b) This man developed the first successful test of adult intelligence, the WAIS. He also developed new intelligence tests for children.

         _____

      (c) In developing his new intelligence tests, this man added many non-verbal items which allowed for the separate assessment of both verbal and non-verbal abilities. He also replaced the IQ score with one based on the normal distribution.

         _____

   Answers: 6-1. (a) Terman (b) Wechsler (c) Wechsler.

BASIC QUESTIONS ABOUT INTELLIGENCE TESTING

7. **List and describe the major functions of intelligence testing.**

   7-1. The text lists three major functions of intelligence testing. They are employed in screening and _____, in selection and _____, and in research and _____. In addition, psychologists also use IQ tests to aid in _____ diagnosis.

   Answers: 7-1. diagnosis, placement, evaluation, clinical.

8. **Discuss the use of IQ tests in non-Western cultures.**

   8-1. Which of the following statements best summarizes the history of IQ testing in non-Western cultures?

      (a) Most non-Western cultures have successfully adapted the IQ tests to their own cultures.

      (b) Many non-Western cultures have different conceptions of what intelligence is and do not necessarily accept Western notions as to how it can be measured.

      (c) While almost all non-Western cultures agree with Western definitions of intelligence, they have been hesitant to develop IQ tests for their own use.

   Answers: 8-1. b.

9. **Explain the meaning of an individual's score on a modern intelligence test.**

   9-1. Answer the following questions regarding intelligence test scores.

      (a) In what manner is human intelligence assumed to be distributed?

      (b) What percentage of people have an IQ score below 100?

—(c) What percentage of persons would score two or more standard deviations above the mean? (see Fig. 9.7 in the text)

Answers: 9-1. (a) It forms a normal distribution. (b) 50% (c) 2 percent.

10. Describe the reliability, validity, and stability of modern intelligence tests.

—**10-1.** Answer the following questions about the reliability of modern intelligence tests.

(a) What kind of reliability estimates (correlation coefficients) are found with most modern intelligence tests?

(b) What might be a problem here with respect to an individual's test score?

10-2. Answer the following questions with respect to the validity and stability of modern intelligence tests.

(a) What is the correlation between IQ tests and grades in school?

‹(b) What is the correlation between IQ tests and the number of years of schooling that people complete?

(c) What might be a general problem with assuming intelligence tests are a valid measure of general mental ability?

__(d) By what age do IQ scores become fairly good predictors of adolescent and adult intelligence?

Answers: 10-1. (a) They are in the low .90's. (b) Temporary conditions could lower the score. **10-2.** (a) .50-.60 (b) .60 to .80 (c) They principally focus on academic/verbal intelligence and ignore other kinds of intelligence (d) By age 7 or 8.

11. Discuss how well inteligence tests predict vocational success.

11-1. Is the ability of intelligence tests to predict vocational success much higher or much lower than their ability to predict academic success?

—**11-2.** What two kinds of intelligence that may be especially important for vocational success are not assessed by IQ tests?

―11-3. Intelligence tests are particularly poor in predicting success within a particular vocational group, such as lawyers. Why is this?

Answers: 11-1. much lower **11-2.** practical intelligence and social intelligence **11-3.** The range of test scores is so restricted.

EXTREMES OF INTELLIGENCE

12. Describe how mental retardation is defined and divided into various levels.

12-1. In addition to having subnormal mental abilities (IQ scores of less than 70 to 75), what else is included in the definition of mental retardation?

12-2. There are four levels of mental retardation; mild, moderate, severe, and profound. Identify each of these levels from the descriptions given below:

(a) These persons have IQ scores below 20 and require total care.

(b) These persons have IQ scores between 50 and 75 may become self-supporting citizens after leaving school and becoming adults.

(c) These persons have IQ scores between 35 and 50 and can be semi-independent in a sheltered environment.

(d) These persons have IQ scores between 20 and 35 and can help to contribute to their self-support under total supervision.

Answers: 12-1. They must show deficiencies in everyday living skills (adaptive skills) originating before age 18.
12-2. (a) profound (b) mild (c) moderate (d) severe.

13. Discuss the causes of mental retardation and the principles that guide programs for the retarded.

―13-1. Although there are over 350 organic syndromes associated with retardation, including Down's syndrome, Phenylketonuria, and hydrocephalacy, organic causes only account for about _____ percent of retardation cases.

―13-2. There are two general hypotheses as to the causes of the remaining 75 percent of retardation cases, most of which are diagnosed as mild. Identify these hypotheses from the descriptions given below:

(a) This hypothesis suggests that retardation is caused by a variety of unfavorable environmental variables.

(b) This hypothesis suggests that retardation results from subtle physiological defects that are difficult to detect.

—13-3.   In recent years treatment programs for the mentally retarded have been guided by the notion that retarded persons should be treated in the least restrictive and most normal environment possible. This notion is called the _____ principle. When this principle is applied to schools, it is known as _____.

Answers: 13-1. 25 **13-2.** (a) environmental (b) biological **13-3.** normalization, mainstreaming.

14. Discuss the role of IQ tests in the identification of gifted children.

—14-1.   Answer the following questions regarding gifted children:

(a) Although it is contrary to federal law, what method is used almost exclusively to identify gifted children?

(b) What is the lower range of IQ scores that is generally needed to qualify children as gifted?

Answers: 14-1. (a) scores on IQ tests (b) 130-145.

—15. Describe the personal characteristics of the gifted.

15-1.   Answer the following questions regarding the personal characteristics of the gifted.

(a) What did Terman's long-term study of gifted children show with respect to the physical, social, and emotional development of these children?

(b) What three factors must intersect and be present to an exceptional degree in order to produce the rarest form of giftedness according to Renzulli?

Answers: 15-1. (a) They were above average in all three areas. (b) intelligence, motivation, creativity (in any order).

HEREDITY AND ENVIRONMENT AS DETERMINANTS OF INTELLIGENCE

16. Summarize the empiracle evidence that heredity affects intelligence.

16-1.   Below are the mean correlations for the intelligence of four different groups of children: siblings reared together, fraternal twins reared together, identical twins reared apart, and identical twins reared together. Match the group with the appropriate correlation.

.86 _____   .60 _____

.72 _____   .44 _____

16-2. What do the above correlations tell us about the role of heredity on intelligence?

Answers: 16-1. (.86) identical twins reared together (.72) identical twins reared apart (.60) fraternal twins reared together (.44) siblings reared together **16-2.** That heredity plays a significant role in intelligence.

17. Discuss the Burt affair and estimates of the heritability of intelligence.

17-1. Answer the following questions regarding the Cyril Burt affair.

(a) While Burt's data may have been flawed, how do they stack up with the data from other similar studies.

(b) What does the Burt affair tell us regarding the dedate about the influence of heredity and environment on intelligence?

17-2. What relationship has been found between the intelligence of children adopted out at birth and their biological parents?

17-3. The consensus estimate of experts is that the heritability ratio for human intelligence hovers around 60 percent. What does this mean?

17-4. Why can you not use a heritability ratio to explain a particular individual's intelligence?

Answers: 17-1. (a) They are in fairly close agreement. (b) The debate has important sociopolitical implications.
17-2. There is a significant correlation in intelligence. **17-3.** The variation in intelligence in a particular group is estimated to be 60% due to heredity, leaving 40% for environmental factors. **17-4.** It is a group statistic and may give misleading results when applied to particular individuals.

18. Describe three lines of research that indicate that environment affects intelligence.

18-1. Complete the statements below that list three findings from adoption studies indicating that environment influences intelligence.

(a) There is a positive correlational relationship beween the intelligence of adopted children and their

_____.

(b) Siblings reared together are more alike than siblings _____.

(c) Unrelated children reared together show a significant positive relationship with respect to their

_____.

18-2. What effects on intelligence have been found among children reared in deprived environments?

18-3. What effects on intelligence have been found among children moved from deprived environments to more enriched environments?

18-4. What relationship has been found between the intellectual quality of home environment and the intelligence of children?

Answers: **18-1.** (a) foster parents (b) reared apart (c) intelligence **18-2.** There is a gradual decrease in intelligence across time. **18-3.** There is a gradual increase in intelligence across time. **18-4.** They are significantly correlated.

19. **Using the concept of reaction range, explain how heredity and the environment interact to affect intelligence.**

   19-1. The notion behind the concept of reaction range is that heredity places an upper and lower _____ on how much an individual can vary with respect to a characteristic such as intelligence. The reaction range for human intelligence is said to be around _____ IQ points.

   19-2. This means that a child with an average IQ of 100 can vary between 90 and 110 IQ points, depending on the kind of _____ he or she experiences.

   19-3. The major point here is that the limits for intelligence are determined by _____ factors and the movement within these limits is determined by _____ factors.

Answers: **19-1.** limit, 20-25 **19-2.** environment **19-3.** genetic or hereditary, environmental.

20. **Discuss heritability and socioeconomic disadvantage as alternative explanations for cultural differences in IQ.**

   20-1. Two explanations for the cultural differences in IQ scores are listed below. Tell what each of these explanations means.

   (a) Jensen's heritability explanation.

   (b) Socioeconomic disadvantage.

   20-2. Which of these two explanations is best supported by research evidence?

Answers: **20-1.** (a) The cultural differences are due to heredity. (b) The cultural differences are due to environmental factors. **20-2.** socioeconomic disadvantage.

21. **Discuss the possible contributions of stereotype vulnerability and cultural bias to ethnic differences in average IQ.**

21-1. Steele's theory of stereotype vulnerability holds that a widely held stereotype that certain racial groups are mentally inferior acts on the members of these groups so as to make them (more/less) vulnerable when confronted with tests assessing intellectual ability. Steele believes that this same vulnerability (does/does not) exist for women entering domains dominated by men. Research so far (does/does not) support this theory.

21-2. What did the text conclude about the possible effects of cultural bias with respect to ethnic differences in IQ scores?

Answers: 21-1. more, does, does **21-2.** It produces only weak and inconsistent effects.

NEW DIRECTIONS IN THE ASSESSMENT AND STUDY OF INTELLIGENCE

22. **Describe new trends in the assessment and study of intelligence.**

22-1. Answer the following questions regarding new trends in the assessment and study of intelligence.

(a) One trend is that two kinds of tests are replacing intelligence tests in many school districts. What kinds of tests are these?

(b) A second trend involves turning away from tests designed to measure general intelligence (Spearmam's "g"). What kinds of tests are replacing them?

(c) A third trend concerns the search for biological correlates of intelligence. Most work here seeks to find correlations between reaction time and IQ. What have been the results so far?

Answers: 22-1. (a) achievement and aptitude tests (b) tests of specific mental abilities (c) the correlations are too low to be of any practical significance.

23. **Describe Sternberg's and Gardner's theories of intelligence.**

23-1. Sternberg's triarchic theory proposes that intelligence is composed of three basic parts. Match these parts with their individual functions:

_____ Contextual subtheory

_____ Experiential subtheory

_____ Componential subtheory

(a) Emphasizes the role played by society.

(b) Emphasizes the cognitive processes underlying intelligence.

(c) Emphasizes the interplay between intelligence and experience.

23-2. Sternberg also theorizes that the componential subtheory is composed of three divisions. Match these divisions with their appropriate function:

_____ Metacomponents

_____ Performance components

_____ Knowledge-acquisition components

(a) Involved in learning and storing information.

(b) The executive processes that govern approaches to problems.

(c) Carries out the instructions of the metacomponents.

23-3. Gardner has proposed seven relatively distinct human intelligences. What does his research show with respect to a "g" factor among these separate intelligences?

Answers: 23-1. contextual (a), experiential (c), componential (b). **23-2.** metacomponents (b), performance components (c), knowledge-acquisition components (a) **23-3.** There does not appear to be a "g" factor; rather, people display a mix of strong, weak, and intermediate abilities.

PUTTING IT IN PERSPECTIVE

24. Discuss how the chapter highlighted three of the text's unifying themes.

24-1. Answer the following questions about the three unifying themes.

(a) What theme is exemplified by the Cyril Burt affair?

(b) What theme is exemplified by the different views about the nature of intelligence held by Western and non-Western cultures

(c) What theme is exemplified by the extensive research using twin studies, adoption studies, and family studies?

Answers: 24-1. (a) Psychology evolves in a sociohistorical context. (b) Cultural factors shape behavior. (c) Heredity and environment jointly influence behavior.

APPLICATION: MEASURING AND UNDERSTANDING CREATIVITY

25. Discuss popular ideas about the nature of creativity.

25-1. Popular notions about creativity would have us believe that creative ideas arise from nowhere, occur in a burst of insight, are not related to hard work, and are unrelated to intelligence. What does the text say about these notions?

Answers: 25-1. They are all false.

26. **Describe creativity tests and summarize how well they predict creative achievement.**

26-1. Most tests of creativity attempt to assess (conventional/ <u>divergent</u>) thinking, such as: List as many uses as you can for a book. Creativity scores are based on the _____ of alternatives generated and the originality and _____ of the suggested alternatives.

26-2. Creativity tests are rather (<u>good/mediocre</u>) predictors of creativity in the real world. One reason for this is that they attempt to treat creativity as a (<u>specific/general</u>) trait while research evidence seems to show it is related to quite _____ domains.

Answers: **26-1.** divergent, number, usefulness (utility) **26-2.** mediocre, general, specific.

27. **Discuss associations between creativity and personality, intelligence, and mental illness.**

27-1. What four personality characteristics are rather consistently found to be related to creativity?

27-2. What is the intelligence level of most highly creative people?

27-3. What form of mental illness appears to be associated with creative achievement?

Answers: **27-1.** autonomy, independence, self-confidence, nonconformity **27-2.** Average to above average. **27-3.** mood disorders

REVIEW OF KEY TERMS

Achievement tests
Aptitude tests
Construct validity
Content validity
Covergent thinking
Correlation coefficient
Creativity
Criterion-related validity
Crystallized intelligence
Deviation IQ scores

Divergent thinking
Eugenics
Factor analysis
Fluid intelligence
Heritability ratio
Intelligence quotient (IQ)
Intelligence tests
Mental age
Mental retardation
Normal distribution

Percentile score
Personality tests
Psychological test
Reaction range
Reliability
Standardization
Test norms
Test-retest reliability
Validity

_____ 1. A standardized measure of a sample of a person's behavior.

_____ 2. Tests that measure general mental ability.

_____ 3. Tests that measure various personality traits.

_____ 4. Tests that assess talent for specific kinds of learning.

_____ 5. Tests that gauge the mastery and knowldege of various subject areas.

_____ 6. The development of uniform procedures for administering and scoring tests, including the development of test norms.

_____ 7. Data that provides information about the relative standing of a particular test score.

_____ 8. Number indicating the percentage of people who score above or below a particular test score.

_____ 9. The measurement consistency of a test.

_____ 10. Estimated by comparing subjects' scores on two administrations of the same test.

_____ 11. The ability of a test to measure what it was designed to measure.

_____ 12. The degree to which the content of a test is representative of the domain it is supposed to measure.

_____ 13. The degree to which the scores on a particualr test correlate with scores on an independent criterion (test).

_____ 14. The degree to which there is evidence that a test measures a hypothetical construct.

_____ 15. The idea of controlling reproduction so as to gradually improve hereditary charcteristics in a population.

_____ 16. A score indicating the mental ability typical of a chronological age group.

_____ 17. Mental age divided by chronological age and multiplied by 100.

_____ 18. A symmetrical, bell-shaped curve that describes the distribution of many physical and psychological attributes.

_____ 19. Scores that translate raw scores into a precise location in the normal distribution.

_____ 20. Subnormal general mental ability accompanied by deficiencies in everyday living skills originating prior to age 18.

_____ 21. An estimate of the percentage of variation in a trait determined by genetic inheritance.

_____ 22. Genetically determined limits on intelligence.

_____ 23. Method that uses the correlation among many variables to identify closely related clusters.

_____ 24. The ability to apply acquired knowledge and skills to problem solving.

_____ 25. Includes reasoning ability, memory capacity, and speed of information processing.

_____ 26. The generation of ideas that are original, novel, and useful.

_____ 27. Thinking that attempts to narrow down a list of alternatives to a single best solution.

_____ 28. Thinking that attempts to expand the range of alternatives by generating many possible solutions.

_____ 29. A numerical index of the degree of relationship between two variables.

Answers: 1. psychological test **2.** intelligence tests **3.** personality tests **4.** aptitude tests **5.** achievement tests **6.** standardization **7.** test norms **8.** percentile score **9.** reliability **10.** test-retest reliability **11.** validity **12.** content validity **13.** criterion-related validity **14.** construct validity **15.** eugenics **16.** mental age **17.** intelligence quotient **18.** normal distribution **19.** deviation IQ scores **20.** mental retardation **21.** heritability ratio **22.** reaction range **23.** factor analysis **24.** crystallized thinking **25.** fluid thinking **26.** creativity **27.** convergent thinking **28.** divergent thinking **29.** correlation coefficient.

REVIEW OF KEY PEOPLE

Alfred Binet
Sir Cyril Burt
Sir Francis Galton
Howard Gardner

Arthur Jensen
Sandra Scarr
Claude Steele

Robert Sternberg
Lewis Terman
David Wechsler

_____ **1.** Developed the Standford-Binet Intelligence Scale.

_____ **2.** Developed the first successful test of adult intelligence.

_____ **3.** Postulated a cognitive triarchic theory of intelligence.

_____ **4.** Used nonexistent data to support the view that intelligence is primarily inherited.

_____ **5.** Proposed a reaction range model for human intelligence.

_____ **6.** Developed the first useful intelligence test.

_____ **7.** Postulated a heritability explanation for cultural differences in intelligence.

_____ **8.** Began the quest to measure intelligence.

_____ **9.** Proposed a stereotype vulnerability theory as an explanation for racial differences on IQ test scores.

_____ **10.** Has suggested the existence of a number of relatively autonomous human intelligences.

Answers: 1. Terman **2.** Wechsler **3.** Sternberg **4.** Burt **5.** Scarr **6.** Binet **7.** Jensen **8.** Galton **9.** Steele **10.** Gardner.

SELF-QUIZ

1. This self-test you are now taking is an example of:
   a. an aptitude test
   b. an achievement test
   c. an intelligence test
   d. a criterion-related test

2. Which of the following statistics is generally used to estimate reliability and validity?
   a. the correlation coefficient
   b. the standard deviation
   c. the percentile score
   d. the median

3. What kind of validity do test such as the SAT and ACT particularly strive for?
   a. content validity
   b. construct validty
   c. absolute validity
   d. criterion-related validity

4. Spearman's "g" infers that":
   a. most kinds of intelligence are highly related
   b. most kinds of intelligence are not highly related
   c. intelligence is highly correlated with personality characteristics
   d. intelligence is primarily inherited

5. With respect to modern intelligence tests:
   a. reliability is generally higher than validity
   b. validity is generally higher than reliability
   c. reliability and validity are about the same
   d. I have no idea what you are talking about

6. If the heritability ratio for intelligence is 80%, this means that for you as an individual 80% of your intelligence is determined by heredity and 20% is determined by your environment. This statement is:
   a. true
   b. false

7. Which of the following explanations for racial differences in intelligence is best supported by research evidence.
   a. Jensen's heritability theory
   b. cultural bias in IQ tests
   c. cultural disadvantage
   d. Watson's differential conditioning theory

8. If the reaction range concept of human intelligence is correct, then a child with exactly normal intelligence will probably not exceed an IQ of:
   a. 100
   b. 110
   c. 120
   d. 130

9. Which of the following retarded groups can often pass for normal as adults?
   a. mild
   b. moderate
   c. profound
   d. both a and b

10. What percentage of mental retardation cases have been definitely linked to organic causes?
    a. approximately 25%
    b. approximately 50%
    c. approximately 75%
    d. approximately 90%

11. Terman's long-term study of gifted children found that they tended to excell in:
    a. physical development
    b. social development
    c. emotional development
    d. all of the above

12. Which of the following groups shows the highest correlation with respect to intelligence?
    a. fraternal twins reared together
    b. fraternal twins reared apart
    c. identical twins reared apart
    d. both a and c

13. The search for biological correlates of intelligence are beginning to prove quite fruitful. This statement is:
   a. true
   b. false

14. What is the role of metacomponents in Sternberg's triarchic theory of intelligence?
   a. learning and storing information
   b. carrying out instructions
   c. giving instructions
   d. all of the above

15. Steele"s theory of stereotype vulnerability is an attempt to explain:
   a. why Asian-Americans score higher than average on IQ tests
   b. why African-Americans score lower than average on IQ tests
   c. both of the above
   d. none of the above

16. Most tests of creativity emphasize:
   a. convergent thinking
   b. divergent thinking
   c. both of the above
   d. none of the above

Answers: 1. b **2.** a **3.** d **4.** a **5.** a **6.** b **7.** c **8.** b **9.** a **10.** a **11.** d **12.** c **13.** b **14.** c **15.** b **16.** b

Chapter Ten

Motivation and Emotion

REVIEW OF KEY IDEAS

MOTIVATIONAL THEORIES AND CONCEPTS

1. **Explain the key elements of evolutionary theory and how it accounts for specific gender differences in mating behavior.**

   1-1. According to evolutionary theorists, the various forms of motivation, like other human and animal characteristics, occur because they have _____ value.

   1-2. Traditional evolutionary theory has had difficulty explaining the survival value of self-sacrifice, however. (E. g., how does falling on a grenade to save a comrade have survival value?) More recently, the evolutionary viewpoint has emphasized adaptive value for the (<u>individual organism/species</u>). Thus, self-sacrifice to save others with similar characteristics helps the species pass its _____ to the next generation.

   1-3. The idea that an organism may sacrifice itself to save others that share the same genes is part of the concept referred to as _____ fitness.

   1-4. Somewhat more controversial is the evolutionary theorists' explanation of gender differences in mating patterns. Evolution favors mechanisms that pass genes on to the next generation. In many mammalian species, including humans, transmission of genes would be maximized for (<u>males/females</u>) by their mating with as many different members of the opposite sex as possible.

   1-5. For females, on the other hand, who are limited in terms of the number of offspring that they can produce in a breeding season, there is no evolutionary advantage to mating with many males. Thus, females tend to be (<u>less/more</u>) selective of mates than males.

   1-6. Buss explains the relationship between infidelity and gender in a similar manner. Paternity (who the father is) is not always certain. Maternity is certain. Thus, if males want to make sure that they pass on their genes, they must be concerned with paternity, and their jealousy relates to (<u>sexual/emotional</u>) infidelity. For females, on the other hand, certain that the child is theirs, the male partner's resources and, hence, his (<u>sexual/emotional</u>) commitment is the more important factor.

   Answers: 1-1. adaptive (survival) **1-2.** species, genes **1-3.** inclusive **1-4.** males **1-5.** less **1-6.** sexual, emotional.

2. Compare and contrast the drive and incentive theoretical perspectives on motivation.

2-1. Review the sections on drive and incentive motivational theories. Then check your understanding by placing the name of the type of theory (drive or incentive) in the blanks below.

_____ Cannot easily account for behavior that *increases* tension.

_____ Motivation to pursue a goal or object depends on the *value* of the object and one's *expectancy* of success at obtaining it.

_____ Emphasizes homeostasis, the pressure to return to a state of equilibrium.

_____ Emphasizes environmental factors in motivation.

_____ Actions result from attempts to reduce internal states of tension.

_____ Emphasizes "pull" from the environment (as opposed to "push" from internal states).

Answers: 2-1. drive, incentive, drive, incentive, drive, incentive.

3. Distinguish between biological and social needs and describe the hierarchy of needs proposed by Maslow.

3-1. Most theories distinguish between _____ needs, such as hunger and thirst, and _____ needs, which are acquired through _____ or the process of socialization. Most biological needs are required for the _____ of the group or individual.

3-2. While there are relatively few _____ needs, an individual may theoretically acquire an unlimited number of _____ needs.

3-3. Note that while aggression is listed in Figure 10.4 as a biological need, some theorists consider aggression to be largely acquired or social. Thus, the distinction between biological and social needs is a useful one but (is/is not) always clear cut.

3-4. Write the names of Maslow's hierarchical levels of needs in the blanks at the right of the pyramid. Start with (a) at the lowest level.

(g) _____

(f) _____

(e) _____

(d) _____

(c) _____

(b) _____

(a) _____

3-5. When or in what circumstance, according to Maslow, does a higher level of need become activated?

3-6. How do needs toward the top of the pyramid differ from those near the bottom?

3-7. Maslow asserted that our highest growth need is our need for self-actualization. What is the need for self-actualization?

Answers: 3-1. biological, social, learning, survival **3-2.** biological, social **3-3.** is not **3-4.** (a) physiological needs (b) safety and security needs (c) belongingness and love needs (d) esteem needs (e) cognitive needs (f) aesthetic needs (g) need for self-actualization **3-5.** A higher level is activated only when a lower level is fairly well satisfied. For example, needs for achievement and recognition are generally activated only after needs for love and belongingness are satisfied. **3-6.** The closer a need is to the top of the pyramid, the more it is socially based; the closer to the bottom, the more it is biologically based. **3-7.** the need to express one's full potential (i.e., to "be all that you can be," although Maslow didn't have in mind joining the Army).

THE MOTIVATION OF HUNGER AND EATING

4. Summarize evidence on the areas of the brain implicated in the regulation of hunger.

4-1. Within the brain the major structure implicated has been the _____. The two main areas of this structure that have been associated with hunger level are the _____ hypothalamus (LH) and the _____ nucleus of the hypothalamus (VMH).

4-2. Different things happen when these two areas are electrically stimulated as opposed to when they are destroyed or lesioned. For example, when the lateral hypothalamus is electrically stimulated, animals tend to (start/stop) eating. When the LH is lesioned, however, the animals (start/stop) eating.

4-3. Summarize the effects of stimulating and lesioning the hypothalamus on eating by writing either "start" or "stop" in the blanks at the right.

Lateral, electrical stimulation: _____

Lateral, lesioning: _____

Ventromedial nucleus, electrical stimulation: _____

Ventromedial nucleus, lesioning: _____

4-4. Starvation is likely to be the result for rats with a lesioned _____ hypothalamus, while obesity is the result for rats that have their _____ hypothalamus destroyed.

4-5. Several recent findings have complicated the issue about brain regulation of eating. For one thing, the neurochemical changes are more complicated than previously thought; for another, there appears to be (only two/more than two) areas of the hypothalamus important for eating behavior. While the ventromedial and lateral parts of the hypothalamus are still regarded as important determinants of eating, the idea of a simple on-off mechanism in the brain is now regarded as (too simplistic/still correct).

Answers: 4-1. hypothalamus, lateral, ventromedial **4-2.** start, stop **4-3.** start, stop, stop, start **4-4.** lateral (LH), ventromedial (VMH) **4-5.** more than two, too simplistic.

5. **Summarize evidence on how fluctuations in blood glucose and insulin affect hunger.**

—5-1.   Much of the food we consume is converted into _____, a simple sugar that is an important source of energy. Manipulations that lower glucose tend to _____ hunger; raising glucose levels generally decreases hunger. Based on this evidence, Mayer proposed that neurons called _____ monitor glucose levels and contribute to the experience of hunger. (While glucostats were originally thought to be exclusively in the brain, their location and exact nature remain obscure.)

—5-2.   For cells to extract glucose from the blood, the hormone insulin must be present. Injections of insulin (in nondiabetics) will produce a (an) _____ in the level of sugar in the blood, with the result that the person experiences a (an) _____ in the sensation of hunger. In addition to insulin, some investigators have suggested that another hormone, abbreviated CCK, is related to (increasing/decreasing) the experience of hunger.

Answers: **5-1.** glucose, increase, brain (hypothalamus), glucostats, liver **5-2.** decrease, increase, decreasing.

6. **Summarize evidence how culture, learning, food cues, and stress influence hunger.**

—6-1.   Although we have some innate taste preferences, it is also clear that _____ affects some of our food choices and even influences the amounts that we eat.

6-2.   In one study an artificial sweetener was substituted in people's diets without their knowledge. If only physiological mechanisms regulated eating behavior, we would expect increased eating to compensate for the caloric loss, yet most subjects (did/did not) increase food consumption. Thus, learning seems to influence both our taste preferences and the _____ we consume.

6-3.   Some people may experience hunger when the clock says it's time to eat. Thus, food-related _____ in our environment, such as the taste of food, the availability or sight of food, and the _____ of day, may influence food consumption.

—6-4.   Besides affecting eating habits and providing cues to eating, the environment may also provide unpleasant or frustrating events that produce emotional _____, a factor that may also trigger eating in many people. Although stress and increased eating are linked, recent evidence suggests that the important factor may be heightened physiological _____ produced by stress rather than the stress itself.

Answers: **6-1.** learning (environment) **6-2.** did not, amounts **6-3.** cues, time **6-4.** stress, arousal.

7. **Discuss the contribution of oversensitivity to external cues, genetic predisposition, dietary restraint, and set point to obesity.**

7-1.   External cues—time of day, the attractiveness of food, the smell of food—influence hunger. Schachter proposed that _____ people are especially sensitive to external cues and not very sensitive to internal, physiological cues that relate to hunger. According to Schachter, then, it is normal weight people who eat as a function of internal cues; the obese are controlled to a greater extent by _____ cues.

7-2. Judith Rodin, one of Schachter's students, found that people sensitive to external food cues tend to secrete insulin, which may reduce blood _____ and increase _____. Rodin's research has blurred the distinction between internal and external cues: Since insulin produces an *internal* signal, it is difficult to argue that the eating occurs simply because of _____ cues.

7-3. Rodin has found that many obese people are not especially responsive to external cues and that many thin or normal-weight people are responsive to such cues. Thus, concerning Schachter's theory, Rodin has concluded that the link between obesity and sensitivity to external cues is (stronger/weaker) than Schachter had proposed.

7-4. It is by now clear that many factors affect body weight and that some of the most important are genetic. For example, Stunkard et al. (1986) found that adopted children were much more similar in weight to their (biological/adoptive) parents than to their (biological/adoptive) parents, even though they were brought up by the latter.

7-5. What are the results of the Stunkard et al. (1990) study of twins?

7-6. Basal or resting metabolism accounts for about two-thirds of an individual's energy output. What has research found with regard to differences between obese and nonobese people in metabolic rates?

7-7. The concept of set point may help explain why body weight remains so stable. The theory proposes that each individual has a "natural" body weight determined in large part by the *number* of _____ that an individual happens to have. Although the number of fat cells in the body may increase through persistent overeating, the number is usually (very stable/highly variable) throughout one's lifetime.

7-8. The larger the (number/size) of fat cells, the higher the set point. When a person diets, fat cells decrease in _____ but not in _____.

7-9. Dieting or weight gain produces a change in the _____ of the fat cells but not, in most cases, the _____ of fat cells. Thus, maintenance of body weight below one's "natural" weight, or _____, is difficult, as is maintenance above one's set point.

7-10. According to the dietary restraint concept, the world is divided into two types of people. Some people eat as much as they want when they want; these people are the _____ eaters. Others monitor their food intake and frequently go hungry; these are the _____ eaters. While restrained eaters are constantly on guard to control their eating, they may also lose control and eat to excess, in which case their restrained eating is said to be _____.

7-11. What does dietary restraint have to do with obesity? Some researchers think that since dietary restraint is frequently disrupted or _____ and thereby results in overeating, restraint may contribute to obesity. Which of the following statements are true, according to the available data? (Place a T or F in the blanks.)

_____ Restrained eaters often overeat after disruptions of self-control.

_____ Restrained eaters experience greater weight fluctuations than unrestrained eaters.

_____ Fluctuations in weight may be just as common among obese people as normal-weight people.

_____ Dietary restraint is a clear cause of obesity.

Answers: 7-1. obese, external **7-2.** glucose (sugar), hunger, external **7-3.** weaker **7-4.** biological, adoptive **7-5.** Identical twins reared apart were found to be far more similar in weight than fraternal twins reared together. Stunkard et al. estimated that approximately 70 percent of the variation in people's weight is due to heredity. **7-6.** No differences have been found in basal metabolism between obese and nonobese people. **7-7.** fat cells, very stable **7-8.** number, size, number **7-9.** size, number, set point **7-10.** unrestrained, restrained, disinhibited **7-11.** disinhibited, T, T, T, F (false because the data are mixed and conclusions are not yet warranted).

SEXUAL MOTIVATION AND BEHAVIOR

8. **Describe the impact of hormones and pheromones in regulating animal and human sexual behavior.**

   8-1. Hormones are clearly linked to sexual behavior. For example, castrated rats have no sexual interest, but if they are injected with the hormone _____ their sexual motivation revives. In humans, the effect of hormones on sexual behavior is considerably (greater/less) than is the case with lower animals.

   8-2. While both of the principal classes of gonadal hormones occur in both sexes, the major female sex hormones are the _____ and the major male sex hormones the _____.

   8-3. Higher levels of the hormone _____, a key androgen, are related to higher levels of sexual activity in (males only/females only/both sexes). The presence of estrogen (is also/is not) correlated with sexual activity.

   8-4. With regard to pheromones:

   (a) What is a pheromone?

   (b) Is there any evidence that pheromones affect *sex drive* in human beings and other higher primates?

   (c) What aspects of human behavior do pheromones seem to affect?

8-5.   Describe the study involving sweat and menstrual synchronization.

Answers: 8-1. testosterone, less **8-2.** estrogens, androgens **8-3.** testosterone, both sexes, is not **8-4.** (a) A chemical secreted by one animal that affects the behavior of other animals. (b) No evidence that pheromones affect the human sex drive. (c) Menstrual cycles: Women who live together tend to have synchronized ovulatory cycles. **8-5.** One study found that a solution of alcohol and sweat taken from some women tended to produce synchronized cycles when rubbed on the lips of other women.

9.   Discuss the role of attraction to a partner in animal and human sexual behavior.

9-1.   Characteristics of a potential partner that may affect sexual interest include the so-called

_____ effect, which refers to the preference for a variety of sexual partners, and the

tendency for many animal species to be selective of partners on the basis of the physical

_____ of a potential partner.

9-2.   While there are wide individual differences, Buss and Schmitt found that on the average college men indicated a desire to have (<u>more/fewer</u>) sexual partners than did college women. In addition, men appear to be more motivated by the desire for (<u>physical gratification/emotional commitment</u>) in sexual relations and women by (<u>physical gratification/emotional commitment</u>).

Answers: 9-1. Coolidge, attractiveness **9-2.** physical gratification, emotional commitment

10.   Describe the Featured Study on culture and mating preferences.

10-1.   According to evolutionary theories, what characteristics do human females look for in a male partner? What do males look for in a female partner?

10-2.   More than 10,000 people participated in Buss's study. The people surveyed were from (<u>the United States/ 37 different cultures</u>).

10-3.   In one or two sentences, summarize the results of Buss's study.

10-4.   What conclusions can reasonably be drawn from Buss's study? Place a checkmark next to all of the statements below that appropriately describe the results.

_____   Some of the differences in mating preferences were universal across cultures.

_____   The data are consistent with evolutionary theories of sexual motivation.

_____   The data may be explained by alternative interpretations that do not derive from evolutionary theory.

_____   One possible alternative explanation of the data is that women value men's economic resources because their own potential has been restricted.

Answers: 10-1. According to the evolutionary theories, women want men who will be able to acquire resources that can be invested in children—men with education, money, status, and ambition. Men, on the other hand, want women who have good breeding potentional, women who are beautiful, youthful, and in good health. **10-2.** 37 different cultures **10-3.** Results supported predictions from the evolutionary theories: women placed more value than men on finding a partner with good financial prospects; men placed more value than women on the characteristics of youth and physical attractiveness (as summed up in the song *Summertime* from Gerschwin's *Porgy and Bess*, "Oh, your daddy's rich, and your ma is good looking.") **10-4.** All of these statements are correct or represent reasonable inferences. Some differences were universal, and the data are consistent with evolutionary theories. At the same time there are alternative explanations involving the fact of discrimination against women in virtually all societies.

11. Summarize the evidence on the impact of erotic materials, including aggressive pornography, on human sexual behavior.

11-1. How do men and women react to erotic materials? Answer this questions in terms of:

(a) reported dislike of the materials

(b) physiological responses

(c) sexual activity after viewing

11-2. In the Zillman and Bryant studies described, male and female undergraduate subjects were exposed to relatively heavy doses of pornography over a period of weeks. What effect did this have on:

(a) attitudes about sexual practices

(b) satisfaction with their sexual partners

11-3. *Aggressive* pornography usually depicts violence against women.

(a) What laboratory evidence indicates that viewing aggressive pornography affects aggression against women?

(b) What is the effect of viewing aggressive pornography on attitudes toward rape?

Answers: 11-1. (a) Women are more likely than men to report disliking erotic materials. (b) Women and men are both physiologically responsive to erotic materials. (As your author notes, differences between reported liking and physiological response may be due to the less sexist nature of the erotica used in laboratory settings.) (c). For a few hours immediately after exposure, the likelihood of sexual activity occurring is somewhat increased (although data on this issue are inconsistent). **11-2.** (a) Attitudes about sexual practices became more liberal; for example, both males and females came to view premarital and extramarital sex as more acceptable. (b) Subjects became less satisfied with their partners in terms of physical appearance and sexual performance. **11-3.** (a) Some studies have found that pornography depicting violence against women increases male subjects' aggressive behavior toward women. In these laboratory studies, aggression is defined as willingness to deliver electric shock to other subjects. (b) Exposure to aggressive pornography appears to make sexual coercion or rape seem less offensive.

12. Summarize evidence on the determinants of sexual orientation.

12-1. What factors determine sexual orientation? Psychoanalysts thought the answer involved some aspect of the parent-child relationship. Behaviorists assumed that it was due to the association of same-sex stimuli with sexual arousal. Thus, both psychoanalytic and behavioral theorists proposed (<u>environmental/ biological</u>) explanations of homosexuality.

12-2. Extensive research on the upbringing of homosexuals has (<u>supported/not supported</u>) the idea that homosexuality is largely explainable in terms of environmental factors.

12-3. Recent studies have produced evidence that homosexuality is in part genetic. Which of the following types of studies have supported this conclusion? (Place Y for yes or N for no in the blanks.)

(a) _____ Studies of hormonal differences between heterosexuals and homosexuals.

(b) _____ Studies of twins and adopted children.

(c) _____ Autopsy studies of the hypothalamus.

12-4. Subjects in one of the studies described were gay men who had either an identical twin brother, a fraternal twin brother, or an adopted brother. For each of the categories what percent of the brothers of the subjects were also gay? Place the appropriate percents in the blanks.

(a) _____ Identical twins   22 percent

(b) _____ Fraternal twins   11 percent

(c) _____ Adopted brothers   52 percent

12-5. LeVay (1991) has reported that a cluster of neurons in the anterior _____ is (<u>smaller/ larger</u>) in gay men than in straight men. Since all of the gay men in this study had died of AIDS, which itself may produce changes in brain structure, these findings should be interpreted with caution. Nonetheless, these data support the idea that there are (<u>environmental/biological</u>) factors that are related to sexual orientation.

Answers: 12-1. environmental **12-2.** not supported **12-3.** (a) N (b) Y (c) Y **12-4.** (a) 52 percent (b) 22 percent (c) 11 percent **12-5.** hypothalamus, smaller, biological.

13. Outline the four phases of the human sexual response.

13-1. Write the names of the four phases of the human sexual response in the order in which they occur. (Hint: I made up a mnemonic device that's hard to forget. The first letter of each phase name produces EPOR, which happens to be ROPE spelled backward.)

(a) _____

(b) _____

(c) _____

(d) _____

13-2. In the blanks below write the first letter of each phase name that correctly labels the descriptions below.

_____   Rapid increase in arousal (respiration, heart rate, blood pressure, etc.)

_____   Vasocongestion of blood vessels in sexual organs; lubrication in female

_____   Continued arousal, but at a slower place

_____   Tightening of the vaginal entrance

_____   Pulsating muscular contractions and ejaculation

_____   Physiological changes produced by arousal subside.

_____   Includes a refractory period for men

Answers: 13-1. (a) excitement (b) plateau (c) orgasm (d) resolution **13-2.** E, E, P, P, O, R, R.

AFFILIATION: IN SEARCH OF BELONGINGNESS

14. Describe the affiliation motive and how it is measured.

14-1. Most human beings seek the company of others, a need referred to as the _____ motive.

14-2. In a recent theoretical review of research on affiliation, Baumeister and Leary assert that the need to affiliate has a strong basis in (<u>learning/evolution</u>). For human beings, as for many other animals, bonding with others permits more effective hunting, defense, and care of offspring. Affiliation, in other words, appears to have to have _____ value

14-3. Need for affiliation may be measured by a test known as the Thematic Apperception Test, or _____ for short. This test involves asking subjects to write or tell _____ in response to pictures of people in various scenes.

14-4. Certain *themes* emerge from the TAT stories that reflect the strengths of various needs or motives. How well does the TAT measure affiliation? Validity studies have shown that people who devote more time to seeking and maintaining friendships do, in fact, tend to score higher on the need for _____ on the TAT.

Answers: 14-1. affiliation **14-2.** evolution, survival (adaptive) **14-3.** TAT, stories **14-4.** affiliation.

ACHIEVEMENT: IN SEARCH OF EXCELLENCE

15. Describe the achievement motive and discuss how individual differences in the need for achievement influence achievement behavior.

15-1. People with high achievement motivation have a need to:

a. master difficult challenges

b. outperform others

c. excel and compete

d. all of the above

15-2. What is the relationship between estimates of achievement motive in a country and the economic growth of that county?

15-3. The procedure used for measuring need for achievement is the same as that used to measure need for affiliation: subjects tell stories about pictures shown in the _____.

15-4. How do people who score high on need for affiliation differ from those who score low?

Answers: 15-1. d **15-2.** Countries with estimated high achievement motivation have higher economic growth (and greater productivity in general). **15-3.** TAT **15-4.** They tend to work hard, compete, be persistent, be successful in their careers, etc.

16. Explain how situational factors and fear of failure affect achievement strivings.

16-1. According to Atkinson's elaboration of McClelland's views, achievement-oriented behavior is determined not only by (1) achievement motivation but by (2) the _____ that success will occur and (3) the _____ of success.

16-2. As the difficulty of a task increases, the _____ of success at the task decreases. At the same time, success at harder tasks may be more satisfying, so the _____ value of the task is likely to increase. Thus, when both the incentive value and probability of success are weighed together, people with a high need for achievement would tend to select tasks of (extreme/moderate) difficulty.

16-3. In addition to success, Atkinson has included fear of failure in the equation. Thus, Atkinson proposes that there are six factors that affect pursuit of achievement: a motivation to achieve (to be successful) and a motivation to avoid _____; perceived *probability* of _____ and the perceived probability of _____; and the *incentive values* of both _____ and _____.

16-4. The motivation to avoid failure may either stimulate achievement or inhibit achievement. Explain.

Answers: 16-1. probability, incentive **16-2.** probability, incentive, moderate **16-3.** failure; success, failure; success, failure **16-4.** One may achieve in order to avoid failure on a task; thus, fear of failure may lead to achievement. On the other hand, one may avoid failure by not pursuing the task at all; thus, fear of failure could also lead to lack of achievement.

THE ELEMENTS OF EMOTIONAL EXPERIENCE

17. Describe the cognitive component of emotion.

17-1. The word *cognition* refers to thoughts, beliefs, or conscious experience. When faced with a large cockroach (or having to make a speech in public), you might say to yourself, "This is terrifying (or maybe disgusting)." This thought or cognition has an evaluative aspect: we assess our emotions as pleasant or unpleasant. Thus, one component of emotion is the _____ component, which includes _____ in terms of pleasantness-unpleasantness.

Answers: **17-1.** cognitive, evaluation.

18. Describe the physiological underpinnings of emotion.

18-1. The second component of emotion is the _____ component, primarily actions of the _____ nervous system. Your encounter with a cockroach might be accompanied by changes in heart rate, breathing, or blood pressure or by increased electrical conductivity of the skin known as the _____ skin response (GSR).

18-2. Lie detectors don't actually detect lies, they detect bodily changes that reflect the _____ component of emotion. One can't be certain, however, that the emotion reflected involves lying. Research has found that lie detectors are inaccurate about _____ of the time.

Answers: **18-1.** physiological, autonomic, galvanic **18-2.** physiological (autonomic arousal), one-fourth to one-third (i.e., about one-third of the innocent suspects were judged guilty by the polygraph, and about one-fourth of the guilty suspects were judged innocent by the polygraph).

19. Discuss the body language of emotions and the facial feedback hypothesis.

19-1. Suppose that you are afraid of cockroaches and that, confronted by an enormous roach, you scream and jump and your face contorts into an expression of fear mixed with disgust. These *actions* represent the _____ component of emotions.

19-2. We communicate emotions not only verbally but _____, through our postures, gestures, and, especially, in our facial _____.

19-3. Ekman and Friesen found that there are at least _____ fundamental facial expressions of emotion and perhaps as many as ten. Since children who have been blind since birth show the same expressions as sighted children, it seems reasonable to believe that basic facial expressions are largely (learned/innate).

19-4. Facial expressions are especially important indicants of emotion that, according to some researchers, not only reflect emotions but help create them. According to the this viewpoint, known as the _____ hypothesis, facial muscles send signals to the brain that help to produce the subjective experience of a particular emotion. Turning up the corners of your mouth, for example, will tend to make you feel _____.

Answers: **19-1.** behavioral (nonverebal) **19-2.** nonverbally (through body language), expressions **19-3.** six, innate **19-4.** facial-feedback, happy.

20. Discuss cross-cultural similarities and variations in emotional experience.

20-1.   Ekman and Friesen asked people in different cultures to label the emotion shown on photographs of faces. How did these studies support the idea that facial expressions tend to be universal across cultures?

20-2.   Different cultures show striking similarities in other aspects of emotional experience as well. For example, regardless of culture, meeting with friends tends to trigger one emotion and encountering failure another. Thus, certain types of _____ trigger the same emotions across cultures.

20-3.   Similarly, events that cause a lump in the throat (or perspiration or tensed muscles, etc.) in one culture will tend to do so in other cultures as well. Thus, the _____ reactions to different stimulus events are also quite similar across cultures.

20-4.   While there are similarities in emotional expression across cultures, there are also striking differences. For example, certain word labels for emotion (e.g., sadness, anger, remorse) that exist in some cultures (also occur/do not occur) in all others.

— 20-5.   Although people in different cultures show the same basic expressions of emotion, *when* they do so is governed by different cultural norms. What emotions are you "supposed to" show at a funeral, or when watching a sporting event? The unwritten rules that regulate our display of emotion, known as _____ rules, vary considerably across cultures.

Answers: **20-1.** People from widely disparate cultures, including cultures that have had virtually no contact with the West, show considerable agreement in labeling photographs of facial expressions with one of approximately six basic emotions. **20-2.** events (experiences, situations) **20-3.** physiological **20-4.** do not occur **20-5.** display.

THEORIES OF EMOTION

21.   Compare and contrast the James-Lange and Cannon-Bard theories of emotion, and explain how Schachter reconciled these conflicting views in his two-factor theory.

21-1.   For each of the following statements indicate the theory being described (James-Lange, Cannon-Bard, or Schachter).

(a)   Each of the different emotions is caused by a different pattern of autonomic arousal.

_____

(b)   Emotions cannot be distinguished on the basis of autonomic arousal; general autonomic arousal causes one to look for an explanation or label. _____

(c)   Emotions originate in subcortical brain structures, which send signals to the autonomic nervous system and to the cortex. _____

(d)   Love is accompanied by a different autonomic pattern from hate; we infer love or hate when we perceive the type of autonomic arousal. _____

(e)   The subjective experience of emotion is caused both by general autonomic arousal and by thoughts about environmental events that occur at the same time. _____

(f) Ralph observe that his heart pounds and that he becomes a little out of breath at times. He also notices that these signs of arousal occur whenever Mary is around, so he figures that he must be in love._____

21-2. In what sense does Schachter's theory reconcile the James-Lange and Cannon-Bard theories?

Answers: 21-1. (a) James-Lange (b) Schachter (c) Cannon-Bard (d) James-Lange (e) Schachter (f) Schachter
21-2. Schachter's view is similar to the James-Lange theory in that in both the perception of arousal contributes to the conscious experience of emotion; it is similar to the Cannon-Bard theory in that there is assumed to be just one general physiological arousal response rather than a different visceral response for each emotion. Since arousal is pretty much the same regardless of the emotion, Schachter proposed that we feel different emotions as a result of inferences we make from events in the environment.

22. Summarize the evolutionary perspective on emotion.

22-1. By preparing an organism for aggression and defense, the emotion of anger helps an organism survive. The emotions of fear, surprise, and interest have similar functions. From an evolutionary perspective, all emotions developed because of the _____ value they have for a species.

22-2. Evolutionary theorists view emotions primarily as a group of (innate/learned) reactions that have been passed on because of their survival value. They also believe that emotions originate in subcortical areas, parts of the brain that evolved before the cortical structures associated with higher mental processes. In the view of the evolutionary theorists, emotion evolved before thought and is largely (dependent on/independent of) thought.

—**22-3.** How many basic, inherited emotions are there? The evolutionary writers assume that the wide range of emotions we experience are blends or variations in intensity of approximately _____ innate or prewired primary emotions.

Answers: 22-1. survival (adaptive) **22-2.** innate, independent of **22-3.** eight (between six and ten).

PUTTING IT IN PERSPECTIVE

23. Explain how this chapter highlighted five of the text's unifying themes.

23-1. Five of the text's organizing themes were prominent in this chapter. Indicate which themes fit the following examples by writing the appropriate abbreviations in the blanks below: C for cultural contexts, SH for sociohistorical context, T for theoretical diversity, HE for heredity and environment, and MC for multiple causation.

(a) Achievement behavior is affected by achievement motivation, the likelihood of success, the likelihood of failure, and so on. _____

(b) Display rules in a culture tell us when and where to express an emotion. _____

(c) Changing attitudes about homosexuality have produced more research on sexual orientation; in turn, data from the research has affected societal attitudes. _____

(d) Body weight seems to be influenced by set point, blood glucose, and inherited metabolism. It is also affected by eating habits and acquired tastes, which vary across cultures. ____, ____, and ____

(e) The James-Lange theory proposed that different emotions reflected different patterns of physiological arousal; Cannon-Bard theory assumed that emotions originate in subcortical structures; Schachter viewed emotion as a combination of physiological arousal and cognition ____.

Answers: 23-1. (a) MC (b) C (c) SH (d) HE, MC, C (e) T.

APPLICATION: UNDERSTANDING HUMAN SEXUALITY

24. Summarize information provided on key factors in rewarding sexual relationships.

24-1. Each of the following statements is based on one of the four key factors that promotes rewarding sexual relationships. Indicate whether the statements are true or false.

____ A college text or course is usually an excellent source of information on human sexuality.

____ Many sexual problems are derived from guilt associated with a value system that views sex as immoral or depraved.

____ Talking about what one likes, asking questions, and in general communicating about sex with one's partner is important in a sexual relationship.

____ It is not unusual for individuals to fantasize about imaginary or former lovers during sexual encounters.

Answers: 24-1. true, true, true, true.

25. Describe three common forms of sexual dysfunction.

25-1. The three most frequent forms of sexual dysfunction are _____ *difficulties*, in which a man is unable to achieve or maintain an erection; _____ *ejaculation*, when a man reaches orgasm too quickly for sexual satisfaction to be achieved; and _____ *difficulties*, involving difficulty in achieving organism.

25-2. The common term for erectile difficulties is _____. Orgasmic difficulties in women used to be referred to as _____. Most researchers and therapists prefer to avoid both of these terms because of their pejorative or derogatory connotations.

Answers: 25-1. erectile, premature, orgasmic 25-2. impotence, frigidity.

26. Summarize the advice provided on coping with sexual problems.

26-1. Sex researchers have developed techniques that have proven helpful in resolving sexual problems. For erectile difficulties, for example, simply having the couple talk openly about the problem may reduce the performance _____ frequently associated with it.

26-2. Sex therapists also use a procedure called _____ focus, in which one partner touches the other in pleasure-producing ways while the second partner provides (physical/verbal) guidance about what feels good.

26-3. Initially, the sensate focus procedure requires that the partners (<u>touch/do not</u>) the genital areas. With pressure to perform removed, a man with erectile difficulties may begin to experience arousals.

26-4. Sensate focus is also used for _____ ejaculation so that over a number of sessions a man may begin to improve control over ejaculation.

26-5. For orgasmic difficulties among women, therapists may try to restructure negative _____ about sex. The technique of sensate focus (<u>has also/has not</u>) been found effective in treating this problem.

Answers: **26-1.** anxiety **26-2.** sensate, verbal **26-3.** do not **26-4.** premature **26-5.** attitudes (emotions, thoughts), has also.

REVIEW OF KEY TERMS

Achievement motive
Affiliation motive
Androgens
Aphrodisiac
Basal metabolic rate
Bisexuals
Display rules
Drive
Emotion
Erectile difficulties
Estrogens
Galvanic skin response (GSR)
Glucose

Glucostats
Heterosexuals
Hierarchy of needs
Homeostasis
Homosexuals
Incentive
Insulin
Intimacy motive
Lie detector
Motivation
Need for self-actualization
Obesity
Orgasm

Orgasmic difficulties
Pheromone
Polygraph
Premature ejaculation
Refractory period
Sensate focus
Set point
Sex therapy
Sexual dysfunction
Sexual orientation
Vasocongestion

motivation   1. Goal-directed behavior that may be affected by needs, wants, interests, desires, and incentives.

display rules   2. Cultural norms that regulate the expression of emotions.

set point   3. A state of physiological equilibrium or balance.

drive   4. An internal state of tension that motivates the organism to reduce the tension and return to homeostasis.

incentive   5. An external goal that motivates behavior.

hierarchy   6. A systematic arrangement of needs according to priority.

self-actual   7. The need to fulfill one's potential.

glucose   8. Blood sugar.

glucostats   9. Neurons that are sensitive to glucose.

insulin   10. A hormone secreted by the pancreas needed for extracting glucose from the blood.

basal metabolic   11. The body's rate of energy output at rest.

set point   12. The theoretical natural point of stability in body weight.

obesity   13. The condition of being overweight.

estrogens   14. The principal class of female sex hormones.

androgens   15. The principal class of male sex hormones.

pheromone _____ 16. A chemical secreted by one animal that affects the behavior of another animal.

intimacy sphr _____ 17. Substance purported to increase sexual desire.

vaso _____ 18. Engorgement of the blood vessels.

orgasm _____ 19. Sexual climax.

refractory period _____ 20. A time following orgasm during which males are unresponsive to sexual stimulation.

sexual orientation _____ 21. Whether a person prefers emotional-sexual relationships with members of the same sex, the other sex, or either sex.

homo _____ 22. People who seek emotional-sexual relationships with members of the same sex.

hetero _____ 23. People who seek emotional-sexual relationships with members of the other sex.

_bi_ _____ 24. People who seek emotional-sexual relationships with members of either sex.

affiliation _____ 25. The motive to associate with others.

intimacy _____ 26. The need to have warm, close exchanges with others marked by open communication.

achievement _____ 27. The need to master difficult challenges and to excel in competition with others.

GSR _____ 28. An increase in the electrical conductivity of the skin related to an increase in sweat gland activity.

emotion _____ 29. A reaction that includes cognitive, physiological, and behavioral components.

polygraph _____ 30. The technical name for the "lie detector."

lie detector _____ 31. The informal name for polygraph, an apparatus that monitors physiological aspects of arousal (e.g., heart rate, GSR).

dysfunction _____ 32. An impairment in sexual functioning that causes subjective distress.

erectile _____ 33. Persistent inability to achieve or maintain an erection adequate for sexual intercourse.

premature _____ 34. Climax in men occurring too quickly.

orgasmic _____ 35. Difficulty in achieving orgasm.

therapy _____ 36. Professional treatment of sexual dysfunctions.

sensate _____ 37. A sexual exercise involving pleasurable touching, verbal feedback, and performance restrictions.

Answers: 1. motivation **2.** display rules **3.** homeostasis **4.** drive **5.** incentive **6.** hierarchy of needs **7.** need for self-actualization **8.** glucose **9.** glucostats **10.** insulin **11.** basal metabolic rate **12.** set point **13.** obesity **14.** estrogens **15.** androgens **16.** pheromone **17.** aphrodisiac **18.** vasocongestion **19.** orgasm **20.** refractory period **21.** sexual orientation **22.** homosexuals **23.** heterosexuals **24.** bisexuals **25.** affiliation motive **26.** intimacy motive **27.** achievement motive **28.** galvanic skin response (GSR) **29.** emotion **30.** polygraph **31.** lie detector **32.** sexual dysfunction **33.** erectile difficulties **34.** premature ejaculation **35.** orgasmic difficulties **36.** sex therapy **37.** sensate focus

REVIEW OF KEY PEOPLE

John Atkinson
Walter Cannon
Paul Ekman & Wallace Friesen
William James

Abraham Maslow
William Masters & Virginia Johnson
David McClelland

Henry Murray
Judith Rodin
Stanley Schachter

Cannon   1. Proposed that emotions arise in subcortical areas of the brain.

_____   2. Compiled an influential catalogue of common social needs; also devised the TAT.

Maslow   3. Proposed a hierarchy of needs; stressed the need for self-actualization.

Schachter   4. Proposed that eating on the part of obese people is controlled by external cues; devised the two-factor theory of emotion.

Rodin   5. Found that external cues may elicit insulin secretions and that the obese are not especially sensitive to external cues.

Masters   6. Did the ground-breaking work on the physiology of the human sexual response.

McClelland   7. Is responsible for most of the early research on achievement motivation.

Atkinson   8. Emphasized additional factors in an elaboration of McClelland's theory of achievement motivation.

_____   9. In a series of cross-cultural studies found that people can identify six or so basic emotions from facial expressions.

_____   10. Thought that emotion arose from one's perception of variations in autonomic arousal.

Answers: 1. Cannon **2.** Murray **3.** Maslow **4.** Schachter **5.** Rodin **6.** Masters & Johnson **7.** McClelland **8.** Atkinson **9.** Ekman & Friesen **10.** James.

SELF-QUIZ

1. Which of the following is unlearned, uniform in expression, and universal within a particular species?
   a. incentive
   b. drive
   c. instinct
   d. motivation

2. In Maslow's hierarchy of needs, which of the following needs would have to be satisfied before the need for self-actualization would become activated?
   a. physiological needs
   b. safety and security needs
   c. esteem needs
   d. all of the above

3. What happens when a rat's lateral hypothalamus is lesioned?
   a. It starts eating.
   b. It looks for a sexual partner.
   c. It stops eating.
   d. It loses bladder and bowel control.

4. What is the effect of insulin on blood glucose?
   a. Glucose level increases.
   b. Glucose level decreases.
   c. Glucose changes to free fatty acids.
   d. CCK increases.

5. Which of the following is thought to be a major determinant of set point?
   a. number of fat cells
   b. size of fat cells
   c. amount of exercise
   d. skill at tennis

6. Estrogens are found in:
   a. males
   b. females
   c. both males and females
   d. androids

7. The presence of testosterone is related to higher levels of sexual activity in:
   a. males
   b. females
   c. both males and females
   d. androids

8. A chemical secreted by one animal that affects the behavior of another animal is known as a (an):
   a. androgen
   b. affiliatrogen
   c. hormone
   d. pheromone

9. Which of the following proposed that emotion arises from one's perception of autonomic arousal?
   a. Schachter
   b. James-Lange
   c. both of the above
   d. neither of the above

10. Stunkard found that adopted children's body weights tended to resemble the body weights of the children's:
    a. biological parents
    b. adoptive parents
    c. nonbiological siblings
    d. mothers and maternal aunts

11. What test is generally used to measure need for achievement?
    a. the TAT
    b. the GSR
    c. the Rorschach
    d. the MMPI

12. Evidence regarding facial expression in different cultures and observation of the blind suggests that:
    a. Schachter's two-factor theory is correct.
    b. Facial expression of emotion is to a large extent innate.
    c. Emotions originate in the cortex.
    d. Learning is the major factor in explaining basic facial expressions.

13. According to Schachter's theory of emotion:
    a. Different emotions are represented by different autonomic reactions.
    b. Emotions originate in subcortical brain structures.
    c. Fear produces a desire to avoid affiliation.
    d. Both arousal and cognition are needed to produce emotion.

14. According to Atkinson, achievement behavior is determined by:
    a. one's need for achievement and fear of failure
    b. one's estimates of the probabilities of success and failure
    c. the incentive values of success and failure
    d. all of the above

15. Evolutionary theories assert that motivations and emotions:
    a. are to a large extent learned
    b. have survival value
    c. are primarily social in origin
    d. all of the above

Answers: **1.** c **2.** d **3.** c **4.** b **5.** a **6.** c **7.** c **8.** d **9.** c **10.** a **11.** a **12.** b **13.** d **14.** d **15.** b.

Human Development Across the Life Span

REVIEW OF KEY IDEAS

PROGRESS BEFORE BIRTH: PRENATAL DEVELOPMENT

1. **Outline the major events of the three phases of prenatal development.**

   1-1. Each box below represents one month in the typical pregnancy; each short line at the top of the boxes represents one week. Indicate the beginning and end of each phase of prenatal development by placing the appropriate capital letters from the diagram in the blanks after the descriptions below.

   a) The germinal stage begins at birth, represented by point _____ in the diagram, and ends at point _____.

   (b) The embryonic stage begins at point _____ and ends at point _____.

   (c) The fetal stage begins at point _____ and ends at point _____.

   1-2. List the names of the three phases of prenatal development in the order in which they occur. In the parentheses at the right indicate the age ranges encompassed by each stage.

   (a) _____   (   )

   (b) _____   (   )

   (c) _____   (   )

   1-3. Match the letter identifying each stage in the previous question with the descriptions below.

   _____ The placenta begins to form.

   _____ At the end of this stage the organism begins to have a human appearance; it is about an inch in length.

   _____ The zygote begins to implant in the uterine wall; about one in five are rejected.

   _____ Muscles and bones develop and physical movements occur.

_____ Most major birth defects probably have their origins in this stage.

_____ The age of viability (about 22 to 26 weeks after conception) occurs during this stage.

Answers: 1-1. (a) A, B (b) B, D (c) D, G **1-2.** (a) germinal (birth to two weeks) (b) embryonic (two weeks to two months) (c) fetal (two months to nine months) **1-3.** a, b, a, c, b, c.

2. Summarize the impact of environmental factors on prenatal development.

2-1. Indicate whether the following statements concerning environmental factors and fetal development are true (T) or false (F).

_____ Severe malnutrition increases the risk of birth complications and neurological deficits.

_____ Studies consistently indicate that moderate malnutrition does not have a harmful effect on infant development.

_____ Few if any drugs consumed by a pregnant woman are able to pass through the placental barrier.

_____ Relative to its affluence the U. S. has a high infant mortality rate.

_____ Recent studies indicate that moderate drinking during pregnancy produces no risk for the developing fetus.

_____ Heavy drinking of alcohol by a pregnant woman may produce microencephaly, heart defects, and retardation in her child.

_____ Smoking during pregnancy is related to increased risk of miscarriage and other birth complications.

_____ The placenta screens out many but not all infectious diseases.

_____ Genital herpes is usually transmitted during the birth process, when newborns come into contact with their mothers' lesions.

_____ AIDS is transmitted primarily during the birth process, when newborns come into contact with their mothers' blood cells.

_____ Good quality prenatal care is associated with fewer premature births and higher infant survival rates.

Answers: 2-1. T, F, F, T, F, T, T, T, T, T, T.

THE WONDROUS YEARS OF CHILDHOOD

3. Summarize evidence on the perceptual abilities of infants.

3-1. Have you ever noticed that newborn babies don't seem to see very well? Newborns actually do have poor visual acuities, about 20/660 (compared to the ideal of 20/20). Newborns see blurred images in large part because, with the eye muscles controlling visual accommodation still developing, they can't _____ their eyes well.

3-2. What is accommodation?

3-3. At about what age does an infant's accommodation become similar to that of adults? _____ By about what age does the newborn's visual acuity improve to 20/20? _____

3-4.   According to the visual cliff studies, at about what age are most infants capable of perceiving depth?

_____

3-5.   At about _____ of age an infant can recognize a photograph of its mother's face. When the child is _____ old it recognize its mother's voice. Thus, the sense of _____ seems to develop more rapidly than the sense of _____.

3-6.   Michael Wertheimer did research on his newborn daughter immediately after he entered the delivery room. What is auditory localization and when do children show an ability to localize?

3-7.   The vision and hearing of newborns have been studied more extensively than the other senses, but available data indicate that the senses of taste, smell, and touch develop reasonably (<u>early/late</u>), especially in comparison with motor skills, considered in the next section.

Answers: 3-1. focus **3-2.** Accommodation involves adjusting the curvature of the lens to change the eye's focus. **3-3.** 6 months; 2 years **3-4.** at about 6 months, or as soon as they can crawl (and some studies suggest even earlier) **3-5.** 3 months, one week, hearing, vision **3-6.** Localization is the ability to detect the direction a sound is coming from, and children show some localization immediately after birth. **3-7.** early.

4. Describe general trends and principals and cultural variations in motor development

4-1.   In the space below, list and describe the two basic trends in motor development described in the text.

Cephalocaudal trend:

Proximodistal trend:

4-2.   The average ages at which children display various behaviors and abilities are referred to as developmental _____. While these averages provide useful information they don't reflect variability, and the age at which children display certain behaviors or abilities varies (<u>enormously/very little</u>) across children.

4-3.   Thus, with regard to the behavior of walking up steps, for example, (Figure 11.6), which of the following is true?

a. children walk up steps at approximately the same age.

b. many normal children don't walk up steps until well after or well before the average age indicated.

4-4.   The process that underlies the developmental norms is *maturation*. What is maturation? (Be specific with regard to the factors of hereditary and environment.)

4-5.   Cross-cultural research has revealed a considerable degree of consistency between cultures in terms of when and in what order motor skills appear. In general, early motor development is much more dependent on (<u>maturation/culture</u>) than is later motor development. As children in a culture grow older, however, the motor skills that they acquire depend to a greater extent on (<u>maturation/culture</u>).

Answers: 4-1. Head to foot: children tend to gain motor control of the upper body before the lower body. Center outward: the tendency to gain control of the torso before the limbs. **4-2.** norms, enormously **4-3.** b **4-4.** Maturation refers to developmental changes that occur in an organism as a result of *genetic*, as opposed to environmental, factors. **4-5.** maturation, culture.

5. Summarize the findings of Thomas and Chess's longitudinal study of infant temperament.

5-1.   Identify the following designs by indicating whether they are longitudinal or cross-sectional.

(a) _____   Groups of subjects of differing ages at a single point in time.

(b) _____   Single group of subjects over a relatively long period of time.

5-2.   Using a longitudinal design Thomas and Chess identified three basic temperaments, described below. Place the names of these temperamental styles in the appropriate blanks.

(a) _____   Happy, regular in sleep and eating, adaptable.

(b) _____   Less cheery, less regular in sleep and eating, more wary of new experiences.

(c) _____   Glum, erratic in sleep and eating, irritable.

5-3.   Approximately what percentages of the children are:

(a) easy? _____

(b) Slow-to-warm-up? _____

(c) Difficult? _____

(d) About what percentage is a mixture of the three basic categories? _____

5-4.   What is the major result and conclusion from the Thomas and Chess study?

Answers: 5-1. (a) cross-sectional (b) longitudinal **5-2.** (a) easy (b) slow-to-warm-up (c) difficult **5-3.** (a) 40 % (b) 15 % (c) 10 % (d) 35 % **5-4.** A child's temperament at 3 months tended to be a fair predictor of temperament at 10 years, which suggests that temperament has a strong biological basis.

6. Summarize theories of attachment and research on patterns of attachment and their effects.

6-1.   Some decades ago behaviorists thought that an infant's attraction to its mother derived from the association between the mother and food. According to this point of view, attachment is (learned/innate), and the mother becomes a (primary/conditioned) reinforcer.

6-2.   This simple conditioning theory of attachment was discarded as a result of the Harlows' famous studies with rhesus monkeys. These studies demonstrated that when infant monkeys were frightened they clung to the "substitute mothers" that (fed them/were soft). Even though they had been reinforced by the wire mothers, the infant monkeys had formed stronger attachments to the (terrycloth/wire) mothers.

6-3.   Bowlby proposed an evolutionary basis for mother-infant attachment, as follows. Human beings have evolved so that infants emit certain behaviors that automatically trigger affectionate and protective responses in adults. What do infants do that make them so adorable to adults? Among the behaviors they emit are _____, cooing, clinging, and so on. The infant's behaviors, and the adult's responses to them, are assumed to be in large part (learned/innate). If smiling in infants causes adults to protect them, then smiling clearly has _____ value in an evolutionary sense.

6-4. Research by Ainsworth and her colleagues indicates that attachments between mothers and their infants tend to fall into three categories. Label each of the following with the pattern of attachment described: secure, anxious-ambivalent, or avoidant.

(a) _____ The infant is anxious even when the mother is near, becomes very agitated when she leaves, and is not comforted when the mother returns.

(b) _____ The infant seeks little contact with the mother and is not distressed when she leaves.

(c) _____ The infant is upset when the mother leaves but is quickly calmed by her when she returns.

6-5. Attachment in infancy has been found to be related to behavior in later childhood. Which of the following tend to describe children who have had secure attachments in infancy?

a. persistence and curiosity

b. leadership ability and self-reliance

c. better social skills and more close friends

d. all of the above

Answers: 6-1. learned, conditioned **6-2.** were soft, terrycloth **6-3.** smiling, innate, survival (adaptive) **6-4.** (a) anxious-ambivalent (b) avoidant (c) secure **6-5.** d.

7. Discuss bonding at birth, day care, and culture in relation to attachment.

7-1. Research on infant-mother bonding during the first few hours after birth indicates that skin to skin contact:

a. Tends to produce stronger attachments later.

b. Results in clear but short-term benefits.

c. Neither of the above.

7-2. Does day care affect infant-mother attachment? Belsky has found that day care for more than 20 hours per week increases the likelihood that a/an (insecure/secure) attachment will form between mother and infant

7-3. Belsky's findings must be put in perspective, however. Which of the following statements are is/true (T) or false (F)?

_____ The proportion of insecure attachments found in the Belsky studies is only slightly higher than the U.S. norm.

_____ Some studies have found that day care can have beneficial effects on children's intellectual and social development.

_____ Negative effects of day care are slight or nonexistent in spacious, adequately staffed and equipped facilities.

7-4. Separation anxiety occurs at roughly the same ages across different cultures. There are cross-cultural differences, however, in the proportion of infants who fall into the three attachment categories (see Table 11.1 in your text).

(a) Which cultural sample (USA, Germany, or Japan) showed the highest proportion of *avoidant* attachments? _____

(b) Which cultural sample evidenced virtually *no avoidant attachments* at all?

_____

(c) Which sample showed the highest levels of *anxious/ambivalent* attachments?

_____

(d) Which two countries had the highest proportion of *secure* attachments?

_____ and _____

Answers: 7-1. c (because, as appealing as the practice may be, research has failed to find convincing evidence that it has either short- or long-term benefits) **7-2.** insecure **7-3.** T, T, T **7-4.** (a) Germany (b) Japan (c) Japan (d) Japan, USA, Japan.

8. **Outline the basic tenets of Erikson's theory and describe his stages of childhood personality development**

8-1.   Erikson's theory is clearly derived from Freudian psychoanalytic theory. Freud asserted that there are five

childhood stages that determine the adult's personality. In contrast, Erikson proposed that there are

_____ stages that influence personality across an individual's (childhood/entire lifespan).

8-2.   Erikson described four childhood stages and four adult stages. In the spaces below write the names of the crises that mark the four *childhood* stages, and indicate in the parentheses the approximate ages at which the crises are supposed to occur.

(a) _____ vs. _____   (   )

(b) _____ vs. _____   (   )

(c) _____ vs. _____   (   )

(d) _____ vs. _____   (   )

8-3.   Below are descriptions of several individuals. In what childhood stage would they have acquired these characteristics, according to Erikson? Use the letters from the question above to indicate the stages.

_____ Jack has trouble functioning effectively in the world outside his family; he is unproductive, and he lacks a sense of competence.

_____ Kristi is insecure and suspicious of everyone.

_____ Larry was torn between being independent of his family and avoiding conflict; as an adult he feels guilty and lacks self-esteem.

_____ From an early age Maureen's parents never seemed satisfied with what she did. Maureen is plagued by a sense of shame and self-doubt.

8-4.   As you may have noted in responding to the previous item, a weakness of Erikson's theory is that it

attempts to account for very (few/many) aspects of personality. Thus, the theory cannot explain the

enormous individual _____ between people.

Answers: 8-1. 8, entire lifespan **8-2.** (a) trust vs. mistrust (first year) (b) autonomy vs. shame and doubt (second year) (c) initiative vs. guilt (ages 3 to 6) (d) industry vs. inferiority (age 6 through puberty) **8-3.** d, a, c, b **8-4.** few, differences.

9. **Outline Piaget's stages of cognitive development and discuss the strengths and weaknesses of Piaget's theory.**

9-1. The diagram below represents Piaget's four main stages of development. Write the names of the stages in the appropriate blanks.

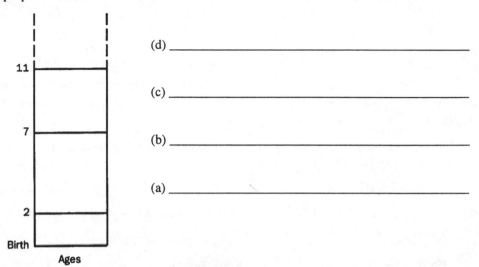

(d) _____

(c) _____

(b) _____

(a) _____

9-2. The stages of development are marked by changes in children's thinking processes brought about by two major processes. If the child interprets a new experience in terms of an *existing* mental structure, then _____ is operating. On the other hand, if the child interprets an experience by *changing* his thinking strategy, then the child has used _____.

9-3. Following is a list of characteristics of children's thinking during various stages. Identify the stage by placing the correct letter (from the diagram above) in the blanks.

_____ At the end of this stage the child is able to think symbolically (e.g., in terms of mental images).

_____ At the beginning of this stage the child's behavior is dominated by reflexes and the ability to coordinate sensory input and movement.

_____ The child understands conservation but cannot handle hierarchical classification.

_____ The child's thought processes are abstract and systematic.

_____ Object permanence occurs toward the end of this stage.

_____ During the first part of this stage, "out of sight, out of mind" might describe the child's reaction to hidden objects.

_____ When water is poured from a wide beaker into a taller beaker, children say there is now more water in the taller beaker.

_____ The child demonstrates a lack of understanding of conservation.

_____ The child shows the shortcomings of centration, irreversibility, egocentrism, and animism.

_____ For the first time the child in this stage is mentally able to undo an action and also is able focus on more than one feature of a problem at the same time.

9-4. When my (R. S.) daughter Vanessa was about 5, I placed two rows of stones on the grass, as illustrated below. Each row contained the same number of stones.

Row A: • • • • • • •

Row B: • • • • • • •

I then spread out one row so that it took up more space:

Row A: • • • • • • • •

Row B: • • • • • • •

(a) I then asked Vanessa to point to the row that now has more stones. If Vanessa behaved like other *preoperational* children, which row would she point to? _____

(b) The preoperational child has not yet mastered the principle that physical quantities remain constant in spite of changes in their shape or, in this case, arrangement. What is the name of this principle? _____

9-5. Some research has demonstrated that certain aspects of Piaget's theory may be incorrect in detail. For example, there is some evidence that object permanence and some aspects of conservation may develop (<u>earlier/later</u>) than Piaget had thought.

9-6. Piaget also had little to say about individual _____ in development or about so-called _____ of stages in which elements of an earlier stage may appear in a later one.

9-7. Piaget thought that people of all cultures would pass through the stages at the same time; subsequent research has found that this (<u>is/is not</u>) the case. While the *sequence* of stages appears to be relatively invariant across cultures, the _____ evidently is not. Nonetheless, Piaget's brilliance, the novelty of his approach, and the wealth of research that his theory inspired assure his place in history as the great child psychologist of the 20th century.

Answers: 9-1. (a) sensorimotor (b) preoperational (c) concrete operations (d) formal operations **9-2.** assimilation, accommodation **9-3.** a, a, c, d, a, a, b, b, b, d **9-4.** (a) Row A (at which point Samantha, then 8 and in the stage of concrete operations, was astonished at her sister's choice and informed her that there were the same number in both!) (b) conservation **9-5.** earlier **9-6.** differences, mixing **9-7.** is not, timetable (timing, age).

10. Describe how the information-processing approach has contributed to our understanding of cognitive development.

10-1. Information-processing theories compare the mind to a _____. This approach has been especially useful in accounting for aspects of _____ developmental involving *attention*, *memory*, and *processing speed*.

10-2. *Attention* is the ability to focus awareness on a narrowed range of stimuli. The *length of time* that an individual can focus attention on a particular task is known as attention _____.

10-3. While children's attention span increases during the preschool years, most four-year-olds still can't attend to a task for very long. Attention span continues to increase during the school years, and children also gradually improve in their ability to filter out irrelevant input, that is, to focus their attention _____.

10-4. Memory also improves throughout childhood, primarily due to the fact that children adopt *strategies* that enhance the storage and retrieval of information. Following are examples of these strategies. Label each strategy and indicate the age at which each tends to appear.

(a) I repeatedly misspelled *friend* on spelling tests in the third grade, and my teacher said to practice, practice, practice. She told me to repeat the spelling over and over in my mind, and I did. This technique is called _____, and most children start using it *routinely* at around age _____.

(b) Sue is trying to remember the names of various types of trees. She organizes them into three groups: those with leaves, those with needles, and those with flowers. She is using the technique of _____. Individuals start using this technique at around age _____.

(c) Suppose you want to commit to memory the names of Piaget's stages. You come up with this mnemonic: Some Psychologists Can't Forget (S, P, C, F). Even better, you think of the meaning of the stage names and create new examples that illustrate each one. You are using _____, which tends to occur only after age _____.

10-5. As children grow older they are able to perform mental tasks more rapidly; in the language of computers, their _____ speed increases.

10-6. As shown in Figure 11.14, processing speed increases with age, and the shape of the curves produced is extremely (different/similar) across a wide variety of cognitive tasks. This similarity suggests that a developmental change has occurred in some very general component of information processing, but the exact nature of this component is (known/unknown).

Answers: 10-1. computer, cognitive **10-2.** span **10-3.** selectively **10-4.** (a) rehearsal, 8 (b) organization, 9 (c) elaboration, 11 **10-5.** processing **10-6.** similar, unknown.

11. Outline Kohlberg's stages of moral development and summarize the strengths and weaknesses of Kohlberg's theory.

11-1. Kohlberg's theory includes three moral levels, each with two stages for a total of six stages. Indicate which of the three moral levels is described in each of the following statements.

(a) Acts are considered wrong because they are punished or right because they lead to positive consequences. _____

(b) Individuals at this level conform very strictly to society's rules, which they accept as absolute and inviolable. _____

(c) This level is characterized by situational or conditional morality, such that stealing might be considered wrong in one circumstance but permissible in another. _____

11-2. The central ideas of Kohlberg's theory have received a fair amount of support. Research has found that children (do/do not) tend to progress through Kohlberg's stages in the order that he indicated. As children get older, stages 1 and 2 reasoning tend to decrease while stages 3 and 4 reasoning tend to _____.

11-3. There have also been several criticisms of Kohlberg's theory. First, moral development is not as consistently uniform as the theory implies. As was the case with other stage theories, there tends to be a "_____" of stages in which characteristics of several stages may appear at once.

11-4. Second, researchers have focused too heavily on (<u>Kohlberg's/newly created</u>) dilemmas, which tends to narrow the scope of research on moral reasoning.

11-5. Third, some critics suggest that Kohlberg's theory reflects liberal, individualistic values that characterize modern _____ societies rather than human beings in general. In other words, the theory may be much more (<u>value-free/culture-specific</u>) than Kohlberg supposed.

11-6. Fourth, Gilligan has asserted that Kohlberg's theory reflects a male point of view, with an emphasis on _____, as opposed to a more feminine morality based on _____ and self-sacrifice. While some evidence supports Gilligan's idea about gender differences in interpretations of moral dilemmas, research thus far (<u>has/has not</u>) found differences in the *ages* at which males and females go through Kohlberg's stages.

Answers: **11-1.** (a) preconventional (b) conventional (c) postconventional **11-2.** do, increase **11-3.** mixing **11-4.** Kohlberg's **11-5.** Western, culture-specific **11-6.** justice, caring, has not.

12. Describe developmental trends in altruism and aggression and explain how both are shaped by heredity, parental modeling, and media role models.

12-1. Altruism involves behavior that is intended to help others. Aggression is intended to hurt others. In general, _____ tends to increase with age, and _____ tends to decrease with age.

12-2. Type of aggression also changes with age. Younger children display more *instrumental* aggression, aggression directed toward obtaining a particular _____. Older children display more *hostile* aggression, aggression directed toward _____ someone rather than accomplishing an objective.

12-3. As individuals age, their aggression also tends to become less physical and more _____.

12-4. There are strong individual differences among children in the degree of altruism and aggression that they exhibit, and there are clear gender differences. At all ages beyond two, _____ tend to be noticeably more aggressive than girls.

12-5. What specific evidence from twin studies indicates that aggression and altruism are influenced by heredity?

12-6. In addition to their genetic inheritance, children acquire aggressive or altruistic behaviors through reinforcement. They also learn by _____ the behavior of their parents and other models. For both altruism and aggression, the evidence indicates that children are much more influenced by what they see their parents (<u>doing/saying</u>) than by hearing what they say.

12-7. Children are also influenced by the mass media, especially by what they see on television. Evidence has indicated that children will tend to model both the altruism and the aggression portrayed on television. Unfortunately, they are exposed much more frequently to _____ than to _____ models.

13. Describe the Featured Study on the effects of exposure to media violence.

13-1. Eron et al. (1983) studied two groups of children in an "overlapping" longitudinal study for a period of three years. The researchers observed one group of children from the first through the

_____ grade and the second group simultaneously from the third through the

_____ grade.

13-2. How did the researchers assess the *amount of television* the children watched?

13-3. How did they assess the degree of *aggressiveness* in the children?

13-4. Indicate true (T) or false (F) for each of the following statements.

_____ The correlations between amount of violent TV viewed and aggressiveness were statistically significant but relatively small in magnitude.

_____ In contrast to the researcher's earlier study, the correlations occurred for girls as well as for boys.

_____ From this study alone one could reasonably conclude that television violence causes aggressive behavior.

_____ The results of this study taken in combination with other studies on media violence justify the conclusion that media violence is causally, if modestly, related to aggressive behavior.

THE TRANSITION OF ADOLESCENCE

14. Describe the major events of puberty and discuss the problem of unusually early or late maturation.

14-1. Read over the section on puberty in the text, then fill in the blanks below with the appropriate terms.

(a) _____ The approximately two-year span preceding puberty that is marked by rapid growth in height and weight.

(b) _____ The period of time during which secondary sex characteristics appear.

(c) _____ The term that refers to physical features that distinguish one sex from another but that are not essential for reproduction (e.g., facial hair in males, breasts in females).

(d) _____ The stage during which sexual functions essential for reproduction reach maturity.

(e) _____ The stage that begins with menarche in females and the production of sperm in males.

(f) _____ The term that refers to the first occurrence of menstruation.

(g) _____ The transitional period between childhood and adulthood in which young people are physiologically mature but have not achieved emotional and economic independence from their parents.

(h) _____ In our society this stage begins at around age 13 and ends at about age 22.

14-2. Adolescents who mature especially early or late may feel uncomfortable about their appearance, particularly girls who mature (early/late) and boys who mature (early/late). For both boys and girls ((early/late) maturation is more likely to be associated with problems involving self-control, emotional stability, and drugs.

Answers: 14-1. (a) pubescence (b) pubescence (c) secondary sex characteristics (d) puberty (e) puberty (f) menarche (g) adolescence (h) adolescence **14-2.** early, late, early.

15. Evaluate the assertion that adolescence is a time of turmoil.

15-1. Imagine that you are at a social gathering. The subject of adolescent stress comes up, and someone says, "It's such a turbulent period, it's no wonder that so many adolescents commit suicide." Suicide at any age is disturbing, but you disagree that adolescence is either so turbulent or characterized by such a large number of suicides. What data would you refer to that back up your assertions?

Answers: 15-1. (1) While suicide among adolescents has increased dramatically in recent decades (Figure 11.20a), the suicide rate for adolescents (ages 15-24 in Figure 11.20b) is *lower than for any older age group.* (Attempted suicide is higher among adolescents than older age groups, however.) Research indicates that, in general, adolescents encounter no more turmoil than people encounter in other periods of life.

16. Explain why the struggle for a sense of identity is particularly intense during adolescence and discuss some common patterns of identity formation.

16-1. Adolescence is a period of change, so it is readily understandable that adolescents tend to focus on the struggle for _____, the question of "Who am I?"

16-2. Recall that Erik Erikson described four crises that mark childhood. What is the crisis that marks adolescence, according to Erikson? _____ vs. _____

16-3. Marcia (1966, 1980) has described four orientations that people may adopt in attempting to resolve the identity crisis. These are not stages that people pass through in an orderly manner but statuses that they may adopt on either a relatively permanent or temporary basis. One possible status is simply to take on the values and roles prescribed by one's parents; this is termed _____. While this may temporarily resolve the crisis, in the long run the individual may not be comfortable with the adopted identity. A second orientation involves a period of experimentation with various ideologies and careers and a delay in commitment to any one; this is termed _____. If the experimentation and lack of commitment become permanent, the individual is said to be in a status of _____ _____. On the other hand, if the consideration of alternatives leads to conviction about a sense of self, one takes on the status referred to as _____ _____.

THE EXPANSE OF ADULTHOOD

17. Summarize evidence on the stability of personality and the prevalence of the mid-life crisis.

17-1. Do people change throughout their lifetimes, or does personality tend to remain the same? Research evidence supports the conclusion that:

    a. personality is stable across one's lifetime

    b. personality changes across one's lifetime

    c. both of the above

    d. neither of the above

17-2. Explain how it is possible that personality appears both to stay the same and to change dramatically over time.

17-3. Two influential studies conducted in the 1970s asserted that people experience a period of emotional turmoil some time between ages 35 and 45, a transitional phase known as the _____ _____.

17-4. The midlife crisis, described as a period of reappraisal and assessment of time left, was thought by the original writers (Gould and Levinson) to be a transitional phase that affected (a minority/most) adults. More recently, a large number of other investigators have found that the midlife crisis characterizes (a minority of/most) adults.

17-5. The disparity between the conclusions of Gould and of Levinson and those of the more recent researchers may have to do with the difference in methods used. Explain.

18. Outline Erikson's stages of development in adulthood.

18-1. In the spaces below write the names of the crises that mark Erikson's three stages of adulthood. In the parentheses indicate the approximate period of adulthood during which the crises are supposed to occur.

(a)_____ vs. _____   (   )

(b)_____ vs. _____   (   )

(c)_____ vs. _____   (   )

18-2. Following are descriptions of the crises occurring in each of the above stages. Indicate the stages by placing the appropriate letters (a, b, or c from the previous question) in the blanks.

_____ Concern for helping future generations versus a self-indulgent concern for meeting one's own desires.

_____ Concern to find meaning in the remainder of one's life versus a preoccupation with earlier failures and eventual death.

_____ Concern for developing a capacity for intimacy with others versus a strategy in which others are manipulated as a means to an end.

Answers: 18-1. (a) intimacy vs. isolation (early adulthood) (b) generativity vs. self-absorption (middle adulthood) (c) integrity vs. despair (aging years) **18-2.** b, c, a.

19. Describe typical transitions in family relations during the adult years.

19-1. In contemporary American society there are many living arrangements other than the traditional family consisting of never-divorced parents, a breadwinner father and homemaker mother, and two or more kids. In fact, only _____ percent of American families fits this image.

19-2. In part as a result of economic factors and in part due to an increased emphasis on personal autonomy, remaining single or postponing marriage is a much more acceptable option today than it was a few decades ago. Nonetheless, people emerge from families and most ultimately form new families. Over _____ % of adults eventually marry.

19-3. While the first few years of married life tend to be quite happy, the current era of changing gender roles is likely to cause tension for the newly married. According to a recent survey, men and women have different views about the meaning of the term *equality*. What do *men* mean by equality in marriage? How do *women* define this concept? What is the evidence about task sharing?

19-4. What event in the family cycle tends to cause the first drop in marital satisfaction? When does marital satisfaction tend to start climbing back?

Answers: 19-1. 7 **19-2.** 90 **19-3.** In one recent survey, half the men were unable to define equality in marriage at all; the other half defined it in psychological terms. Women defined it more concretely—in terms of sharing tasks and responsibilities. The evidence indicates that women are still doing the bulk of the housework in America even when employed outside the home. **19-4.** Although most parents report having no regrets about having children, marital satisfaction tends to drop at the birth of the first child. Marital satisfaction tends to increase when children leave home. The "empty nest" seems to have little lasting negative impact.

20. Discuss patterns of career development in both men and women.

20-1. Donald Super breaks career development into five major stages. List these stages in the spaces below next to the approximate ages at which they occur. (See Table 11.2.)

_____ (birth to adolescence)

_____ (adolescence to mid 20s)

_____ (mid 20s to mid 40s)

_____ (mid 40s to mid 60s)

_____ (mid 60s on)

20-2. Following are descriptions of events that may occur during the five stages. Place the names of the stages described in the appropriate blanks. (Refer to your text and Table 11.2.)

_____ This stage ranges from no thought about vocation to thought based on fantasy, then likes and dislikes, then ability.

_____ The individual finishes school, may try out various work experiences, shifts jobs if the first are not gratifying.

_____ The person is likely to receive support and guidance from a mentor.

_____ Future job moves almost always take place within the same occupational area.

_____ The concern is with retaining achieved status rather than improving it.

_____ Energy may shift from work to the family or leisure activities.

_____ Involves preparation to leave the work place.

20-3. Most of the research findings on career development summarized above are based on (men/women). Although it was originally believed that these findings would apply equally well to women, evidence has indicated that this (is/is not) the case. The pattern for men frequently reveals a clear, consistent path toward vocational success; the pattern for women is much less predictable and may be characterized as nearly _____.

20-4. Which of the following are factors that contribute to the less direct career paths of women? Place a T next to statements that are likely factors, an F next to those that are not.

_____ Women are more likely than men to interrupt their careers for child rearing or other family reasons.

_____ Women place as much priority on their own career goals as those of their husbands.

_____ Women are less likely than men to enjoy the benefits of mentoring (e.g., "old boy" network).

_____ Women face discrimination, especially at upper management levels (the "glass ceiling").

Answers: 20-1. growth, exploration, establishment, maintenance, decline **20-2.** growth, exploration, establishment, establishment, maintenance, maintenance, decline **20-3.** men, is not, random **20-4.** T, F, T, T.

21. Describe the physical changes associated with aging.

21-1.   As we age, our physical and cognitive characteristics change. Indicate which of the following physical traits increase and which decrease by placing checkmarks in the appropriate blanks.

	INCREASES	DECREASES
Physical changes		
Proportion of body fat:	_____	_____
Overall weight:	_____	_____
Number of neurons in the brain :	_____	_____
Visual acuity:	_____	_____
Ability to see close:	_____	_____
Hearing:	_____	_____

Answers: 21-1. Body fat and overall weight increase (except that overall weight may decrease somewhat after the mid-50s); the rest decrease.

22. Describe the cognitive changes associated with aging.

22-1.   Indicate which of the following cognitive traits and which decrease by placing checkmarks in the appropriate blanks.

	INCREASES	DECREASES
Cognitive changes		
Memory:	_____	_____
Speed of learning:	_____	_____
Processing speed:	_____	_____
Speed of solving problems:	_____	_____

22-2.   Despite the decline in physical and cognitive capacities, aging is not so bad as it may at first seem. The increase in body fat is largely (<u>cosmetic/debilitating</u>) rather than functional, and the loss of visual and hearing acuity may be compensated for with glasses and hearing aids.

22-3.   With regard to loss of brain cells, it's not so much a matter of "who needs 'em" as that the gradual loss appears to have (<u>little/a strong</u>) effect on functioning. Women's reaction to menopause varies a great deal, but the evidence in general is that menopause is accompanied by (<u>intense/little</u>) emotional distress.

22-4.   Intellectual performance and memory decline (<u>modestly/sharply</u>) with advancing age and (<u>are/are not</u>) universal. Speed of problem solving generally does (<u>increase/decrease</u>) with age, but problem solving ability is largely unimpaired if time is not a factor.

Answers: 22-1. All of these cognitive characteristics decrease. **22-2.** cosmetic **22-3.** little, little **22-4.** modestly, are not, decreases.

PUTTING IT IN PERSPECTIVE

23. Explain how this chapter highlighted the interaction of heredity and environment.

23-1.   The behavior of a child is the result of the child's genetic inheritance and its environment, which includes the behavior of the child's parents. In turn, the behavior of the parents toward the child is affected both by their inherited characteristics and by the behavior of the child. Thus, behavior is the result not of heredity or environment operating separately but of an _____ between the two factors.

23-2. To understand the concept of *interaction* consider this problem: There is a form of mental retardation that results from phenylketonuria, an inherited inability to metabolize a common amino acid in milk. When fed milk, children born with phenylketonuria become mentally retarded. Is this type of retardation an inherited disorder?

a. Yes, it's genetic.

b. No, it's caused by the environment.

c. A certain proportion of the causal factors are hereditary and the remainder due to the environment.

d. The disorder results from heredity and environment operating jointly.

23-3. This chapter has been concerned with changes in human behavior across the life span. The theme being stressed here is that these changes result from an *interaction* of heredity and environment. In your own words, explain how the interaction operates.

Answers: 23-1. interaction **23-2.** d. (This disorder might at first seem to be inherited, since there is a genetic trait involved. But the retardation does not occur if the infant is not fed milk products, which involves the environment. The point is that this disorder, like behavior in general, cannot be attributed solely to nature or to nurture or even to relative weights of each: It is a function of an *interaction* between the two. **23-3.** The interaction of heredity and environment refers to the fact that we are a product of both factors. It means more than that, however. Heredity and environment don't operate separately. Interaction means that the genetic factors affect the operation of the environment and that environmental factors affect genetic predispositions. The influence of one factor *depends on* the effects of the other.

APPLICATION: UNDERSTANDING GENDER DIFFERENCES

24. Summarize evidence on gender differences in behavior and discuss the significance of these differences.

24-1. Which gender tends to show more of (or score higher on tests of) the following abilities or traits? Circle the correct answer at the right.

Cognitive

verbal skills	MALES	FEMALES	NEITHER
mathematical skills	MALES	FEMALES	NEITHER
visual-spatial skills	MALES	FEMALES	NEITHER

Social

aggression	MALES	FEMALES	NEITHER
sensitivity to nonverbal cues	MALES	FEMALES	NEITHER
susceptibility to influence	MALES	FEMALES	NEITHER
sexually permissiveness	MALES	FEMALES	NEITHER
assertiveness	MALES	FEMALES	NEITHER
anxiety	MALES	FEMALES	NEITHER
nurturance	MALES	FEMALES	NEITHER

24-2. There is an enormous overlap between the genders with regard to these traits. There are, of course, many females who are more aggressive than the average male and many males who are more sensitive to nonverbal cues than the average female. Thus, it is important to note that the differences referred to in this section are differences between group _____ and that the size of the differences is relatively _____.

Answers: 24-1. cognitive: females, males, males; social: males, females, females, males, males, females, females **24-2.** averages (means), small.

25. Explain how biological factors are thought to contribute to gender differences.

25-1. For evolutionary theorists, the relative invariance of gender differences found across cultures reflects natural selection. From this perspective males are more sexually active and permissive than females because reproductive success for males is maximized by seeking (<u>few/many</u>) sexual partners. Greater aggressiveness has survival value for males because it enhances their ability to acquire material _____ sought by females selecting a mate.

25-2. Evolutionary theorists also assert that ability differences between the genders reflect the division of labor in our ancestral past. Males were primarily the hunters and females the gatherers, and the adaptive demands of hunting may have produced males' superiority at most _____ tasks.

25-3. The evolutionary view of gender is certainly an interesting and plausible explanation of the remarkable similarity in gender differences across cultures. For several reasons, however, the theory is (<u>controversial/universally accepted</u>). For one thing, there are reasonable alternative theories of gender differences; for another, the evolutionary explanation is relatively (<u>easy/difficult</u>) to test empirically.

25-4. In addition, evolutionary analysis can be used to explain almost anything. What if females had happened, on the average, to be more aggressive and more sexually permissive than males? Could you come up with a plausible-sounding evolutionary explanation of gender differences in this case?

25-5. Several studies suggest that hormones are a major factor in shaping gender differences. For example, females exposed prenatally to high levels of an _____-like drug given their mothers during pregnancy tend to show more male-typical behavior than do other females. Recent studies have also found that normal aging men given testosterone to enhance their sexual function also show increases in _____ perception.

25-6. While the research just described supports the role of biology in gender development it is, for several reasons, not conclusive. For one thing, the studies are based on small samples of people who have abnormal conditions. For another, most of the research is by necessity (<u>experimental/correlational</u>), and there are plausible alternative explanations for the findings.

25-7. Other biological evidence suggests that males depend more heavily on the left hemisphere for verbal processing and the right for spatial processing than is the case with females. In other words, males may tend to exhibit more cerebral _____ than females. Results on this topic have been mixed, however. Even if future research eventually supports the idea that males have more cerebral specialization than females, it would be difficult to see how that would account for the observed gender differences, such as the superiority of males on spatial tasks and the superiority of females on _____ tasks.

Answers: 25-1. many, resources 25-2. spatial (visual-spatial) 25-3. controversial, difficult 25-4. Yes, you probably could. I don't think I'll venture forth with some possibilities in this answer space, however. 25-5. androgen, spatial (visual-spatial) 25-6. correlational 25-7. specialization, verbal

26. Explain how environmental factors are thought to contribute to gender differences.

26-1.   Research on the role of biology in determining gender is intriguing but still open to dispute. The effect of environmental factors on gender roles is less controversial. Children learn as a result of the consequences for their behavior, the rewards and punishments that they receive in the process of _____ conditioning.

26-2.   Children also acquire information by seeing what others do, the process of _____ learning. While children imitate both males and females, they are more likely to imitate the behavior of (same-sex/opposite-sex) models.

26-3.   In addition to operant conditioning and observational learning, children are active participants in their own gender-role socialization, the process referred to as _____-socialization. First, once they discover (at age 5 or 6) that being a boy or girl is a permanent condition, they will then _____ themselves as boys or girls. Second, following classification in terms of gender children will _____ characteristics and behaviors associated with their gender. Third, they will bring their _____ in line with their values by engaging in "sex-appropriate" behaviors.

26-4.   Whether through operant conditioning, observational learning, or self-socialization, the major forces for gender-role socialization occur in three main aspects of the child's environment: in their _____, in _____, and in the _____.

Answers: 26-1. operant 26-2. observational (modeling), same-sex 26-3. self, classify (categorize), value, behavior 26-4. families, schools, media.

REVIEW OF KEY TERMS

Accommodation	Epigenetic principle —	Object permanence
Age of viability	Family life cycle	Placenta
Aggression	Fetal alcohol syndrome	Prenatal period
Altruism	Fetal stage	Primary sex characteristics
Animism	Gender	Proximodistal trend
Assimilation	Gender differences	Puberty
Attachment	Gender roles	Pubescence
Centration	Gender stereotypes	Secondary sex characteristics
Cephalocaudal trend	Germinal stage	Separation anxiety
Cognitive development	Irreversibility	Sex
Conservation	Longitudinal design	Social clock
Cross-sectional design	Maturation	Socialization
Dementia	Menarche	Stage
Development	Mentor	Temperament
Developmental norms	Meta-analysis	Visual cliff
Egocentrism	Motor development	Zygote
Embryonic stage		

_____ 1. The sequence of age-related changes that occurs as a person progresses from conception to death.

_____ 2. The period of pregnancy, extending from conception to birth.

_____ 3. The first two weeks after conception.

_____ 4. The structure that connects the circulation of the fetus and the mother but that blocks passage of blood cells.

_____ 5. The second stage of prenatal development, lasting from two weeks after conception until the end of the second month.

_____ 6. The third stage of prenatal development, lasting from two months after conception through birth.

_____ 7. The age at which the baby can first survive in the event of a premature birth.

_____ 8. A collection of congenital problems associated with a mother's excessive use of alcohol during pregnancy.

_____ 9. An experimental apparatus that includes a glass platform extending over a several-foot drop.

_____ 10. Developmental changes in muscular coordination required for physical movement.

_____ 11. The head-to-foot direction of motor development.

_____ 12. The center-outward direction of motor development.

_____ 13. The average ages at which people display certain behaviors and abilities.

_____ 14. Characteristic mood, energy level, and reactivity.

_____ 15. One group of subjects is observed over a long period of time.

_____ 16. Investigators compare groups of subjects of differing ages at a single point in time.

_____ 17. The idea that parts give rise to the whole; in Erikson's theory, the notion that each stage contributes to the ultimate personality.

_____ 18. Emotional distress displayed by an infant when separated from a person with whom it has formed an attachment.

_____ 19. Culturally constructed distinctions between femininity and masculinity.

_____ 20. Widely held beliefs about females' and males' abilities, personality traits, and social behavior.

_____ 21. Development of thinking, reasoning, remembering, and problem solving.

_____ 22. Interpreting new experiences in terms of mental structures already available.

_____ 23. Altering existing mental structures to explain new experiences.

_____ 24. A mental capacity that involves recognizing that objects continue to exist even when they are no longer visible.

_____ 25. Piaget's term for the awareness that physical quantities remain constant in spite of changes in their shape or appearance.

_____ 26. The Piagetian term for the tendency to focus on just one feature of a problem and neglect other important features.

_____ 27. The inability to cognitively visualize reversing an action.

_____ 28. Thinking characterized by a limited ability to share another person's viewpoint.

_____ 29. A sequence of stages that families tend to progress through.

_____ 30. Someone with a senior position in an organization who serves as a role model, tutor, and advisor to a younger worker.

_____ 31. The attribution of lifelike qualities to inanimate objects.

_____ 32. A developmental period during which certain behaviors and capacities occur.

_____ 33. The biologically based categories of male and female.

_____ 34. Any behavior, either physical or verbal, that is intended to hurt someone.

_____ 35. Concern with the welfare of others, cooperation, and helping of others.

_____ 36. A close, emotional bond of affection between an infant and its caregiver.

_____ 37. Physical features associated with gender that are not directly needed for reproduction.

_____ 38. The physical structures necessary for reproduction.

_____ 39. The two-year span preceding puberty marked by the appearance of secondary sex characteristics and by rapid growth.

_____ 40. The first occurrence of menstruation.

_____ 41. The stage during which reproductive functions reach maturity.

_____ 42. A person's notion of a developmental schedule that specifies what he or she should have accomplished by certain points in life.

_____ 43. Developmental changes that reflect one's genetic blueprint rather than environment.

_____ 44. A one-celled organism created by the process of fertilization, the union of sperm and egg.

_____ 45. Behavioral differences between females and males.

_____ 46. A statistical procedure for combining data from different studies to estimate the size of a particular variable's effects.

_____ 47. The acquisition of norms, roles, and behaviors expected of people in a particular group.

_____ 48. Expectations concerning what is the appropriate behavior for each sex.

_____ 49. An abnormal condition marked by multiple cognitive deficits; more prevalent in older adults but not a product of normal aging but.

Answers: 1. development **2.** prenatal period **3.** germinal stage **4.** placenta **5.** embryonic stage **6.** fetal stage **7.** age of viability **8.** fetal alcohol syndrome **9.** visual cliff **10.** motor development **11.** cephalocaudal trend **12.** proximodistal trend **13.** developmental norms **14.** temperament **15.** longitudinal design **16.** cross-sectional design **17.** epigenetic principle **18.** separation anxiety **19.** gender **20.** gender stereotypes **21.** cognitive development **22.** assimilation **23.** accommodation **24.** object permanence **25.** conservation **26.** centration **27** irreversibility **28.** egocentrism **29.** family life cycle **30.** mentor **31.** animism **32.** stage **33.** sex **34.** aggression **35.** altruism **36.** attachment **37.** secondary sex characteristics **38.** primary sex characteristics **39.** pubescence **40.** menarche **41.** puberty **42.** social clock **43.** maturation **44.** zygote **45.** gender differences **46.** meta-analysis **47.** socialization **48.** gender roles **49.** dementia.

REVIEW OF KEY PEOPLE

Mary Ainsworth   Harry & Margaret Harlow Jean Piaget
John Bowlby   Lawrence Kohlberg   Alexander Thomas & Stella Chess
Erik Erikson

_____   1. Conducted a major longitudinal study in which they identified three basic styles of children's temperament.

_____   2. Used cloth and wire "substitute mothers" to study attachment in infant rhesus monkeys.

_____   3. Theorized that there are critical periods in human infants' lives during which attachments must occur for normal development to take place.

_____   4. Partitioned the life span into eight stages, each accompanied by a psychosocial crisis.

_____   5. Pioneered the study of children's cognitive development.

_____   6. Developed a stage theory of moral development.

_____   7. Described three categories of infant-mother attachment.

Answers: 1. Thomas & Chess **2.** Harlow & Harlow **3.** Bowlby **4.** Erikson **5.** Piaget **6.** Kohlberg **7.** Ainsworth.

SELF-QUIZ

1. Which prenatal period begins at the second week and ends at the second month of pregnancy?
   a. germinal stage
   b. embryonic stage
   c. fetal stage
   d. none of the above

2. In which prenatal stage do most major birth defects probably have their origins?
   a. germinal stage
   b. embryonic stage
   c. fetal stage
   d. none of the above

3. Which of the following senses seems to be weakest in the newborn?
   a. vision
   b. hearing
   c. smell
   d. touch

4. Maturation refers to developmental changes that occur in an organism as a result of:
   a. accommodation and assimilation
   b. genetic factors
   c. environmental factors
   d. parental and peer pressures

5. What is the major conclusion from Thomas and Chess's longitudinal study of temperament?
   a. Children's temperaments tend to go through predictable stages.
   b. The temperament of the child is not a good predictor of the temperament of the adult.
   c. Opposites attract.
   d. Children's temperaments tend to be consistent over the years.

6. The crisis occurring in the first year, according to Erikson, is one involving:
   a. trust versus mistrust
   b. initiative versus guilt
   c. industry versus inferiority
   d. all of the above

7. During which stage in Piaget's system is the child able to understand conservation but unable to handle hierarchical classification?
   a. sensorimotor
   b. preoperational
   c. concrete operations
   d. formal operations

8. A child in the early sensorimotor period is shown a ball, which she watches intensely. The ball is then hidden under a pillow. What will the child do?
   a. ask, "Where is the pillow?"
   b. stare at the pillow but not pick it up
   c. move the pillow and pick up the ball
   d. ignore the pillow, as if the ball didn't exist

9. Who developed a stage theory of moral development?
   a. Piaget
   b. Kohlberg
   c. Gould
   d. Bowlby

10. Aggressiveness in human beings seems to be caused by:
    a. watching aggressive acts on TV
    b. biological (genetic) factors
    c. parental modeling
    d. all of the above

11. Suicide in the 15–24 age group occurs:
    a. more frequently than in any other age group
    b. less frequently than in any other age group
    c. more frequently than the 65–74 age group
    d. at the same level as the 65–74 age group

12. Which of the following factors tends to be accompanied by a drop in ratings of marital satisfaction?
    a. childlessness during early married life
    b. the birth of the first child
    c. the first child's departure for college
    d. when the last child leaves home

13. Females tend to score slightly higher than males on tests of:
    a. verbal ability
    b. mathematical ability
    c. visual-spatial ability
    d. none of the above

14. Females exposed to high levels of androgen during prenatal development tend to show:
    a. more male-typical behavior than other females
    b. more stereotypic female behavior than other females
    c. less cerebral specialization than other females
    d. a larger corpus collosum than other females

15. Once children discover that their gender is permanent, they are likely to want to engage in behavior that is "sex appropriate" as defined by the culture. This process is referred to as:
    a. operant conditioning
    b. observational learning
    c. self-socialization
    d. none of the above

Answers: 1. b **2.** b **3.** c **4.** b **5.** d **6.** a **7.** c **8.** d **9.** b **10.** d **11.** b **12.** b **13.** a **14.** a **15.** c.

Chapter Twelve

Personality: Theory, Research, and Assessment

REVIEW OF KEY IDEAS

THE NATURE OF PERSONALITY

1-1. I can always tell when my colleague across the hall has finished for the day because I hear squeaking as he carefully moves his computer table under his bookcase. And I know what follows: He closes and reshelves his books, sorts the papers on his desk into two piles, and slides the pens and pencils into his desk drawer bin. The fact that my colleague engages in the *same behaviors* almost every day illustrates the feature of personality termed _____.

1-2. When I'm done, on the other hand, I usually just stand up and walk out, leaving my generally messy desk behind. The fact that my colleague and I *differ* with respect to office neatness illustrates the feature of personality termed _____.

Answers: **1-1.** consistency (stability) **1-2.** distinctiveness (behavioral differences).

2. Explain what is meant by a personality trait and describe proposed systems for organizing traits.

2-1. A consistent tendency to behave in a particular way is referred to as a personality _____. Personality trait descriptions frequently consist of a series of _____, such as anxious, excitable, shy, aggressive, and so on.

2-2. There are an enormous number of trait words that could be used to describe people, and psychologists have devised several different systems in an attempt to classify these terms. For example, Gordon Allport proposed 4500 personality traits classified into three levels: _____ traits, which characterize almost all of a person's behavior (but are displayed by very few people); _____ traits, the five or ten dominant traits possessed by most people; and _____ traits, the less-consistent dispositions that occur in some situations but not others.

2-3. Using factor analysis Raymond Cattell reduced Allport's list of 4500 trait words to just _____ basic traits. McCrae and Costa, also using the factor-analysis technique, have come up with yet a simpler model involving only _____

2-4. Some researchers contend that more than five factors are needed to describe personality and others maintain that fewer than five are needed. Of the various models, however, the dominant conception of personality structure is currently the _____-factor model.

2-5. Below are listed some of the adjectives that describe each of the five factors. List the name of each of the factors next to the appropriate adjectives. (The five factors are relatively easy to remember if one thinks of NEO, which may mean "new," and adds AC: NEOAC.)

_____: outgoing, sociable

_____: imaginative, nonconforming

_____: anxious, insecure

_____: dependable, disciplined

_____: sympathetic, trusting

Answers: 2-1. traits, adjectives **2-2.** cardinal, central, secondary **2-3.** 16, five **2-4.** five **2-5.** extraversion, openness to experience, neuroticism, conscientiousness, agreeableness.

PSYCHODYNAMIC PERSPECTIVES

3. List and describe the three components into which Freud divided the personality and indicate how these are distributed across three levels of awareness.

— **3-1.** Below is a schematic illustration of the three Freudian structures of personality. Label each.

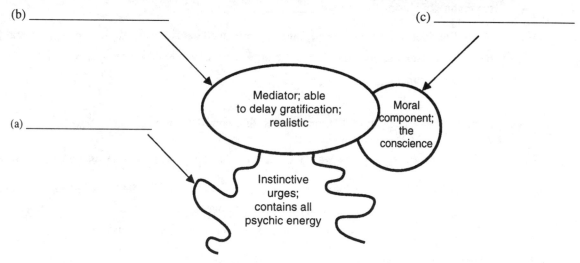

(b) _____

(c) _____

(a) _____

Mediator; able to delay gratification; realistic

Moral component; the conscience

Instinctive urges; contains all psychic energy

3-2. Freud superimposed the levels of consciousness on the psychic structures. The following illustration makes clear that two of the structures exist at all three levels while one is entirely unconscious. Label the levels.

(a) _____

(b) _____

(c) _____

Answers: **3-1.** (a) id (b) ego (c) superego **3-2.** (a) conscious (b) preconscious (c) unconscious. (The diagram shows that the ego emerges from the id and that the superego grows out of the ego.)

---

4. **Explain the preeminence of sexual and aggressive conflicts in Freud's theory and describe the operation of defense mechanisms.**

4-1. Freud believed that most of our conflicts arise from _____ and _____ urges. Conflicts relating to these areas were preeminent in his mind because (1) they are subject to subtle social _____ and, for that reason, are a source of confusion; and (2) they are less likely to be immediately gratified and more apt to be _____ than other urges.

4-2. Following is a list of the defense mechanisms. Match each with the correct description by placing the appropriate letters in the blanks.

A. rationalization D. displacement F. regression

B. repression   E. reaction formation G. identification

C. projection

_____ A return to an earlier, less mature stage of development.

_____ Forming an imaginary or real alliance with a person or group; becoming like them.

_____ Creating false but reasonable-sounding excuses.

_____ Pushing distressing thoughts into the unconscious.

_____ Attributing ones own thoughts, feelings, or conflicts to another.

_____ Expressing an emotion that is the exact opposite of the way one really, but unconsciously, feels.

_____ Diverting emotional feelings from their original source to a substitute target.

4-3. Using the letters from the previous question, match the defense mechanisms with the following examples.

_____ After John and Marsha break up, John says he hates Marsha; this statement helps him defend against his real feelings of affection.

_____ "Society is filled with perverts," says the preacher; but later evidence suggests that he is the one with the sexual conflicts.

_____ In reaction to the stress of entering college, Alice starts acting like a grade-school kid.

_____ Bruce acts like John Wayne, and he owns tapes of all the Duke's movies.

_____ Mary is angry at her mother, so she kicks her baby brother.

5. Outline Freud's psychosexual stages of development and their theorized relations to adult personality.

5-1. List Freud's stages of psychosexual development, in the order in which they are supposed to occur, in the blanks below. Place the ages in the parentheses.

(a) _____ ( )

(b) _____ ( )

(c) _____ ( )

(d) _____ ( )

(e) _____ ( )

5-2. The following behaviors or personality characteristics are supposed to result from fixation at a particular psychosexual stage. Place the names of the correct stages in the blanks.

(a) She has problems with anger control, is hostile toward people in authority, and defies any attempt at regulation of her behavior. _____

(b) He eats too much, drinks too much, and smokes. _____

(c) He has occasional outbursts of hostility toward his father that he can't understand. In family arguments he sides with his mother. _____

5-3. The Oedipus complex occurs during the _____ stage, between the ages of _____ and _____. This complex theoretically involves an erotically tinged attraction toward the (<u>same-sex/opposite-sex</u>) parent and a strong hostility toward the (<u>same-sex/opposite-sex</u>) parent. Resolution of the Oedipus complex involves (<u>increasing/stopping</u>) both the child's erotic attraction and the child's hostility.

6. Summarize the revisions of Freud's theory proposed by Jung and Adler.

6-1. Freud devised the theory and method of treatment termed *psychoanalysis*. To differentiate his approach from Freud's, Jung called his theory _____ _____. Like Freud, Jung emphasized the unconscious determinants of personality. Unlike Freud, he proposed that the unconscious consists of two layers, a _____ unconscious and a _____ unconscious. The personal unconscious is similar to Freud's unconscious, but it has less emphasis on sexuality. The collective unconscious is a repository of inherited, ancestral memories that Jung termed

_____.

6-2. Jung's major contribution to psychology is considered by many to be his description of two major personality types: _____, reserved, contemplative people who tend to be concerned with their own internal world of thoughts; and _____, outgoing people who are more interested in the external world of others.

6-3. For Freud, the driving energy behind the human personality was sexuality; for Jung it may have been the collective unconscious. For Adler, it was striving for _____ and the attempt to overcome childhood feelings of inferiority. Efforts to overcome imagined or real inferiorities involve _____ through development of one's abilities. While Adler considered compensation to be a normal mechanism, he saw _____ as an abnormal attempt to conceal feelings of inferiority.

6-4. Adler is associated with the term _____ _____, an exaggerated feeling of inadequacy supposedly caused by parental pampering or neglect in early childhood. To a greater extent than either Freud or Jung, Adler emphasized the effects of the social context on personality development. For example, he thought that _____ _____ (that is, whether one is an only child, first-born, second-born, etc.) had a major effect on personality. Although the concept created considerable interest, birth order has turned out to be a (<u>weaker/ stronger</u>) and (<u>more/less</u>) consistent factor than he had supposed.

Answers: 6-1. analytical psychology, personal, collective, archetypes **6-2.** introverts, extraverts **6-3.** superiority, compensation, overcompensation **6-4.** inferiority complex, birth order, weaker, less.

7. Summarize the strengths and weaknesses of the psychodynamic approach to personality.

7-1. Psychoanalytic formulations have had a major impact on the field of psychology. List the three contributions discussed in your text.

7-2. Psychoanalytic formulations have also been extensively criticized. After each of the following statements list the particular criticism, from the discussion in your text, that the statement represents.

(a) Freud proposed that females develop weaker superegos and that they have a chronic sense of inferiority caused by penis envy. _____

(b) Although he discussed some characteristics associated with the psychosexual stages, Freud didn't really specify which events, occurring during which childhood stages, produce which sets of personality traits. _____ _____

(c) Support for the theories has been provided solely by clinical case studies and by clinical intuition.
_____ _____

Answers: 7-1. the discovery that *unconscious forces* can influence behavior, that *internal conflict* may generate psychological distress, and that *early childhood experiences* influence the adult personality **7-2.** (a) sexism (b) poor testability (c) inadequate evidence.

8. **Discuss how Skinner's principles of operant conditioning can be applied to the structure and development of personality.**

   8-1. Which of the following processes plays an important part in Skinner's ideas about human behavior?

   a. mental conflict

   b. the mind

   c. free will

   d. none of the above

   8-2. According to Skinner, much of our behavior is affected by reinforcement, punishment, or extinction—in other words, by the environmental _____ that follow our behavior. For example, if someone behaves aggressively (i.e., has an aggressive personality trait) it is because he or she has been _____ for behaving aggressively in the past.

   8-3. Skinner recognized the concept of personality, that there are differences between people and that behavior is relatively consistent over time. The distinctiveness and consistency of personality occurs, however, not because of what's going on in an individual's *mind* but because of what occurs in their _____.

   8-4. Thus, for Skinner, personality is not mental, but environmental. People do not change their minds, their environment changes. Skinner makes a strong case for the point of view that our behavior is caused or _____ rather than free and that the determinants are largely _____ rather than genetic.

   Answers: 8-1. d **8-2.** consequences (stimuli, events), reinforced **8-3.** environment **8-4.** determined, environmental.

9. **Describe Bandura's social-learning theory and compare it to Skinner's viewpoint.**

   9-1. In what respect is Bandura's point of view similar to Skinner's?

   9-2. Three of the major differences between Bandura's and Skinner's viewpoints involve the concepts listed below. Carefully define and explain these concepts and indicate how they represent a difference from Skinner's position.

   (a) reciprocal determinism:

   (b) observational learning:

   (c) self-efficacy:

9-3. According to Bandura whom do we imitate, and in what circumstances?

Answers: 9-1. It is similar in that Bandura believes that personality is largely shaped through learning. **9-2.** (a) *Reciprocal determinism* refers to the point of view that not only does environment determine behavior, as Skinner asserted, but that behavior determines environment, and, further, that behavior, environment, and mental processes all mutually affect one another. (b) *Observational learning* is the process through which we learn behaviors by observing the consequences of someone else's (i.e., a model's) behavior. For example, we learn not only by being reinforced, as Skinner proposed, but by observing someone else being reinforced. (c) *Self-efficacy* is a belief in our ability to perform certain behaviors. This belief affects whether we undertake those behaviors and how well we perform them. Skinner makes no allowance for mentalistic concepts such as self-efficacy. **9-3.** We tend to imitate models whom we like, consider attractive and powerful, view as similar to ourselves, and observe being reinforced.

10. **Identify Mischel's major contribution to personality theory and indicate why his ideas have generated so much controversy.**

10-1. Mischel's major contribution to personality theory is his contention that human behavior is determined to a much greater extent by the _____ than by _____.

10-2. Why is this such a controversial idea for personality theory?

Answers: 10-1. situation (situational factors), personality (personality traits) **10-2.** The notion is controversial because the very definition of personality involves the word *consistency*. Mischel's findings suggest that behavior is not as consistent as personality theorists may have thought, that it is strongly affected by an ever-changing situation.

11. **Summarize the strengths and weaknesses of the behavioral approach to personality.**

11-1. The major strengths of the behavioral approach have been its commitment to empirical _____. Empirical means observable, and for the behaviorists the subject matter of the science of human behavior must be, at some level, _____.

11-2. The major weaknesses of the behavioral approach, according to its critics, have been its overdependence on research involving _____ subjects, the _____ nature of its objection to the concepts of free will and cognition, and its _____ view of personality.

Answers: 11-1. research, observable **11-2.** animal, dehumanizing, fragmented.

HUMANISTIC PERSPECTIVES

12. **Explain how humanism was a reaction against both the behavioral and psychodynamic approaches and discuss the assumptions of the humanistic view.**

12-1. The humanistic movement reacted (a) against the behavioral approach because of its mechanistic, fragmented view of personality and its emphasis on _____ research, and (b) against the psychoanalytic approach because of its emphasis on _____ drives.

12-2. In addition, the humanistic viewpoint found fault with both movements because of their emphasis on _____, or absolute causation. The humanists also thought that the behaviorists and the Freudians failed to recognize the (<u>unique</u>/<u>common</u>) qualities of human behavior.

12-3. Humanistic psychology emphasizes the (<u>similarities</u>/<u>differences</u>) between human beings and the other animal species; believes we (<u>are controlled by</u>/<u>can rise above</u>) our biological heritage; asserts that we are largely (<u>rational</u>/<u>irrational</u>) creatures; and stresses a (<u>subjective</u>/<u>objective</u>) approach that emphasizes people's impressions over the realities of the situation.

Answers: 12-1. animal, primitive (animalistic) **12-2.** determinism, unique **12-3.** differences, can rise above, rational, subjective.

13. Identify the single structural construct in Rogers's person-centered theory and summarize his view of personality development.

13-1. Who are you? What are you like? What are your unique qualities? What is your typical behavior? Your answers to these questions are likely to reflect what Roger's called the _____.

13-2. Although Ralph tends to be a submissive and somewhat lazy person (and that is the way his friends, family, and co-workers describe him), he views himself as hard-working and dynamic, a leader both on the job and at home.

    (a) What is Ralph 's self-concept?

    (b) Is his self-concept congruent or incongruent?

    (c) According to Rogers, what parental behavior may have led to this incongruence?

    (d) According to Rogers, what parental behavior would have resulted in Ralph's achieving congruence rather than incongruence?

13-3. Define the following Rogerian concepts.

    (a) conditional love:

    (b) unconditional love:

13-4. What is defensiveness for Rogers?

Answers: 13-1. self or self-concept **13-2.** (a) that he is hard-working, dynamic, and a leader (b) incongruent (c) conditional love or acceptance (d) unconditional love or acceptance **13-3.** (a) affection given conditionally, the condition being that the child or adult must live up to another's expectations (b) affection given without conditions, full acceptance of the person that is not dependent on what he or she is or does. **13-4.** As with Freud, people defend against anxiety by distorting or denying reality. For Rogers, people's defensiveness arises when people defend their self-concepts against inconsistent experiences. Thus, defensiveness is related to incongruence.

14. Explain what Maslow meant by self-actualization, and summarize his findings on the characteristics of self-actualizing people.

14-1. In a few words, what did Maslow mean by self-actualization?

14-2. Suppose a woman had the talent and ambition to be a mathematician but followed the urging of others and became a nurse instead. How does her behavior relate to self-actualization and mental health, according to Maslow?

14-3. Which of the following, according to Maslow, are characteristic of self-actualized people? Place Y in the blank if the description applies, N if it does not.

_____ Spontaneous

_____ Has more profound emotional experiences than others

_____ Uncomfortable being alone

_____ Not dependent on others for approval

_____ Enjoys strong friendships that are few in number

_____ Extreme in personality (e.g., either conforming or rebellious)

Answers: 14-1. the need to fulfill one's potential **14-2.** She is not self-actualized, so she is not as healthy as she could be. **14-3.** Y, Y, N, Y, Y, N.

15. Summarize the strengths and weaknesses of the humanistic approach to personality.

15-1. To its credit, the humanistic movement called attention to the possibility that a person's _____ views may be more important than objective reality. The movement also emphasized the importance of the _____ or self-concept and stressed the study of the (normal/abnormal) personality.

15-2. Critics have also identified several weaknesses of the humanistic formulations. Match the weaknesses listed below with the statements by placing the appropriate letters in the blanks.

A. poor testability

B. unrealistic view of human nature

C. inadequate evidence

_____ Humanistic psychologists tend to scorn research, so little experimental support for their views has emerged.

_____ Even without research, some of the descriptions, such as of self-actualized personalities, have an idealized, perfectionistic ring.

_____ Humanistic ideas are frequently difficult to define, so research on some concepts is difficult or impossible.

Answers: 15-1. subjective, self, normal **15-2.** C, B, A.

BIOLOGICAL PERSPECTIVES

16. **Describe Sheldon's and Eysenck's biological theories of personality.**

16-1. Following are a list of physical characteristics. Which Sheldon body type is associated with each? Identify the body type by placing the appropriate letters in the blanks below.

A. thin   Endomorph: _____

B. fat   Mesomorph: _____

C. muscular   Ectomorph: _____

16-2. Sheldon proposed that *personality* was strongly related to the *type of physique* that one has. Match the personality characteristics listed below with the Sheldon body type by placing the appropriate letters in the blanks. (See Figure 12.11.)

A. inhibited, intellectual   Endomorph: _____

B. domineering, competitive   Mesomorph: _____

C. relaxed, sociable   Ectomorph: _____

16-3. The major flaw in Sheldon's procedures was that Sheldon himself made the personality ratings. Thus, there was no double blind (Chapter 2), and the research probably suffered from _____ bias. Sheldon's findings (have/have not) been supported by subsequent research.

16-4. According to Eysenck, individual differences in personality can be understood in terms of a heirarchy of traits. At the top of the heirarchy are three fundamental higher-order traits from which all other traits derive: _____, _____, and _____.

16-5. Eysenck asserts that a major factor in personality involves the ease with which people can be _____. Eysenck believes that differences in conditionability, like personality differences in general, are to a large extent (environmentally/genetically) determined.

16-6. Conditionability, in turn, is related to extraversion-introversion. According to Eysenck (extraverts/ introverts) have higher levels of physiological arousal, a characteristic that makes them (more/less) readily conditioned.

16-7. Why would it be that people who are more easily conditioned tend to be introverts?

16-8. What is the research evidence regarding Eysenck's idea about the relationship between introversion and physiological arousal level?

a. The data is mixed, with some studies supporting and others failing to support the relationship.

b. Evidence has generally supported the relationship.

c. Evidence has generally failed to support the relationship.

17. **Describe the Featured Study on personality similarity in twins and other research on heritability of personality.**

17-1.   Which of the following groups were included in the Featured Study?

   a. identical twins reared together

   b. identical twins reared apart

   c. fraternal twins reared together

   d. fraternal twins reared apart

   e. all of the above

17-2.   The most telling finding of this study was that the personalities of ____ were more similar than those of

   _____.

   a. identical twins reared together, identical twins reared apart

   b. fraternal twins reared together, fraternal twins reared apart

   c. identical twins reared apart, fraternal twins reared together

   d. identical twins reared together, fraternal twins reared together

17-3.   Approximately what percentage of the variance in personality was attributable to genetic factors?

   a. 5 to 10 percent

   b. 10 to 22 percent

   c. 40 to 58 percent

   d. 70 to 76 percent

17-4.   How important a determinant of personality was family environment found to be in this study?

   a. more important than heredity

   b. equal to heredity

   c. of little importance

17-5.   The recent twin studies are likely to have a major impact on the way psychologists think about the causes of human behavior. Why are the results so important and so surprising?

17-6.   Evolutionary theorists assert that the biological basis of personality exists because of the evolutionary importance of the "Big Five" traits. It is easy to understand that low neuroticism and high conscientiousness, agreeableness, openness, and extraversion have _____ value. Unexplained, however, is the fact that so many human beings survived who lack these characteristics! In other words, the evolutionary theorists have not yet confronted the issue, of critical importance for personality theory, of the origins of _____ differences.

Answers: 17-1. e **17-2.** c (This is the most important comparison because: even though the fraternal twins shared the same environment, their common environment did not make them nearly as similar as twins who did not have a common environment *but who shared the same heredity*.) **17-3.** c **17-4.** c **17-5.** Theories of development and personality have tended to stress the importance of the environment, especially the family environment; the recent twin studies find heredity to be very important and family environment to be of little importance. Thus, the results are contrary to the expectations of most of us and of much of the theorizing in the field of personality. **17-6.** survival (adaptive), individual.

18. Summarize the strengths and weaknesses of the biological approach to personality.

18-1. People frequently blame parents for kids' personalities. I recently asked a friend of mine why she thought a mutual acquaintance of ours was so obnoxious. She said, "Well, raised with such crazy parents, what would you expect?" I said, "Is that an argument for environment or heredity?" That is one of the benefits of the twin studies: They put data in place of speculation.

But what are some of the weaknesses of the biological approach? One is that heritability ratios should be regarded only as _____ that will vary depending on sampling and other procedures. Another is that the attempt to apportion variance into heredity and environment is artificial since heredity and environment always _____. Finally, there is no truly comprehensive biological _____ of personality.

Answers: 18-1. estimates, interact, theory.

CONTEMPORARY EMPIRICAL APPROACHES TO PERSONALITY

19. Discuss the meaning and significance of locus of control.

19-1. Locus of control is a fairly stable personality trait that is strongly related to behavior. Indicate which of the following statements describe internals and which externals by placing an I or an E in the blanks.

_____ They are more likely to have high academic achievement.

_____ They believe that their successes and failures are due to fate or luck.

_____ They are more likely to develop psychological disorders.

_____ They are more likely to experience depression.

_____ They believe that the consequences of their behaviors are due to their actions or abilities.

_____ They are more likely to give up smoking.

_____ They are more likely to take up an exercise program.

19-2. Are you an "Internal" or an "External"? Why do you think so? In the space below give a brief definition of the concepts of internal and external locus of control.

Answers: 19-1. I, E, E, E, I, I, I **19-2.** Locus of control is the extent to which people believe that their *actions* affect *outcomes*. Do you tend to believe that *what you do* in large part determines your success or failure? If so, you are an internal. Do you think that *external events*, such as luck or fate, are the major determinant of what happens to you? Then you are an external. (Of course, like any other dimension of personality, this trait occurs along a continuum.)

20. **Discuss the meaning of sensation seeking and identify the characteristics of high sensation seekers.**

20-1. Sensation seeking refers to the degree to which people tend to seek or avoid high levels of sensory stimulation, a tendency that is to a large extent genetically inherited, according to Zuckerman. Indicate which of the following characteristics describe high-sensation seekers and which describe low by placing an H or L in the blanks.

_____ Risk taking

_____ Easily bored

_____ Takes comfort in the routine

_____ More likely to drink heavily

_____ More likely to engage in recreational drug use

_____ Tends to ignore middle class rules and conventions

_____ Relishes extensive travel, finding new and unusual friends

_____ Tends toward sexual experimentation

_____ Tends to like mountain climbing, skydiving, scuba diving

_____ Relatively tolerant of stress

_____ More likely to have difficulty in school, exhibit poor health habits

20-2. Sensation seeking seems to be a fairly potent personality characteristic that may influence the course of romantic relationships. Do people tend to prefer partners who are similar to themselves in sensation seeking, or do opposites attract with regard to this characteristic?

Answers: 20-1. H, H, L, H, H, H, H, H, H, H, H **20-2.** As is the case with personality traits in general, people prefer partners who are similar to themselves in sensation seeking.

21. **Explain what is meant by self-monitoring and discuss the effects of self-monitoring on interpersonal relationships.**

21-1. Describe the characteristics of people who are high in self-monitoring with regard to the following situations:

(a) impression management: They are relatively (good at/poor at) creating the desired impression.

(b) control of facial expressions: They are (able/not able) to feign emotion by controlling their facial expressions.

(c) spotting deception: They are (good at/poor at) spotting deception in others.

(d) dating and sexual relationships: They tend to have (more/fewer) partners and (stronger/weaker) emotional commitments.

21-2. The three personality traits reviewed in this section overlap to some extent and may be easily confused. To review these concepts, match the specific trait with the behavioral descriptions by placing the appropriate abbreviations in the blanks.

I   internal locus of control

E   external locus of control

Hi-SS   high sensation seeking

Lo-SS   low sensation seeking

Hi-SM   high self-monitoring

Lo-SM   low self-monitoring.

(a) ____   Last summer Ralph decided on the spur of the moment to sell his car and spend two months traveling by foot in India. Ralph's hobbies include sky-diving and gambling.

(b) ____   Floyd never seems to get the breaks in life. He feels somewhat depressed and hopes that fate will be kind to him. He is certain that there is nothing he can do to change the position he is in.

(c) ____   Margie figures she knows what people want and she successfully adjusts her personality to fit the occasion or person she is with. She is good at feigning emotion and also good at detecting deception in others. She changes sexual partners frequently and avoids emotional commitments.

(d) ____   Alice usually doesn't try to hide her feelings and isn't very good at it when she does try. She prefers close relationships with the opposite sex to playing the field. She isn't especially gullible, but she also isn't really good at figuring out when people are trying to deceive her.

(e) ____   Ruppert had a considerable amount of difficulty on the first test in his advanced calculus course, which surprised him since he generally did well in school. So, after going over the problems that he missed, he adopted a different study strategy.

(f) ____   Jan hates it when her boyfriend drives too fast, and she refuses to go skiing with him because she thinks it's too dangerous.

Answers: 21-1. (a) good at (b) able (c) good at (d) more, weaker **21-2.** (a) Hi-SS (b) E (c) Hi-SM (d) Lo-SM (e) I (f) Lo-SS.

CULTURE AND PERSONALITY

22. **Summarize research on culture and personality.**

22-1.   I believe that Europeans tend to describe people in terms of nationality—as being typically English, French, German, and so on. If my observations are correct, Europeans show more blatant interest than do Americans in modal _____ types that supposedly reflect national character.

22-2.   Of course, I'm generalizing about the European character, and my generalizations may be as incorrect as other generalizations about nationality and character. For a decade or so after World War II, researchers using the Freudian model attempted to find a single, dominant personality type representative of each culture. This attempt was (successful/not successful).

22-3.   With the current increased attention to cultural factors, interest in the relationship between personality and culture has again surfaced. The new data reveal both similarities and differences across cultures. With regard to similarities, precisely the same _____ personality factors tend to emerge in different cultures.

22-4.   Concerning differences, people in Western cultures tend to have a more (internal/external) locus of control than do people in Asian cultures; and people in the United States and in Australia tend to be (lower/higher) in self-monitoring than people in Asian countries.

22-5.   Research by Markus and Kitayama also indicates that the individualistic orientation characteristic of the West is not at all universal across cultures. Thus, while Americans tend to value (independence/connectedness), Asians value (interdependence/uniqueness) among people. While American parents urge their children to (stand out/blend in), Asian parents encourage their children to take pride in the accomplishments of (each individual/the group).

Answers: 22-1. personality **22-2.** not successful **22-3.** five **22-4.** external, higher **22-5.** independence, connectedness, stand out, the group.

PUTTING IT IN PERSPECTIVE

23. **Explain how this chapter highlighted three of the text's unifying themes.**

23-1. We've just discussed one of the three themes emphasized in this chapter, that our behavior is influenced by our cultural heritage. The two other themes are that the field is theoretically _____ and that psychology evolves in a _____ context.

23-2.   Freudian, behavioral, and biological perspectives of personality assume that behavior is determined; the humanistic perspective emphasizes (causation/free will). The biological perspective stresses genetic inheritance; the behavior perspectives stresses (heredity/environment) factors. As these examples illustrate, the study of personality involves an enormous amount of theoretical _____.

23-3. Concerning sociohistorical context, it is clear that theories of personality have strongly affected our culture. For example, the surrealist art movement, begun in the 1920s, derives directly from _____ psychology, as do other movements in literature and the arts. And the current debate on the effects of media violence is to a large extent a product of research in social _____ theory.

23-4. In turn, culture has affected psychology. For example, it seems quite likely that the sexually repressive climate of Victorian Vienna caused Freud to emphasize the _____ aspects of human behavior; and it is clear, from Freud's own description, that World War I influenced his development of the second Freudian instinct, the _____ instinct. Thus, psychology evolves in a _____ context.

Answers: 23-1. diverse, sociohistorical **23-2.** free will, environment, diversity **23-3.** psychoanalytic (Freudian), learning **23-4.** sexual, aggression, sociohistorical.

APPLICATION: UNDERSTANDING PERSONALITY ASSESSMENT

24. **Outline the four principal uses of personality tests.**

24-1. List the four principal uses of personality tests in the blanks next to the correct descriptions.

   (a) Psychological _____: Measuring personality traits in empirical studies.

   (b) _____: Advising people on career plans and decisions.

   (c) _____ selection: Choosing employees in business and government.

   (d) Clinical _____: Assessing psychological disorders.

Answers: 24-1. (a) research (b) Counseling (c) Personnel (d) diagnosis.

25. **Describe the MMPI, 16PF, and NEO Personality Inventory and summarize the strengths and weaknesses of self-report inventories.**

25-1. The MMPI, 16PF, and NEO Personality Inventories are (projective/self-report) tests. All three tests are also used to measure (single/multiple) traits.

25-2. Identify which tests (MMPI, 16PF, or NEO) are described by each of the following.

(a) _____ Originally designed to diagnose psychological disorders.

(b) _____, _____ Originally designed to assess the normal personality.

(c) _____ Measures the "big five" personality traits.

(d) _____ Includes four validity scales to help detect deception or carelessness.

25-3. The major strength of self-report inventories, in comparison with simply asking a person what they are like, is that they provide a more precise and more (objective/personal) measure of personality.

25-4. The major weakness of self-report inventories is that they are subject to several sources of error, including the following: (1) Test-takers may intentionally fake responses, that is, may engage in deliberate _____. (2) While not realizing it, people may answer questions in ways to make themselves "look good," the _____ _____ bias. (3) In addition, some people tend either to agree or to disagree with nearly every statement on a test, a source of error involving _____ sets.

Answers: 25-1. self-report, multiple **25-2.** (a) MMPI (b) 16PF, NEO (c) NEO (d) MMPI **25-3.** objective **25-4.** deception, social desirability, response.

26. **Describe the projective hypothesis and summarize the strengths and weaknesses of projective tests.**

26-1. If you have ever looked at clouds and described the images you've seen, you've done something similar to taking a projective test. If you thought that the images you saw reflected something about your personality, then you also accepted the *projective hypothesis*. The projective hypothesis is the idea that people will tend to _____ their characteristics onto ambiguous stimuli, so that what they see reveals something about their personalities and problems.

26-2. Two major projective tests are the Rorschach, a series of _____, and the TAT, a series of _____ or scenes.

26-3. The advantages of projective tests are that (1) since the way the tests are interpreted is not at all obvious, it is difficult for people to engage in intentional _____; and (2) projective tests may help tap problems or aspects of personality of which people are _____.

26-4. The major weakness of projective tests concerns inadequate evidence that they are either _____ (consistent) or _____ (measure what they are intended to measure). Nonetheless, the tests are still valued and used by many clinicians. It should also be noted that when users agree on a systematic scoring procedure, some projective tests have shown adequate reliability and validity. Thus, as discussed in Chapter 10, the _____ has proven to be a particularly useful test in research on achievement motivation.

Answers: 26-1. project **26-2.** inkblots, pictures **26-3.** deception, unconscious (unaware) **26-4.** reliability, validity, TAT.

Archetypes
Behaviorism
Cardinal trait
Central trait
Collective unconscious
Compensation
Conscious
Defense mechanisms
Displacement
Ego
Extraverts
Factor analysis
Fixation
Humanism
Id
Identification
Incongruence

Introverts
Locus of control
Model
Need for self-actualization
Observational learning
Oedipal complex
Personality
Personality trait
Personal unconscious
Phenomenological approach
Pleasure principle
Preconscious
Projection
Projective tests
Psychodynamic theories
Psychosexual stages

Rationalization
Reaction formation
Reality principle
Reciprocal determinism
Regression
Repression
Secondary traits
Self-actualizing persons
Self-concept
Self-efficacy
Self-monitoring
Self-report inventories
Sensation seeking
Striving for superiority
Superego
Unconscious

_____   1. An individual's unique constellation of consistent behavioral traits.

_____   2. A characteristic that represents a durable disposition to behave in a particular way in a variety of situations.

_____   3. A dominant trait that permeates nearly all of a person's behavior.

_____   4. Prominent, general dispositions found in anyone.

_____   5. Less consistent dispositions that surface in some situations but not in others.

_____   6. All the diverse theories, descended from the work of Sigmund Freud, that focus on unconscious mental forces.

_____   7. The primitive, instinctive component of personality that operates according to the pleasure principle.

_____   8. The id's demands for immediate gratification of its urges.

_____   9. The decision-making component of personality that operates according to the reality principle.

_____ 10. The ego's delay of gratification of the id's urges until appropriate outlets and situations can be found.

_____ 11. The moral component of personality that incorporates social standards about what represents right and wrong.

_____ 12. Consists of whatever you are aware of at a particular point in time.

_____ 13. Contains material just beneath the surface of awareness that can be easily retrieved.

_____ 14. Contains thoughts, memories, and desires that are well below the surface of conscious awareness.

_____ 15. The series of largely unconscious Freudian reactions that protect a person from unpleasant emotions such as anxiety or guilt.

_____ 16. The defense mechanism that pushes distressing thoughts and feelings into the unconscious or keeps them from emerging into consciousness.

_____ 17. Attributing your own thoughts, feelings, or motives to another.

_____ **18.** Creating false but plausible excuses to justify unacceptable behavior.

_____ **19.** Diverting emotional feelings (usually anger) from their original source to a substitute target.

_____ **20.** Behaving in a way that is exactly the opposite of one's true (but unconscious) feelings.

_____ **21.** Reverting to immature patterns of behavior.

_____ **22.** Bolstering self-esteem by forming an imaginary or real alliance with some person or group.

_____ **23.** Developmental periods with a characteristic sexual focus that leave their mark on adult personality

_____ **24.** A failure to move forward from one stage to another as expected.

_____ **25.** Characterized by erotically tinged desires for one's opposite-sex parent and hostility toward one's same-sex parent.

_____ **26.** Jungian concept referring to the structure holding material that is not in one's awareness because it has been repressed or forgotten.

_____ **27.** A storehouse of latent memory traces inherited from our ancestral past.

_____ **28.** Emotionally charged images and thought forms that have universal meaning.

_____ **29.** People who tend to be preoccupied with the internal world of their own thoughts, feelings, and experiences.

_____ **30.** People who tend to be interested in the external world of people and things.

_____ **31.** An Adlerian concept referring to a universal drive to adapt, to improve oneself, and to master life's challenges.

_____ **32.** Efforts to overcome imagined or real inferiorities by developing one's abilities.

_____ **33.** Personality tests that ask people a series of questions about their characteristic behavior.

_____ **34.** A statistical procedure that identifies clusters of variables that are highly correlated with one another.

_____ **35.** A theoretical orientation based on the premise that scientific psychology should study only observable behavior.

_____ **36.** The assumption that internal mental events, external environmental events, and overt behavior all influence one another.

_____ **37.** Learning that occurs when an organism's responding is influenced by the observation of others.

_____ **38.** A person whose behavior is observed by another.

_____ **39.** Our belief about our ability to perform behaviors that should lead to expected outcomes.

_____ **40.** A theoretical orientation that emphasizes the unique qualities of humans, especially their freedom and potential for personal growth.

_____ **41.** Approach that assumes we have to appreciate individuals' personal, subjective experiences to truly understand their behavior.

_____ **42.** A collection of beliefs about one's own nature, unique qualities, and typical behavior.

_____ **43.** A Rogerian concept referring to the degree of disparity between one's self-concept and one's actual experience.

_____ **44.** The need to fulfill one's potential.

_____ 45. People with exceptionally healthy personalities, marked by continued personal growth.

_____ 46. A generalized expectancy about the degree to which we control our outcomes.

_____ 47. A generalized preference for high or low levels of sensory stimulation.

_____ 48. The degree to which people attend to and control the impression they make on others in social interactions.

_____ 49. A person's overall assessment of her or his personal adequacy or worth.

Answers: 1. personality **2.** personality trait **3.** cardinal trait **4.** central trait **5.** secondary traits **6.** psychodynamic theories **7.** id **8.** pleasure principle **9.** ego **10.** reality principle **11.** superego **12.** conscious **13.** preconscious **14.** unconscious **15.** defense mechanisms **16.** repression **17.** projection **18.** rationalization **19.** displacement **20.** reaction formation **21.** regression **22.** identification **23.** psychosexual stages **24.** fixation **25.** Oedipal complex **26.** personal unconscious **27.** collective unconscious **28.** archetypes **29.** introverts **30.** extraverts **31.** striving for superiority **32.** compensation **33.** self-report inventories **34.** factor analysis **35.** behaviorism **36.** reciprocal determinism **37.** observational learning **38.** model **39.** self-efficacy **40.** humanism **41.** phenomenological approach **42.** self-concept **43.** incongruence **44.** need for self-actualization **45.** self-actualizing persons **46.** locus of control **47.** sensation seeking **48.** self-monitoring **49.** self-esteem.

REVIEW OF KEY PEOPLE

Alfred Adler   Hans Eysenck   Walter Mischel
Gordon Allport   Sigmund Freud   Carl Rogers
Albert Bandura   Carl Jung   B. F. Skinner
Raymond Cattell   Abraham Maslow

_____ 1. One of the first theorists to make systematic distinctions between traits in terms of their relative importance.

_____ 2. The founder of psychoanalysis.

_____ 3. Developed the theory called analytical psychology; anticipated the humanists' emphasis on personal growth and self-actualization.

_____ 4. Founder of an approach to personality named individual psychology.

_____ 5. Modern behaviorism's most prominent theorist, recognized for his theories of operant conditioning.

_____ 6. A contemporary behavioral theorist who elaborated the concept of observational learning.

_____ 7. His chief contribution to personality theory has been to focus attention on the extent to which situational factors govern behavior.

_____ 8. One of the fathers of the human potential movement, he called his approach a person-centered theory.

_____ 9. The humanist who developed a theory of self-actualization.

_____ 10. Theorist who proposed that there are 16 basic personality factors.

_____ 11. He went against the spirit of the times by proposing a biologically oriented theory of personality.

Answers: 1. Allport **2.** Freud **3.** Jung **4.** Adler **5.** Skinner **6.** Bandura **7.** Mischel **8.** Rogers **9.** Maslow **10.** Cattell **11.** Eysenck

SELF-QUIZ

1. Personality traits are characterized by:
   a. consistency and distinctiveness
   b. charm and wit
   c. change as a function of the situation
   d. lack of individual differences

2. Which of the following are among the basic issues around which personality theories have been constructed?
   a. determinism versus free will
   b. consciousness versus the unconscious
   c. nature versus nurture
   d. all of the above

3. Which of the following is entirely unconscious, according to Freud?
   a. the id
   b. the ego
   c. the superego
   d. the archetype

4. Although Osmo at an unconscious level has great hatred for Cosmo, he says he likes Cosmo and, to the outside world, gives all the appearance of liking him. Which defense mechanism is Osmo using?
   a. regression
   b. reaction formation
   c. projection
   d. rationalization

5. The Oedipal complex occurs during the:
   a. oral stage
   b. anal stage
   c. phallic stage
   d. genital stage

6. Which of the following concepts did Carl Jung develop?
   a. archetypes
   b. the collective unconscious
   c. introversion-extraversion
   d. all of the above

7. Which of the following did Adler emphasize in his theory of personality?
   a. striving for superiority
   b. castration anxiety
   c. introversion-extraversion
   d. all of the above

8. Much of the behavior that we call personality results from reinforcement and observational learning, according to:
   a. Jung
   b. Skinner
   c. Bandura
   d. Adler

9. Which of the following accepts a deterministic view of human behavior?
   a. the psychoanalytic approach
   b. the biological approach
   c. the behavioral approach
   d. all of the above

10. According to Rogers, what causes incongruence?
    a. an inherited sense of irony
    b. conditional acceptance or affection
    c. unconditional acceptance or affection
    d. unconditioned stimuli

11. Herb had the desire and potential to be a violinist but became, instead, a trader in hog futures. He decided never to touch the violin again. What is wrong with Herb, according to Maslow?
    a. He suffers from incongruence.
    b. He suffers from castration anxiety.
    c. He has not achieved self-actualization.
    d. He has an inferiority complex.

12. According to Eysenck, differences in personality result in large part from differences in:
    a. introversion-extraversion
    b. genetic inheritance
    c. conditionability
    d. all of the above

13. Recent studies of the personalities of identical and fraternal twins are surprising and important because they indicate that:
    a. personality is in large part genetically determined
    b. environment is more important than heredity
    c. birth order is critical in personality formation
    d. monads and archetypes can be accounted for genetically

14. Sally believes that whatever happens to her, be it good or bad, is largely a matter of luck or fate. Sally has:
    a. an internal locus of control
    b. an external locus of control
    c. high self-monitoring
    d. a sensation-seeking tendency

15. Amanda is extraverted, impulsive, and risk-taking, and she likes fast cars, spicy food, and adventurous men. She is also nonconforming, especially in the sense that she will not adapt her personality to the person she happens to be with. Amanda is high on:
    a. external locus of control
    b. self-monitoring
    c. sensation seeking
    d. illegal substances

Answers: 1. a **2.** d **3.** a **4.** b **5.** c **6.** d **7.** a **8.** c **9.** d **10.** b **11.** c **12.** d **13.** a **14.** b **15.** c.

Chapter Thirteen

Stress, Coping, and Health

REVIEW OF KEY IDEAS

THE NATURE OF STRESS

1. **Discuss the nature of stress.**

   1-1. The text defines stress as any circumstances that threaten or are <u>perceived</u> to threaten one's well-being and thereby tax one's coping abilities. This definition would indicate that the sources of stress are quite (<u>subjective/objective</u>). Or to put it another way, stress lies in the mind of the _____.

   1-2. Why might minor hassles have significant harmful effects?

   Answers: 1-1. subjective, beholder or individual **1-2.** Because of the cumulative nature of stress.

2. **Describe key processes and factors in our appraisals of stress.**

   2-1. When you appraise an event as either irrelevant, relevant but not threatening, or stressful, you are making a _____ appraisal.

   2-2. When you appraise an event as stressful and then you evaluate your coping resources and options, you are making a _____ appraisal.

   2-3. While a variety of factors influence stress evaluation, two are particularly important. Identify them in the situations described below.

   (a) A salesperson friend of mine is a frequent flyer, yet she still finds flying is stressful and can quickly tell you why this is so. What do you think she says?

   (b) Why are natural disasters such as earthquakes and tornadoes particularly stressful?

Answers: **2-1.** primary **2-2.** secondary **2-3.** (a) She feels a lack of personal control when she flys. (b) because they are unpredictable.

MAJOR TYPES OF STRESS

3. Describe frustration as a form of stress.

    3-1. Which of the following three situations best illustrates what is meant by frustration?

        (a) Your family moves from a large city to a rather small, rural community.

        (b) You are late for an appointment and stuck in a traffic jam.

        (c) Your are forced to choose between two good movies on television.

    3-2. If you picked choice "b" then you have caught on that frustration always involves the _____ of the pursuit of some goal.

Answers: **3-1.** b **3-2.** thawarting or blocking.

4. Identify the three basic types of conflict and discuss which types are most troublesome.

    4-1. Many persons do not want to pay their income taxes, but, on the other hand, they don't want to go to jail either. These persons are faced with an _____-_____ conflict.

    4-2. Getting married has both positive and negative aspects that make it an excellent example of an_____-_____ conflict.

    4-3. Consider the problem of the studemt who has to choose between scholarships for two different universities. Since he can't accept both, he's faced with an_____-_____ conflict.

    4-4. Now that you have correctly identified the three basic types of conflict, list them below in their order of troublesomeness, beginning with the least troublesome.

        (a) _____

        (b) _____

        (c) _____

Answers: **4-1.** avoidance-avoidance **4-2.** approach-avoidance **4-3.** approach-approach **4-4.** (a) approach-approach (b) approach-avoidance (c) avoidance-avoidance.

5. Summarize evidence on life change and pressure as forms of stress.

    5-1. The Social Readjustment Rating Scale (SRRS), measures the stress induced by _____ in daily living routines. The developers of this scale theorized that all kinds of life changes, both pleasant and unpleasant, would induce stress. Early research showed that high scores on the SRRS were correlated with psychological disturbances and many kinds of physical _____.

5-2. Later research began to indicate that high scores on the SRRS were primarily the result of (pleasant/unpleasant) life changes. Other independent research has found that change by itself can induce stress, but the greatest stress appears to be induced by _____ life changes.

5-3. There are two kinds of pressure. One is the pressure to get things accomplished, or the pressure to _____. The other is the pressure to abide by rules, or the pressure to _____.

Answers: 5-1. changes, illness **5-2.** unpleasant, unpleasant **5-3.** perform, conform.

RESPONDING TO STRESS

6. Identify some common emotional responses to stress and discuss the effects of emotional arousal.

6-1. The text describes three different dimensions of emotions that are particularly likely to be triggered by stress. Identify which of these dimensions is most likely to be present in the following situations.

   (a) The emotions in this dimension are likely to be found as a person begins to feel more and more helpless and unable to cope.

   (b) The emotions in this dimension are likely to be found as a person begins to feel increasingly put upon and treated unfairly.

   (c) The emotions in this dimension are likely to be found as a person faces increasing degrees of conflict or uncertainty.

6-2. What does the inverted U hypothesis say about what happens to the optimal arousal level as tasks become more complex?

Answers: 6-1. (a) dejection, sadness, and grief (b) annoyance, anger, and rage (c) apprehension, anxiety, and fear
6-2. The optimal arousal level decreases.

7. Describe the fight-or-flight response and the three stages of the General Adaptation Syndrome.

7-1. What division of the autonomic nervous system mediates the fight-or-flight response?

7-2. Although our bodies' fight-or-flight response appears to be an evolutionary carry-over from our past, why is it perhaps of more harm than help to modern human beings?

7-3. Indicate which of the three stages of the General Adaptation Syndrome is being described in each of the following.

(a) This is the initial stage in which the body prepares for the fight-or-flight response.

(b) This is the second stage in which the body stabilizes its physiological changes as it begins to effectively cope with the stress.

(c) This is the third stage in which the body's coping resources are becoming depleted and the resistance to many diseases declines.

7-4. Why did Hans Selye call this body defense system the General Adaptation Syndrome?

Answers: 7-1. sympathetic nervous system **7-2.** Because most stressful situations generally require a more complex response than simple fight or flight. **7-3.** (a) stage of alarm (b) stage of resistance (c) stage of exhaustion **7-4.** Because it is a general response to all kinds of stressful situations.

8. **Discuss the two major pathways along which the brain sends signals to the endocrine system in response to stress.**

8-1. Fill in the missing parts in the diagram below detailing the two major pathways along which the brain sends signals to the endocrine system.

CEREBRAL CORTEX

(a) _____

SYMPATHETIC NS   PITUITARY GLAND

ACTH

(b) _____ (GLAND)   (c) _____ (GLAND)

CATECHOLAMINES   CORTICOSTEROIDS
Increases heart rate &   Increases energy, inhibits
respiration, etc.   tissue inflammation, etc.

Answers: 8-1. (a) hypothalamus (b) adrenal medulla (c) adrenal cortex.

9. **Describe and evaluate aggression, giving up, and self-indulgence as behavioral responses to stress.**

9-1. Answer the following questions regarding aggression, giving up, and self-indulgence as responses to stress.

(a) Which of these responses is frequently, but not always, triggered by frustration? _____

(b) Which of these responses often results from a cognitive appraisal that one lacks control over problems? _____

(c) Which of these responses is illustrated by the saying, "When the going gets tough, the tough go shopping"? _____

9-2. What is a common fault of all three of these behavioral responses to stress?

Answers: 9-1. (a) aggression (b) giving up (c) self-indulgence **9-2.** They divert effort away from solutions to problems.

10. **Discuss the value of defensive coping and positive illusions.**

10-1. Indicate whether each of the following statements regarding defensive coping is true or false.

_____ (a) Although they are largely unconscious, defense mechanisms can operate at any level of consciousness.

_____ (b) Only neurotic persons use defensive mechanisms.

_____ (c) Defense mechanisms are used to shield against emotional discomfort that often occurs with stress, particularly anxiety.

10-2. What two major problems arise from using defensive coping?

10-3. What conclusion does the text draw regarding small and extreme positive illusions?

Answers: 10-1. (a) true (b) false (c) true **10-2.** They avoid the problem and they are related to poor health. **10-3.** Small positive illusions may be beneficial while extreme illusions may be harmful.

THE EFFECTS OF STRESS ON PSYCHOLOGICAL FUNCTIONING

11. **Discuss the effects of stress on task performance and the burnout syndrome.**

11-1. Baumeister's theory as to why stress affects task performance is that pressure to perform makes us self-conscious and this elevated self-consciousness disrupts our _____. The term we commonly use for this is _____ under pressure.

11-2. Indicate whether each of the following statements regarding the burnout syndrome is true or false.

   (a) Burnout appers to reult from events that undermine the belief that one's life is meaningful and important.

   (b) The onset of of burnout is usually sudden.

Answers: **11-1.** attention, choking **11-2.** (a) true (b) false.

12. Discuss posttraumatic stress disorder and other psychological problems and disorders that may result from stress.

12-1. Answer the following questions regarding post-traumatic stress syndrome.

   (a) What is unique about post-traumatic stress disorder?

   (b) What are the two most common causes of this syndrome among men?

   (c) What is the most common cause of this syndrome among women?

12-2. In addition to alcohol abuse and unhappiness, what four other psychological problems have been shown to be related to chronic stress? (One of them has to do with school, two have to do with sleep, and one involves intimate relationships.)

12-3. Stress has also been implicated in the onset of serious psychological disorders. In addition to schizophrenia, what three other disorders are mentioned?

Answers: **12-1.** (a) It occurs somtime after the stressful event (b) combat experience and seeing someone die (c) rape (or physical attack) **12-2.** poor academic performance, insomnia, nightmares, sexual difficulties **12-3.** anxiety disorders, depression, eating disorders.

THE EFFECTS OF STRESS ON PHYSICAL HEALTH

13. Describe the Type A behavior pattern and summarize the evidence linking it to coronary heart disease.

13-1. Tell whether the following characteristics are found in Type A or Type B persons.

   _____ (a) easygoing

   _____ (b) competitive

   _____ (c) impatient

   _____ (d) amicable

   _____ (e) hostile

13-2. Which aspect of the Type A behavior seems to be most highly related to coronary heart disorder.

13-3. Early research indicated that Type A persons were _____ times more likely to suffer from coronary heart disease than were Type B persons. Continuing research has since shown that the coronary risk is more (<u>severe/moderate</u>) than originally thought. It now appears that Type A persons are approximately _____ as likely to suffer from coronary heart disease compared to Type B persons.

Answers: 13-1. (a) Type B (b) Type A (c) Type A (d) Type B (e) Type A **13-2.** cynical hostility **13-3.** six, moderate, twice.

14. Discuss and evaluate other evidence linking stress to immunosuppression and a variety of physical illnesses.

14-1. Research has found stress to be related to numerous diseases and disorders. What effect on the lymphocytes (the specialized white blood cells that are important in initiating the immune response) appears to be the link between stress and so many disorders?

Answers: 14-1. Stress appears to suppress the proliferation of the lymphocytes (thus suppressing the immune system in general).

15. Describe the Featured Study on stress and the common cold.

15-1. Answer the following questions about the Featured Study.

(a) What two groups were the subjects divided into on the basis of their answers to stress inventories?

(b) Which group showed a significantly higher incidence of colds, after controlling for the roommate effect?

(c) What is rather unique about this particular study?

15-2. While many studies have shown a relationship between stress and numerous physical illness, we can still not state definitely that stress leads to physical illness. Why is this?

Answers: 15-1. (a) high-stress and low-stress (b) the high-stress group (c) It was able to control for so many possibly confounding variables. **15-2.** Because almost all of the data are correlational (and you cannot infer cause and effect relationships with these kinds of data).

FACTORS MODERATING THE IMPACT OF STRESS

16. Discuss how social support and hardiness moderate the impact of stress.

16-1. What two areas of our health appear to benefit from having strong social support groups?

16-2. What three personality characteristics were found to differentiate hardy executives from less hardy executives?

Answers: 16-1. Both mental and physical health. **16-2.** high commitment, seeking challenge, a feeling of being in control.

17. Discuss how personality and physiological factors are related to stress tolerance.

17-1. What difference was found between optimists and pessimists with respect to good physical health?

17-2. What personality characteristic was found to be related to longevity in a recent study from a sample of Terman's gifted children?

17-3. What condition triggered by autonomic reactivity may also contribute to heart disease?

Answers: 17-1. Optimists were more likely to enjoy good physical health. **17-2.** conscientiousness **17-3.** cardiovascular reactivity (an increase in heart rate and blood pressure).

HEALTH-IMPAIRING BEHAVIOR

18. Discuss the negative impact of smoking, poor nutrition, and lack of exercise on physical health.

18-1. Answer the following questions regarding the negative impact of smoking on physical health.

(a) How many fewer years can a 25-year-old male smoker expect to live than a 25-year-old nonsmoker?

(b) What are the two most frequent diseases that kill smokers?

(c) What appears to happen with respect to readiness to give up as smokers cycle through periods of abstinence and relapse?

18-2. Answer the following true-false questions.

_____ (a) Among Americans most deficiences in diet are because of inability to afford appropriate food.

_____ (b) Regular exercise appears to increase longevity.

_____ (c) Alcohol causes the most damage of all the recreational drugs.

Answers: 18-1. (a) 8 years (or 8.3 years) (b) lung cancer and heart disease (c) Readiness to give up smoking builds gradually. **18-2.** (a) false (b) true (c) true.

19. Discuss the relationship between behavioral styles and AIDS.

19-1. What two bodily fluids are most likely to transmit AIDS?

19-2. What two general groups have the highest incidence of AIDS in the United States?

19-3. How can one virtually guarantee that he or she will not contact AIDS?

Answers: 19-1. blood and semen **19-2.** Gay & bisexual males and intravenous drug users. **19-3.** Stay with only one sexual partner (known to prefer this same lifestyle) and don't use intravenous drugs.

20. Explain how health-impairing lifestyles develop.

20-1. The text list four complementary explanations as to why health-impairing lifestyles develop. Given the hints below, list these four reasons.

(a) slowly

(b) immediate

(c) delayed

(d) "not me"

REACTIONS TO ILLNESS

21. Discuss individual differences in willingness to seek medical treatment.

> **21-1.** Indicate whether the following statements regarding individual differences in willingness to seek medical treatment are true or false.
>
> _____ (a) Delay in seeking treatment is perhaps the biggest problem here.
>
> _____ (b) The perception of pain and illness is very subjective.
>
> _____ (c) Some persons seek treatment because they actually like the "sick role".

Answers: **21-1.** (a) true (b) true (c) true.

22. Discuss the extent to which people tend to adhere to medical advice.

> **22-1.** The text lists three reasons for failure to comply with medical advice. One is that patients often fail to completely _____ treatment instructions. A second is that the treatment may prove to be quite _____. The third reason is not directly related to either instructions or treatment, but rather to the attitude towards the _____. A negative attitude makes compliance (more/less) likely.

Answers: **22-1.** understand, unpleasant (or aversive), physician or doctor, less.

PUTTING IT IN PERSPECTIVE

23. Explain how this chapter highlighted two of the text's unifying themes.

> **23-1.** The fact that the amount of stress in any given situation primarily lies in the eyes of the beholder nicely illustrates the theme that experience is _____.
>
> **23-2.** The fact that stress interacts with numerous other factors that affect health illustrates the theme of multifactorial _____.

Answers: **23-1.** subjective **23-2.** causation.

APPLICATION: IMPROVING COPING AND STRESS MANAGEMENT

24. Summarize Albert Ellis's ideas about controlling one's emotions.

> **24-1.** The main idea behind Albert Ellis's rational-emotive therapy is that stress is largely caused by _____ thinking. Therefore, by changing one's catastrophic thinking and taking a more rational approach, one can then reduce.
>
> **24-2.** Ellis illustrates this theory by postulating an A-B-C series of events. Describe below what is going on during each of these events.
>
> (A) activating event:

(B) belief:

(C) consequence:

24-3. Since the emotional turmoil in the A-B-C sequence is caused by the sequence, effort must be directed towards changing irrational beliefs. Ellis proposes two techniques for doing this. One must first learn to _____ instances of irrational beliefs. Then one must learn to actively _____ these irrational beliefs.

Answers: 24-1. catastrophic, stress **24-2.** (A) The activating event that precedes the stress. (B) One's belief about the event. (C) The emotional consequences that result from the belief. **24-3.** B, detect, dispute.

25. Discuss the adaptive value of humor and releasing pent-up emotions.

25-1. What dual role does humor appear to play in easing stress in difficult situations.

25-2. Why might talking or writing about a problem with a sympathetic friend prove useful when experiencing stress?

Answers: 25-1. It allows for both redefining the problem in a less threatening way and the releasing of tension. **25-2.** It may help to release pent-up tension.

26. Discuss the adaptive value of relaxation and exercise.

26-1. Complete the following statements regarding the adaptive value of relaxation and exercise.

(a) A quiet environment environment, a mental device, a passive attitude, and a comfortable position are conditions that facilitate:

(b) Eating a balanced diet, getting adequate sleep and exercise, and staying away from overeating and harmful drugs can help to minimize:

Answers: 26-1. (a) learning to relax (b) physical vulnerability.

REVIEW OF KEY TERMS

Acquired Immune Deficiency
   Syndrome (AIDS)
Aggression
Approach-approach conflict
Approach-avoidance conflict
Avoidance-avoidance conflict
Biopsychosocial model
Burnout
Catastrophic thinking
Catharsis
Conflict

Constructive coping
Coping
Defense mechanisms
Fight-or-flight response
Frustration
General adaptation syndrome
Hardiness
Health psychology
Immune response
Learned helplessness
Life changes

Optimism
Posttraumatic stress disorder (PTSD)
Pressure
Primary appraisal
Psychosomatic diseases
Rational-emotive therapy
Secondary appraisal
Social support
Stress
Type A personality
Type B personality

_____ 1. Holds that physical illness is caused by a complex interaction of biological, psychological, and sociocultural factors.

_____ 2. Concerned with how psychosocial forces relate to the promotion and maintenance of health, and the causation, prevention and treatment of illness.

_____ 3. Any circumstances that threaten or are perceived to threaten our well-being and thereby tax our coping abilities.

_____ 4. An initial evaluation of whether an event is irrelevant, relevant but not threatening, or stressful.

_____ 5. An evaluation of one's coping resources and options for dealing with a particular stress.

_____ 6. Occurs in any situation in which the pursuit of some goal is thwarted.

_____ 7. Occurs when two or more incompatible motivations or behavioral impulses compete for expression.

_____ 8. Occurs when a choice must be made between two attractive goals.

_____ 9. Occurs when a choice must be made between two unattractive goals.

_____ 10. Occurs when a choice must be made whether to pursue a single goal that has both attractive and unattractive aspects.

_____ 11. Any noticeable alterations in one's living circumstances that require readjustment.

_____ 12. Expectations or demands that one behave in a certain way.

_____ 13. A physiological reaction to threat in which the autonomic nervous system mobilizes an organism for either attacking or fleeing an enemy.

_____ 14. A model of the body's stress response consisting of three stages: alarm, resistance and exhaustion.

_____ 15. An active effort to master, reduce or tolerate the demands created by stress.

_____ 16. Involves any behavior that is intended to hurt someone, either physically or verbally.

_____ 17. Passive behavior produced by exposure to unavoidable aversive events.

_____ 18. Largely unconscious reactions that protect a person from unpleasant emotions such as anxiety and guilt.

_____ 19. Relatively healthy efforts to deal with stressful events.

_____ 20. Involves physical, mental and emotional exhaustion that is attributable to work-related stress.

_____ 21. Disturbed behavior that emerges after a major stressful event is over.

_____ 22. A behavior pattern marked by competitive, aggressive, impatient, hostile behavior.

_____ 23. A behavior pattern marked by relaxed, patient, easy-going, amicable behavior.

_____ 24. The body's defensive reaction to invasion by bacteria, viral agents, or other foreign substances.

_____ 25. Various types of aid and succor provided by members of one's social network.

_____ 26. A personality syndrome marked by commitment, challenge, and control that is purportedly associated with strong stress resistance.

_____ 27. A general tendency to expect good outcomes.

_____ 28. An approach to therapy that focuses on altering clients' patterns of irrational thinking to reduce maladaptive emotions and behavior.

_____ 29. The release of emotional tension.

_____ 30. Unrealistic and pessimistic appraisal of stress that exaggerates the magnitude of a problem.

_____ 31. Physical ailments caused in part by psychological factors, especially emotional distress.

_____ 32. A disorder in which the immune system is gradually weakened and eventually disabled by the human immunodeficiency virus (HIV).

Answers: 1. biopsychosocial model **2.** health psychology **3.** stress **4.** primary appraisal **5.** secondary appraisal **6.** frustration **7.** conflict **8.** approach-approach conflict **9.** avoidance-avoidance conflict **10.** approach-avoidance conflict **11.** life changes **12.** pressure **13.** fight-or-flight response **14.** general adaptation syndrome **15.** coping **16.** aggression **17.** learned helplessness **18.** defense mechanisms **19.** constructive coping **20.** burnout **21.** posttraumatic stress disorder **22.** Type A pattern **23.** Type B pattern **24.** immune response **25.** social support **26.** hardiness **27.** optimism **28.** rational-emotive therapy **29.** catharsis **30.** catastrophic thinking **31.** psychosomatic diseases **32.** Acquired Immune Deficiency Syndrome (AIDS).

REVIEW OF KEY PEOPLE

Walter Cannon

Robin DiMatteo

Albert Ellis

Meyer Friedman & Ray Rosenman

Thomas Holmes & Richard Rahe

Richard Lazarus

Neal Miller

Suzanne Ouellette (formerly Kobasa)

Michael Scheier & Charles Carver

Hans Selye

Shelley Taylor

_____ 1. Observed that minor hassles were more closely related to mental health than were major stressful events.

_____ 2. Noted for his extensive investigations of the three types of conflict.

_____ 3. These researchers developed the Social Readjustment Rating Scale.

_____ 4. One of the first theorists to describe the "fight-or-flight" response.

_____ 5. Coined the word "stress" and described the General Adaptation Syndrome.

_____ 6. These researchers found a connection between coronary risk and what they called Type A behavior.

7. Researched the notion that some persons may be hardier than others in resisting stress.

8. The developer of Rational-Emotive Therapy.

9. These researchers observed a correlation between optimism and good health in a sample of college students.

10. A leading expert on patient behavior.

11. Showed several lines of evidence indicating that illusions may sometimes be adaptive for mental and physical health.

Answers: 1. Lazarus **2.** Miller **3.** Holmes & Rahe **4.** Cannon **5.** Selye **6.** Friedman & Rosenman **7.** Ouellette (Kobasa) **8.** Ellis **9.** Scheier & Carver **10.** DiMatteo **11.** Taylor.

SELF-QUIZ

1. Which of the following statements is incorrect?
   a. stress is a subjective experience
   b. stress involves both primary and secondary appraisals
   c. minor hassles may prove more stressful than major ones
   d. one should seek to avoid all stress

2. You've been invited to dinner at a nice restaurant on the final night of a TV mini series you've been watching and thus find yourself confronted with:
   a. pressure
   b. frustration
   c. an approach-avoidance conflict
   d. an approach-approach conflict

3. The week of final exams subjects most students to what kind of stress?
   a. pressure
   b. change
   c. frustration
   d. conflict

4. High scores on the Social Readjustment Rating Scale were found to be correlated with psychological disturbances and:
   a. type A behavior patterns
   b. physical illness
   c. pessimistic attitudes
   d. all of the above

5. According to optimal-arousal theories, which of the following situations would be least affected by a high optimal-arousal level?
   a. taking a psychology exam
   b. typing a term paper
   c. buttoning a shirt
   d. learning to drive a car

6. The General Adaptation Syndrome shows that the body eventually successfully adapts to long-term stress. This statement is:
   a. true
   b. false

7. Which of the following organs is involved in both of the body's two major stress pathways?
   a. the adrenal gland
   b. the sympathetic nervous system
   c. the pituitary gland
   d. the pineal gland

8. Aggression is frequently triggered by:
   a. helplessness
   b. frustration
   c. loneliness
   d. change

9. Seeing someone die is one of the principal causes of:
   a. post-traumatic stress disorder
   b. burnout
   c. learned helplessness
   d. coronary heart disorder

10. Fred Fritz owns his own business to which he is highly committed. He loves it because he likes the challenge and the feeling that he is in control. Fred Fritz has the characteristics found in:
    a. Type A executives
    b. Type B executives
    c. hardy executives

11. One of the key links between stress and physical illness may be that the body's response to stress:
    a. increases the optimal-arousal level
    c. decreases the optimal-arousal level
    d. suppresses the adrenal gland

12. Smoking is to lung cancer as Type A behavior is to:
    a. coronary disease
    b. AIDS
    c. defensive coping
    d. mental disorders

13. A major idea behind Rational-Emotive Therapy is that stress is caused by:
    a. conflict
    b. frustration
    c. catastrophic thinking
    d. pressure

14. Social support, hardiness, and optimism are all related to:
    a. the Type B personality pattern
    b. a low level of stress
    c. defensive-coping strategies
    d. good physical health

15. Employing small positive illusions to alleviate stress:
    a. should always be avoided
    b. is a sign that one is neurotic
    c. may prove useful on occasion
    d. both a and b

Answers: 1. d **2.** d **3.** a **4.** b **5.** c **6.** b **7.** a **8.** b **9.** a **10.** c **11.** b **12.** a **13.** c **14.** d **15.** c.

Chapter Fourteen

Psychological Disorders

REVIEW OF KEY IDEAS

ABNORMAL BEHAVIOR: MYTHS, REALITIES, AND CONTROVERSIES

1. **Describe and evaluate the medical model of abnormal behavior.**

   1-1. The medical model uses physical illness as a model or metaphor to explain psychological disorders. Under the medical model, maladaptive behavior is referred to as mental _____.

   1-2. The term "mental illness" is so familiar to all of us that we rarely think about the meaning of the concept and whether or not the analogy with disease is a good one. Among the model's detractors, Thomas Szasz asserts that words such as *sickness*, *Illness*, and *disease* are correctly used only in reference to the _____, and that it is more appropriate to view abnormal behavior as a deviation from accepted social _____ than as an illness.

   1-3. Other critics object to the disease model because they believe that the derogatory _____ inherent in medical diagnosis tends to carry a strong social stigma. People tend to be _____ against those who are labeled mentally ill.

   1-4. Some critics also suggest that the medical model encourages sufferers to adopt the _____ role of patient, waiting for the doctor to produce a cure, rather than a more active role as problem solver.

   1-5. The text takes an intermediate position: while there certainly are problems with the medical model it can be useful as long as one understands that it is just an _____ and not a true explanation. (For example, the medical concepts of diagnosis, etiology, and prognosis have proven useful in treatment and study of psychological disorders.)

   Answers: **1-1.** illness (disease, sickness) **1-2.** body, norms (behavior, standards) **1-3.** stigma, prejudiced (biased) **1-4.** passive **1-5.** analogy (model).

2. **Explain the most commonly used criteria of abnormality and complexities that arise in their application.**

2-1.   What does abnormal mean? The three criteria most frequently used are *deviance*, *maladaptive behavior*, and *personal distress*.

(a) _____: Does not *conform* to cultural norms or standards.

(b) _____: Behavior that *interferes with* the individual's social or occupational functioning.

(c) _____: Intense *discomfort* produced by depression or anxiety.

2-2.   Following are three statements that describe a person with a particular type of disorder. Which criterion of abnormal behavior is illustrated by each statement? Place the letters from the list above in the appropriate blanks.

_____ Ralph washes his hands several dozen times a day. His handwashing interferes with his work and prevents him from establishing normal friendships.

_____ Even if Ralph's handwashing compulsion did not interfere with his work and social life, his behavior still would be considered strange. That is, most people do not do what he does.

_____ It is also the case that Ralph's skin is very raw, and he becomes extremely anxious when he does not have immediate access to a sink.

2-3.   In some cultures, hearing voices or speaking with gods may be valued. In our culture, however, such behavior is likely to be considered abnormal. While the major categories of disorder may transcend culture, our assessments of abnormality are nonetheless value judgments that are strongly influenced by our _____. Thus, one of the problems involved in defining abnormality is that there are no criteria for psychological disorders that are entirely _____ -free.

2-4.   Another complexity is that we all have *some* behaviors that fit the criteria referred to above *to some degree*: they interfere with our lives, cause us discomfort, and do not conform to cultural norms. Thus, the difference between normal and abnormal is not black and white but exists along a

_____.

2-5.   The fact that before 1973 the American Psychiatric Association listed homosexuality as a disorder but in 1973 decided it was not a disorder illustrates yet another complexity: Cultural norms vary not only as a function of culture but also change across _____.

Answers: 2-1. (a) deviance (b) maladaptive behavior (c) personal distress **2-2.** b, a, c **2-3.** culture (society), value (culture) **2-4.** continuum **2-5.** time.

3. **List three stereotypes of people with psychological disorders.**

3-1.   In the space below list three stereotypes of people with psychological disorders:

(a) The disorders are _____.

(b) People with the disorders are _____ and dangerous.

(c) People with the disorders behave in a bizarre manner and are very _____ from normal people.

Answers: 3-1. (a) incurable (b) violent (c) different.

4. Summarize the Featured Study on the admission of pseudopatients to mental hospitals.

4-1.   What type of people did Rosenhan seek to have admitted to mental hospitals?

4-2.   Once they were admitted, did the pseudopatients continue to complain of hearing voices, or did they behave normally?

4-3.   What proportion of the pseudopatients were admitted to the hospital?

4-4.   Indicate *true* of *false* for each of the following statements.

_____ (a) Once the patients no longer claimed to hear voices, the professional staff rapidly recognized that they were not abnormal.

_____ (b) Most of the pseudopatients were dismissed within a couple of days.

_____ (c) The diagnosis for most of the pseudopatients was that they suffered from a relatively mild form of mental disorder.

4-5.   What is the major implication to be drawn from Rosenhan's study?

Answers: 4-1. normal individuals **4-2.** behaved normally **4-3.** all of them (Eight people sought admission to mental hospitals in five states, and all of them were admitted.) **4-4.** (a) false (b) false (The shortest stay was 7 days, the longest 52 days, and the average 19 days.) (c) false (Most were diagnosed with schizophrenia, a severe form of mental illness.) **4-5.** The major implication is that it is difficult, even for mental health professionals, to distinguish normal from abnormal behavior. (The study may also be interpreted to mean that there is a bias toward seeing abnormality where it may not exist or that abnormality is easily feigned.)

5. List the five diagnostic axes of DSM-IV and discuss some of the controversial aspects of this classification system.

5-1.   Below are descriptions of the five axes of the DSM-IV classification system. Label each with the correct axis number (I through V).

_____ Listing of physical disorders

_____ Diagnosis of milder, long-running personality disturbances

_____ Diagnosis of the major disorders

_____ Estimates of the individual's current general level of adaptive functioning

_____ Notes concerning the severity of stress experienced by the individual in the past year

5-2.   The new DSM system has produced praise but some criticism as well. While the consistency it brought to diagnosis is a critically important step, it is important only to the extent that the categories accurately describe real conditions. Some critics have argued that consistency came at the price of sacrificing interest in the _____ of the diagnostic categories.

5-3.   Second, decisions about revision of the DSM are made by committees, committees that, it is argued, may be more persuaded by the rhetorical skills of a few committee members than the available _____ evidence.

5-4.   Third, the recent DSMs include everyday problems that are not traditionally thought of as mental illnesses (such as nicotine-dependence disorder and gambling disorder). Although it may seem odd to include these in the DSM, what is the advantage of doing so?

Answers: 5-1. III, II, I, V, IV **5-2.** validity **5-3.** empirical **5-4.** Since many health insurance policies reimburse only for treatment of disorders listed in the DSM, including these "everyday" problems may permit people to bill their insurance companies for treatment.

6. Discuss estimates of the prevalence of psychological disorders.

6-1.   Epidemiological studies assess the prevalence of various disorders across a specific period of time. Prevalence refers to the _____ of a population that exhibits a disorder during a specified period of time. For mental disorders, the time period is usually (<u>one year/the entire lifespan</u>).

6-2.   According to our best (if still approximate) estimates, what is the prevalence of mental illness in the United States? _____

Answers: 6-1. percentage (proportion), the entire lifespan **6-2.** Approximately one-third of our population suffers from some form of mental illness at some point in their lives.

ANXIETY DISORDERS

7. List four types of anxiety disorders and describe the symptoms associated with each.

7-1.   List the names of the four anxiety syndromes in the space below. As hints, the initial letters of some key words are listed at the left.

GAD: _____

PhD: _____

OCD: _____

PDA: _____ and _____

7-2.   Match the anxiety disorders with the symptoms that follow by placing the appropriate letters (from the previous question) in the blanks.

(a) _PDA_   Sudden, unexpected, and paralyzing attacks of anxiety

(b) _GAD_   Not tied to a specific object or event

(c) _OCD_   Senseless, repetitive rituals

(d) _GAD_   Brooding over decisions

(e) _PhD_   Fear of specific objects or situations

(f) _PDA_   Persistent intrusion of distressing and unwanted thoughts

(g) _GAD_   Free-floating anxiety

(h) _PDA_   Frequently includes fear of going out in public

8. **Discuss the contribution of biological, cognitive, and personality factors, conditioning, and stress to the etiology of anxiety disorders.**

8-1. Several types of studies indicate that there is a genetic factor in anxiety disorders. For example, twin studies find higher concordance rates for anxiety among _____ twins than _____ twins. In addition, infants who display a temperament described as _____, thought to have a strong genetic basis, appear to have a predisposition to anxiety disorders.

8-2. Other biological evidence implicates disturbances at synapses using GABA for several types of anxiety disorders and of serotonin for panic attacks and obsessive-compulsive disorder. Thus, the body chemicals known as _____ appear to play an important role in anxiety.

8-3. Conditioning or learning clearly plays a role as well. For example, if an individual is bitten by a dog, he or she may develop a fear of dogs through the process of _____ conditioning. The individual may then avoid dogs in the future, a response maintained by _____ conditioning.

8-4. People are more likely to be afraid of snakes than of hot irons. Using Seligman's notion of preparedness, explain why.

8-5. Two types of anecdotal evidence do not support the conditioning point of view. For example, people with phobias (<u>always can/frequently cannot</u>) recall a traumatic incident, and people who have experienced extreme traumas (<u>always/frequently do not</u>) develop phobias.

8-6. As discussed in Chapter 6, the conditioning models are being extended to include a larger role for cognitive factors. For example, children probably acquire fears by _____ the behavior of anxious parents.

8-7. In addition, cognitive theorists indicate that certain *thinking styles* contribute to anxiety. For example, as indicated in your text, the sentence "The doctor examined little Emma's Growth" could refer either to height or to a tumor. People who are high in anxiety will tend to perceive the (<u>tumor/height</u>) interpretation. People's tendency to experience anxiety, in other words, appears to be related to their readiness to perceive threat _____.

8-8. Personality also plays a role. Not surprisingly, people who score high on the _____ trait of the "big five" personality factors have an elevated prevalence of anxiety disorders and a poorer prognosis for recovery.

8-9. Finally, stress is related to the anxiety disorders. For example, one study found that men who experienced stress were 8.5 times as likely to develop generalized _____ disorders as men under low stress. In another study, patients with _____ disorder were found to have experienced a dramatic increase in stress in the month prior to the onset of their disorder.

SOMATOFORM DISORDERS

9. **Compare and contrast the three somatoform disorders and discuss their etiology.**

9-1. For each of the following symptoms, indicate which disorder is described by placing the appropriate letters in the blanks: S for somatization, C for conversion, and H for hypochondriasis.

_____ Serious disability that may include paralysis, loss of vision or hearing, loss of feeling, and so on

_____ Many different minor physical ailments accompanied by a long history of medical treatment

_____ Cannot believe the doctors report that the person is not really ill

_____ Symptoms that appear to be organic in origin but don't match underlying anatomical organization

_____ Diverse complaints that implicate many different organ systems

_____ Usually does not involve disability so much as overinterpreting slight possible signs of illness

_____ "Glove anesthesia"; seizures without loss of bladder control

9-2. In the film *Hannah and Her Sisters* Woody Allen is convinced that certain minor physical changes are a sign of cancer. When tests eventually find no evidence of cancer, he is sure the tests have been done incorrectly. Which of the somatoform disorders does this seem to represent? _____

9-3. The somatoform disorders are associated with certain personality types, with particular cognitive styles, and with learning. Among personality types, the self-centered, excitable, and overly dramatic _____ personalities are more at risk for developing these disorders.

9-4. With regard to cognitive factors, focusing excessive attention on internal _____ factors, or believing that good health should involve a complete lack of discomfort, may contribute to somatoform disorders.

9-5. With regard to learning, the sick role may be positively reinforced through, for example, _____ from others or negatively reinforced by _____ certain of life's problems or unpleasant aspects..

DISSOCIATIVE DISORDERS

10. **Describe three dissociative disorders and discuss their etiology.**

10-1. The three dissociative disorders involve memory and identity. Two of the disorders involve fairly massive amounts of forgetting, dissociative _____ and dissociative _____.

10-2. People who have been in serious accidents frequently can't remember the accident or events surrounding the accident. This type of memory loss, which involves specific traumatic events, is known as dissociative _____.

10-3. An even greater memory loss, in which people lose their memories for their entire lives along with their sense of identity, is termed dissociative _____.

10-4. You may have seen media characterizations of individuals who can't remember who they are—what their names are, where they live, who their family is, and so on. While popularly referred to as amnesia, this type of dissociative disorder is more correctly called dissociative _____.

10-5. A few years ago there was a spate of appearances on talk shows by guests who claimed to have more than one identity or personality. This disorder is still widely known as _____- _____ disorder (MPD), but the formal name in the DSM-IV is _____ _____ disorder. The disorder is also often (correctly/mistakenly) called schizophrenia.

10-6. What causes dissociative disorders? Dissociative amnesia and dissociative fugue are related to excessive _____, but little else is known about why these extreme reactions occur in a tiny minority of people.

10-7. With regard to multiple-personality disorder, the diagnosis is controversial. Although many clinicians believe that the disorder is authentic, Spanos argues that it is the product of media attention and the misguided probings of a small minority of psychotherapists. In other words, Spanos believes that MPD (is/is not) a genuine disorder.

10-8. While the majority of people with multiple-personality disorders report having been emotionally and sexually _____ in childhood, little is known about the causes of this controversial diagnosis.

Answers: 10-1. amnesia, fugue **10-2.** amnesia **10-3.** fugue **10-4.** is **10-5.** multiple-personality, dissociative identity disorder, mistakenly **10-6.** stress **10-7.** is not **10-8.** abused.

MOOD DISORDERS

11. Describe the two major mood disorders: depressive disorder and bipolar disorder.

11-1. While the terms manic and depressive describe mood, they refer to a number of other characteristics as well, listed below. With one or two words for each characteristic describe the *manic* and *depressive* episodes. (Before you make the lists, it may be a good idea to review Table 14.2 and the sections on depressive and bipolar mood disorders.)

	Manic	*Depressive*
mood:	_____	_____
sleep:	_____	_____
activity:	_____	_____
speech:	_____	_____
sex drive:	_____	_____

11-2. Be sure to note that mania and depression are not the names of the two affective disorders. What is the name of the disorders accompanied only by depressive states? _____ By both manic and depressive states? _____

11-3. The DSM refers to persistent but relatively mild symptoms of depressive disorder as _____ disorder and to persistent but mild symptoms of bipolar disorder as _____ disorder.

Answers: 11-1. mood: euphoric (elated, extremely happy, etc.) vs. depressed (blue, extremely sad); sleep: goes without or doesn't want to vs. can't (insomnia); activity: very active vs. sluggish, slow, inactive; speech: very fast vs. very slow; sex drive: increased vs. decreased **11-2.** depressive disorders (or unipolar disorders), bipolar mood disorders **11-3.** dysthymic, cyclothymic.

12. Explain how genetic and neurochemical factors may be related to the development of mood disorders.

12-1. Twin studies implicate genetic factors in the development of mood disorders. In a sentence, summarize the results of these studies.

12-2. While the exact mechanism is not known, the activities of norepinephrine, serotonin, and other _____ are associated with mood disorders. In support of the role played by these body chemicals, it has been found that administering certain _____ known to affect the availability of neurotransmitters in the brain tends to lessen the severity of mood disorders.

Answers: 12-1. For mood disorders, the concordance rate for identical twins is much higher than that for fraternal twins (actually a huge difference, as shown in Figure 14.15, about 67% for the former compared to 15% for the latter). **12-2.** neurotransmitters, drugs.

13. Explain how cognitive factors, interpersonal factors, and stress may be related to the development of mood disorders.

13-1. Martin Seligman's model of depression is referred to as the _____ _____ model. While he originally based his theory of depression on an animal conditioning model involving exposure to unavoidable aversive stimuli, he has more recently emphasized (cognitive/behavioral) factors.

13-2. The reformulated version of learned helplessness involves people's patterns of _____, the inferences people make about the causes of their own and others' behavior.

13-3. Below are possible thoughts that a person might have after performing poorly-on a test in school, in an athletic event, in a social encounter, etc. Following each thought are three dimensions of attributional style. Circle the one pole from each pair that best describes the sample cognition.

(a) "I've never been very good at this type of thing and I'm not doing well now."

internal ——————————————— external

stable ——————————————— unstable

global ——————————————— specific

(b) "I messed up the test this time because I was lazy, but next time I'll work harder."

internal ———————————————————— external

stable ———————————————————— unstable

global ———————————————————— specific

(c) "I just can't ever seem to do anything well."

internal ———————————————————— external

stable ———————————————————— unstable

global ———————————————————— specific

(d) "I messed up, but on the day of the event I had the flu and a high fever. I'm rarely sick."

internal ———————————————————— external

stable ———————————————————— unstable

global ———————————————————— specific

13-4. Which of the above attributional styles (represented by a, b, c, or d) is most likely to characterize depressed people? _____ Least likely to characterize depressed people? _____

13-5. With regard to interpersonal factors, depressed people tend to lack _____ skills. How does this characteristic affect the ability to obtain reinforcers?

13-6. Why do we tend to reject depressed people?

13-7. What is the relationship between stress and the onset of mood disorders?

Answers: 13-1. learned helplessness, cognitive **13-2.** attributions **13-3.** (a) internal, stable, specific (b) internal, unstable, specific (c) internal, stable, global (d) external, unstable, specific **13-4.** c, d **13-5.** social (interpersonal); lack of social skills makes it difficult to obtain certain reinforcers, such as good friends and desirable jobs. **13-6.** Because they are not pleasant to be around. Depressed people complain a lot, are irritable, and tend to pass their mood along to others. **13-7.** There is a moderately strong link between stress and the onset of mood disorders.

SCHIZOPHRENIC DISORDERS

14. Describe the general characteristics (symptoms) of schizophrenia.

14-1. Before we review the different types of schizophrenia, consider some general characteristics of the schizophrenic disorders, as follows.

(a) Irrational thought: Disturbed thought processes may include false beliefs, known as

_____ (e.g., the false belief that one is a world-famous political figure who is being pursued by terrorists).

(b) Deterioration of adaptive behavior: The deterioration usually involves social relationships, work, and neglect of personal _____.

(c) Distorted perception: This category may include hearing (or sometimes seeing) things that aren't really there. These sensory experiences are known as _____.

⌐ (d) Disturbed emotion: Emotional responsiveness may be disturbed in a variety of ways. The person may have little or no responsiveness, referred to as _____ affect, or they may show _____ emotional responses, such as laughing at news of a tragic death.

Answers: 14-1. (a) delusions (b) hygiene (cleanliness) (c) hallucinations (d) flat (flattened, blunted), inappropriate.

15. **Describe two classification systems for schizophrenic subtypes and discuss the course of schizophrenia (including factors related to prognosis).**

⌐ **15-1.** Write the names of the four recognized subcategories of schizophrenia next to the descriptions that follow.

(a) _____ type: Particularly severe deterioration, incoherence, complete social withdrawal, aimless babbling and giggling, delusions centering on bodily functions.

(b) _____ type: Muscular rigidity and stupor at one extreme or random motor activity, hyperactivity, and incoherence at the other; now quite rare.

(c) _____ type: Delusions of persecution and grandeur.

(d) _____ type: Clearly schizophrenic but doesn't fit other three categories.

⌐ **15-2.** Many critics have asserted that there are no meaningful differences among the categories listed above and have proposed an alternative classification system. Nancy Andreasen and others have described a classification system consisting of only two categories, one that consists of _____ symptoms and the other of _____ symptoms.

15-3. In Andreasen's system, "positive" and "negative" do not mean pleasant and unpleasant. Positive symptoms *add* something to "normal" behavior (like chaotic speech), and negative symptoms *subtract* something (like social withdrawal). Indicate which of the following are positive and which negative by placing a P or an N in the appropriate blanks.

_____ flattened emotions

_____ hallucinations

_____ bizarre behavior

_____ social withdrawal

_____ apathy

⌐ **15-4.** When does schizophrenia tend to emerge?

⌐ **15-5.** Mark the following T (true) or F (false).

_____ Schizophrenia may have either a sudden or gradual onset.

_____ A schizophrenic can never truly recover from the disorder.

_____ About half of schizophrenic patients experience a significant degree of recovery.

_____ Males tend to have an earlier onset of schizophrenia than females.

_____ Males tend to have more hospitalizations and higher relapse rates than females.

15-6. What characteristics tend to predict recovery from schizophrenia? In the list below indicate the favorable and unfavorable prognostic indicators by placing a plus (+) or minus (-) in the appropriate blanks.

_____ Has a rapid onset

_____ Occurs at a young age

_____ Accompanied by good previous social and work adjustment

_____ A supportive family to return to

Answers: 15-1. (a) disorganized (b) catatonic (c) paranoid (d) undifferentiated **15-2.** positive, negative **15-3.** N, P, P, N, N, P, N **15-4.** generally during adolescence and early adulthood, rarely after age 45 **15-5.** T, F, T, T, T **15-6.** +, -, +, +.

16. Explain how genetic vulnerability, neurochemical factors, and structural abnormalities in the brain may contribute to the etiology of schizophrenia.

16-1. As with mood disorders, twin studies implicate genetic factors in the development of schizophrenia. In a sentence, summarize the general results of these studies.

16-2. As with mood disorders, neurotransmitter substances in the brain are implicated in the etiology of schizophrenia. Although the evidence is somewhat clouded, what is the name of the neurotransmitter thought to be involved? _____

16-3. In addition to possible neurochemical factors, certain differences in brain structure may be associated with schizophrenia. One of these differences involves enlarged brain _____, which are hollow fluid-filled cavities in the brain. Current thinking, however, is that this brain abnormality is an _____ rather than a cause of schizophrenia.

16-4. Current research points to the thalamus as a possible structural factor in schizophrenia. The thalamus in schizophrenics tends to be (smaller/larger) and show (less/more) metabolic activity than is the case for normals.

Answers: 16-1. For schizophrenia, the concordance rate is higher for identical than for fraternal twins (about 48% for identical compared with about 17% for fraternal twins. (For comparison, recall that the respective percentages for mood disorders are 67% and 15%.) **16-2.** dopamine (thought to be a factor because most drugs useful in treating schizophrenia decrease dopamine activity in the brain) **16-3.** ventricles, effect **16-4.** smaller, less.

17. Summarize evidence on how family dynamics and stress may be related to the development of schizophrenia.

17-1. Families that communicate in an unintelligible manner (e.g., in vague, muddled, contradictory, or fragmented sentences) have a communication style that is referred to as communication _____. Children brought up in these families are somewhat more likely to develop _____ than those brought up with a more normal communication pattern.

17-2. Expressed emotion refers to the extent to which a patient's relatives are overly critical or protective or are in other ways overly emotionally involved with the patient. Patients returning to families that are high in expressed emotion have a relapse rate that is much (higher/lower) than that of families low in expressed emotion.

17-3. Obviously, many people who are subjected to intense stress do not develop schizophrenia. As with several other disorders, stress does seem to be a factor in schizophrenia but only for who are already _____ to the disorder.

Answers: **17-1.** deviance, schizophrenia **17-2.** higher **17-3.** vulnerable (predisposed).

PERSONALITY DISORDERS

18. **Discuss the nature of personality disorders and describe the three broad clusters of such disorders.**

18-1. The personality disorders, which are recorded on Axis II, are (<u>less/more</u>) severe than most of the disorders on Axis I. They consist of relatively extreme and (<u>flexible/inflexible</u>) sets of personality traits that cause subjective distress or impaired functioning.

18-2. Complete the terms used to describe the three broad clusters of personality disorders.

(a) _____-fearful cluster

(b) _____-eccentric cluster

(c) _____-impulsive cluster

18-3. Match the clusters listed in the previous question with the following descriptions by placing the appropriate letters in the blanks.

_____ Distrustful, aloof, unable to connect emotionally with others

_____ Maladaptive efforts to control fear of social rejection

_____ Overly dramatic or impulsive

18-4. The majority of patients diagnosed as having a histrionic personality disorder (one of the dramatic-impulsive clusters) also qualifies for two or more other personality disorders. As this example illustrates, a major problem with the classification of personality disorders is that there is an enormous _____ among the disorders.

18-5. In hopes of remedying these problems, some theorists have suggested that personality disorders be described in terms a limited number of personality _____, such as the five-factor model discussed in Chapter 12. While this approach has many advocates, psychologists are not in agreement about which personality dimensions to use or even whether or not this approach has clinical utility.

Answers: **18-1.** less, inflexible **18-2.** anxious, odd, dramatic **18-3.** b, a, c **18-4.** overlap **18-5.** dimensions (factors, traits).

19. **Describe the antisocial personality disorder and discuss its etiology.**

19-1. The *antisocial* personality disorder is more extensively researched than are the other personality disorders and is described in more detail in your text. Check the concepts from the following list that are likely to correctly describe this disorder.

_____ sexually promiscuous   _____ genuinely affectionate

_____ manipulative   _____ impulsive

_____ feels guilty   _____ lacks an adequate conscience

_____ much more likely to occur in males than females   _____ may appear charming

_____ may be a con artist, thug, or unprincipled business executive

19-2. What types of studies support the idea that biological factors are involved in the etiology of the antisocial personality?

19-3. What environmental factors seem to be related to development of an antisocial personality?

Answers: 19-1. All the terms describe the antisocial personality except for *feels guilty* and *genuinely affectionate*. **19-2.** Twin and adoption studies. (There also has been mixed support for Eysenck's idea that antisocial personalities are chronically lower in autonomic arousal and therefore less likely to develop conditioned inhibitions.) **19-3.** Studies suggest that inconsistent, ineffective, or abusive parental discipline may be involved. Since one or both parents may also exhibit antisocial characteristics, observational learning may also be a factor.

PSYCHOLOGICAL DISORDERS AND THE LAW

20. **Distinguish between the legal concepts of insanity and incompetence and explain the grounds for involuntary commitment.**

20-1. While the words *schizophrenic, insane*, and *incompetent* may, in some cases, apply to the same person, the terms do not mean the same thing. Only the term *schizophrenic* is a psychological diagnosis; the other two words are legal terms. Distinguish between these terms by placing them in the blanks next to the descriptions below.

(a) _____ An individual that a court has declared to be mentally unfit to stand trial

(b) _____ An individual who is troubled by delusions and who in general seems out of touch with reality

(c) _____ A person that a court has declared mentally ill at the time of the crime and therefore not responsible for his criminal actions

20-2. What is the difference between the legal concepts of *insanity* and *incompetence?*

20-3. Roughly, how is insanity defined under the M'naghten rule?

20-4. Answer the following questions concerning the procedures needed for involuntary commitment to a psychiatric facility.

(a) What three criteria are used to determine whether an individual should be committed?

___ (b) What is required to temporarily commit an individual for one to three days?

(c) What is required for longer-term commitment?

Answers: 20-1. (a) incompetent (b) schizophrenic (c) insane **20-2.** The M'naghten rule says that insanity exists when a person cannot distinguish right from wrong. **20-3.** *Insane* means that a court has declared an individual not responsible for his or her actions because of a mental illness. *Incompetent* means that the court has decided that the individual does not have the capacity to understand the nature of the legal proceedings at trial. Thus, *insane* refers to mental state at the time of the alleged crime; *incompetent* refers to mental state at the time of the trial. **20-4.** (a) In general, for people to be involuntarily committed, mental health and legal authorities must judge them to be (1) dangerous to themselves or (2) dangerous to others or (3) in extreme need of treatment. (b) Temporary commitment (usually 24 to 72 hours) may be done in emergencies by a psychologist or psychiatrist. (c) Longer-term commitments are issued by a court and require a formal hearing.

CULTURE AND PATHOLOGY

21. **Discuss the evidence on three issues related to culture and pathology.**

21-1.   Your text divides viewpoints about culture and pathology into *relativists* and *panculturalists*. The
_____ believe that there are basic standards of mental health that are *universal* across
cultures. The _____ believe that psychological disorders *vary as a function of culture*.

21-2.   Several questions reflect on this issue. First, are the *same disorders* found in different cultures? To some
extent, yes. The three most severe disorders, listed below, are identifiable throughout the world:

_____

_____

_____

21-3.   On the other hand, some of the milder disorders listed in the DSM, such as hypochondriasis, narcissistic
personality, and generalized _____ disorder, go unrecognized in some cultures.

21-4.   In addition, there are (<u>no disorders/some disorders</u>) that are unique to particular cultures. For example,
the obsessive fear about one's penis withdrawing into one's abdomen is found only among Chinese males
in Malaya, and _____ nervosa is found only in affluent Western societies.

21-5.   The second question concerns whether or not *patterns of symptoms* are similar across cultures. In general,
they are. But while delusions are characteristic of schizophrenia in (<u>only Western/all</u>) cultures, the
specific delusions reported (<u>vary/are invariant</u>) across culture. For example, satellites or microwaves
would not be a part of the delusional systems of people in less technologically advanced countries. .

21-6.   The third question concerns prevalence rates. For two of the major disorders, _____ and
_____ disorder, prevalence rates are quite similar across cultures, about 1 percent which
may be attributable to the strong biological component of these disorders. For most of the other disorders
prevalence rates (<u>vary considerably/are fairly constant</u>) across cultures.

21-7.   In summary, are psychological disorders universal, or do they vary across cultures?

a. There are some universal standards of normality and abnormality.

b. There are some disorders that are specific to particular cultures.

c. Both of the above: some aspects of psychopathology are universal, some vary as a function of culture.

Answers: 21-1. panculturalists, relativists **21-2.** schizophrenia, depression, bipolar disorder **21-3.** anxiety **21-4.** some disorders, anorexia **21-5.** all, vary **21-6.** schizophrenia, bipolar, vary considerably **21-7.** c.

PUTTING IT IN PERSPECTIVE

22. Explain how this chapter highlighted four of the text's organizing themes.

22-1. Below are examples of the highlighted themes. Indicate which theme fits each example by writing the appropriate abbreviations in the blanks: MC for multifactorial causation, HE for the interplay of heredity and environment, SH for sociohistorical context, and C for the influence of culture.

(a) Mood and schizophrenic disorders will occur if one has a genetic vulnerability to the disorder *and* if one experiences a considerable amount of stress. ____

(b) Psychological disorders are caused by neurochemical factors, brain abnormalities, styles of child rearing, life stress, and so on. ____

(c) Bipolar disorder occurs in all societies; anorexia nervosa occurs only in affluent Western societies. ____

(d) Homosexuality is no longer classified as a disorder in the DSM. ____ and ____

Answers: 22-1. (a) HE (b) MC (c) C (d) SH, C.

APPLICATION: UNDERSTANDING AND PREVENTING SUICIDE

23. Summarize how age, sex, marital status, and occupation are related to the prevalence of suicide.

23-1. Which marital status is associated with the fewest suicides?

a. single

b. divorced

c. married

d. bereaved

23-2. Across which age range does the largest number of suicide *attempts* occur?

a. 14 to 24

b. 24 to 44

c. over 55

23-3. Suicide attempts are more common among ____; actual (successful) suicides are more common among ____.

a. males, females

b. females, males

23-4. See Figure 14.25. After age 55 the suicide rate increases:

a. only among men

b. only among women

c. for both men and women

23-5. In terms of occupational status, suicides are particularly frequent among:

a. the unemployed

b. pressured professionals (e.g., doctors and lawyers)

c. both of the above

Answers: 23-1. c 23-2. b 23-3. b 23-4. a 23-5. c.

24. **List four myths about suicidal behavior.**

24-1.   For each of the following statements, indicate whether it is true of false.

____ (a) Many suicidal individuals talk about committing suicide before they actually make the attempt.

____ (b) The majority of suicides are preceded by some kind of warning.

____ (c) A small minority of those who attempt suicide are fully intent on dying.

____ (d) Many people are suicidal for a limited period of time, not for their entire lives.

Answers: 24-1. All of these statements are true and are thus contrary to the four myths of suicide.

25. **Summarize advice provided on preventing a suicide.**

25-1.   While it is probably true that no one knows exactly what to do about suicide, your text makes some suggestions that may be useful if you ever find yourself face to face with someone contemplating suicide. Label each of the following statements with one of the six suggestions for dealing with a suicidal person.

1. Take suicidal talk seriously.

2. Provide empathy and social support.

3. Identify and clarify the crucial problem.

4. Suggest alternative courses of action.

5. Capitalize on any doubts.

6. Encourage professional consultation.

(a) "Look, there's a number I want you to call, so that you can talk with someone about this and make an appointment for professional help."

(b) "You say you're worried about how your family would react. You're right—this would be really tough for them."

(c) "You think no one cares. I know that I care, and that's why I'm here. I think I can understand what you've been going through, and I want to help."

(d) "O.K., let's really try to put a finger on what's the main issue here. Did you say that you think you've failed your family? Does that seem to be the main problem?"

(e) "Let's try to come up with some alternative possibilities about what to do to solve this situation. I've got some suggestions."

(f) "You've been talking about things that sound like they're related to suicide. Are you contemplating suicide? Because if you are, I want to talk to you about it."

Answers: 25-1. (a) 6. Encourage professional consultation. (b) 5. Capitalize on any doubts. (c) 2. Provide empathy and social support. (d) 3. Identify and clarify the crucial problem. (e) 4. Suggest alternative courses of action. (f) 1. Take suicidal talk seriously.

REVIEW OF KEY TERMS

Agoraphobia
Antisocial personality disorder
Anxiety disorders
Attributions
Bipolar disorders
Catatonic schizophrenia
Competency
Concordance rate
Conversion disorder
Culture-bound disorders
Cyclothymic disorder
Delusions
Depressive disorders
Diagnosis
Disorganized schizophrenia

Dissociative amnesia
Dissociative disorders
Dissociative fugue
Dissociative identity disorder
Dysthymic disorder
Epidemiology
Etiology
Generalized anxiety disorder
Hallucinations
Hypochondriasis
Insanity
Involuntary commitment
Medical model
Mood disorders
Multiple-personality disorder

Obsessive-compulsive disorder (OCD)
Panic disorder
Paranoid schizophrenia
Personality disorders
Phobic disorder
Prevalence
Prognosis
Psychosomatic diseases
Schizophrenic disorders
Seasonal affective disorder (SAD)
Somatization disorder
Somatoform disorders
Transvestism
Undifferentiated schizophrenia

_____ 1. Proposes that it is useful to think of abnormal behavior as a disease.

_____ 2. Involves distinguishing one illness from another.

_____ 3. Refers to the apparent causation and developmental history of an illness.

_____ 4. A forecast about the possible course of an illness.

_____ 5. A sexual disorder in which a man achieves sexual arousal by dressing in women's clothing.

_____ 6. The study of the distribution of mental or physical disorders in a population.

_____ 7. Refers to the percentage of a population that exhibits a disorder during a specified time period.

_____ 8. A class of disorders marked by feelings of excessive apprehension and anxiety.

_____ 9. Disorder marked by a chronic high level of anxiety that is not tied to any specific threat.

_____ 10. Disorder marked by a persistent and irrational fear of an object or situation that presents no realistic danger.

_____ 11. Disorder that involves recurrent attacks of overwhelming anxiety that usually occur suddenly and unexpectedly.

_____ 12. Disorder marked by persistent uncontrollable intrusions of unwanted thoughts and urges to engage in senseless rituals.

_____ 13. A fear of going out in public places.

_____ 14. Physical ailments with a genuine organic basis that are caused in part by psychological factors.

_____ 15. A class of disorders involving physical ailments that have no authentic organic basis and are due to psychological factors.

_____ 16. Disorder marked by a history of diverse physical complaints that appear to be psychological in origin.

_____ 17. Disorder that involves a significant loss of physical function (with no apparent organic basis), usually in a single-organ system.

_____ **18.** Disorder that involves excessive preoccupation with health concerns and incessant worrying about developing physical illnesses.

_____ **19.** A class of disorders in which people lose contact with portions of their consciousness or memory, resulting in disruptions in their sense of identity.

_____ **20.** A sudden loss of memory for important personal information that is too extensive to be due to normal forgetting.

_____ **21.** People's loss of memory for their entire lives along with their sense of personal identity.

_____ **22.** Older term, still widely used, that describes the coexistence in one person of two or more personalities.

_____ **23.** The new term that replaced multiple-personality disorder in the DSM-IV.

_____ **24.** A class of disorders marked by depressed or elevated mood disturbances that may spill over to disrupt physical, perceptual, social, and thought processes.

_____ **25.** Mood disorder that tends to repeatedly occur at about the same time of the year.

_____ **26.** Disorders marked by persistent feelings of sadness and despair and a loss of interest in previous sources of pleasure.

_____ **27.** Disorders marked by the experience of both depressive and manic periods.

_____ **28.** Statistic indicating the percentage of twin pairs or other pairs of relatives who exhibit the same disorder.

_____ **29.** Inferences that people draw about the causes of events, others' behavior, and their own behavior.

_____ **30.** A class of disorders marked by disturbances in thought that spill over to affect perceptual, social, and emotional processes.

_____ **31.** False beliefs that are maintained even though they clearly are out of touch with reality.

_____ **32.** Sensory perceptions that occur in the absence of a real, external stimulus, or gross distortions of perceptual input.

_____ **33.** Type of schizophrenia dominated by delusions of persecution, along with delusions of grandeur.

_____ **34.** Type of schizophrenia marked by striking motor disturbances, ranging from muscular rigidity to random motor activity.

_____ **35.** Type of schizophrenia marked by a particularly severe deterioration of adaptive behavior.

_____ **36.** Type of schizophrenia marked by idiosyncratic mixtures of schizophrenic symptoms.

_____ **37.** A class of disorders marked by extreme, inflexible personality traits that cause subjective distress or impaired social and occupational functioning.

_____ **38.** Disorder marked by impulsive, callous, manipulative, aggressive, and irresponsible behavior; reflects a failure to accept social norms.

_____ **39.** A legal status indicating that a person cannot be held responsible for his or her actions because of mental illness.

_____ **40.** A defendant's capacity to stand trial.

_____ **41.** Legal situation in which people are hospitalized in psychiatric facilities against their will.

_____ **42.** Chronic but relatively mild symptoms of bipolar disturbance.

	43.	Abnormal syndromes found only in a few cultural groups.
	44.	Chronic depression that is insufficient in severity to merit diagnosis of a major depressive episode.

Answers: 1. medical model **2.** diagnosis **3.** etiology **4.** prognosis **5.** transvestism **6.** epidemiology **7.** prevalence **8.** anxiety disorders **9.** generalized anxiety disorder **10.** phobic disorder **11.** panic disorder **12.** obsessive-compulsive disorder **13.** agoraphobia **14.** psychosomatic diseases **15.** somatoform disorders **16.** somatization disorder **17.** conversion disorder **18.** hypochondriasis **19.** dissociative disorders **20.** dissociative amnesia **21.** dissociative fugue **22.** multiple-personality disorder **23.** dissociative identity disorder **24.** mood disorders **25.** seasonal affective disorder (SAD) **26.** depressive disorders **27.** bipolar disorders **28.** concordance rate **29.** attributions **30.** schizophrenic disorders **31.** delusions **32.** hallucinations **33.** paranoid schizophrenia **34.** catatonic schizophrenia **35.** disorganized schizophrenia **36.** undifferentiated schizophrenia **37.** personality disorders **38.** antisocial personality disorder **39.** insanity **40.** competency **41.** involuntary commitment **42.** cyclothymia **43.** culture-bound disorders **44.** dysthymia.

REVIEW OF KEY PEOPLE

Nancy Andreasen   Thomas Szasz
David Rosenhan   Martin Seligman

	1.	Critic of the medical model; argues that abnormal behavior usually involves a deviation from social norms rather than an illness.
	2.	Did a study on admission of pseudopatients to a mental hospital; concluded that our mental health system is biased toward seeing pathology where it doesn't exist.
	3.	Developed the concept of "preparedness"; believes that classical conditioning creates most phobic responses.
	4.	Proposed an alternative approach to subtyping that divides schizophrenic disorders into just two categories based on the presence of negative versus positive symptoms.

Answers: 1. Szasz **2.** Rosenhan **3.** Seligman **4.** Andreasen.

SELF-QUIZ

1. Which of the following concepts or people asserts that abnormal behavior is best thought of as an illness?
   a. the behavioral model
   b. the medical model
   c. Thomas Szasz
   d. Arthur Staats

2. Judgments of abnormality are usually based on assessments of:
   a. deviance from cultural standards
   b. degree of emotional distress
   c. the extent to which the behavior is maladaptive
   d. all of the above

3. In Rosenhan's study involving admission of pseudopatients to psychiatric facilities, most of the "patients" were:
   a. diagnosed as seriously disturbed
   b. diagnosed as suffering from a mild neurosis
   c. dismissed within two days
   d. misdiagnosed by the ward attendants but correctly diagnosed by the professional staff

4. An individual gets sudden, paralyzing attacks of anxiety and fears going out in public away from her house. Which anxiety disorder does this describe?
   a. generalized anxiety disorder
   b. phobic disorder
   c. obsessive-compulsive disorder
   d. agoraphobia

5. Ralph cleans and scrubs the cupboards in his house seven times each day. Which anxiety disorder does this describe?
   a. generalized anxiety disorder
   b. phobic disorder
   c. obsessive-compulsive disorder
   d. panic disorder

6. Human beings may have evolved to be more easily conditioned to fear some stimuli than others. This is Seligman's notion of:
   a. preparedness
   b. anxiety differentiation
   c. somatization
   d. learned helplessness

7. Which of the following is included under the somatoform disorders?
   a. bipolar mood disorders
   b. hypochondriasis
   c. phobias
   d. schizophrenia

8. Paralysis or loss of feeling that does not match underlying anatomical organization is a symptom of:
   a. somatization disorder
   b. conversion disorder
   c. hypochondriasis
   d. malingering

9. Multiple personality is:
   a. an anxiety disorder
   b. a dissociative disorder
   c. a mood disorder
   d. a somatoform disorder

10. The disorder marked by striking motor disturbances ranging from rigidity to random motor activity and incoherence is termed:
    a. catatonic schizophrenia
    b. multiple personality
    c. dissociative disorder
    d. paranoid schizophrenia

11. Which of the following tends to be associated with recovery from schizophrenia?
    a. rapid, as opposed to gradual, onset of the disorder
    b. onset at an early age
    c. a family high in expressed emotion
    d. all of the above

12. Genetic factors appear to play a role in causing:
    a. anxiety disorders
    b. mood disorders
    c. schizophrenic disorders
    d. all of the above

13. An individual thinks he is Jesus Christ. He also believes that, because he is Christ, people are trying to kill him. Assume that this individual is not correct—he is not Christ, and people are not trying to kill him. Which of the following would be the most likely diagnosis?
    a. multiple personality
    b. paranoid schizophrenia
    c. obsessive-compulsive disorder
    d. catatonic schizophrenia

14. A court declares that, because of a mental illness, an individual is not responsible for his criminal actions. The individual is:
    a. insane
    b. incompetent to stand trial
    c. psychotic
    d. all of the above

15. Among males suicide is committed most frequently:
    a. between the ages of 15 to 19
    b. between the ages of 20 to 24
    c. between the ages of 24 to 44
    d. after age 55

Answers: 1. b **2.** d **3.** a **4.** d **5.** c **6.** a **7.** b **8.** b **9.** b **10.** a **11.** a **12.** d **13.** b **14.** a **15.** d.

Psychotherapy

REVIEW OF KEY IDEAS

THE ELEMENTS OF PSYCHOTHERAPY: TREATMENT, CLIENTS, AND THERAPISTS

1. **Identify the three categories of therapy and discuss how various demographic variables relate to the likelihood of treatment.**

   1-1. Even though she already owns more than a thousand pairs of of shoes, Imelba cannot resist the urge to buy more. She checks the Yellow Pages and calls three different psychotherapists regarding possible treatment for her compulsion.

       (a) One therapist tells her that treatment will require her to talk with the therapist so as to develop a better understanding of her inner feelings. This therapist probably belongs to the _____ school of psychotherapy.

       (b) Another therapist suggests that some form of medication may help alleviate her compulsion. This therapist probably pursues the _____ approach to psychotherapy.

       (c) The third therapist is of the opinion that her urge to buy shoes results from learning and correcting it requires that she unlearn this compulsion. This therapist probably pursues the _____ approach to psychotherapy.

   1-2. Indicate whether the following statements about people who seek and choose not to seek psychotherapy are true or false.

   _____ Men are more likely than women to seek psychotherapy.

   _____ The two most common presenting symptoms are excessive anxiety and depression.

   _____ Persons seeking psychotherapy always have identifiable disorders.

   _____ Only a minority of persons needing psychotherapy actually receive treatment.

   _____ Many people feel that seeking psychotherapy is an admission of personal weakness.

   Answers: 1-1. (a) insight (b) biomedical (c) behavioral **1-2.** false, true, false, true, true.

2. **Describe the various types of mental health professionals involved in the provision of psychotherapy.**

    2-1.   Identify the following kinds of mental health professionals:

        (a) Medically trained persons (physicians) who generally use biomedical and insight approaches to psychotherapy.

        (b) Persons with doctoral degrees who emphasize behavioral and insight approaches to psychotherapy in treating a full range of psychological problems (two types).

        (c) Nurses who usually work as part of the treatment team in a hospital setting.

        (d) These persons often work with both the patient and family to reintegrate the patient back into society.

        (e) Persons who usually specialize in particular types of problems; such as, vocational, drug, or marital counseling.

Answers: 2-1. (a) psychiatrists (b) clinical and counseling psychologists (c) psychiatric nurses (d) clinical social workers (e) counselors

INSIGHT THERAPIES

3. **Explain the logic of psychoanalysis and describe the techniques by which analysts probe the unconscious.**

    3-1.   Freud believed that psychological disturbances originate from unresolved conflicts deep in the unconscious levels of the mind. His theory of personality, which he called _____ , would be classified as an _____ approach to psychotherapy. The psychoanalyst plays the role of psychological detective, seeking out problems thought to originate from conflicts left over from early _____ .

    3-2.   The psychoanalyst employs two techniques to probe the unconscious. One technique requires the patient to tell whatever comes to mind no matter how trivial. This technique is called _____. The other technique requires the patient to learn to remember his or her dreams which are then probed for their hidden meaning by the psychoanalyst. This technique is called _____.

Answers: 3-1. psychoanalysis, insight, childhood **3-2.** free association, dream analysis.

4. **Discuss resistance and transference in psychoanalysis.**

   —4-1.   Freud believed most people (<u>do/do not</u>) want to know the true nature of their inner conflicts and will
   employ various strategies so as to offer _____ to the progress of therapy. As therapy
   progresses, the patient often begins to relate to the therapist as though he or she was actually one of the
   significant persons (mother, father, spouse, etc.,) in the patient's life. This phenomenon is called
   _____.

   Answers: 4-1. do not, resistance, transference.

5. **Discuss trends in modern psychodynamic approaches to therapy.**

   5-1.   Indicate whether the following statements about trends in modern psychodynamic approaches to therapy
   are true or false.

   _____   The new approaches have sought to decrease the number of visits per week.

   _____   The new approaches have deemphasized the couch and free association in favor of more
   direct and varried communicative techniques.

   _____   The new approaches place a greater emphasis on character reconstruction.

   _____   The new approaches place a greater emphasis on neutrality and nonintrusion by the analyst.

   Answers: 5-1. true, true, false, false.

6. **Identify the elements of therapeutic climate and discuss therapeutic process in Rogers's client-centered therapy.**

   6-1.   Client-centered therapy, as developed by Carl Rogers, holds that there are three important aspects
   necessary for a good therapeutic climate. These are genuineness, unconditional positive regard, and
   empathy. Match these terms with their correct definitions as given below.

   (a)   The ability to truly see the world from the client's point of view and communicate this understanding
   to the client.

   (b)   The therapist's openness and honesty with the client.

   (c)   The complete and nonjudgemental acceptance of the client as a person without necessarily agreeing
   with what the client has to say.

   6-2.   For client-centered therapy, the major emphasis is to provide feedback and _____ as the client
   expresses his or her thoughts and feelings. The idea here is that the client (does/does not) need direct
   advice. What it needed is help in sorting through personal confusion in order to gain greater
   _____ into true inner feelings.

   Answers: 6-1. (a) empathy (b) genuineness (c) unconditional positive regard **6-2.** clarification, does not, insight or
   understanding.

7. **Discuss the logic, goals, and techniques of cognitive therapy.**

7-1.   Answer the following questions regarding the logic, goals and techniques of cognitive therapy.

(a) What is the basic logic behind cognitive therapy? Or to put it another way, what is the origin of many psychological problems according to cognitive therapy?

(b) What is the primary goal of cognitive therapy?

(c) How do cognitive therapists go about trying to change a client's negative illogical thinking?

(d) Cognitive therapy is actually a blend of insight therapy and behavior therapy. What technique from behavior therapy do cognitive therapists frequently employ?

Answers: 7-1. (a) negative illogical thinking (b) to change the client's negative illogical thinking (c) through argument and persuasion (d) homework assignments.

8. **Describe how group therapy is generally conducted and identify some advantages of this approach.**

8-1.   When conducting group therapy, the therapist generally plays a (an) (<u>active/subtle</u>) role, one that is primarily aimed at promoting _____ cohesiveness. Participants essentially function as _____ for each other, providing acceptance and emotional support.

8-2.   Besides being less expensive, group therapy also has three other advantages: (1) the realization by the participants that their problems (<u>are/are not</u>) unique, (2) the opportunity to work in a safe environment to build _____ skills, and (3) the fact that group therapy is particularly appropriate for certain kinds of problems. Many peer _____ groups work with such diverse problems as alcoholism, overeating, child abuse, etc.

Answers: 8-1. subtle, group, therapists **8-2.** are not, social, self-help.

9. **Discuss Eysenck's critique of insight therapy and more recent evidence on the efficacy of insight therapies.**

9-1.   In his review of therapeutic outcome studies with neurotic patients, Eysenck found that about _____ of all treated patients recovered within 2 years. The rate of recovery for untreated patients during this same time period was (<u>lower than/the same as</u>) untreated patients. Eysenck concluded that _____ emission accounted for most of the cures ascribed to insight therapies.

9-2.   After reexamining Eysenck's data, Bergin concluded that spontaneous remission accounts for approximately _____ percent of the "recoveries" from neurotic disorders. Recent studies have also concluded that when compared to untreated controls, insight therapies appear to be _____ to no treatment or placebo treatment.

Answers: 9-1. two-thirds, the same, spontaneous **9-2.** 30-40, superior.

10. **Summarize the general principles underlying behavioral approaches to therapy.**

   10-1.   In contrast to insight therapists who believe that pathological symptoms are signs of an underlying problem, behavior therapists believe that the _____ are the problem. Thus, behavior therapists focus on employing the principles of learning to directly change maladaptive _____. The two general principles underlying this approach are (1) one's behavior is a product of _____, and (2) what has been learned can be _____.

   Answers: 10-1. symptoms, behavior, learning, unlearned.

11. **Describe the goals and procedures of systematic desensitization and aversion therapy.**

   11-1.   State whether the following situations would be most applicable to systematic desensitization or to aversion therapy.

   (a)   The treatment goal is to lessen the attractiveness of particular stimuli and behaviors that are personally or socially harmful.

   (b)   The treatment goal is to reduce irrational fears such as found in phobias and other anxiety disorders.

   (c)   The three-step treatment involves pairing an imagined anxiety hierarchy with deep muscle relaxation.

   (d)   Treatment involves presenting an unpleasant stimulus, such as electric shock, while a person is engaged in performing a self-destructive, but personally appealing, act.

   (e)   This would be the treatment of choice for students who are unduly anxious about public speaking.

   Answers: 11-1. (a) aversion therapy (b) systematic desensitization (c) systematic desensitization (d) aversion therapy (e) systematic desensitization.

12. **Describe the goals and techniques of social skills training and biofeedback.**

   12-1.   As the name implies, social skills training is a behavior therapy designed to improve a client's social or _____ skills. Three different behavioral techniques are employed. First, one is required to closely watch the behavior of socially skilled persons, a technique called _____. Next the client is expected to imitate and practice the behavior he or she has just witnessed, a technique called behavior _____. Finally, the client is expected to perform in social situations requiring increasingly more difficult social skills, a technique called _____.

12-2. Biofeedback works by providing the client with immediate _____ about some bodily function, such as blood pressure or muscle tension, thus leading to better control of these functions. For example, it has been found that clients can lessen the intensity and frequency of tension headaches by learning to _____ the muscle tension in their neck and facial muscles.

Answers: **12-1.** interpersonal, modeling, rehearsal, shaping **12-2.** feedback, lessen (reduce).

13. Discuss evidence on the effectiveness of behavior therapies.

13-1. Compared to the evidence in support of insight therapies, the evidence in favor of behavior therapy is somewhat (weaker/stronger). It is important to remember, however, that behavior therapies are best suited for treating (specific/general) psychological disorders and that all of the various behavioral techniques (are/are not) equally effective.

Answers: **13-1.** stronger, specific, are not.

BIOMEDICAL THERAPIES

14. Describe the principal categories of drugs used in the biomedical treatment of psychological disorders.

14-1. Valium and Xanax, popularly called tranquilizers, are used to treat psychological disorders in which anxiety is a major feature. Thus, they are collectively called _____ drugs.

14-2. Another class of drugs is used to treat severe psychotic symptoms, such as hallucinations and confusion. These drugs are collectively called _____ drugs.

14-3. Three classes of drugs - tricyclics, MAO inhibitors, and selective serotonin reuptake inhibitors - have been found to be useful in alleviating depression. These drugs are collectively called _____ drugs.

14-4. A rather unique drug can function as both an antidepressant and antimanic agent and thus is effective in treating bipolar mood disorders. This drug is _____.

Answers: **14-1.** antianxiety **14-2.** antipsychotic **14-3.** antidepressant **14-4.** lithium.

15. Discuss evidence on the effects and problems of drug treatments for psychological disorders.

15-1. Drug therapies have proven useful in the treatment of many psychological disorders. However, they remain controversial for at least three reasons. Use the hints below to describe these three reasons.

(a) resolve problems

(b) two areas having to do with excess

(c) cure is worse than the disease

16. **Describe ECT and discuss its therapeutic effects and its risks.**

   16-1.   Answer the following questions about the nature, therapeutic effects, and risks of ECT.

   (a) What is the physical effect of the electric shock on the patient?

   (b) What general class of disorders warrant conservative use of ECT as a treatment technique?

   (c) Why does ECT work?

   (d) What is the major risk of ECT?

BLENDING APPROACHES TO PSYCHOTHERAPY

17. **Discuss the merits of blending or combining different approaches to therapy.**

   17-1.   A significant trend in modern psychotherapy is to blend or combine many different treatment approaches. Psychologists who advocate and use this approach are said to be _____. One outcome study cited by the text suggests there may be merit to this approach. In this study, three different groups of depressed patients were treated by either insight therapy, drug therapy, or both. The greatest improvement was found in patients treated by _____.

CULTURE AND THERAPY

18. **Discuss the barriers that lead to underutilization of mental health services by ethnic minorities and possible solutions to the problem.**

   18-1.   The text lists four general barriers (cultural, language, access, and institutional) to mental health services for ethnic minorities. Indicate which of these barriers is represented in the following statements.

   _____ (a) Many of the ethnic minorities are in low-paying jobs and without health insurance.

   _____ (b) Very few mental health facilities are equipped to provide culturally responsive services.

   _____ (c) There is a limited number of bilingual therapists.

   _____ (d) Psychotherapy was developed by whites in the Western world to treat whites in the Western world.

18-2. What would be an optimal, but perhaps impractical, solution to the problems of language and cultural differences betweem therapists and clients?

18-3. What kind of training was recommended for therapists?

18-4. What suggestion was made with respect to traditional therapies?

Answers. 18-1. (a) access (b) institutional (c) language (d) cultural **18-2.** Ethnically match therapists and clients. **18-3.** cultural sensitivity training **18-4.** That they be modified to be more compatible with specific ethnic groups.

INSTITUTIONAL TREATMENT IN TRANSITION

19. **Explain why people grew disenchanted with mental hospitals and describe the community mental health movement.**

19-1. After more than a century of reliance on state mental hospitals, the evidence began to grow that these institutions were not helping the patients; rather, in many instances, they were worsening their condition. What two conditions, unrelated to funding, were said to be responsible for this state of affairs?

19-2. In order to correct for these shortcomings, the community mental health movement arose as an alternative treatment option. The four key services they generally provide are (select the correct four from the following):

a. long-term inpatient therapy

b. short-term inpatient therapy

c. extensive outpatient therapy

d. crisis intervention services

e. education about mental health

f. vocational rehabilitation

Answers: 19-1. The paternalistic care made the patients feel helpless, and the removal of patients from their communities separated them from essential support groups. **19-2.** b, c, d, e.

20. **Describe the deinstitutionalization trend and evaluate its effects.**

20-1. The transferring of mental health care from large state institutions to community based facilities is what is meant by the term _____. As a result of deinstitutionalization, the number of mental patients in large institutional hospitals has _____ remarkably. The length of stay by patients in mental hospitals has also _____.

20-2. While deinstitutionalization has resulted in a decrease in the number of patients, as well as their length of stay, the number of admissions to psychiatric hospitals has actually _____. This is because of a large number of readmissions for short-term care, which the text calls "the _____ problem". Another problem brought about by deinstitutionalization is that a large number of discharged patients who have meager job skills and no close support groups make up a large portion of the nation's _____ persons.

Answers: 20-1. deinstitutionalization, declined (or decreased), declined **20-2.** increased, revolving door, homeless.

21. Describe the Featured Study on homelessness among the mentally ill.

21-1. Answer the following questions regarding the Featured Study.

(a) How did the study systematically estimate the number of persons suffering from mental illness among the nation's homeless?

(b) What was the median age of the guests?

(c) While 91 percent of the guests were found to have psychological disorders, only 28 percent had been previously hospitalized. What possible explanation did the authors give to account for the large percentage of untreated guests.

(d) What did the authors conclude about the current status of community shelters?

Answers: 21-1. (a) They interviewed all guests at a selected homeless facility in Boston. (b) 34 (c) They came into adulthood after deinstitutionalization. (d) Community shelters often serve as open asylums.

PUTTING IT IN PERSPECTIVE

22. Explain how this chapter highlighted two of the text's unifying themes.

22-1. What point does the text make about how theoretical diversity influenced psychotherapy?

22-2. The approaches to psychotherapy discussed in this chapter are not universally accepted or used, and some are actually counterproductive in many cultures. Why is this?

Answers: 22-1. The many diverse approaches have resulted in better treatment techniques. **22-2.** cultural influences and differences.

23. Discuss when and where to seek therapy, and the potential importance of a therapist's sex, professional background, and cost.

23-1. While one might seek psychotherapy just to get more out of life, serious thinking about seeking psychotherapy should begin when you have talked to friends and family and still feel _____ about a problem that is severely disrupting your life. In addition to talking to friends and acquaintances, the text lists many places (Table 15.5) where one might seek psychotherapy. The general idea here is to _____ around when looking for a therapist.

23-2. The text concludes that the kind of degree held by the psychotherapist (is/is not) crucial, although a verifiable degree indicating some kind of professional training is important. The sex of the therapist should be chosen according to the feelings of the _____; it is unwise to engage a therapist whose sex makes the client feel uncomfortable.

23-3. Answer the following questions regarding the cost of psychotherapy.

(a) How does the cost of therapists involved in private practice compare with the fees charged by similar professional groups?

(b) Many community agencies use a sliding scale to assess therapy costs. What does this mean?

Answers: 23-1. uncomfortable (helpless, overwhelmed), shop **23-2.** is not, client **23-3.** (a) The costs are similar. (b) Fees are assessed acording to the ability to pay.

24. Discuss the importance of a therapist's theoretical approach.

24-1. Studies of the effectiveness of various theoretical approaches to therapy show they are (unequal/equal) in overall success. This equality of results among all theoretical approaches (does/does not) apply to all types of problems. The theoretical approach may make a difference for specific types of problem

Answers: 24-1. equal, does not.

25. Summarize what one should look for in a prospective therapist and what one should expect out of therapy.

25-1. The text lists three areas to evaluate when looking for a therapist. Complete the following statements describing these areas.

(a) Can you talk to the therapist _____?

(b) Does the therapist appear to have _____?

(c) Does the therapist appear to be _____ _?

25-2. What should one consider before terminating therapy because of lack of progress?

25-3. What did the Ehrenbergs say about what to expect from psychotherapy?

Answers: 25-1. (a) openly (in a candid, nondefensive manner) (b) empathy and understanding (c) self-assured and confident. **25-2.** The lack of progress may be due to resistance on your part. **25-3.** It takes time, effort and courage.

REVIEW OF KEY TERMS

Antianxiety drugs
Antidepressant drugs
Antipsychotic drugs
Aversion therapy
Behavior therapies
Biofeedback
Biomedical therapies
Client-centered therapy
Clinical psychologists
Cognitive therapy

Community mental health centers
Counseling psychologists
Deinstitutionalization
Dream analysis
Electroconvulsive therapy (ECT)
Free association
Group therapy
Insight therapies
Interpretation
Lithium

Mental hospitals
Psychiatrists
Psychoanalysis
Psychopharmacotherapy
Resistance
Social skills training
Spontaneous remission
Systematic desensitization
Tardive dyskinesia
Transference

_____   1. Two groups of professionals that specialize in the diagnosis and treatment of psychological disorders and everyday behavioral problems.

_____   2. Physicians who specialize in the treatment of psychological disorders.

_____   3. Therapies that involve verbal interactions intended to enhance client's self-knowledge and thus produce healthful changes in personality and behavior.

_____   4. An insight therapy that emphasizes the recovery of unconscious conflicts, motives and defenses through techniques such as free association and transference.

_____   5. A technique in which clients are urged to spontaneously express their thoughts and feelings with as little personal censorship as possible.

_____   6. A technique for interpreting the symbolic meaning of dreams.

_____   7. A therapist's attempts to explain the inner significance of a client's thoughts, feelings, memories and behavior.

_____   8. A client's largely unconscious defensive maneuvers intended to hinder the progress of therapy.

_____   9. A process that occurs when clients start relating to their therapist in ways that mimic critical relationships in their lives.

_____ 10. An insight therapy that emphasizes providing a supportive emotional climate for clients who play a major role in determining the pace and direction of their therapy.

_____ 11. An insight therapy that emphasizes recognizing and changing negative thoughts and maladaptive beliefs.

_____ 12. The simultaneous treatment of several clients.

_____ 13. Therapies that involve the application of learning principles to change a client's maladaptive behaviors.

_____ 14. A behavior therapy used to reduce clients' anxiety responses through counterconditioning.

_____ 15. A behavior therapy in which an aversive stimulus is paired with a stimulus that elicits an undesirable response.

_____ 16. Recovery from a disorder that occurs without formal treatment.

_____ 17. A behavior therapy designed to improve interpersonal skills that emphasizes shaping, modeling, and behavioral rehearsal.

_____ 18. A behavioral technique in which a bodily function is monitored and information about it is fed back to a person to facilitate control of the physiological process.

_____ 19. Therapies that use physiological interventions intended to reduce symptoms associated with psychological disorders.

_____ 20. The treatment of mental disorders with drug therapy.

_____ 21. Drugs that relieve tension, apprehension and nervousness.

_____ 22. Drugs that gradually reduce psychotic symptoms.

_____ 23. A neurological disorder marked by chronic tremors and involuntary spastic movements.

_____ 24. Drugs that gradually elevate mood and help bring people out of a depression.

_____ 25. A chemical used to control mood swings in patients with bipolar mood disorder.

_____ 26. A treatment in which electric shock is used to produce cortical seizure accompanied by convulsions.

_____ 27. A medical institution specializing in the provision of inpatient care for psychological disorders.

_____ 28. Centers that provide mental health care for their local communities.

_____ 29. Transfering the treatment of mental illness from inpatient institutions to community-based facilities that emphasize outpatient care.

Answers: 1. clinical and counseling psychologists **2.** psychiatrists **3.** insight therapies **4.** psychoanalysis **5.** free association **6.** dream analysis **7.** interpretation **8.** resistance **9.** transference **10.** client-centered therapy **11.** cognitive therapy **12.** group therapy **13.** behavior therapies **14.** systematic desensitization **15.** aversion therapy **16.** spontaneous remission **17.** social skills training **18.** biofeedback **19.** biomedical therapies **20.** psychopharmacotherapy **21.** antianxiety drugs **22.** antipsychotic drugs **23.** tardive dyskinesa **24.** antidepressant drugs **25.** lithium **26.** electroconvulsive therapy (ECT) **27.** mental hospitals **28.** community mental health centers **29.** deinstitutionalization.

REVIEW OF KEY PEOPLE

Aaron Beck   Sigmund Freud   Joseph Wolpe
Hans Eysenck   Carl Rogers

_____ 1. Developed a systematic treatment procedure that he called psychoanalysis.

_____ 2. The developer of client-centered therapy.

_____ 3. Noted for his work in the development of cognitive therapy.

_____ 4. His early research showed that insight therapies were ineffective.

_____ 5. The developer of systematic desensitization.

Answers: 1. Freud **2.** Rogers **3.** Beck **4.** Eysenck **5.** Wolpe.

SELF-QUIZ

1. Psychotherapy as developed in the Western world has for the most part been found to be applicable to all cultures. This statement is:
   a. true
   b. false

2. Which of the following is not a true statement?
   a. women seek psychotherapy more than men
   b. the two most common problems that lead to psychotherapy are sexual problems and depression
   c. persons seeking psychotherapy don't always have identifiable problems
   d. many people feel that seeking psychotherapy is an admission of personal weakness

3. Which of the following mental health professionals must have medical degrees?
   a. psychiatric social workers
   b. clinical psychologists
   c. psychiatric nurses
   d. psychiatrists

4. Psychoanalysis is an example of what kind of approach to psychotherapy?
   a. insight
   b. learning
   c. biomedical
   d. a combination of learning and biomedical

5. When a client begins relating to his psychoanalyst as though she were his mother, we have an example of:
   a. transference
   b. free association
   c. catharsis
   d. restructuring

6. Which of the following is correct concerning trends in modern psychodynamic approaches to therapy?
   a. the therapeutic process has been lengthened
   b. a greater emphasis has been placed on unconscious forces
   c. a greater emphasis on direct communication
   d. all of the above are correct

7. The major emphasis in client-centered therapy is to provide the client with:
   a. interpretation of unconscious thinking
   b. cognitive restructuring
   c. feedback and clarification
   d. good advice

8. Which of the following therapies would be most likely to employ aversive conditioning?
   a. insight therapies
   b. behavior therapies
   c. biomedical therapies
   d. none of the above

9. Which of the following is likely to be found in cognitive therapy?
   a. a search for automatic negative thoughts
   b. reality testing
   c. an emphasis on rational thinking
   d. all of the above

10. Which kind of therapists are likely to play the least active (most subtle) role in conducting therapy?
   a. behavior therapists
   b. cognitive therapists
   c. group therapists
   d. pychoanalytic therapists

11. Eysenck's study of outcome studies with neurotic patients found that the recovery rate:
   a. was best for treated patients
   b. was best for untreated patients
   c. was the same for treated and untreated patients

12. Which of the following therapies is most likely to see the symptom as the problem?
   a. psychoanalysis
   b. gestalt
   c. behavior
   d. cognitive

13. Which of the following behavior therapy techniques would most likely be used to treat a fear of flying?
   a. systematic desensitization
   b. aversive conditioning
   c. modeling
   d. biofeedback

14. Behavior therapy, in comparison to other forms of therapy, is the most applicable to all kinds of psychological disorders. This statement is:
   a. true
   b. false

15. Electroconvulsive therapy (ECT) is now primarily used to treat patients suffering from:
   a. anxiety
   b. phobias
   c. severe mood disorders
   d. psychosis

16. Psychotherapists who combine several different approaches in their approach to therapy are said to be:
   a. enigmatic
   b. eclectic
   c. unspecific
   d. imaginative

17. The trend toward deinstitutionalization mainly came about because large mental institutions:
   a. were becoming too expensive
   b. were actually worsening the condition of many patients
   c. could not be properly staffed
   d. both a and c

Answers: 1. b 2. b 3. d 4. a 5. a 6. c 7. c 8. b 9. d 10. c 11. c 12. c 13. a 14. b 15. c 16. b 17. b

Chapter Sixteen

Social Behavior

REVIEW OF KEY IDEAS

PERSON PERCEPTION: FORMING IMPRESSIONS OF OTHERS

1. **Describe how various aspects of physical appearance may influence our impressions of others**.

    1-1.   In general, we tend to attribute _____ characteristics to good-looking people. With regard to personality, we see attractive people as friendlier, better-adjusted, and more poised. Although differences are not as great for competence, we also tend to see attractive people as (<u>less/more</u>) intelligent and successful than less attractive people.

    1-2.   In addition, we make inferences about people based on their nonverbal behavior—how they move, talk, and gesture. For example, people with a youthful gait are judged to be _____ and more powerful than those with a stiffer, older gait.

    1-3.   While good looks in general have relatively little impact on judgments of honesty, people do have a tendency to view baby-faced individuals (large eyes, rounded chin) as more _____ than others but also as more helpless and submissive. (Hey, what about the notorious criminal Baby-faced Nelson? Well, it's a general rule of thumb, not an absolute principle.)

    Answers: 1-1. positive (desirable, favorable) characteristics (e.g., more friendly, sociable, poised, warm, and well-adjusted) **1-2.** happier **1-3.** honest.

2. **Explain how schemas, stereotypes, and other factors contribute to subjectivity in person perception.**

    2-1.   Briefly define the following:

    (a) schemas:

    (b) stereotypes:

2-2. Men are competitive, women are sensitive: these are stereotypes. Stereotypes are broad generalizations that tend to ignore the _____ within a group. People who hold stereotypes do not necessarily assume that all members of a particular group have the same characteristics but merely that there is an increased _____ that they do.

2-3. Whether probabilistic or absolute, schemas in general and stereotypes in particular direct our perception, so that we tend to see the things we expect to see. Such selective perception results in an overestimation of the degree to which our expectations match actual events, a phenomenon referred to as _____ correlation.

2-4. In one study discussed in the text subjects watched a videotape of a woman engaged in various activities (including drinking beer and listening to classical music). For one set of subjects she was described as a librarian and for another as a waitress. What effect did the occupational labels have on subjects' recall of the woman's *activities*?

a. Subjects in the "librarian" condition tended to recall her listening to classical music.

b. Subjects in the "waitress" condition tended to recall her drinking beer.

c. Both of the above.

2-5. The study just described illustrates subjectivity in person perception. Our schemas, in this case the _____ that we have about categories of people, affect how we perceive and what we remember.

Answers: 2-1. (a) Social schemas are cognitive structures or *clusters of ideas* about people and events. (b) Stereotypes are a type of schema about groups or categories of people. **2-2.** diversity (variability), probability (likelihood) **2-3.** illusory **2-4.** c **2-5.** stereotypes.

3. Explain the evolutionary perspective on bias in person perception.

3-1. How does one explain bias or prejudice in terms of evolution? The answer is to assume that bias in some way had _____ value in our evolutionary past. For example, physical attractiveness was associated with health, which was associated with reproductive potential in _____ and the ability to acquire resources in _____.

3-2. Evolutionary theorists also assert that we needed a quick way to categorize people as friend or enemy or, in more technical terms, as members of our _____ or members of the _____.

3-3. The question still remains: how could prejudice and bias be adaptive? It must be clear that what was adaptive in our evolutionary past (is also/may not be) adaptive now. Nonetheless, from the point of view of evolutionary theory, cognitive mechanisms involving bias have been shaped by natural _____.

Answers: 3-1. adaptive (survival), women, men **3-2.** ingroup, outgroup **3-3.** may not be, selection.

ATTRIBUTION PROCESSES: EXPLAINING BEHAVIOR

4. **Explain what attributions are and why and when we make them.**

   4-1. Why are you reading this book? The search for causes of events and of our own and others' behavior is termed _____. For example, you might _____ your behavior to an upcoming test (or to personal interest, lust for knowledge, fear, etc.).

   4-2. What are attributions? Attributions are inferences that people make about the _____ of events and about the their own and others' behavior.

   4-3. Why do we make attributions? We seem to have a strong need to _____ our experiences, possibly because such understanding may enhance our chances of success in the future.

   4-4. When do we make attributions? We tend to make attributions, that is, to look for explanations, under the following circumstance:

   (a) When _____ events grab our attention.

   (b) When events have _____ consequences for us.

   (c) When people behave in _____ ways.

   (d) When we are suspicious about the _____ underlying someone's behavior.

   Answers: 4-1. attribution, attribute **4-2.** causes (origin, source, explanation) **4-3.** understand (explain) **4-4.** (a) unusual (unexpected) (b) personal (c) unexpected (unusual) (d) motives.

5. **Describe the distinction between internal and external attributions.**

   5-1. Which of the following involve internal and which external attributions? Label each sentence with an I or an E.

   _____ He flunked because he's lazy.

   _____ Our team lost because the officials were biased against us.

   _____ The accident was caused by poor road conditions.

   _____ He achieved by the sweat of his brow.

   _____ Criminal behavior is caused by poverty.

   _____ His success is directly derived from his parents' wealth and influence.

   Answers: 5-1. I, E, E, I, E, E

6. **Summarize Kelley's and Weiner's theories of attribution.**

   6-1. See Figure 16.3. Kelley's theory is tough to follow, but here's a sample problem. Ralph cried when he watched the Santa Claus parade. *No one else* seemed to be crying, so according to Kelley's model Ralph's behavior would be <u>low</u> in (<u>consistency/distinctiveness/consensus</u>). Further, Ralph *always cries* when he watches parades, so Ralph's crying is <u>high</u> in (<u>consistency/distinctiveness/consensus</u>). Ralph also cries when he watches a movie, attends the ballet, watches a sporting event, or on almost any other occasion; thus, Ralph's crying is <u>low</u> in (<u>consistency/distinctiveness/consensus</u>).

6-2. According to Kelley, *low* consistency favors an external attribution. *High* consistency is compatible with either an external or internal attribution: internal if distinctiveness and consensus are low and external if distinctive and consensus are high. So, people will tend to attribute Ralph's crying to _____ factors.

6-3. Weiner proposed that attributions are made not only in terms of an internal-external dimension but also in terms of a stable-unstable dimension. Suppose that Sally makes a high score on an exam. Her score could be attributed to the fact that she is a hard worker, an (internal/external) factor. If she always works hard, the factor is also (stable/unstable).

6-4. Alternatively, Sally's high score might be attributed to an easy test, an (internal/external) factor. If the tests are always easy, then this factor is also (stable/unstable); if the tests are sometimes easy and sometimes difficult, then the factor is (stable/unstable).

6-5. Weiner eventually added another dimension, controllability, to his model. Other theorists have added a *global-specific* factor. As discussed in Chapter 14, these three dimensions allow one to make certain predictions about personality. For example, which of the following attributional styles are most likely to characterize depressed people?

a. internal, stable, and global

b. external, unstable, and specific

c. internal, unstable, and specific

Answers: 6-1. consensus, consistency, distinctiveness **6-2.** internal. (I said this was a tough theory. The idea is that if Ralph cries on many occasions, regardless of the event, when no one else is crying—then we begin to think it's something about Ralph.) **6-3.** internal, stable **6-4.** external, stable, unstable **6-5.** a. (For more practice with these concepts see item 13 in Chapter 14 of this study guide.)

7. Describe several types of attributional bias and cultural variations in attributional tendencies.

7-1. Define or describe the following:

(a) fundamental attribution error:

(b) actor-observer bias:

(c) defensive attribution:

(d) self-serving bias:

7-2. Recent research has indicated that the attributional biases described above may not apply to all cultures. Since collectivist societies emphasize accomplishing the goals of the group over individual achievement, collectivist cultures are (less/more) likely to attribute other's behavior to personal traits. In other words, people from collectivist cultures tend to be (less/more) prone to the fundamental attribution error.

7-3. Some evidence also indicates that people from collectivist societies would be more likely to attribute their *successes* to (the ease of a task/unusual ability). Similarly, they would be more likely to attribute their *failures* to (bad luck/lack of effort). Thus, in contrast with people from individualistic societies, people from collectivist cultures appear to be (less/more) prone to the self-serving bias.

Answers: 7-1. (a) the tendency for observers to attribute an individual's behavior to *internal* rather than *external* factors (b) the tendency for observers to attribute an actor's behavior to internal rather than external factors *and the tendency for actors to attribute their own behavior to external causes* (Yes, there is overlap between these two concepts. The fundamental attribution error is part of the actor-observer bias.) (c) the tendency to attribute other people's misfortunes to internal causes, that is, the tendency to blame the victim (d) the tendency to attribute our *successes* to internal factors and our *failures* to situational factors **7-2.** less, less **7-3.** the ease of a task, lack of effort, less.

INTERPERSONAL ATTRACTION: LIKING AND LOVING

8. Summarize evidence on the role of proximity and physical attractiveness in attraction.

8-1. What factors influence liking, friendship, and love? One of the factors is simple spatial _____. We are more likely to form friendships, and romantic relationships, with people who are _____ to us, people who live, shop, sit, or work nearby.

8-2. A second factor is physical _____. Other things being equal, we prefer to have (romantic relationships/friendships/both) with people who are good looking.

—**8-3.** While everyone might prefer to have a relationship with the most attractive people, that isn't the way it works out. What is the matching hypothesis? Does it apply to same-sex friendships as well as romantic relationships?

9 17 19 22 28 37

Answers: 8-1. proximity, close **8-2.** attractiveness, both **8-3.** The matching hypothesis: people tend to have romantic relationships with others of the opposite sex who are *approximately equal* to themselves in physical attractiveness. The matching hypothesis also seems to apply to same-sex friendships among men but not among women.

9. Summarize evidence on the role of similarity and reciprocity in attraction.

9-1. Do opposites attract, or do birds of a feather flock together? An overwhelming amount of research supports the idea that we are attracted to others who are (similar to/different from) us in attitudes, personality, social background, etc.

9-2. Similarity appears to cause attraction. In experiments in which the degree of attitude similarity between a subject and an ostensible "stranger" is manipulated, liking is proportional to similarity: the greater the similarity, the greater the _____.

— **9-3.** We also tend to like others who like us, the principle of _____. In many cases we are particularly fond of those who exaggerate our good characteristics and overlook our bad. For married or dating couples, for example, the happiest couples seem to be those who have an (accurate/idealized) view of their partners.

Answers: 9-1. similar to **9-2.** attraction (liking) **9-3.** reciprocity, idealized.

10. **List several myths about love described by Berscheid and Hatfield.**

    10-1.   List the three myths about love described in your text.

    Answers: 10-1. When you fall in love you'll know it. Love is a purely positive experience. True love lasts forever.

11. **Describe Sternberg's triangular theory of love.**

    11-1.   Hatfield and Berscheid divide love into two types: _____ and _____

        love. Sternberg further divides companionate love into two subtypes, so that there are these three factors

        in his theory of love: _____, _____, and _____.

    11-2.   Which of Sternberg's three factors tends to peak early and drop off rapidly? _____

        Which tend to increase gradually over time? _____ and _____.

    Answers: 11-1. passionate, companionate; passion, intimacy, commitment **11-2.** passion; intimacy, commitment.

12. **Summarize the evidence on love as a form of attachment.**

    12-1.   In Chapter 11 we discussed types of attachment styles between infants and their caregivers. What *general* conclusion did Hazen and Shaver reach concerning the association between types of infant attachment and the love relationships of adults?

    12-2.   Write the names of the three infant attachment styles next to the appropriate letters below.

        S: _____

        A-A: _____

        A: _____

    12-3.   Using the letters from the previous question, identify the types of romantic relations predicted by the infant attachment styles.

        _____ As adults these people have difficulty getting close to others, tend to use casual sex to avoid intimacy and commitment.

        _____ These adults are preoccupied with love, have volatile relationships, are expectant of rejection, are jealous.

        _____ These individuals easily develop close relationships, are trusting, and tend not to worry about being abandoned.

    Answers: 12-1. The three types of infant-caretaker attachments (also described in Chapter 11) tend to predict the love relationships that children have as adults. **12-2.** secure, anxious-ambivalent, avoidant **12-3.** A, A-A, S.

13. **Discuss cross-cultural research on romantic relationship and evolutionary analyses of mating patterns.**

13-1. According to David Buss, as discussed in Chapter 10, males and females do not look for the same attributes in prospective mates. Buss's data indicate that _____ want mates who can acquire resources that can be invested in children, while _____ want mates who are beautiful, youthful, and in good health. These gender differences in mate preference appear to occur (<u>in virtually all/only in Western</u>) societies.

13-2. While there is cross-cultural similarity in preferences involving mate selection, there are differences among cultures in their views of the relationship between romantic love and marriage. The idea that one should be in love in order to marry is in large part an 18th-century invention of (<u>Eastern/Western</u>) culture.

13-3. Like the song says, we in the West assume that love and marriage go together (like a horse and carriage). There is little empirical support for our belief in the superiority of our system, however. In fact, some data indicate that love in arranged marriages tends to (<u>increase/decrease</u>) over the years, while love among couples who marry for love tends to (<u>increase/decrease</u>)

13-4. If men seek physical attractiveness and women resources, how does this affect *tactics* that people use in pursuing the opposite sex? In support of the evolutionary perspective, Buss has found that men tend to use tactics that emphasize their (<u>looks/resources</u>) and women tactics that emphasize their (<u>looks/resources</u>).

13-5. A recent study by Schmitt and Buss further specifies that the tactic used by the two sexes may depend in part on the type of romance they are looking for. Signals of sexual availability (e.g., dressing seductively) were rated as most effective for women seeking a _____ -term relationship. Signals of sexual exclusivity (e.g., rejecting overtures from other men) were considered most effective for women seeking a _____ -term relationship.

13-6. For men an immediate display of resources was rated the most effective tactic for a _____ -term relationship and an emphasis on potential for acquiring resources as most effective for a _____ - term relationship.

Answers: **13-1.** women, men, in virtually all **13-2.** Western **13-3.** increase, decrease **13-4.** resources, looks **13-5.** short, long **13-6.** short, long.

ATTITUDES: MAKING SOCIAL JUDGMENTS

14. **Describe the components of attitudes and the relations between attitudes and behavior.**

14-1. Attitudes are said to be made up of three components: cognition, affect, and behavior. What do the words *cognition* and *affect* refer to? List synonyms (one or two words for each) in the blanks below.

(a) cognition: _____

(b) affect: _____

14-2. The behavioral component refers, of course, to behavior. When expressed, it is the component we can readily observe, but it is not always expressed. Thus, this component is described in terms of behavioral _____ or tendencies.

14-3. People can have attitudes toward almost anything—political views, art, other people, cottage cheese. Take cottage cheese. List the three components of attitudes illustrated next to the examples below.

_____ He hates cottage cheese.

_____ If cottage cheese touches his plate he scrapes it into the garbage.

_____ He thinks: "Cottage cheese seems kind of lumpy."

14-4. As LaPiere found in his travels with the Chinese couple, attitudes (are/are not) particularly good predictors of behavior. In part this seems to be true because attitudes and cognitions are highly general, while _____ tend to be quite specific.

14-5. In addition, attitudes may be only mediocre predictors because the behavioral component is just a *predisposition* that may be changed by norms or other *aspects of the immediate situation*. For example, why might the restaurateurs have *said* that they would not serve the Chinese couple but in fact have served them when confronted with the actual situation?

Answers: 14-1. (a) beliefs (thoughts, thinking) (b) emotion (feelings) **14-2.** predispositions **14-3.** affect, behavior, cognition. (Note that the components may be remembered as the ABCs of attitude.) **14-4.** are not, behaviors **14-5.** The actual situation is likely to present new information, such as: the possible embarrassment of confrontation, pressure from others present, the unanticipated pleasant characteristics of the couple, and so on.

15. Summarize evidence on source factors, message factors, and receiver factors that influence the process of persuasion.

15-1. If you are the *source* of a communication, the message giver:

(a) What factors mentioned in your text would you use to make yourself more *credible*? _____ and _____

(b) What else would you hope to emphasize about yourself? _____

15-2. With regard to *message* factors:

(a) Which is more effective, a one-sided message or a two-sided message more effective?

_____

(b) In presenting your argument, should you use every argument that you can think of or emphasize just the stronger arguments? _____

(c) Is simple repetition a good strategy, or should you say something just once? _____

(d) Do fear appeals tend to work? _____

15-3. With regard to *receiver* factors in persuasive communications:

(a) If you know that someone is going to attempt to persuade you on a particular topic you will be (harder/easier) to persuade. This is the factor referred to as _____

(b) Resistance to persuasion is greater when an audience holds an attitude incompatible with the one being presented. In this case the receiver will also tend to scrutinize arguments longer and with more skepticism, an effect referred to as (confirmation/disconfirmation) bias.

—(c) People will be persuaded only if the message is not too different from their original position. This *range* of potentially acceptable positions is referred to as people's _____ of acceptance.

Answers: 15-1. (a) expertise, trustworthiness (b) likability (for example, by increasing your physical attractiveness or emphasizing your similarity with the message receiver) **15-2.** (a) In general, two-sided (That's the kind of speech Mark Antony gave over the body of Caesar in Shakespeare's *Julius Caesar*.) (b) stronger only (c) repetition (causes people to believe it's true, whether it is or isn't) (d) yes, if they arouse fear (and especially if the audience is persuaded that the effects are exceedingly unpleasant, likely to occur, and avoidable) **15-3.** (a) easier (b) disconfirmation (c) latitude.

16. Discuss how learning processes can contribute to attitudes.

16-1. Following are examples that relate learning theory to attitude change. Indicate which type of learning—classical conditioning (CC), operant conditioning (OC), or observational learning (OL)—is being illustrated.

_____ Ralph hears a speaker express a particular political attitude that is followed by thunderous applause. Thereafter, Ralph tends to express the same attitude.

_____ Advertisers pair soft drinks (and just about any other product) with attractive models. The audience likes the models and develops a stronger liking for the product.

_____ If you express an attitude that I like, I will agree with you, nod, say "mm-hmm," and so on. This will tend to strengthen your expression of that attitude.

Answers: 16-1. OL, CC, OC

17. Explain how cognitive dissonance can account for the effects of counterattitudinal behavior and effort justification.

17-1. (Dissonance is another truly complicated theory. Read over the text and see how you do on these questions. Here's a hint: Both problems that follow are contrary to common-sense ideas of reward and punishment; dissonance theory prides itself on making predictions contrary to these common-sense ideas. Item 17-1 indicates that we like behaviors accompanied by less, not more, reward; item 17-2 indicates that we like behaviors accompanied by more, not less, discomfort.)

Ralph bought a used car. However, the car uses a lot of gas, which he doesn't like because he strongly supports conserving energy. He rapidly concludes that conserving fuel isn't so important after all.

(a) Ralph has engaged in counterattitudinal behavior. What were the two contradictory cognitions? (One is a thought about his *behavior*. The other is a thought about an important *attitude*.)

(b) Suppose the car was a real beauty, a rare antique worth much more than the price paid. Alternatively, suppose that the car was only marginally worth what was paid for it. In which case would dissonance be stronger? In which case would the attitude about gas guzzling be more likely to change?

17-2. Suppose Bruce decides to join a particular club. (1) One possible scenario is that he must travel a great distance to attend, the club is very expensive, and he must give up much of his free time to become a member. (2) Alternatively, suppose that the traveling time is short, the club is inexpensive, and he need not give up any free time. In which case (1 or 2) will he tend to value his membership more, according to dissonance theory? Briefly, why?

Answers: 17-1. (a) I know I bought the car. I'm against the purchase of cars that waste gas. (b) The additional reward in the first situation produces less dissonance and will tend to leave Ralph's original attitude about gas consumption intact. Ralph's attitude about gas consumption will change more when there is less justification (in terms of the value of the car) for his action. As described in your text, we tend to have greater dissonance, and greater attitude change, when *less reward* accompanies our counterattitudinal behavior. **17-2.** According to dissonance theory, he will value the membership more under alternative 1, even if the benefits of membership are slight, because people attempt to *justify the effort* expended in terms of the benefits received. (While dissonance is a true phenomenon with many of the characteristics that Festinger described in 1957, several other variables are operating, so it is difficult to predict when dissonance will occur.)

18. Relate self-perception theory and the elaboration likelihood model to attitude change.

18-1. At a cocktail party Bruce eats caviar. When asked whether he likes caviar he responds, "I'm eating it, so I guess I must like it." This example illustrates _____ theory.

18-2. According to self-perception theory, people infer their attitudes by observing their own _____. Thus, if people engage in a behavior that is not accompanied by high rewards, they are likely to infer that they (enjoy/do not enjoy) the behavior.

18-3. To illustrate the elaboration likelihood model: Suppose that you are to travel in Europe and must decide between two options, whether to rent a car or go by train (e.g., on a Eurailpass, to be specific). In the blanks below indicate which persuasive route, central (C) or peripheral (P), is referred to in these examples.

_____ : After looking at train brochures showing apparently wealthy and dignified travelers dining in luxury on the train while viewing the Alps, you opt for the train.

_____ : Your travel agent, whose expertise you value and who usually knows what she is talking about, strongly recommends that you take the train. You decide on the train.

_____ : You examine the costs of each mode of transportation, taking into account that four people will travel together. You interview several people who have used both methods. You factor in time, convenience, standing in line, the difficulty of reserving seats, and the cost of cab rides for the train option. You decide to rent a car.

18-4. In the elaboration likelihood model, the route that is easier, that involves the least amount of thinking, is the _____ route. The route in which relevant information is sought out and carefully pondered is the _____ route. Elaboration, which involves thinking about the various complexities of the situation, is more likely to occur when the _____ route is used.

18-5. Elaboration leads to (more enduring/transient) changes in attitudes. In addition, elaboration (i.e., the more central route) is (more/less) likely to predict behavior.

Answers: 18-1. self-perception **18-2.** behavior, enjoy **18-3.** P, P, C **18-4.** peripheral, central, central **18-5.** more enduring, more.

CONFORMITY AND OBEDIENCE: YIELDING TO OTHERS

19. Summarize research on the determinants of conformity.

> **19-1.** Briefly summarize the general procedure and results of the Asch line-judging studies.

> **19-2.** Conformity increased as number of accomplices increased, up to a point. At what number did conformity seem to peak? _____

> **19-3.** Suppose there are five accomplices, one real subject, and another accomplice who dissents from the majority. What effect will this "dissenter" have on conformity by the real subject?

> **19-4.** Did subjects in the Asch study really change their beliefs about the lines, or were they just pretending to change them in response to social pressure? Subsequent research in which subjects made their responses anonymously supported the conclusion that subjects changed their (<u>public behavior/private beliefs</u>) but not their (<u>public behavior/private beliefs</u>).

> **19-5.** Conformity which involves only public acceptance rather than a true change in private beliefs is termed _____.

Answers: 19-1. Subjects were asked to judge which of three lines matched a standard line, a judgment that was actually quite easy to make. Only one of the subjects was a real subject, however; the others were accomplices of the experimenter, who gave wrong answers on key trials. The result was that a majority of the real subjects tended to conform to the wrong judgments of the majority on at least some trials. **19-2.** 7 **19-3.** Conformity will be dramatically reduced, to about one-fourth of its peak. **19-4.** public behavior, private beliefs **19-5.** compliance.

20. Describe the Featured Study on obedience to authority and the ensuing controversy generated by Milgram's research.

> **20-1.** Two individuals at a time participated in Milgram's initial study, but only one was a real subject. The other "subject" was an accomplice of the experimenter, an actor. By a rigged drawing of slips of paper the real subject became the _____ and the accomplice became the _____. There were a total of _____ subjects, or "teachers," in the initial study.

> **20-2.** The experimenter strapped the learner into a chair and stationed the teacher at an apparatus from which he could, supposedly, deliver electric shocks to the learner. The teacher was to start at 15 volts, and each time the learner made a mistake the teacher was supposed to _____ the level of shock by 15 volts—up to a level of 450 volts.

> **20-3.** At 300 volts, the learner pounded on the wall and demanded to be released. Of the 40 subjects, how many quit the experiment at that point? _____ How many subjects had quit prior to that point? _____ What percentage of the subjects continued to obey instructions, thereby increasing the shock all the way up to 450 volts? _____

20-4. What is the major conclusion to be drawn from this study? Why are the results of interest?

20-5. As you might imagine, Milgram's studies on obedience were controversial, producing both detractors and defenders. Following are three objections raised against Milgram's studies. Beneath each are possible *counter-arguments* raised by either Milgram or his supporters. Complete the counter-arguments by filling in the blanks.

(a) "Subjects knew it was an experiment, so they went along only because they assumed everything must be okay."

If subjects had thought everything was okay, they would not have shown the enormous

_____ that they did.

—(b) "Subjects in an experiment expect to obey an experimenter, so the results don't generalize to the real world."

The flaw in this argument is that in many aspects of the real world, including the military and

business worlds, _____ is also considered appropriate.

(c) "Milgram's procedure, by which subjects were allowed to think that they had caved in to commands to harm an innocent victim, was potentially emotionally damaging to the subjects."

The brief distress experienced by the subjects was a _____ price to pay for the

insights that emerged. Furthermore, the subjects were thoroughly _____ at the end

of the experiment.

Answers: 20-1. teacher, learner, 40 **20-2.** increase **20-3.** 5, none, 65 percent **20-4.** The major conclusion is that ordinary people will tend to obey an authority even when their obedience could result in considerable harm (and perhaps even death) to others. The result is of interest because it suggests that such obedience as occurs in war atrocities (e.g., in World War II, at Mai Lai in Viet Nam, in Cambodia, Rwanda, and throughout history) may be due not to the evil *character* of the participants so much as pressures in the *situation*. Note that the obedience results reflect the actor-observer attributional bias. (Milgram's results are also of interest because most people would not expect them: even psychiatric experts predicted that fewer than 1% of the subjects would go all the way to 450 volts.) **20-5.** (a) distress (b) obedience (c) small, debriefed.

21. Discuss cultural variations in conformity and obedience.

21-1. As with other cross-cultural comparisons, replications in other countries yield some similarities and some differences. Indicate true (T) or false (F) for the following statements.

_____ The obedience effect found by Milgram seems to be a uniquely American phenomenon.

_____ In replications of the Milgram studies in several European countries, obedience levels were even higher than those in the United States.

_____ Replications of the Asch line-judging studies have found that cultures that emphasize collectivism are more conforming than are those that emphasize individualism.

Answers: 21-1. F, T, T.

22. **Discuss the nature of groups and the bystander effect.**

22-1. The word *group* doesn't have the same meaning for social psychologists that it does for everyone else. As I look out across my social psychology class on a Tuesday morning, I might say to myself, "Hm, quite a large group we have here today." Actually, my class is *not* a group in social psychological terms because it lacks one, and perhaps two, of the essential characteristics of a group. A group consists of two or more individuals who (a) _____ and (b) are _____.

22-2. Which of the following are groups, as defined by social psychologists?

_____ A husband and wife.

_____ The board of directors of a corporation.

_____ A sports team.

_____ Spectators at an athletic event.

_____ Shoppers at a mall.

22-3. What is the bystander effect?

22-4. Why does the bystander effect occur? In part because onlookers produce a certain _____ about the situation (i.e., no one else is doing anything, so maybe it's not an emergency). In addition, the presence of others causes a _____ of responsibility (i.e., we're all responsible, or someone else will do it.)

Answers: 22-1. (a) interact (b) interdependent **22-2.** The first three are groups and the last two are not. **22-3.** When people are in groups (or at least in the presence of others), they are less likely to help than when they are alone. Or, the greater the number of onlookers in an emergency, the less likely any one of them is to assist the person in need. **22-4.** ambiguity, diffusion.

23. **Summarize evidence on group productivity, including social loafing.**

23-1. Individual productivity in large groups is frequently less than it is in small groups. Two factors contribute to this decreased efficiency: a loss of _____ among workers in larger groups (e.g., efforts of one person interfere with those of another) and _____ loafing.

23-2. Social loafing is the reduction in _____ expended by individuals working in groups as compared to people working alone.

23-3. Social loafing and the bystander effect seem to share a common cause: _____ of responsibility.

23-4. In some cases (e.g., if the task is important and a person is concerned about the output of co-workers) individuals may expend more rather than less effort in a group, a phenomenon called social _____. Cultural factors may also have an effect; social loafing is less common in (collectivistic/individualistic) societies.

24. **Describe group polarization and groupthink.**

24-1. This problem should help you understand the concept of group polarization. Suppose that a group of five corporate executives meet to decide whether to raise or lower the cost of their product, and by how much. Before they meet as a group, the decisions of the five executives (expressed as a percentage) are as follows: +32%, +17%, +13%, +11%, and +2%. After they meet as a group, which of the following is most likely to be the result? Assume that group polarization occurs.

   a. +30%, +10%, +3%, +3%, and +2%

   b. +32%, +29%, +22%, +15%, and +20%

   c. +3%, +13%, +11%, +9%, and +2%

   d. −10%, −7%, −3%, 0%, and +7%

24-2. What is group polarization?

24-3. Have you ever been in a group when you thought to yourself, "This is a stupid idea, but my best friend seems to be going along with it, so I won't say anything." If so, you may have been in a group afflicted with groupthink. Groupthink is characterized by, among other things, an intense pressure to _____ to group opinions accompanied by very low tolerance for dissent.

24-4. According to Janis, the major cause of groupthink is high group _____. Tetlock and other writers have recently argued, however, that cohesiveness (is/is not) a crucial factor and may in some cases reduce groupthink. The groupthink theory has intuitive appeal but evaluation of its generality awaits future research.

Answers: 24-1. b **24-2.** Group polarization is the tendency for a group's decision to shift toward a more extreme position in the direction that individual members are already leaning. **24-3.** conform **24-4.** cohesiveness (i.e., the degree of liking that members have for each other and for the group), is not.

PUTTING IT IN PERSPECTIVE

25. **Explain how the chapter highlighted three of the text's unifying themes.**

25-1. This chapter again illustrates psychology's commitment to empirical research. When people hear the results of psychological studies they frequently conclude that the research just confirms common sense. Dispute this view by listing and describing *at least one study* with results that are not predictable from common sense assumptions.

25-2. Cross-cultural differences and similarities also reflect one of the unifying themes. People conform, obey, attribute, and love throughout the world, but the manner and extent to which they do so are affected by cultural factors. Important among these factors is the degree to which a culture has an _____ or _____ orientation.

25-3. Finally, the chapter provides several illustrations of the way in which our view of the world is highly subjective. For example, we tend to make ability and personality judgments based on people's physical _____; see what we expect to see as a result of the cognitive structures termed social _____; distort judgments of physical lines based on pressures to _____; and make foolish decisions when we become enmeshed in the group phenomenon known as _____.

Answers: 25-1. This chapter described at least three studies that defy the predictions of common sense. (1) Milgram's research. Psychiatrists incorrectly predicted that fewer than 1% of the subjects would go to 450 volts. (2) Cognitive dissonance studies. Common sense would suggest that the more people are paid, the more they would like the tasks they are paid for. Dissonance researchers found the opposite, that people paid *more* liked the tasks *less*. (3) Bystander effect. Common sense might predict that the larger the number of people who see someone in need of help, the more likely any one is to offer help. Research on the bystander effect consistently finds the opposite result. **25-2.** individualistic, collectivistic **25-3.** attractiveness (appearance), schemas, conform, groupthink.

APPLICATION: UNDERSTANDING PREJUDICE

26. Relate person perception processes and attributional bias to prejudice.

26-1. Prejudice is a negative _____ toward others based on group membership.

26-2. The cognitive component of prejudice is comprised of schemas about groups. This type of schema is frequently referred to as a _____

26-3. Stereotypes are part of the *subjectivity* of person perception. People tend to see what they expect to see, and when stereotypes are activated people see and remember information that (is/is not) congruent with their stereotype.

26-4. Stereotypes are highly accessible and frequently are activated automatically, so that even though people reject prejudiced ideas, stereotypes (can not/may still) influence behavior

26-5. People's *attributional biases* are also likely to maintain or augment prejudice. For example, observers tend to attribute success in men to (ability/luck) but success in women to (ability/luck).

26-6. People are also predisposed to attribute other people's behavior to internal traits, the bias referred to as the _____ attribution error.

26-7. When people experience misfortune, we are also likely to attribute their misfortune to (personal traits/ environmental events). This type of attributional bias is referred to as defensive attribution or _____ blaming. By extension, people who are victims of prejudice may be _____ for the prejudice against them.

Answers: 26-1. attitude **26-2.** stereotype **26-3.** is **26-4.** may still **26-5.** ability, luck **26-6.** fundamental **26-7.** personal traits, victim, blamed.

27. Relate principles of attraction, attitude formation, and group processes to prejudice.

27-1. Two factors discussed under interpersonal attraction are related to prejudice. According to the principle of *proximity*, people tend to become friends with those who live near them. Segregated housing patterns eliminate _____ and so also reduce chances for friendship formation among the races.

27-2. *Similarity* between people, especially with regard to attitudes, is also a major factor in friendship formation. If Rosenbaum is correct, perceived _____ may be an even more important than similarity in creating and maintaining prejudice.

27-3. Principles of attitude formation also contribute to our understanding of prejudice. If someone makes racial epithets that are followed by reinforcers (such as attention or approval), then these remarks are more likely to occur in the future. In this way attitudes are developed and maintained through the learning process known as _____ conditioning.

27-4. In addition, when people see others engage in discriminatory behavior, they may model that behavior through the process known as _____ learning.

27-5. Ingroup members perceive themselves differently from outgroup members. One difference in perception involves the tendency of ingroup members to view outgroup members less favorably. Further, the more that one identifies with an ingroup, the (more/less) prejudiced one is toward the outgroup.

27-6. Another important difference in the perception of ingroups and outgroups is termed the *illusion of outgroup homogeneity*. Explain this concept.

Answers: **27-1.** Proximity **27-2.** dissimilarity **27-3.** operant **27-4.** observational **27-5.** more **27-6.** We overestimate the homogeneity of outgroups. That is, we tend to think that they all look alike, and they tend to think that we all look alike. It goes beyond appearance—ingroups tend to view outgroup members as similar in behavior and attitudes as well.

REVIEW OF KEY TERMS

Attitudes
Attributions
Bystander effect
Channel
Cognitive dissonance
Collectivism
Commitment
Companionate love
Compliance
Conformity
Defensive attribution
Discrimination
Ethnocentrism
External attributions
Fundamental attribution error

Group
Group cohesiveness
Group polarization
Groupthink
Illusory correlation
Individualism
Ingratiation
Ingroup
Internal attributions
Interpersonal attraction
Intimacy
Latitude of acceptance
Matching hypothesis
Message

Obedience
Outgroup
Passionate love
Person perception
Prejudice
Proximity
Receiver
Reciprocity
Self-serving bias
Social loafing
Social psychology
Social schemas
Source
Stereotypes

_____ 1. The branch of psychology concerned with the way individuals' thoughts, feelings, and behaviors are influenced by others.

_____ 2. The process of forming impressions of others.

_____ **3.** Clusters of ideas about categories of social events and people that we use to organize the world around us.

_____ **4.** Widely held beliefs that people have certain characteristics because of their membership in a particular group.

_____ **5.** Error that occurs when we estimate that we have encountered more confirmations of an association between social traits than we have actually seen.

_____ **6.** Inferences that people draw about the causes of events, others' behavior, and their own behavior.

_____ **7.** Attributing the causes of behavior to personal dispositions, traits, abilities, and feelings.

_____ **8.** Attributing the causes of behavior to situational demands and environmental constraints.

_____ **9.** The tendency of an observer to favor internal attributions in explaining the behavior of an actor.

_____ **10.** The tendency to blame victims for their misfortune so that we feel less likely to be victimized in a similar way.

_____ **11.** The tendency to attribute our positive outcomes to personal factors and our negative outcomes to situational factors.

_____ **12.** Liking or positive feelings toward another.

_____ **13.** Geographic, residential, and other forms of spatial closeness.

_____ **14.** The observation that males and females of approximately equal physical attractiveness are likely to select each other as partners.

_____ **15.** Liking those who show that they like us.

_____ **16.** A conscious effort to cultivate others' liking by complimenting them, agreeing with them, doing favors for them, and so on.

_____ **17.** A complete absorption in another person that includes tender sexual feelings and the agony and ecstasy of intense emotion.

_____ **18.** A warm, trusting, tolerant affection for another whose life is deeply intertwined with one's own.

_____ **19.** Warmth, closeness, and sharing in a relationship.

_____ **20.** The intent to maintain a relationship in spite of the difficulties and costs that may arise.

_____ **21.** Responses that locate the objects of thought on dimensions of judgment; have cognitive, behavioral, and emotional components.

_____ **22.** The person who sends a communication.

_____ **23.** The person to whom the message is sent.

_____ **24.** The information transmitted by the source.

_____ **25.** The medium through which the message is sent.

_____ **26.** A range of potentially acceptable positions on an issue centered around one's initial attitude position.

_____ **27.** A tendency to evaluate people in outgroups less favorably than those in one's ingroup.

_____ **28.** Situation that exists when related cognitions are inconsistent.

_____ **29.** Yielding to real or imagined social pressure.

_____ 30. Yielding to social pressure in one's public behavior even though one's private beliefs have not changed.

_____ 31. A form of compliance that occurs when people follow direct commands, usually from someone in a position of authority.

_____ 32. Involves putting group goals ahead of personal goals and defining one's identity in terms of the group one belongs to.

_____ 33. Involves putting personal goals ahead of group goals and defining one's identity in terms of personal attributes rather than group memberships.

_____ 34. Two or more individuals who interact and are interdependent.

_____ 35. The apparent paradox that people are less likely to provide needed help when they are in groups than when they are alone.

_____ 36. A reduction in effort by individuals when they work together as compared to when they work by themselves.

_____ 37. Situation that occurs when group discussion strengthens a group's dominant point of view and produces a shift toward a more extreme decision in that direction.

_____ 38. Phenomenon that occurs when members of a cohesive group emphasize concurrence at the expense of critical thinking in arriving at a decision.

_____ 39. The group one belongs to and identifies with.

_____ 40. People who are not a part of the ingroup.

_____ 41. The strength of the liking relationships linking group members to each other and to the group itself.

_____ 42. A negative attitude held toward members of a group.

_____ 43. Behaving differently, usually unfairly, toward the members of a group.

Answers: 1. social psychology **2.** person perception **3.** social schemas **4.** stereotypes **5.** illusory correlation **6.** attributions **7.** internal attribution **8.** external attribution **9.** fundamental attribution error **10.** defensive attribution **11.** self-serving bias **12.** interpersonal attraction **13.** proximity **14.** matching hypothesis **15.** reciprocity **16.** ingratiation **17.** passionate love **18.** companionate love **19.** intimacy **20.** commitment **21.** attitudes **22.** source **23.** receiver **24.** message **25.** channel **26.** latitude of acceptance **27.** ethnocentrism **28.** cognitive dissonance **29.** conformity **30.** compliance **31.** obedience **32.** collectivism **33.** individualism **34.** group **35.** bystander effect **36.** social loafing **37.** group polarization **38.** groupthink **39.** ingroup **40.** outgroup **41.** group cohesiveness **42.** prejudice **43.** discrimination.

REVIEW OF KEY PEOPLE

Solomon Asch	Elaine Hatfield	Harold Kelley
Ellen Berscheid	Fritz Heider	Stanley Milgram
Leon Festinger	Irving Janis	Bernard Weiner

_____ 1. Was the first to describe the crucial dimension along which we make attributions; developed balance theory.

_____ 2. Devised a theory that identifies important factors relating to internal and external attributions.

_____ 3. With Hatfield did research describing two types of romantic love: passionate and companionate.

_____ 4. Originator of the theory of cognitive dissonance.

_____ 5. Devised the "line-judging" procedure in pioneering investigations of conformity.

_____ 6. In a series of "fake shock" experiments studied the tendency to obey authority figures.

_____ 7. Developed the concept of groupthink.

_____ 8. Under the name of Walster did early study on dating and physical attractiveness; with Berscheid, described types of romantic love.

_____ 9. Concluded that attribution has not only on internal-external dimension but a stable-unstable dimension.

Answers: **1.** Heider **2.** Kelley **3.** Berscheid **4.** Festinger **5.** Asch **6.** Milgram **7.** Janis **8.** Hatfield **9.** Weiner.

SELF-QUIZ

1. Which of the following characteristics do we tend to attribute to physically attractive people?
   a. coldness
   b. happiness
   c. unpleasantness
   d. all of the above

2. Cognitive structures that guide our perceptions of people and events are termed:
   a. attributions
   b. stigmata
   c. schemas
   d. denkmals

3. Inferences that we make about the causes of our own and others' behavior are termed:
   a. attributions
   b. stigmata
   c. schemas
   d. denkmals

4. Bruce performed very well on the examination, which he attributed to native ability and hard work. Which bias does this illustrate?
   a. the fundamental attribution error
   b. the actor-observer bias
   c. the self-serving bias
   d. all of the above

5. Which of the following are related to interpersonal attraction?
   a. proximity
   b. similarity
   c. physical attractiveness
   d. all of the above

6. Which of the following could be an example of the fundamental attribution error?
a. Ralph described himself as a failure.
b. Ralph thought that the reason he failed was that he was sick that day.
c. Jayne said Ralph failed because the test was unfair.
d. Sue explained Ralph's failure in terms of his incompetence and laziness.

7. Bruce had what could be described as a secure attachment to his parents during his infancy. What kind of relationship is he likely to develop as an adult?
a. trusting and close
b. jealous
c. volatile and preoccupied with love
d. difficult

8. Which of the following is, in general, likely to reduce the persuasiveness of a message?
a. The receiver's viewpoint is already fairly close to that of the message.
b. The receiver has been forewarned about the message.
c. A two-sided appeal is used.
d. The source is physically attractive.

9. Osmo is frequently seen in the company of Cosmo. When asked if he likes Cosmo, Osmo replies, "I guess I must, since I hang out with him." Which theory does this example best illustrate?
a. balance
b. cognitive dissonance
c. self-perception
d. observational learning

10. In making a decision you rely on the opinion of experts and the behavior of your best friends. According to the elaboration likelihood model, which route to persuasion have you used?
a. central
b. peripheral
c. attributional
d. 66

11. Which of the following is the best statement of conclusion concerning Milgram's classic study involving the learner, teacher, and ostensible shock?
a. Under certain circumstances, people seem to enjoy the opportunity to be cruel to others.
b. People have a strong tendency to obey an authority even if their actions may harm others.
c. The more people there are who observe someone in need of help, the less likely any one is to help.
d. Aggression seems to be a more potent force in human nature than had previously been suspected.

12. Which of the following is most likely to function as a group?
a. shoppers at a mall
b. the audience in a theater
c. the board of trustees of a college
d. passengers in an airplane

13. Vanessa witnesses a car accident. In which of the following cases is she most likely to stop and render assistance?
a. Only she saw the accident.
b. She and one other individual saw the accident.
c. She and 18 others saw the accident.
d. The other observers are pedestrians.

14. Suppose the original decisions of members of a group are represented by the following numbers in a group polarization study: 9, 7, 5, 5, 4. The range of numbers possible in the study is from 0 to 9. Which of the following possible shifts in decisions would demonstrate polarization?
    a. 2, 3, 3, 4, 5
    b. 7, 7, 6, 5, 5
    c. 5, 4, 0, 2, 3
    d. 9, 9, 7, 7, 5

15. According to Janis, what is the major cause of groupthink?
    a. strong group cohesion
    b. weak group cohesion
    c. the tendency of group members to grandstand
    d. group conflict

Answers: 1. b **2.** c **3.** a **4.** c **5.** d **6.** d **7.** a **8.** b **9.** c **10.** b **11.** b **12.** c **13.** a **14.** d **15.** a.

Appendix B
Statistical Methods

REVIEW OF KEY IDEAS

1. **Describe several ways to use frequency distributions and graphs to organize numerical data.**

   1-1.   Identify the following methods that are commonly used to present numerical data.

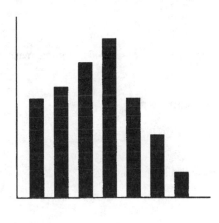   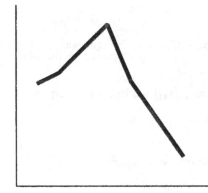

   (a) _____   (b) _____

   1-2.   What data are usually plotted along the:

   (a) horizontal axis?

   (b) vertical axis?

   Answers: 1-1. (a) histogram (b) frequency polygram **1-2.** (a) the possible scores (b) the frequency of each score.

2. Describe the measures of central tendency and variability discussed in the text.

2-1. Tell which measure of central tendency - the mean, median, or mode - would be most useful in the following situations.

(a) Which measure would be best for analyzing the salaries of all workers in a small, low-paying printshop that includes two high-salaried managers? Explain your answer.

(b) Which measure would tell us the most common shoe size for men?

(c) Which measure would be best for pairing players at a bowling match, using their individual past scores, so that equals play against equals?

(d) Where do most of the scores pile up in a positively skewed distribution?

Answers: 2-1. (a) the median, because the high salaries of the two management persons would distort the mean (b) the mode (c) the mean (d) at the bottom end of the distribution.

3. Describe the normal distribution and its use in psychological testing.

3-1. Answer the following questions regarding the normal distribution.

(a) Where do the mean, median, and mode fall in a normal distribution?

(b) What is the unit of measurement in a normal distribution?

(c) Where are most of the scores located in a normal distribution?

(d) Approximately what percentage of scores falls above 2 standard deviations in a normal distribution?

(e) If your percentile ranking on the SAT was 84, what would your SAT score be (see Fig. B.7 in the text)?

Answers: **3-1.** (a) at the center (b) the standard deviation (c) around the mean (plus or minus 1 standard deviation) (d) 2.3% (e) 600 (approximately).

4. Explain how the magnitude and direction of a correlation is reflected in scatter diagrams and how correlation is related to predictive power.

4-1. Answer the following questions about the magnitude and direction of a correlation as reflected in scattergrams.

(a) Where do the data points fall in a scattergram that shows a perfect correlation?

(b) What happens to the data points in a scattergram when the magnitude of correlation decreases?

(c) What does a high negative correlation indicate?

4-2. Answer the following questions regarding the predictive power of correlations.

(a) How does one compute the coefficient of determination?

(b) What does the coefficient of determination tell us?

(c) What could we say if the sample study used in the text showed a correlation of -.50 between SAT scores and time watching television?

Answers: **4-1.** (a) in a straight line (b) They scatter away from a straight line. (c) High scores on one variable (X) are accompanied by low scores on the other variable (Y). **4-2.** (a) by squaring the correlation coefficient (b) It indicates the percentage of variation in one variable that can be predicted based on the other variable. (c) Knowledge of TV viewing allows one to predict 25% of the variation on SAT scores (.50 x .50 = .25).

5. Explain how the null hypothesis is used in hypothesis testing and relate it to statistical significance.

    5-1.   Answer the following questions regarding the null hypothesis and statistical significance.

        (a) In the sample study correlating SAT scores and television viewing, the findings supported the null hypothesis. What does this mean?

        (b) What level of significance do most researchers demand as a minimum before rejecting the null hypothesis?

        (c) What is the probability of making an error when a researcher rejects the null hypothesis at the .01 level of significance?

Answers: 5-1. (a) We cannot conclude that there is a significant negative correlation between SAT scores and television viewing. (b) the .05 level (c) 1 in 100.

REVIEW OF KEY TERMS

Coefficient of determination
Correlation coefficient
Descriptive statistics
Frequency distribution
Frequency polygon
Histogram
Inferential statistics

Mean
Median
Mode
Negatively skewed distribution
Normal distribution
Null hypothesis
Percentile score

Positively skewed distribution
Scatter diagram
Standard deviation
Statistics
Statistical significance
Variability

_____   **1.** The use of mathematics to organize, summarize and interpret numerical data.

_____   **2.** An orderly arrangement of scores indicating the frequency of each score or group of scores.

_____   **3.** A bar graph that presents data from a frequency distribution.

_____   **4.** A line figure used to present data from a frequency distribution.

_____   **5.** Type of statistics used to organize and summarize data.

_____   **6.** The arithmetic average of a group of scores.

_____   **7.** The score that falls in the center of a group of scores.

_____   **8.** The score that occurs most frequently in a group of scores.

_____   **9.** A distribution in which most scores pile up at the high end of the scale.

_____   **10.** A distribution in which most scores pile up at the low end of the scale.

_____   **11.** The extent to which the scores in a distribution tend to vary or depart from the mean.

_____   **12.** An index of the amount of variability in a set of data.

_____   **13.** A bell-shaped curve that represents the pattern in which many human characteristics are dispersed in the population.

_____   **14.** Figure representing the percentage of persons who score below (or above) any particular score.

_____   **15.** A numerical index of the degree of relationship between two variables.

_____   **16.** A graph in which paired X and Y scores for each subject are plotted as single points.

_____   **17.** The percentage of variation in one variable that can be predicted based on another variable.

_____   **18.** Statistics employed to interpret data and draw conclusions.

_____   **19.** The hypothesis that there is no relationship between two variables.

_____   **20.** Said to exist when the probability is very low that observed findings can be attributed to chance.

Answers: 1. statistics **2.** frequency distribution **3.** histogram **4.** frequency polygon **5.** descriptive statistics **6.** mean **7.** median **8.** mode **9.** negatively skewed distribution **10.** positively skewed distribution **11.** variability **12.** standard deviation **13.** normal distribution **14.** percentile score **15.** correlation coefficient **16.** scatter diagram **17.** coefficient of determination **18.** inferential statistics **19.** null hypothesis **20.** statistical significance.

Appendix C

Industrial/Organizational Psychology

REVIEW OF KEY IDEAS

1. **Discuss the settings, procedures, and content areas of I/O psychology.**

   1-1.   In a humorous commentary a few years ago psychologist Jerry Burger said he longed to hear, just once, someone in a theater asking, "Is there a social psychologist in the house?" (Burger, 1986). Burger's comments reflected not only his wish that psychology be recognized somewhere outside the halls of academia but his desire for application. Of course, the settings for the four applied fields of psychology (Chapter 1) frequently are outside university settings—clinical psychology and counseling psychology take place in mental health settings, school psychology occurs in educational settings, and I/O psychology is conducted in _____ settings.

   1-2.   While research and application of I/O psychology may occur in the work place, many of its principles derive from academic fields such as social psychology. I/O psychologists also use (<u>much the same/very different</u>) research methods and statistics as the other fields of psychology.

   1-3.   There are three primary areas of interest for the industrial psychologists. Write the names of these subareas in the blanks below next to the initial letters that represent them.

   P: _____ psychology

   O: _____ psychology

   HF: _____ _____ psychology

   1-4.   Below are descriptions of the three subareas of I/O psychology. Match the subareas with the descriptions by placing the letters from the previous question in the appropriate blanks.

   _____ Examines the way human beings fit the work environment; concerned with the interface between human beings and the tools and resources they use.

   _____ Tests and selects employees, tries to match the abilities of the person to the job requirements.

   _____ Concerned with job satisfaction, relationships among employees, social adaptation of the worker to the workplace.

1-5.   Below are possible problems encountered in a workplace. Match the subareas with the problems.

_____ The employees intentionally work at a slow pace.

_____ Several employees unintentionally push the wrong buttons on the machines in their work environments.

_____ Ralph tests out poorly in accounting but has potential for working with the gyroplex machine.

Answers: 1-1. work (employment, industrial, business) **1-2.** much the same **1-3.** personnel, organizational, human factors (or human engineering) **1-4.** HF, P, O **1-5.** O, HF, P.

2. Discuss how the systems approach relates to the subfields of I/O psychology.

2-1.   Your text makes the point that the three subareas of I/O psychology do not operate independently. For example, making a human factors change (is likely to/will not) affect personnel and organizational functions as well.

2-2.   Replacing a secretary's typewriter with a computer may affect not only the way the employee interfaces with the machine (the _____ _____ subarea), but interactions among employees (the _____ subarea) and the characteristics of the employee (the _____ subarea).

2-3.   It is clear, then, that changes in one part of the sociotechnical system affect other parts. For this reason the approach of I/O psychology is termed a _____ approach.

Answers: 2-1. is likely to **2-2.** human factors (human engineering), organizational, personnel **2-3.** systems.

3. Describe how the three subfields of I/O psychology emerged historically.

3-1.   The first of the three subareas of I/O psychology to appear historically was _____ psychology. One could mark the origin of this field at the turn of the century, at about the time of Binet's development of the _____ test.

3-2.   Two major historical events of the twentieth century spurred the use of ability testing on a massive scale and enhanced the importance of personnel psychology. What were these two events?

3-3.   Prior to 1930, the cost-benefit theories of Frederick _____ dominated industry's thinking about behavior in the workplace. Productivity was thought to be determined solely by identifying efficient movements, finding employees capable and willing to work, and paying amounts that were exactly proportionate to rate of _____.

3-4.   In 1930 a now-famous study at a Western Electric plant near Chicago found that productivity was affected by workers' _____ toward their supervisors. This result was surprising because it had previously been thought that only physical factors, such as pay and working conditions, would affect productivity. This experiment marks the beginning of the _____ _____ movement in industrial psychology.

3-5.   The subarea directed toward developing workplace environments that fit the human beings who use them is known as _____ _____ psychology.

3-6. Human factors developed in large part in response to the need to understand the best and safest ways for human beings to interact with airplanes and other weapons of war. What historical event may be used to mark the beginning of human factors psychology? _____.

Answers: **3-1.** personnel, intelligence **3-2.** World War I and World War II **3-3.** Taylor, production (work) **3-4.** attitudes, human relations **3-5.** human factors (human engineering) **3-6.** World War II.

4. Discuss the role of psychological testing in personnel psychology, and discuss job analysis and performance evaluation.

4-1. The function of personnel psychology is to match the abilities of people with characteristics of the job.

(a) If there are more applicants than jobs, what is the role of the personnel psychologist?

(b) If there are no applicants who have the skills needed for the job, what is likely to be the task of the personnel psychologist? What is the function of testing in this case?

4-2. While the task of personnel psychology is to match the person to the job, characteristics of the job (<u>are/ are not</u>) always obvious. We know that accountants do accounting and managers do managing and so on, but these rough descriptions are not specific enough to permit prediction from tests. A more precise description is provided by the process known as job _____, a method for breaking a job into its constituent parts.

4-3. Job analysis determines not only what tasks a person does for a particular job but which of the tasks are _____ to the job and which are _____. Once the analysis has determined the components of the job and the skills needed, the personnel psychologist administers psychological _____ to assess those skills.

4-4. Tests used must be both consistent and measure what they are supposed to measure. That is, the tests must show an appropriate level of _____ and _____ (see Chapter 9).

4-5. In part as a result of the popularity of the "_____" theory of personality, the last few years there has seen renewed interest in using _____ tests (see Chapter 12).

4-6. After selection and hiring have taken place, the next step is to assess the quality of employees' work. The _____ evaluation should be guided by the job analysis and should emphasize job aspects that are important rather than trivial.

4-7. While in some instances it is possible to evaluate performance on the basis of objective products, in most cases it is not; output is usually attributable to more than one person. Thus, the most common form of performance evaluation is _____ ratings.

4-8. With regard to supervisor ratings:

(a) What are the major advantages of using this method?

(b) A major disadvantage of using ratings is that they can be influenced by irrelevant factors. Give one or two examples of these irrelevant factors.

(c) What steps can be taken to help prevent such rating errors?

Answers: 4-1. (a) To use psychological testing to select the applicant with the best skills for the job. (b) To develop training programs designed to provide candidates with the needed skills. In this case, the testing objective is to find individuals who have the capacity to develop the needed skills. **4-2.** are not, analysis **4-3.** central, peripheral, tests **4-4.** reliability, validity **4-5.** Big Five, personality **4-6.** performance **4-7.** supervisor **4-8.** (a) The supervisor may know the employee's work best, and evaluations are based on observations made over a long period of time. (b) Some supervisors are more lenient than others; supervisors may be influenced by how much they like the person. (c) Rating errors may be lessened by providing supervisors with training and by designing scales that eliminate some of the pitfalls of the rating process.

5. **Describe and compare the equity and expectancy theories of work motivation.**

5-1. Equity theory assumes that workers attempt to match inputs with outcomes. The workers' efforts (and skills, experience, loyalty, and so on) are considered _____; their wages (and other rewards) are the _____. To the extent that inputs match outcomes a state of _____ is said to exist.

5-2. If employees perceive that the rewards do not match their efforts, and therefore that balance does not exist, equity theory indicates that they will make changes directed at producing equity. For example, what adjustments might they make if they perceive that they are *underpaid*?

5-3. If employees are *overpaid*, equity theory suggests that they will (increase/decrease) output or ask for (lower/higher) wages. The evidence indicates, however, that this type of adjustment (is/is not) likely to occur.

5-4. Expectancy theory has a different approach to understanding work motivation. It assumes that effort is in large part a function of an employee's evaluation of two main questions relating to the reward. What are these questions?

5-5. Following are possible thoughts running through the minds of imaginary employees. Indicate which theory of work motivation, equity or expectancy, is reflected in these examples.

_____: The boss has promised me a big raise if I increase sales by 10 percent. I could sure use the money. I don't think he will give it to me, though, so I'm not going to expend the extra effort.

_____: It's unfair that I'm the one with the skill but he's the one who gets the raise! I'm not going to work so hard in the future.

_____: My supervisor says that I'd become employee of the month if I could average two widgets per hour. Big deal! I can't eat employee of the month—what I need is cash.

_____: Next year's salary is just 5 percent higher than this year's. Considering my loyalty and the money I've made for the company, that just isn't enough. Next year I'm going to slow down and be sure to take all of my sick leave.

Answers: 5-1. inputs (investments), outcomes (rewards), equity (balance, homeostasis) **5-2.** They could reduce effort, or they could ask for higher wages. **5-3.** increase, lower, is not **5-4.** Is the reward of value to me? Is it likely that I will receive the reward? (In other words: Do I want it, and will I get it?) **5-5.** expectancy, equity, expectancy, equity.

6. Summarize research on job satisfaction.

6-1. What do people want in a job? Place check-marks to indicate which of the following are primary factors associated with job satisfaction.

_____ interesting and challenging work

_____ pleasant co-workers

_____ adequate salary

_____ opportunities for advancement

_____ effective and supportive supervisors

_____ acceptable company policies

6-2. To assess job satisfaction most organizations distribute questionnaires that ask employees to rate their job satisfaction. Results indicate that satisfaction is positively correlated with three factors: low <u>absenteeism</u>, low <u>turnover</u>, and high <u>productivity</u>. Thus, employees who are happy with their jobs tend to be absent less often, look for new jobs less frequently, and tend to be more productive. These correlational data do not indicate causal direction, however. While it is probably the case that satisfaction reduces _____ and _____, it may have little effect on _____.

6-3. Managers might hope, and it would seem reasonable to expect, that job satisfaction would result in greater productivity. A great deal of research has failed to find this to be the case, however. There is, however, some evidence that the reverse is true, that _____ leads to more _____.

Answers: 6-1. Thousands of studies have found that all of these are primary sources of job satisfaction! **6-2.** absenteeism, turnover, productivity **6-3.** productivity, job satisfaction

7. Discuss how human engineering can enhance work environments.

7-1. There are two major points of interaction, or interface, between humans and machines: the first involves the devices that _____ information; the second is the action taken by the person, the _____ part of the system.

7-2. For example, dashboards in cars provide the _____ part of the system. Based on that information, the human being operates the pedals and knobs that provide the _____ part of the system.

7-3. The major problems encountered in using machines result from confusion that may involve either the _____ or the _____ parts of the system. To reduce these interface problems, human factors specialists design display panels easily understood at a glance or control components shaped like the functions they control. For example, after World War II the knobs that operated the flaps on airplanes were redesigned to be shaped like _____.

7-4. Most people have certain expectations about the way things work. For example, people generally expect to unscrew things in a counterclockwise direction. Thus, a major design principle is to build in accordance with response _____, people's natural expectations about the way controls work.

7-5. As I sit here writing the last paragraph of this study guide, I am well aware that my computer and software are user-friendly. Probably some nice human factors psychologist designed them that way, and for that I am grateful. They make my life easier. How can human engineering enhance work environments? Well designed machines permit greater efficiency and are less confusing and less frustrating. Thus, they reduce _____, a potential cause of both health problems and _____ in the workplace.

Answers 7-1. display, control **7-2.** display, control **7-3.** display, control, flaps **7-4.** stereotypy **7-5.** stress, accidents (mistakes)

Reference: Burger, J. M. (1986) Is there a Ph. D. in the house? *APA Monitor, 17*, 4.